The Viceroy's Daughters

Also by Anne de Courcy

The English in Love
1939: The Last Season
Circe: The Life of Edith, Marchioness of Londonderry

The Viceroy's Daughters

THE LIVES OF
THE CURZON SISTERS

~

Anne de Courcy

Weidenfeld & Nicolson
LONDON

First published in 2000 by
Weidenfeld & Nicolson

© 2000 Anne de Courcy

A CIP catalogue record for this book is available
from the British Library.

ISBN 0 297 81977 1

Typeset by Selwood Systems, Midsomer Norton

Printed in Great Britain by Butler & Tanner Ltd, Frome and London

Weidenfeld & Nicolson
The Orion Publishing Group Ltd
Orion House
5 Upper Saint Martin's Lane
London WC2H 9EA

Contents

Illustrations

The author and publishers would like to thank the following for their kind permission to reproduce photographs: David Metcalfe, 3, 4, 8, 9, 10, 11, 21, 23, 24, 25, 33, 34, 36, 37, 39, 41, 42, 44, 45, 46, 47, 48, 49, 50, 51, 52, 53, 54, 57; Mary Evans Picture Library, 5; Topham Picturepoint, 15, 16, 43, 56; Frank Cakebread, 30; Hulton Getty, 17, 20, 22, 27, 28, 35, 40.

Preface

The great proconsular figure of Lord Curzon holds immense fascination for anyone as interested in the quirks and byways of human nature as in brilliance of intellect and ferocity of will. A man noted for the splendour of his way of life even in an age of magnificos, unable to resist women while regarding them in no way as the equal of men, as capable of poring over a butcher's bill at 2.30 in the morning as of planning a great enterprise of state, Curzon often bewildered those around him. What must he have been like as a parent? And how would the legacy of such a father affect his three daughters, daughters of a man who longed above all for a male heir. Would he inspire or overwhelm them, and would they discover the happiness he found with their mother, or the disharmony that overtook his second marriage?

In writing their story I am above all grateful to their children: to Lord Ravensdale (Nicholas Mosley) for making available to me the whole of his aunt Irene's copious diaries, early family letters and photographs; to David Metcalfe for his generosity in allowing me access to his family papers and letters, his mother's diaries and his wonderful collection of her photographs; to Davina Eastwood for all her help with memories and reminiscences, and particularly for her friendship, despite her reservations about the writing of such an intimate family portrait; and to Vivien Forbes Adam for many fascinating talks and memories of her parents.

I would also like to offer my most grateful thanks to Lord Holderness for so kindly allowing me to quote from the letters of his father, Lord Halifax; to Francis Sitwell for letting me read and quote from the diaries of his mother, Georgia Sitwell; to Sir Edward

Cazalet for generously sending me copies of the diaries of his uncle, Victor Cazalet to read and quote from; and to Christopher Davson for allowing me access to the papers of his grandmother, Elinor Glyn, and the essays sent to her by Professor Thomas Lindsay. Lord Rosslyn was extremely kind in allowing me to see the unpublished memoir of his mother, Lady Loughborough and to quote from it. I am most grateful to Lord Romsey for permission to quote from the diaries of Lord and Lady Mountbatten, to Hugo Vickers for his extracts from the diary of Gladys Duchess of Marlborough, to Mrs Westropp for the loan of the late Miss Monica Sheriffe's Melton Mowbray photograph albums, and to Mr Frank Cakebread for the loan of his photographs of Savehay Farm, Denham.

I am very grateful to Robert Barrett for his genealogical research; to Janet Tomlinson for her help with photographs; to Miss Betty Hanley for photographs and descriptions of the Château de Candé in the time of her aunt, Fern Bedaux; to Sir Dudley and Lady Forwood for their hospitality and reminiscences of the Duke of Windsor; to Dame Gillian Wagner for information and letters relating to her uncle, General Sir Miles Graham, and for photographs; and to Count Franco Grandi for all he told me about his father.

Among those who helped me with their memories of the sisters, their families, their friends and their times were Michael Clayton, Lady Clarissa Collin – whom I must also thank for photographs of her father – the late Quentin Crewe, Lady Kitty and Mr Frank Giles, Viscount Monckton of Brenchley, the Hon. Lady Mosley, Nigel Nicolson, the Countess of Plymouth, Kenneth Rose, Alfred Shaughnessy, Lady Thorneycroft, the late Michael Tree, Alice Winn and Elizabeth Winn, all of whom I would like to thank. As always the staffs of the British Library, the London Library and the Kensington and Chelsea Library were immensely helpful, as was Mollie Chalk, archivist at Broadlands, and Helen Langley, head of Modern Political Papers at the Bodleian.

I am also immensely grateful to David Metcalfe and to Nicholas Mosley for kindly reading my manuscript and offering their comments and, last but not least, to the superlative editing of Benjamin Buchan of Weidenfeld & Nicolson. Any mistakes are mine, not his.

Anne de Courcy
June 2000

I

Curzon and His Circle

~

The Curzon daughters were born when the wealth and privilege of the British upper classes were at their zenith. Powdered footmen in brilliant liveries stood behind chairs at dinner parties of ten courses. The pavement outside a grand house was covered with sound-deadening straw if the occupant was ill, or with a red carpet if there was a ball, so that guests in tiaras or tailcoats could proceed in style to a ballroom filled with flowers from the hothouses of the host's country estate. Most of them, born into this tight and exclusive circle threaded through with networks of cousinage, already knew each other, their friendships flowering during the long Saturdays to Mondays spent at each other's country houses.

The grandeur, the sports, the pleasures, the elaborate clothes washed, ironed, mended and packed by lady's maid or valet, the dressing gongs, the carriages, the silver tea-things on a white lace cloth beneath a cypress tree on the lawn, were expressions of a society secure in its own power – a power which extended over roughly a quarter of the world and which was, equally securely, held in the hands of its ruling class.

No one epitomised the concept of the Englishman born to rule better than George Nathaniel Curzon. As Lady Cynthia Asquith, the daughter of Curzon's friend, Lady Elcho, tartly observed: 'It certainly needed no trained psychologist's eye to diagnose him at a glance as a man who would prefer to be mounted on an elephant rather than a donkey.' When his daughters Irene, Cynthia and Alexandra were born, in 1896, 1898 and 1904 respectively, he was at the height of his powers and influence.

The Hon. George Curzon, the eldest of four brothers and six

sisters, was born on 11 January 1859, at Kedleston, the Derbyshire estate that had belonged to the Curzons for more than seven hundred years. The house, a northern palace, was built by Robert Adam, its saloon based on the Pantheon in Rome, and with a park surrounding it. George's father, the fourth Lord Scarsdale, who as a younger son had not expected to succeed, was the village rector. All his life Curzon was passionate about Kedleston and constantly sought to enrich and improve it, a passion that expanded to embrace the other grand houses which he later bought or rented.

Curzon's brilliance and belief in himself were apparent from an early age; the future Prime Minister Herbert Henry Asquith, who met him while he was at Eton, was more struck by his self-confidence than by any other quality. Brought up by a sadistic governess, a cold mother, who died when he was sixteen, and a distant, eccentric father, the realisation that he could depend only upon himself and on what he could make of his life had come to him early.

Just before his mother died, George had taken a fall while riding in the Kedleston woods, hurt his back badly and spent three days lying in bed in great pain. Like any fifteen-year-old, when he got better he forgot about it. Then, on holiday in France just before going up to Oxford in the autumn of 1878, he was suddenly struck by agonising pain in the lower back. His right hip, he realised, had altered shape. He went straight back to London where he immediately consulted a specialist, who told him that he was suffering from curvature of the spine and that in future he must wear a corset or brace and avoid violent exercise. From then on, he was in more or less constant pain, often having to take to his bed as the only alleviation. Work provided distraction, consolation and a lifeline out of the self-pity into which he occasionally fell.

The effect of this constant suffering permeated Curzon's character, aggravated by the steel corset he was obliged to wear. This rigid framework made him literally stiff-necked, giving him an appearance of pride veering on self-importance, a man prepared to stand on his dignity on all occasions. And, just as stiffness of body is often reflected in rigidity of mind, so his attitudes and prejudices all too easily became set in stone while his will dominated his emotions.

This did not stop him from becoming the centre of a notable

group of friends both as an undergraduate at Oxford and after. There was the masculine society of the Crabbet Club – founded by the traveller, poet and womaniser Wilfrid Scawen Blunt at his home in Sussex – which would meet for what Curzon called 'bay-arnos' (he was under the impression that 'beano' was Italian for a festivity) in the first weekend of July, when around twenty members arrived bringing with them presents of wine, cigars and other delicacies. In 1883 he was elected a Fellow of All Souls; and three years later became the Conservative MP for Southport in Lancashire.

Curzon was also a founder member of the coterie of aristocratic and intellectual men and women known as 'the Souls'. Though the nude tennis-playing of the Crabbet Club after a long night of talk had no place among the Souls, they were equally impressed by an elegance of intellectual style. They were not afraid of expressing emotion – indeed, they had been christened the Souls by Lord Charles Beresford in 1888 since, as he said: 'You all sit and talk about each other's souls'; and the name was confirmed by Curzon's banquet for them of 1889 at the Bachelors' Club, where each guest found on their chair a set of his verses describing the characteristics of each individual Soul. Their articulateness, freedom of expression and extravagant expressions of affection made their conversation the very opposite of the convention and banality that had trickled down from Court circles. One favourite after-dinner game was Styles, in which guests were given half an hour to write something in the style of Shakespeare, Macaulay, Wordsworth or Tennyson.

Their influence, especially that of the female Souls, on the young Curzon was immense. Beauty, if possible accompanied by voluptuousness, chic and charm, became for him a prerequisite in a woman. Many years later, when Lord Peel was being considered as a possible Viceroy, he remarked in Cabinet: 'I need hardly say that I have no objection whatsoever to our friend Willy Peel but I feel bound to remind those of my colleagues who may not be personally acquainted with his wife that whilst she is undoubtedly a lady of colossal wealth, she has a calamitous appearance.'

Women, he felt, should be the brilliant, decorative adjuncts of a husband's career, the solace and relaxation of his private moments, rather than individuals in their own right. Even while at Oxford he spoke in the Union against a proposal to allow women students to use the university library (unavailingly: the motion was carried by 254 votes to 238). Although he preferred spending what leisure time he had with women rather than with men, he liked them, as his lover Elinor Glyn shrewdly wrote, 'rather in the spirit in which other men like good horses or fine wine, or beautiful things to embellish a man's leisure but not as equal souls worthy of being seriously considered or treated with that scrupulous sense of honour with which he would deal with a man'.

His attitude to women was contradictory in other ways. Emotional, even sometimes sentimental, his cool, aloof façade belied the longing for affection behind his imperious demeanour. He was drawn to the feminine qualities of warmth, softness and decorative serenity as to a fire. His libido was powerful, impelling him into flirtations – one young woman complained that when he found himself alone with her at a country-house breakfast he immediately tried to kiss her – and full-blown affairs where sex, rather than love, was the motivation. In his early years he was the subject of would-be blackmail by a lady of very easy virtue; later, he chose mistresses – notably the romantic novelist Elinor Glyn – from his own world where discretion would be assured.

As a wife, he selected one of the richest and most beautiful young women in America. Mary Leiter, mother of the three Curzon daughters, was the daughter of Levi Ziegler Leiter, a Chicago millionaire whose forebears had come from Switzerland and who, in 1811, founded the village of Leitersburg in Maryland. In 1854, Levi Leiter had left Leitersburg for Chicago to work for a firm of merchants; there, he met a friend of his own age called Marshall Field who, like him, had begun his commercial life by working in a country store. Both of them were intelligent, hard-working and ambitious. Together, in January 1865, they founded the American store today known as Marshall Field. By the time Mary was born, in 1870, her father was hugely wealthy.

Mary was educated as befitted the family's new status. She was taught dancing, music, singing and art; she learned French from a French governess and history, chemistry and arithmetic from a Columbia University don. She was tall and slim, with large grey eyes in an oval face, glossy chestnut-brown hair drawn back into a loose knot at the nape of her neck and small, pretty hands and feet. Everything that could be done, through her father's wealth and her mother's social ambition, to turn her into the debutante of the year was done; and when she became a friend of the attractive 23-year-old Frances Cleveland, wife of the President of the United States, success was assured.

Thanks to the Cleveland connection, when the Leiter family arrived in New York at the end of the 1888 Washington season, Mary was adopted on to the all-important Social Register. In New York, too, she triumphed and then, fascinated by the idea of the English aristocracy, with its titles and country houses, she determined to conquer London as well.

Thanks to her beauty and letters of introduction, Mary was soon launched. When Asquith's wife Margot saw the eighteen-year-old Mary in a black lace dress with a huge picture hat trimmed with roses she was 'struck dumb' by her loveliness. At the Duchess of Westminster's ball in July 1890, which Mary had the signal honour of opening by dancing a quadrille with the Prince of Wales, she met George Curzon. When they saw each other again at a house party, Mary, now twenty, fell in love.

As for Curzon, 'I had a strong inclination to kiss you, with difficulty restrained', he told her later – but then, it was an inclination he often experienced. Although they wrote to each other daily during the ten days before Mary left England and saw each other as often as possible, their courtship hung fire. While Mary ached for him to propose to her, Curzon was too busy travelling through the Pamir mountains and thence into Afghanistan, gathering material for an eventual five volumes on Asia.

After three years of sporadic contact Curzon, returning home from Cairo via Paris, learned that Mary was there too. Her mother invited him to dine with them at the Hôtel Vendôme. After dinner, while Mrs Leiter tactfully left them alone, Mary told Curzon how she had pined for him during this period, rejecting countless suitors as she waited for him to make up his mind. It was enough: Curzon proposed on the spot but he stipulated that the engagement must remain secret until he had finished his travels in the Pamirs. During the next two years, they were to meet for just two days and a few hours.

Mary's superhuman devotion and submissiveness was exactly what Curzon wanted. Here was a beautiful, loving, faithful woman, who knew her place. 'The terrace of the House is as crowded with women as the Royal Enclosure at Ascot,' he wrote disgustedly to Mary on 21 June 1893, 'and the encroachment of the sex fills me with indignation which no blandishments can allay. Give me a girl that knows a woman's place and does not yearn for trousers. Give me, in fact, Mary.' That she was also immensely rich was an understood part of the bargain: the tide of American heiresses marrying British titles was then in full flood. Ironically, it was this very wealth that would later drive a wedge between those whom its owner loved most – her husband and children.

The question of the Leiter fortune arose well before the official announcement of their engagement on 4 March 1895. (Describing the engagement, the *St James's Gazette* wrote of the bridegroom: 'He is superbly clever and not unconscious of the fact.') Lord Scarsdale gave his son an allowance of £1,000 a year and promised to settle on him land worth £7,000 a year in income. After much discussion, Levi Leiter made a marriage settlement on his daughter of $700,000, invested in railway fixed interest stock, to give her an annual income of $33,000. Should she predecease Curzon, he was entitled to one-third of this income, with another third to go to any children they might have. The remaining third was to be left as appointed by Mary or, in default of that, by Curzon. Levi Leiter also promised Mary a further £1 million either during his lifetime or in his will.

They were married on the morning of 22 April 1895 at St John's Church, opposite the White House, in Washington DC, Mary in a white dress from Worth and the Scarsdale diamonds, and a few days later they sailed for England from New York. Mary never saw America again. Their first house in London was No. 5 Carlton House Terrace off Pall Mall. Curzon, setting a precedent that was to endure through both his marriages, was more familiar with its domestic minutiae than Mary.

In June 1895 he was appointed Under Secretary of State at the Foreign Office. The following month there was a general election; Curzon, his campaign funded by his father-in-law and aided by the charm and beauty of his young wife, increased his majority.

Within a few months the young couple had decided they could not afford Carlton House Terrace; and instead leased No. 4 Carlton Gardens from a fellow Soul, Arthur Balfour, renting a

Georgian house in Reigate, The Priory, while Balfour's house was being made ready for them. Mary was not allowed to choose so much as a single curtain; Curzon, although working a sixteen-hour day, took the whole of the decoration out of her hands, despite the fact that she would have enjoyed it – and that her father was paying. In many ways, it was the template for their marriage.

For the next few years Mary was miserable, alone in a foreign country, with little to do and a husband hardly ever there. Because his work prevented him from escorting her, the ordinary social round passed her by. During the London Season of 1896 they went out to dinner only twice and it was the same during the Jubilee year that followed. Only Mary's baby, Mary Irene, born on 20 January 1896, lightened her wretchedness. She pronounced the child's name Ireen, in the American fashion; Curzon, a classicist, gritted his teeth every time he heard this but loyally said nothing.

A fortnight before her second child, Cynthia Blanche (always known as Cimmie), was born on 28 August 1898 it was announced that Curzon was to succeed Lord Elgin as Viceroy of India. For a man as young as thirty-eight, who had held no senior government position before, it was an extraordinary post to be offered. It was given to him in part because he asked for it – Curzon believed, with reason, that he could fill it better than anyone else – but chiefly because he was quite clearly the best available candidate. He had visited India four times, his knowledge of its culture, problems and history was immense, he had written about it at length, and he was on terms of friendship with many of its potentates, as well as the Emir who ruled its powerful neighbour, Afghanistan.

His triumph was crowned by the award of the peerage considered fitting for the greatness of the office; he was now Baron Curzon of Kedleston (in the peerage of Ireland). But although as Viceroy of India he would be one of the most powerful rulers in the world, holding the destinies of millions in his hand, financially he would be worse off rather than better. Maintaining the huge staffs considered essential at Viceregal Lodge in Calcutta and the Viceroy's summer palace at the hill station of Simla mopped up the £25,000 viceregal annual salary; in addition, the Curzons were expected to buy all plate, wine, carriages and horses from the outgoing Viceroy, as well as paying their own fares and freight to India.

As Vicereine, Mary had to be dressed as befitted a queen in a country where status was indicated by sumptuous clothing and jewels. Her trousseau from Paris cost over £1,000* (the average weekly wage of an agricultural labourer then was 90p). Levi Leiter gave her a parure of diamonds, including a tiara, and £3,000 to the couple jointly. It was at this moment that Curzon, perhaps feeling that once touched by destiny nothing could harm him, decided to buy a 25-year lease on a neighbouring house, No. 1 Carlton House Terrace. It cost him £25,000 and a further £1,500 was needed to put it in decent repair, which he did not hesitate to borrow from the bank (guaranteed by his long-suffering father-in-law).

On 10 December 1898, Mary, Irene, Cimmie, aged $3\frac{1}{2}$ months, and their nanny (engaged, needless to say, by Curzon), left Plymouth on the three-week voyage for India. Curzon joined them at Marseilles. His departure was known to his coterie of friends as 'the passing of a Soul'.

---

*Well over £54,000 in today's money.

2

Viceroy and Vicereine

~

On the way to India Mary Curzon made her will. Datelined 'The Indian Ocean, 29 December 1898', it is a pathetically brief document, seemingly written largely to safeguard her jewellery.

> I devise and bequeath my four rows of white pearls my large tiara made by Boucheron my second diamond tiara made by the Goldsmiths Co my diamond necklace made by Watherston and all my old laces to my husband George Nathaniel Lord Curzon of Kedleston to be held by him upon trust during his life for my son if I have one or for the eldest surviving of my sons if I have more than one. And upon my husband's death to be similarly held upon trust by my son or eldest son whichever it be as heirlooms inalienable from the Kedleston title. Failing my son I bequeath the above mentioned articles to my husband upon trust during his life for my daughters to be distributed by him among them either during his life or upon his death at his discretion.

She wished the same for her diamond star tiara and diamond brooch.

Moving on to the rest of her jewellery – notably a ring, clasp and brooch of rubies and diamonds, brooches, crescent and belt of turquoise and a sapphire-and-diamond bracelet – she left these to Curzon, to keep or dispose of as gifts as he thought fit, as well as her plate and personal belongings. To her father went a book and a picture by Millet; to her mother, her sables, silver fox, chinchilla and other furs. This will would later add to the conflict between Curzon and his daughters.

In India, as in England, the two little girls led a life with a strict nursery routine. Outside the home, their parents moved through the formalities expected of them. Levees, dances, a Drawing Room, a garden party, official dinners for 120 every Thursday and innumerable smaller dinner and luncheon parties were crammed into the three months spent in Calcutta. Bejewelled princes walked along marble floors past motionless rows of uniformed viceregal guards to where the Viceroy, seated on a dais in the Throne Room, awaited them. If the visitor were of sufficiently high rank Curzon would descend the steps to meet him.

Simla, in the Darjeeling Hills, was a different matter altogether. The wives and children of army officers and administrators in the Indian Civil Service came here to escape the stifling, enervating heat of the plains while their husbands sweltered below, escaping for short breaks to join them, and life was freer and less formal. Young officers flirted with grass widows during early-morning rides, picnics and dances, gossip was rife and the atmosphere frivolous.

The nearest Curzon came to relaxation was at another Viceregal refuge, Naldera, a camp seventeen miles from Simla where he could eat and work out of doors. The stream of orders, reports, diplomatic messages and reforms that flowed unceasingly from his pen were varied by letters to friends in England and a copious correspondence with his agent on the need to find a tenant prepared to pay the highest possible rent for No. 1 Carlton House Terrace. Eventually they settled on Mr Choate,* who offered £2,000 a year.

India, with its superabundance of eligible single men, was a paradise for young unmarried women. When Mary's sisters came to stay with the Curzons in 1899 the youngest, Daisy, became engaged to one of the Viceroy's ADCs, Lord Suffolk's eldest son (whom she married in 1904).

Mary took her two young children back to England for a visit of six months in 1901, during which time she and Curzon wrote to each other almost every day. He also wrote to his daughters, loving little notes with exactly the sort of news they would like. 'My sweet Simmy, Daddy is going to write you a line while he is sitting out under the trees at Naldera,' he wrote on 10 June 1901. 'It is so hot that he has got no coat on. Little Fluffy is lying at my

---

*Joseph Hodges Choate was the US Ambassador to London 1899–1905.

feet stretched out on her side pretending to be asleep. She never leaves me and has quite recovered her looks now that she is back in Simla. I am all alone now in the morning when I get up. No itty girls to come in and see me and help me to shave. Isn't it sad? Kisses to Irene and Simmy from loving Daddy.' The letters continued in a stream, from Viceregal Lodge, Simla, and the heat of Government House in Calcutta ('When I came back here little Danny recognised me at once and he came trotting to me and never leaves my side at luncheon and dinner.')

In England Mary was feted, dining with the King and Queen – of whom she became a close friend – and enchanting men like the future Prime Minister, Arthur Balfour, who described her as 'intoxicating'.

She was back in India for the Coronation Durbar (to proclaim Edward VII King-Emperor) held in India's capital, Delhi, in 1902. The viceregal couple entered the city on an elephant, sitting in a silver howdah beneath the golden umbrella of state. The assemblage awaiting them displayed possibly the greatest collection of jewels ever to be seen in one place: each of the Indian princes was adorned with the most spectacular of his gems from the collections of centuries, while the English had been advised that protocol demanded their most splendid, opulent pieces. The only unplanned moment in the magnificence of the proceedings occurred when a fox terrier belonging to one of the bandsmen in a Highland regiment trotted across the great horseshoe-shaped arena, mounted the dais, leapt into the empty throne awaiting Curzon and began barking.

Parades, march-pasts and polo culminated in the State Ball, where Mary outshone everyone in the famous Peacock Dress – cloth of gold embroidered with tiny peacock feathers, each eye an emerald, the skirt trimmed with white roses and the bodice with lace. She glittered with diamonds, pearls and precious stones: a huge necklace of diamonds around her throat, others of diamonds and pearls and a crown-like tiara, a pearl tipping each of its high diamond points. As she walked through the hall, Curzon beside her in white satin knee breeches, the gasps were almost audible.

It was at Naldera, in the summer of 1903, that Mary conceived her third child. She returned to England early in January 1904 for the birth; the Curzons' third daughter was born on 20 March

1904. She was christened Alexandra Naldera, after her godmother Queen Alexandra and the place of which Mary had such idyllic memories. Neither of the Curzons regarded their family as complete, however; both were anxious for an heir.

Very shortly, Mary was pregnant again. Curzon, who had come back to England in May, began to look for a country house, which had to be reasonably easy to reach from London and grand enough to suit his tastes. One day he was taken to lunch at Hackwood, near Basingstoke, a beautiful eighteenth-century house set in a finely timbered deer park of 700 acres. Lord Wilton, to whom it had been leased by its owner, Lord Bolton, was anxious to reassign the lease. With his usual thoroughness, Curzon, who had been immediately attracted by the place, set himself the task of finding out as much as he could about it.

In August their hopes for an heir were dashed when Mary suffered a miscarriage, followed by complications. In those pre-antibiotic days, any infection was dangerous and by September her life was despaired of. She rallied, succumbed, and rallied again, Curzon distraught at her bedside and her daughters brought in to say goodbye to her. Finally, after her life had been five times given up for lost, she recovered and by the end of October 1904 was considered out of danger, though very weak.

A month later Curzon tore himself away from his family to return to India. Although no previous Viceroy had served a second term, he had requested an extension in order to see through the reforms he had inaugurated and, having gained Cabinet agreement, felt he could not renege on this. He missed Mary bitterly ('I have not dared go into your room for fear I should burst out crying'), as she did him.

In February 1905 Mary, her three daughters, two nannies, and a live cow in the hold to give fresh milk for eleven-month-old Alexandra, left for India. They went straight to the health-giving air of Simla – where almost at once Mary narrowly escaped death from an earthquake – and, at last, settled down for what they hoped would be a uninterrupted spell of family life at Naldera. It was here that Alexandra was given the name that would stay with her all her life: Baba, the Indian word for baby or little one.

They were there less than a year. Curzon may have been India's greatest Viceroy but his imperious attitude had made him enemies.

The chief of these was Lord Kitchener, whom Curzon himself had proposed as Commander-in-Chief of the Indian Army. Although, ironically, Kitchener was one of Mary's greatest admirers, it was almost inevitable that two men of such dominating character would fall out. In the ensuing battle of wills Kitchener, politically more manipulative than Curzon and soon with the Cabinet on his side, became the victor. On 14 August 1905, Curzon resigned. 'Today you will see Curzon's resignation in the papers and Minto's appointment,' wrote Lord Esher to a friend. 'What a confusion, a new viceroy on the eve of the Prince of Wales's visit.

'Of course it is bound to take the gilt off that, as Curzon would have done the whole thing magnificently. Perhaps, in one sense, from the P. of Wales's point of view, it has this advantage, that he would have played ALMOST second fiddle to Curzon.'

When the Curzons left Simla in October, their carriage was dragged through the streets by the townspeople and they were given a triumphant send-off. By contrast, Curzon arrived home in December 1905 to a cool, shabby welcome. There was no earldom (given to every previous Viceroy) and his friend Arthur Balfour, now Prime Minister, refused to support his candidacy in the various parliamentary constituencies which invited him to stand.

Bitterly wounded, puzzled and humiliated he retired with Mary and their daughters to the South of France, returning to 1 Carlton House Terrace the following March. Here, once more, he took over the management of the house, even inspecting all the servants every morning to check that their uniforms were in perfect condition and their fingernails clean. This time, Mary did not mind so much. She had never really recovered her health after her illness eighteen months earlier and it was now steadily deteriorating, so much so that in June 1906 she wrote to her brother: 'I fear I shall never be well again.'

Less than a month later she put her final letter on Curzon's pillow. 'What causes me such acute agony is that I should be a burden to you whom I worship, just when I would give my very soul to be a help.' Ten days later, on 18 July 1906, she died of a heart attack, with Curzon's arm around her. She was only thirty-six.

3

The Schoolroom at Hackwood

~

Devastated by the death of his wife and the miserable, ignominious end to his viceroyalty, Curzon virtually retired from public life, devoting most of his intellectual energy to the Chancellorship of Oxford University, to which he had been nominated in 1907, and to the Rectorship of Glasgow University, to which he was elected in 1908. More importantly for his daughters, he installed himself in the house that was to become their home. For, ignoring his father's adverse reports on its size and expense, he had finally leased Hackwood.

Palatial enough to suit even Curzon, who had acquired its lease for a premium of £8,000 (the original asking price was £14,000), its rent of £3,050 a year included the wages of keepers for the excellent shoot. There were nine lodges and cottages, vineries, greenhouses, a cricket ground, kitchen garden, coach-house and infirmary. The entrance hall was 52ft long, with tapestry panels, there was a ballroom, a large library, an oak-panelled saloon of 45 × 33ft and a morning-room almost as big, a dining-room 60ft long, bedrooms galore, with a large nursery suite in the east wing above the billiard room and the smoking-room, servants' bedrooms, a steward's room, a housekeeper's room, furnace rooms, dairies, sculleries, bakehouses, cellars, larders, a lamp room, a plate room and a boot room.

Curzon immediately set about improving those aspects of the house which he considered needed remodelling. A large mound outside interfered with his view; he had it lowered, necessitating the removal of almost 15,000 cubic feet of earth before it was level. The drains, which gave trouble, were cleaned – Curzon devoted many letters to the question of sludge in the filters – and the lake was dredged. A ratcatcher was called in, the breakfast room and library painted, two bell-pushes, with ivory labels marked 'Maid' and 'Valet', fitted in all the family and guest bed-rooms. Four radiators were fitted in the icy ballroom, and in an Organ Hall covered with Persian carpets he installed an Aeolian organ on which he would play with childlike gusto and enjoyment.

The house was furnished with the utmost grandeur. Curzon's tastes ran to the imperial – gilded furniture, crimson velvet hang-ings, gold tassels and huge chandeliers. There were crimson silk damask curtains with cords and tassels, a carved gilt threefold Louis XIV screen and panels of crimson velvet with appliqué borders in the saloon. Even the billiard table had a cover of crimson velvet with a design in gold and silver thread. Tapestry curtains set off the more exotic fruits of his travels – ivories, Persian rugs, ebony chairs and tigerskins.

Almost at once he began the great house parties for which the Edwardians are known. His most famous ones were at Whitsun-tide, in late May or early June, with firework displays in the park, charades, games, croquet, tennis, walking, talking and the clan-destine love-affairs that were a feature of Edwardian high society.

For this was a world of rigid etiquette but flexible morals, where anything was permissible if there was no public scandal. Thus certain conventions took on the force of iron rules. Letters, for instance, always had to be left out to be stamped and posted by servants: if a woman posted her own it suggested a secret correspondent. Every well-brought-up girl was taught from child-hood to close the door of her bedroom as she left it – open doors could be thought to signal availability – and forbidden to look into the windows of gentlemen's clubs as this could also be inter-preted as invitation (although the same young women were expected to use every art, including the sidelong glance, to allure those same gentlemen when seated next to them at dinner). Going on the stage was disreputable yet the private equivalent – charades, tableaux and amateur dramatics – was popular in the grandest and most respectable houses.

Provided one observed these outward forms, romantic pos-sibilities were ever-present. The formality between the sexes was such that friendships, always ostensibly platonic, between men and married women were a recognised social relationship. Many *were* truly platonic – Lady Desborough, for instance, had a host of male friends with whom she corresponded, many of whom wrote to her for years without ever using her Christian name. Others were the cover for a love-affair under the accepted convention that they were nothing more than friendship.

Curzon, like the rest of his circle, viewed his friends' liaisons with sympathy, relished hearing the latest gossip about them, and pursued his own affairs wholeheartedly but discreetly. It was different, of course, for the lower classes. When Curzon found that one of the housemaids in his employ at Carlton House Terrace had allowed a footman to spend the night with her he sacked her without hesitation ('I put the wretched little slut out in the street at a moment's notice') and years later believed that Edith Thompson (of the famous Thompson–Bywaters murder case) should be hanged, not because he thought she was guilty of murder but because of her 'flagrant and outrageous adultery'. This regard for the outward form while pursuing private inclination was an ethos which was later to colour the thinking of his daughters.

Curzon was a loving and thoughtful, if distant, father to his three children, interested in every detail of their clothes, education and health. 'My darling Twinkums,' reads a note brought up to the nursery in February 1908. 'I am so sorry my pretty is whooping worse. This afternoon as I was lying with the window slightly open, I just caught a sound of it in the distance, like the cry of a far away owl. Love to all the kittens. Your loving Daddy.'

Whenever he was away, letters scribbled on small black-bordered sheets of paper arrived for all of them in turn. Frequently – as, later, with his second wife Grace – they contained an admonition to write to him more often. 'Darling Cim, What is Mrs Simkin doing? I get long and beautiful and well written letters from Irene but where is little Cim? Silent as a mouse. Not even the sound of a nibble.' Only Mary, viewed as a perfect, saint-like figure in death, had written to him as copiously and frequently as even he could wish.

Long letters came when he and the children's Aunt Blanche took a restorative sea voyage in the autumn of 1908 to Las Palmas, Majorca, where his fame preceded him but the lack of occupation made his stay nearly intolerable.

Auntie Blanche and I have been here for over five days and are already rather tired of it. The roads are abominable and driving upon them almost a torture. The surroundings of the town are bare and brown and barren – all thrown up by some ancient volcano – and there is nothing to do.

The Spanish authorities have found me out and write splendid articles about me in the local newspapers. The Governor and the Mayor called upon me in tight trousers and top hats with gold canes in their hands and tonight they have organised a special performance at the theatre in my honour. When I go out young Spanish boys pursue me with postcards on which they request me to write my autograph.

It was not surprising that the girls grew up with the idea of their father as a majestic being of immense importance and all-seeing knowledge.

When Mary Curzon died, the main presence in the children's lives was their devoted Nanny Sibley, who from then on gave up her life to her three charges, refusing to return to the fiancé she had left in India. As the girls grew older, they spent most of their time in the grey-carpeted schoolroom with a succession of governesses.

One of the first of these had taught Lady Cynthia Charteris (now Lady Cynthia Asquith). 'Can you', asked Curzon of Cynthia, 'recommend this daughter of Austria, your sometime preceptress, as a suitable person to be entrusted with the upbringing of three high-minded orphans?' Lady Cynthia could. She did not, however, tell him about her former governess's report of how Curzon would 'enter the schoolroom in a procession of one at the beginning of the term, arrange all the books and pictures, and draw up the timetable of lessons'.

His interest in his children's education did not stop at organising their timetable. Luncheon would be treated as an impromptu lesson or, more often, an examination. Day after day events in the history of the nation would be described in Gibbonian prose, in the Derbyshire accent with its short *a*'s which their father retained all his life ('the gr*a*ss on that p*a*th needs cutting'). Then came the questioning, dreaded most perhaps by Irene, the eldest, who frequently felt so nervous she could hardly swallow her food.

It was often disguised as a game. 'I see a battlefield,' Curzon would intone. 'I see a man in armour, on a large, heavy horse, richly caparisoned ...' The children would be asked in turn which incident their father had been describing and where it fitted into the pattern of history. When they could not answer, he would turn to the quaking governess who was usually equally at sea. The only response that any of them could give was: 'We have not got as far as that', to which Curzon would reply that they never seemed to move beyond William the Conqueror. It was the same with geography, Bible studies or other subjects in which he thought they should be educated. Interestingly, the one subject of which he never spoke and in which he felt women should never 'meddle' was the one that later attracted all three girls – politics.

Out of doors, their hair in pigtails and dressed in navy blue serge sailor suits, the children would help their father in an activity characteristic both of his energy and of his attention to detail. When Curzon had first arrived at Hackwood he had told the astonished head gardener, who had kept the gardens there for many years, that he did not know how to keep lawns free of plantains and that he, Lord Curzon, would show him the correct way.

Accordingly, preceded by a footman carrying a small rush mat on which Curzon could rest his right knee and a narrow pronged spike for the removal of the enemy, the former Viceroy and his daughters would emerge on to the Hackwood lawns. There he would vigorously attack the hated weed while the girls stood round him, each holding a little wicker basket in which to put the debris of roots and leaves. Anyone who spotted a plantain their father had not seen was given sixpence – a thistle rated one shilling. Indoors, Curzon showed the same dedication to removing grubby fingermarks from doors and walls, leading his children round bedrooms and drawing-rooms with handfuls of breadcrumbs to remove any stains they found.

His eldest daughter, Irene, was already enthralled by the sport that would dominate her life for the next twenty-five years. Horses and hunting had become her passion. The hunts local to Hackwood were the Tyne and the Garth and in her first season at the age of twelve, out with the Tyne on 14 November 1908, riding first Dandy and then Topsy, she was awarded the fox's brush (tail). She went home ecstatic.

At the end of the season there was an even greater triumph, this time with the Garth, who met seven miles from Hackwood at Long Sutton House. Hounds found in nearby gorse, ran for two hours covering seven miles of country, and Irene – again riding first Dandy then Topsy – was this time given the ultimate accolade, the mask (head).

Later, her sisters came out hunting with her. Irene's Hunting Journal, laboriously filled with handwriting that had not yet become atrocious, records that on 29 October 1910, during her third season, 'Cim got the mask and Baba the brush.' As it was a cub-hunting day it was, no doubt, an easy way of maintaining cordial relations with a local grandee: halfway through the season, on 21 January 1911, there was a lawn meet at Hackwood (followed by a six-mile point), both of which Irene must have adored.

Cimmie preferred the activities at her boarding school, The Links, in Eastbourne, where the thirty-seven pupils wore a uniform of white blouses and striped ties, played cricket, tennis, lacrosse and roller-skated, swam in the summer and skated in the winter. It was run by Miss Jane Potts, governess to Queen Victoria's granddaughter Princess Alice, and it aimed to produce happy, healthy, well-brought-up young women who could embroider and play the piano – exactly fitting the Curzonian feminine ideal of accomplishment rather than education. Cimmie loved it.

4

Elinor Glyn

~

Curzon was not one of those fathers who felt that his children must have a stepmother. To him, the wife he had loved so much was a paragon of all the virtues; he mourned Mary deeply and sincerely and he encouraged his children to think of their dead mother in the same way. 'Darling Cim, I have been looking out the photos of darling Mummie for you and Irene and I will have some beautiful ones framed and sent to you before long,' said one note sent from his study in Carlton House Terrace to the nursery upstairs.

Upper-class Edwardian children seldom saw much of their parents and Curzon's own upbringing, given over to the mercy of a sadistic governess, had been particularly brutal in that respect. The Curzon daughters viewed their father as someone loving but distant, an Olympian figure whose letters expressed the affection he was too busy to show by companionship. When they were living in the same house he would usually see them in the mornings; if not, they would frequently receive a note.

He was not a man to do without women for long, not only because of his powerful libido but because he loved female company. 'A dinner party without a woman present is nothing more than a meeting of masticating and chunnering males,' he once wrote. They had to be beautiful and, if possible, red-haired (all the locks of hair he kept were of some shade of red). Two attachments, in particular, were to have a lasting effect on his children's lives.

He had first met Elinor Glyn at a weekend house party in early 1908. At forty-three, she was extraordinarily youthful-looking and an acknowledged beauty. With her white skin, green eyes fringed with thick black lashes and red hair ('No really *nice* woman would have colouring like that', she once said of herself), she was everything that Curzon admired physically in a woman, from the 'snowy amplitudes' revealed in her *décolletée* dresses to the colour of her hair. This was so long and thick that when she had first married her husband, Clayton Glyn, he had hired the Brighton Baths for two days so that she could swim up and down naked, her hair streaming out behind her. Alas, it was his sole romantic gesture – and Elinor lived for romance. Years later she was to write in her autobiography: 'On looking back at my life, I see that the dominant interest, in fact the fundamental impulse behind every action, has been the desire for romance.'

Thwarted of it in her relationship with her husband, a placid, good-natured man whose absorbing interest was food – one of his nieces remarked that rather than go to bed with his wife he would sit up all night with a pear in order to eat it at the exact moment of perfect ripeness – Elinor turned instead to clothes. Into them she poured all her love of beauty, her search for perfection, her thwarted romanticism.

She had the perfect excuse – 'helping Lucy'. Her sister Lucy, married to the baronet Sir Cosmo Duff Gordon, was the fashionable society dressmaker 'Lucile' and, as Elinor pointed out to her husband, if Lucy's dresses were seen to advantage on Elinor, more customers would follow.

It was an era when clothes had never been more lavish or important. For the smart woman, several changes of costume a day were essential: tweed walking-dresses for the morning; chiffon and lace dresses surmounted by enormous picture hats for Ascot; cotton or linen dresses to go on the river; white muslin with silk sashes for tea on the lawn and teagowns for an afternoon in the boudoir; fur-trimmed velvet coats to which bunches of Parma violets were pinned for winter; handmade peach or pink crêpe-de-chine underwear trimmed with coffee-coloured Brussels lace.

Men's clothes were equally elaborate: black morning coats with beautifully-fitting dark blue or black overalls strapped down over polished black boots with blunt silver spurs for Rotten Row; tweed knickerbocker suits for shooting, often with the Tyrolean-style hats made popular by the King; frock-coats for the House of Commons; white tie and tails for dinner parties.

Elinor was always superbly dressed, frequently in her favourite shades of purple, mauve or lilac that set off her dramatic colouring. On every possible pretext she acquired new outfits – later, some of her family were to say that she ruined Clayton by her extravagance. This sense of a passion barely restrained – albeit for what the men of those days called 'feminine fripperies' – flashed from her green eyes and informed her manner. She was completely faithful to her husband, but around her hung an aura of sensuality and sexual suggestiveness. She had just written the novel *Three Weeks*, which had scandalised Edwardian society with its tale of the erotic passion between a beautiful and mysterious older woman and a young man, its highlight the seduction by the 'Lady' of her younger lover Paul on a tigerskin.

Elinor found it difficult to understand the furore caused by *Three Weeks*. All her life, she believed not only that sensual passion could be the pathway to the highest appreciation of the beautiful and the good, and could awaken both idealism and nobility in the young, but also that it was the mysterious, necessary fertile soil from which sprang intellectual development and creative thought. For Elinor, love – real love – between a man and a woman meant the complete and rapturous union of body, mind and spirit, the noblest state to which humankind could aspire with, naturally, faithfulness to the object of such a supreme passion as the inevitable corollary. It was an attitude that found little echo in the society around her.

When Curzon met the famous Mrs Glyn, he was immediately intrigued and attracted. The fact that his friend Alfred, Lord Milner, was supposedly madly in love with her only added a competitive edge to his feelings. His chance for an opening move soon came.

Owing to her husband's financial losses, the Glyns were largely dependent on Elinor's earnings. Elinor decided to cash in on the notoriety of *Three Weeks* and dramatise it for a charity matinée on 23 July 1908 in the hope that this would prompt a professional manager to stage it commercially. As no actress could be found to play the part of the heroine, Elinor took this herself. Curzon was one of the large invited audience. There, lying in voluptuous abandon on a tigerskin in the centre of the Adelphi stage, her red hair tumbling over flimsy draperies, was the author and incarnation of the most famous love story of the decade, seemingly offering herself to the beholder. The effect on Curzon was immediate.

He rushed back to Carlton House Terrace where he unpacked from a trunk one of the five tigerskins he had brought back from India. It was a particularly fine one, shot in Gwalior by Curzon himself. Within days, the Lord Chamberlain had refused permission for *Three Weeks* to be shown in public, a ban that only enhanced the exotic reputation of the book – and its author. Curzon despatched his present to Elinor (Alfred Milner, he was put out to learn a few days later, had had exactly the same idea).

Nothing could have been more effective. Elinor had felt a particular affinity with this jungle beast ever since an early admirer had murmured 'Belle tigresse!' in her ear. It was a message loaded with erotic symbolism; it came, too, from a man she already admired. Curzon's aristocratic mien, dignity and cool, patrician good looks represented to her the highest type of Englishman – the hero of her books come to life (all her life she was to call him 'Milor').

She wrote to thank him, mentioning the admiration she felt for his work as Viceroy, a tribute that was balm to a man still chewing over the soreness of his rejection by an ungrateful government. He wrote back suggesting that they met; to his delight, he found that she was cultivated, intelligent and well-read as well as beautiful. The long, clandestine pursuit of her began over chance meetings, secret lunches and dinners.

Curzon's second important female friendship was open and sunny. In 1906 Waldorf Astor, son of the immensely wealthy American businessman, the widowed William Waldorf Astor, had fallen in love with Nancy Shaw, born Nancy Langhorne, from a well-known Virginian family. Nancy – like Waldorf, born on 19 May 1879 – had been briefly and unhappily married to Robert Gould Shaw, by whom her first son Bobbie was born in 1898. When she realised that Shaw was a hopeless alcoholic she left him, only agreeing to a divorce when his parents begged her to do so in order that he could marry his pregnant mistress. In 1906 she married the 27-year-old Waldorf and his father, now the first Lord Astor, gave the young couple Cliveden, his palatial house on the Thames.

Almost at once, Nancy began to entertain on a grand scale.

There were two or three balls for up to five hundred guests given every Season, frequent dinners for fifty or sixty people and hardly a weekend without a house party for twenty or thirty. Cliveden was run like a small principality, with its own home farm, its outdoor servants – from forty to fifty gardeners and a dozen stablemen at any one time – living in cottages with their families, its own football and cricket teams, its own tennis courts and golf courses. One hundred tons of coal a year were burned in the bedroom fires alone; the French chef had five kitchenmaids; a legion of housemaids serviced the house; the lawns were mowed by horses with leather boots over their shoes and when a car passed through the park gates the lodgekeeper telephoned the house on a special hand-wound telephone.

Nancy's great charm as a hostess was her American freshness, vitality and relaxed approach. In contrast to the organised formality pertaining in most other great houses, she never appeared before luncheon and guests were free to do exactly what they wanted, from bathing or tennis to walking and talking. She was pretty, witty, warm and funny, she came from the same great country as Curzon's beloved Mary, and he fell under her spell immediately.

'My dear Nancy, I know you are all you describe (and a lot more besides),' he wrote to her in September 1909. 'Virtue and frailty – can there be a more irresistible combination? Why can't a man be fond of a woman without wanting to be her lover? Why can't a woman be fond of a man without being bound to crawl into bed with him? Therefore I am always bound to you by ties of love and abandoned decorum. It is so good to find a woman who is witty and tender and withal domestic.' He loved Cliveden, too, its Palladian elegance, its spaciousness, the Italian stonework installed in the garden by Lord Astor.

Nancy loved her Waldorf, so Curzon had to be content with a romantic friendship. Her relationship with the Curzon daughters was semi-maternal, often shot through with the same squabbles and furious accusations that bedevil family relationships, but the bond was similarly deep, loving and enduring. Cliveden was a house where children were welcome – a special table for them at tea with the grown-ups was set with bread and butter and a plain cake instead of the pastrycook's confections.

Meanwhile, Elinor Glyn was falling deeply in love with Curzon. She still clung to the idea of marital fidelity but her idealism had been sorely tested by the behaviour of Clayton, sinking into alcoholism and debt and trying to cover up both by lies and deceptions. When Clayton was 'lent' £1,200 by Curzon, who knew he would never see it again, it was a moral milestone for Elinor. She felt not only that Clayton had betrayed the marriage but that she had in some sense been 'sold' by him. She now felt herself free of obligation towards him. When she went to Dresden in the late summer of 1908 to look for a *pension* where her older daughter Margot could stay while being 'finished', she made a detour afterwards to Heidelberg, where Curzon met her. They spent several passionate days together before returning home separately. It was the first time Elinor had been unfaithful to Clayton.

Back in England, there was an idyllic weekend with Curzon and his three daughters at a house he had leased from Lord Derby, Crag Hall in Derbyshire, where she and Curzon and their five children picnicked, walked and played games. After dinner, *à deux*, Curzon read Aristotle to her; soon afterwards, he gave her a pair of sapphire earrings, saying that these were 'our stone of love and faith,' and a Della Robbia Venus, saying that it reminded him of her.

She leased a small suite at the Ritz so that her lover could visit her, and she and her two daughters made discreet visits to Hackwood. In one of her journals, all bound in green leather, locked with a gold key and kept in purple velvet bags, she wrote rhapsodically: 'A King dwells in the stately house and he is a wizard, because he touched a poor sad and weary travelling Queen, who had never been allowed a throne in her own land – and lo! she became a Queen indeed, reigning with crown and sceptre, and her kingdom was his heart.'

Without in any way understanding the relationship, the three Curzon daughters soon accepted it as a settled part of their world, thinking of Elinor's daughters in the light of cousins. As for Elinor, faithful by nature, she regarded herself as bound body and soul to Curzon and, naturally warm-hearted, was prepared to love his children as her own. With Cimmie especially she formed a deep bond, strengthened when Cimmie was confined first to bed and then to the house with a back problem. 'We talked often of the soul, and of the meaning of things,' said Elinor later.

Cimmie was the only one of Curzon's children to have inherited his congenital malformation of the spine, albeit in much milder form. Curzon sent her at once to the best orthopaedic specialist he could find and she had to begin a strict corrective regime. 'I find by placing a block $\frac{1}{3}$ of an inch beneath the left foot when standing and a pad half an inch thick beneath the left side when sitting, Miss Cynthia's back is much improved,' reported this man, who prescribed bedrest, massage, lying flat first on her front, then her back, for half an hour each, followed by a drive. After a spinal support was made she was allowed to play quiet outdoor games.

Elinor would have made an admirable stepmother. She taught Baba to paint, she told the endless stories that children love and she was genuinely fond of them all. Clayton's health was declining and she had begun to cherish hopes that if she was widowed Curzon would propose to her. She did everything she could to cement the bond between them, from reading translations of the classics to interesting him in the spiritualist séances then fashionable. Being good at psychic games such as table-turning (when 'spirits' were invited to answer questions by rapping or moving tables, in darkened rooms) was a social asset in those days when the physicist Oliver Lodge had made 'piercing the veil' respectable. Curzon, like most of his friends, enjoyed this dabbling in the supernatural and Elinor prided herself on her psychic abilities.

Curzon's feelings were more complicated. In modern parlance, he blew hot and cold. Elinor was a bewitching mistress but his women friends, whose influence in such matters was powerful, disapproved of her. Some schisms, especially those inspired by politics, could be ignored and the Souls did not allow their political differences to interfere with their friendships. But the female Souls were ferociously possessive of their 'dear George' (shortly after her marriage, Mary had told her mother, 'My path is strewn with roses and the only thorns are unforgiving women') and they disapproved of Elinor. She did not come from their tightly-linked circle, she was notorious for the sexual explicitness of *Three Weeks* (ironically, the only erotic book she ever wrote) and she took dear George away from them. Mary Leiter had at least been extremely rich.

Like Mary, Elinor was totally adoring. 'Oh! my heart! to see you there master of those ten thousand people, calm, aloof, unmoved,' she wrote in her journal in early December 1910. 'To hear your noble voice and listen to your masterly argument. To sit there, one of a rough crowd, gazing up at your splendid face and to know that in other moments that proud head can lie upon my breast even as a little child. Ah me! these are the moments in life worth living for. And what matter that sometimes you are cruel and aloof even to me. Have you not a right to be since you are entirely king of my very being?'

It was at this moment that Curzon chose to tell Elinor that their affair should end and that they should be no more than 'tender friends'. One of the reasons, he told her, was the 'chattering of servants'. Another was more probable: he was an ambitious man and he did not wish to present any avoidable weakness that might stand in the way of his return to high office. A mistress known for a book that had been castigated as immoral by reviewers and which had caused her exclusion from the grander house parties would offer plenty of chances for both scandal and ridicule. His parting present of a pair of diamond-and-emerald earrings did nothing to soothe her. 'How can either you or I crush the longing in our veins for each other's arms and lips?' wails her journal. 'I am free and you are free and now we must starve and ache because the situation is too difficult and interferes with your life.'

Elinor could hardly believe that Curzon's decree was final ('You in the prime of life with the red blood rushing in your veins'), especially after receiving a wistful letter from him. As she crossed the Atlantic on a brief visit to New York, her entry for 15 February 1911 records sadly: 'I can never love you less. However you will, you can come back to me and I will love and soothe you and be tender and true.' These words came true sooner than either of them expected.

5

Enter Grace Duggan

~

The rupture with Elinor gave Curzon more time for his friendship with Nancy Astor, who still showed no sign of anything but complete marital fidelity. His letters, with their amorous but resigned undertone, show the extent of his devotion. 'It has just come to me to say that I am truly dearly devotedly fond of you and that I wouldn't lose your affection and your confidence for anything in heaven above or the earth beneath,' he wrote just after Christmas 1910. But chaste adoration was not enough for Curzon and he soon resumed his affair with Elinor. She had no illusions as to the excitement which her voluptuous proportions could evoke in him ('he is a most passionate physical lover') but she wanted her idol to love her as completely as she did him and she laid herself out to please him in as many ways as she could.

She was a clever woman and she talked to political friends like Lord Milner so that she could discuss affairs of the day with perception and acumen; she read the Greek authors to whom Curzon had introduced her; she even indulged the broad vein of bawdiness which she had discovered lurked beneath what Margot Asquith called his 'expression of enamelled assurance'. Just as the nude in art did not shock if it was given the pretext of a classical background, so writing that would otherwise be condemned as salacious could be accepted if presented with sufficient intellectual and historical gloss. Where *Three Weeks* outraged with its open description of adultery, the libidinous goings-on of fifteenth-century castle-dwellers and peasants as described by her friend, the respected medievalist Professor Thomas Lindsay of Edinburgh University, would not.

Lindsay responded admirably to her request for an essay on the more esoteric of these customs. 'I'll not apologise for the very great coarseness of much that I have written,' ran his letter, 'as you asked me not to withhold real information on that account.' The accompanying bundle of manuscript, covering such subjects as 'Priest or Knight, the Better Lover?', 'Nudity' and 'Indecent Games', lived up to his promise, with its mingling of chivalrous custom, louche behaviour and – of particular appeal to Elinor – its exposition of the Renaissance belief that the sexual act was not a thing apart but the *only* complete and perfect form of love.

While Curzon pursued his varied interests, the life of his daughters was one of routine, mostly revolving around governesses and schools and, for Cimmie, long months of treatment for her back which ultimately proved successful. The summers were spent at Curzon's villa, also called Naldera, at the seaside resort of Broadstairs, where their father would join them for a day or so.

In 1911 Curzon was turning over in his mind the question of 'finishing' his eldest daughter, now sixteen. 'I have been over to Paris to see about Irene's education,' he wrote to Nancy in August 1911. 'I plan to place her with a French lady to study certain aspects (only) of Gallic life.' In the event, he sent Irene to Dresden, noted for its music, buildings and general culture and, thanks to German links with the royal family and many members of the aristocracy, then at least as popular as Paris for the cultural education of a young woman. For Irene, music was to remain an abiding passion that not only gave her joy and consolation but influenced many future friendships – and love affairs.

She had been sent to Dresden with the children's governess as chaperone. At home, Curzon was occupied in interviewing a replacement. Baba wrote excitedly to Irene: 'Darling sweet Nina, Miss L came this evening. We talked about lessons and after played ball, she has brought a bike with her! She seems very nice, she is so jolly, she does lovely painting on chiffon and does all sorts of nice things. We are going to take her round the woods this morning, she is very sad we have no dog or cat. Goodbye sweet Nina from your loving Baba.'

Perhaps the governess's influence caused Curzon finally to relent and allow Baba the dog she had been begging for – naturally, chosen by him rather than her. He selected one on a basis that to him seemed quite logical: the first dog had trotted confidently in and relieved itself against the red Foreign Office box, after which every other dog followed suit. The only one that did not was a Pomeranian. Baba named it Bobby.

Curzon believed that he led a quiet life, dedicated to duty in spite of constant pain and an ambition shattered by the débâcle of his resignation as Viceroy. 'I am supposed to seek the footlights. Little do they know what a business it is to get me on to the stage. How many of them, I wonder, have any idea of the long hours spent in bed and the aching back, of the vicious and severe pain in the leg, of the fearful steel cage in which I have to be incased when I undergo any strain in which standing up is involved.' His belated earldom in 1911 did little to modify these feelings while those for Elinor grew stronger. By the time he took a house in Green Street, Mayfair, to bring out her daughter Margot in the spring of 1912, Curzon appeared to be deeply in love again, marking his return with a sapphire-and-diamond ring to match the earrings he had given her earlier.

But the relationship was still on a sporadic and clandestine basis. Elinor was never invited to Curzon's large house parties at Hackwood, for instance, when up to twenty of his friends arrived with an equal or greater number of servants – and she was certainly not asked to the dinner he gave at the end of June 1912 to celebrate the completion of 1 Carlton House Terrace, attended by eighty-six of his friends, including most of the Souls and a miscellany of others ranging from potentates like Lord Derby to hostesses like Lady Cunard.

Instead, Curzon would dine with her secretly, though never as often as she wished, leaving her with the longing ache with which she was by now so familiar. She would sit waiting for a word from him. 'I am listening – for what? a telephone ringing? it rang at that moment but it was only a shop. Here is the footman with a telegram – my pulse thunders in my ears but it is only an unimportant missive about tonight.' She did not fool herself. 'What a man most desires to do *that he will find time for* even if he snatch it from sleep. Realise that if he does not write it is because writing is *not* what he most desires to do. He may love you just the same but the subtle thought of whether he makes you happy or unhappy does not enter into his scheme of things.'

By the end of July she had come to a clear vision and was chiding herself: 'Fool to sit there and eat your heart out. Why live like a nun away from the world? for ever brooding on one thought, the concentrated essence of fidelity to one man. He does not value you the more for it. He enjoys his life and his friends, his life is full of interesting things, he does not rebuff the admiration of women as you do of men.' It was true: to Nancy Astor he would respond immediately, especially if he thought there was the slightest chance of seeing her. 'Faithful dog that I am I reply at once though it is past 1 am. Of course this is because I love and think of you and to hear from you means that faithful little girl has turned a thought to me.'

Nancy was never too busy for his daughters and often asked them to Cliveden. 'Dearest Cim and Baba, It was so awfully kind of you to write me and I loved getting your letters,' came one note in February 1914 when she was indisposed. 'Perhaps your Papa will motor you over next week just to see me in the afternoon. I shall write and beg him to do so because it is so dull lying in bed. I feel it is your duty to come and visit your old Governess, who has been so kind to you for many years. You and Baba will I hope be careful hunting. With a great deal of love, Affectionately Yours, Nancy Astor. Love to Irene.'

Elinor, meanwhile, began to see other men and in 1913 even, gently, to encourage their friendship. The following year, she decided to make herself less available and early in 1914 went to live in Paris where, thanks to French relatives and a court of admirers, she felt happy and at home. Curzon's devotion seemed assured: that spring, he commissioned a portrait of her by the fashionable society painter Philip de Laszlo and when his daughters asked for Elinor's address so that they could write to her, he gave it to them immediately: her influence could bring nothing but good to motherless girls.

In many ways, Elinor fulfilled his ideal of womanhood: she was beautiful, intelligent, discreet, she did not attempt to interfere with his life and above all – though she earned her living by her pen – she was not tiresomely independent. All his life Curzon spent much time and energy in trying to keep women in what he regarded as their proper place – drawing-room, bedroom, boudoir and, if they were of the lower classes, kitchen. In the House of Lords he brought the heavy artillery of his classically-trained mind to bear on their demand for the vote ('I believe that the great majority of men hold that female suffrage will be injurious to the Empire and the State'). He did concede that it should be the electorate rather than Parliament which should decide whether women got the vote but as the electorate was entirely male there was little danger there.

He himself produced fifteen reasons why 'woman suffrage' was undesirable, concluding with the effect on India if women were seen to have any hand at all in the government of the mother country. Small wonder that the Prime Minister Herbert Asquith was to note of Irene (in a letter to Venetia Stanley, the young woman he adored, a month after the outbreak of war): 'The Curzon daughter seemed quiet and a trifle gauche. I expect he is rather an overwhelming father.' Curzon was even reluctant to ask women who openly disagreed with him on this important point to the great coming-out ball he was giving for Irene, writing plaintively to Nancy Astor: 'Must I ask that red-haired little tiger cat Frances Balfour who abuses me on every suffragist platform?' Otherwise, he brought all his characteristic attention to detail to this important rite of passage.

The ball took place at Carlton House Terrace on 4 May 1914. Nothing was spared to make it a success. A supper room was created in the garden, its 70-foot-long walls covered inside with blue canvas, lace curtains at its window, eight chandeliers, the drawing-room carpet on the ground and with tapestries brought up from Hackwood hung on the walls. The first-floor drawing-room, its floor cleaned, polished and waxed, was turned into the ballroom, with small gilt chairs for the chaperones all round. To reach it, a special covered staircase, lined in blue and buff muslin, was constructed from the pavement to the drawing-room balcony with its French windows. The library doors were removed so that this could be used as a passage through to the cloakrooms. Casano's band (considered the smartest), with twenty musicians led by the great man himself, was hired at a cost of 43 guineas, including the bringing and removal of three grand pianos.

There were flowers everywhere – carnations and lilies-of-the-valley on the supper tables, golden hanging baskets overflowing with white roses in the hall, massed hydrangeas in the fireplaces and orchids in every alcove – and almost as many dukes and duchesses: the Marlboroughs, Devonshires, Rutlands, Sutherlands and Portlands were among the fifty-two guests at the dinner party beforehand (the cost, noted Curzon carefully, was 25s a head). The setting alone cost £438 6s 6d and Gunter's supplied supper for four hundred and a full staff of waiters for £230. The wine was from Curzon's cellars. 'The Queen', he noted, 'drinks sparkling Moselle at dinner and supper, the King whisky and Berlin seltzer.' But at the last minute the royal couple had to absent themselves owing to the death of the Duke of Argyll, Princess Louise's husband; instead they came to tea with Curzon and Irene that afternoon.

It was a polished and appreciated entertainment; as he told Nancy afterwards: 'People were very good about [it] and I think it repaid all the trouble.' Irene, dark and graceful, 'with a great look of the mother she lost', reported one society paper, wore the obligatory white with a single string of the magnificent pearls that had belonged to Mary. Unfortunately, as she knew no young men owing to her father's Victorian belief that these dangerous creatures should be kept away from girls until they came out, her only dancing partners were elderly uncles.

When war was declared on 4 August 1914, Curzon offered his services to Asquith immediately but was rejected. 'Pitiful that at 39 one was thought fit to rule 300 millions of people, and at 55 is not wanted to do anything in an emergency in which our whole national existence is at stake,' he reflected bitterly. His children were loyally indignant for him. Baba drew a pen-and-ink sketch of the head of her father's nemesis, Lord Kitchener (now at the peak of his fame as Secretary for War), marking it phrenologically, its different sections labelled with various qualities such as 'mis-judgement', 'short-sightedness', 'ambition', 'egotism'.

To Elinor, who had returned from France, he lent his holiday villa Naldera at Broadstairs. Here her daughter Margot would listen to the guns booming on the other side of the Channel. He also invited the Belgian royal family, whom he had met with Mary in the South of France, to stay at Hackwood for as long as they wished. Though the King of the Belgians returned to the unoccupied part of Belgium, his three children – Charles, Albert and Marie-José – remained at Hackwood throughout the war.

Baba was the one who saw most of them; she and Marie-José played piano duets together, were exactly the same age and remained friends all their lives. Baba disliked Albert, largely because of his unkindness to her beloved dog Bobby, into whom, to annoy her, he would attempt to stick pins.

Curzon was solicitous about the welfare of his Belgian guests. He supervised the princes' education and, one weekend in 1915, invited a famous Belgian cellist who had taught Queen Elizabeth of the Belgians to play the violin to stay at Hackwood for the weekend and make music to entertain her three children.

With him came the young Artur Rubinstein, later to achieve worldwide fame as a pianist, and two other members of the quartet. They arrived on Saturday, to be greeted by Irene with the news that her father was still in London but would arrive in time for dinner and that the two Belgian princes were away. 'That leaves us only with little Princess Marie-José,' said Irene, 'but she is the one who really loves music.'

Curzon greeted his guests in the drawing-room before dinner. The impression he made on Rubinstein was indelible. 'Lord Curzon entered like a supreme judge ready to pronounce a death sentence. His bald head, cold steel-grey eyes and thin, tight mouth made his face bland and expressionless, and he walked with pompous dignity.' (Rubinstein was unaware of Curzon's steel spinal corset, though this sometimes creaked when he walked.) It was too late for music that night, Curzon told them, and Rubinstein spent the following morning in the company of the Curzon daughters and little Princess Marie-José. At teatime Curzon said: 'Gentlemen, if you are not tired, it would be delightful to hear some music.'

They played a quartet by Dvořák, listened to attentively by the girls while Curzon sat in a comfortable armchair in a corner of the room. 'At the end of the first movement we saw him peacefully asleep,' recorded Rubinstein. 'He woke up brusquely when we had finished. "That was quite, quite delightful. Thank you very much, gentlemen." We took a train before dinner and arrived in London a little tired but in good humour. "It was quite, quite delightful, gentlemen," we repeated many times to each other.'

For Rubinstein it was even more delightful than for the others.

He had made a mental note of the young Irene's charms in the hope that they would encounter each other on more neutral ground in the future. He was not the only man to admire Irene at that time. Comte Willy de Grunne, in charge of the King of the Belgians' household, fell deeply in love with her and longed to marry her. 'Ah! Irene! I loved her so much,' he told her nieces years later. 'She was such a wonderful dancer – how we waltzed together!' But though Irene enjoyed dancing with him, she scarcely noticed him otherwise and quickly forgot him.

Elinor, away from London, was unaware of a development that was to devastate her emotionally. The Souls had not given up their efforts to prise their 'dear George' away from the hated Mrs Glyn and one of them, his friend Violet, the Duchess of Rutland, gave a luncheon party in June 1915 for him to meet someone who might effect this. Curzon had already noticed Grace Duggan, wearing a pink dress and leaning against a pillar, at a ball given by Lady Londesborough. She was married to a wealthy Argentinian of suspect health who was an honorary attaché at the Argentinian Embassy, a post that gave his beautiful wife plenty of scope for the fashionable, frivolous, amorous life she enjoyed.

When the Duchess's letter told him she was inviting 'that pretty Mrs Duggan', Curzon accepted at once and at the luncheon asked Grace Duggan if he might call on her a few days later at her house at 32 Grosvenor Square, where she ran a convalescent home for Belgian officers.

Within a month of dining at the ultra-respectable RAC, they had plunged into a passionate love affair. 'My heart is just calling to you all day,' wrote Grace on 26 August 1915, on her silver-and-black monogrammed paper. 'Believe me my darling great big man, I think I must have been waiting for you always as I can't describe how complete I feel. You call me a flower, dear heart; I do feel a wide open full-blown rose with every petal open to you, my sun. George darling, my love for you is so big that it frightens me. Help me and keep me. Your Grace.'

War did not halt another of Curzon's passions: houses and castles. In 1911 he had bought the fifteenth-century Tattershall Castle in Lincolnshire and was restoring it, but he believed the most 'truly British style' ran from the second half of Queen Elizabeth's reign to the end of James I's. For him, the most perfect of the smaller stately homes of that period was Montacute House, in Somerset, with its tall chimneys, armoured figures in niches below the balustrading, stone staircases and panelled baronial hall. He itched to restore it and when its lease became available he consulted Irene and Cimmie about its purchase – it was, after all, their money that would buy it and it would, ostensibly, be their home as well.

His daughters' share of the Leiter Trust, the fortune left by their maternal grandfather, brought in an annual income of more than £10,000 each* of which Curzon had the handling until they came of age (his own income from Mary's marriage settlement was £4,000 a year). Because the three girls were such substantial heiresses, the trustees had insisted that they be made wards of court, with their father as their official guardian; every year, he had to appear before a judge for the necessary permission to use their incomes for housing, upkeep, education and general maintenance of the Curzonian style of living.

Curzon's view was that the purchase of the Montacute lease meant a substantial house for each daughter but, viewing Hackwood as home, they showed little enthusiasm for this new interest. He went ahead anyway and acquired the lease in 1914. Montacute fulfilled all his ideals of architectural beauty. He badgered the long-suffering owner with questions: Did any of the oak chests have any particular significance? Was the Hall ever used as a living room? When was the asphalt tennis court laid? How old was the kitchen garden? Who planted the broad avenue leading to the east entrance?

He put in a first-floor bathroom, restored the original stonework and filled the house with Elizabethan furniture bought locally so that, as he put it, 'without being fine, it is contemporary and harmonious'. Then he asked Elinor to decorate it.

She was thrilled. Convincing proof of his adoration, she felt, could go no further. To seek her help in creating a home must surely mean that he intended to share it with her if her circumstances altered – and Clayton's health was deteriorating fast.

---

*Just under half a million pounds in today's terms.

Elinor felt convinced that if, as seemed likely, she was widowed, Curzon would ask her to marry him.

She stuck to Milor's imperial theme for his own bedroom, with a crimson carpet and hangings, silver Louis XIV mirror and Spanish candlesticks and, in the intervals between decorating, wrote a tribute to the man with whom she hoped to spend the rest of her life – a *Pen Portrait of a Great Man, by One who knows the Greatness of his Soul*, bound in green leather with a gilt C and coronet in one corner.

She put as much effort into designing the interiors of his daughters' bedrooms, with a pink carpet and chintzes in Irene's and parrots on the walls of Baba's. Elsewhere she gave free rein to her own romantic tastes, a mélange of rich colour and luxurious fabrics that evoked an almost oriental sensuality. Her signature purples and mauves were everywhere – even the governess's room had a mauve carpet. In the Great Chamber there were silk hangings on the walls, a sofa, chairs and curtains of purple and orange velvet, green silk velvet cushions and four smaller chairs in purple velvet. Here, too, she replaced in their original niches the female nude statues removed for their supposed indelicacy in the mid-Victorian era and persuaded Curzon to strew three of his tigerskins on the purple carpet. It was a temple to the erotic love she hoped to share with him for the rest of her life.

When Clayton died in November 1915 this hope must have been reaffirmed every time Curzon visited her at Montacute during the customary year's mourning that followed. His visits were often unannounced; in order to preserve the character of Montacute he had refused to have a telephone installed.

What Elinor did not know was that a fortnight before Clayton's death Grace Duggan's husband had also died. In 1916, the widowed Grace left their house in Grosvenor Square, and leased Trent Park, in Middlesex, with its exquisite gardens, pink pillars and flamingos, from the rich and social Sir Philip Sassoon. She kept up the house in lavish pre-war style – 'four footmen in the hall and dinner beginning with caviar', reported one visitor, Edward Marsh – and Curzon would come and see her there.

Curzon, with the choice of two adoring red-haired beauties, had no hesitation in proposing to the younger, richer and more frivolous of the two. One day he invited Grace to accompany him to the ruined Bodiam Castle in Sussex, which he had just bought from Lord Ashcombe and intended to restore. They ate their luncheon, which they had brought with them, in a private room at the Castle Inn opposite and looked over at the castle ruins. Curzon then drove Grace to Winchelsea where, in one of its beautiful churches, he asked her to marry him. Afterwards he wrote: 'May I be worthy of the love of my girl and make her truly happy.'

On 17 December 1916, Elinor was standing on a stepladder straightening some of the newly-hung curtains she had chosen when a servant brought her a six-days-old copy of *The Times*. Opening it, she began to read. On the Court page it held the news of Curzon's engagement to Mrs Duggan.

Elinor climbed down from the ladder, burnt Curzon's letters, packed her belongings and left Montacute – and his life.

6

Growing Up

~

Grace Duggan was rich, kind, beautiful and, although comparatively brainless, approved of by the Souls. Unlike Elinor, she was still young enough to have the son Curzon longed for. He desperately wanted an heir not only to inherit his hard-won earldom but to forge a similarly brilliant career – daughters did not count as it was inconceivable to him that a woman could attain distinction in public life. His liaison with Grace had already assured him of their sexual compatibility and she was exactly the physical type that he admired: a voluptuous redhead with an ample bosom.

In addition, she had an exquisite complexion, huge dark eyes and the small hands and feet (size three-and-a-half) considered such a mark of delicate femininity. He still hoped to re-attain high office and – again unlike Elinor – Grace was untainted by notoriety. Though money was a subject they did not discuss, her wealth would allow him to maintain the grandeur of his way of life. He must, too, have been encouraged by the fact that she had already borne two sons, Alfred and Hubert, as well as a daughter, Marcella.

The separations that were so to plague him started almost at once. The first was one that both agreed was essential: Grace had to return to the Argentine to settle her affairs there, despite the delay it would cause to their wedding plans. 'I long for the day ever drawing nearer when my girl will come home to be with me as long as life shall last,' wrote Curzon in the first of many loving letters, 'and we will do our best to give peace and happiness to each other and perhaps to do something worthy in so much of life as may be left to me. It is an age since her dear kisses trembled on my mouth.'

On 23 March 1916, while Grace was away, Lord Scarsdale died. Curzon, as his heir, inherited the ancestral home of Kedleston. It was the fulfilment of a long-held dream: Curzon had always felt passionately about Kedleston but while his father was alive all his suggestions for the refurbishment and upkeep of this Palladian palace had been firmly rebuffed.

Kedleston, almost more than any other of Curzon's houses, exactly fulfilled his taste. Commissioned by Sir Nathaniel Curzon from Robert Adam in 1759, it appealed to what Elinor Glyn had called the Roman in him. The saloon, with its huge domed rotunda rising to 62 feet, was full of statues, pediments, friezes, columns, urns and garlands. The marble hall had twenty Corinthian columns; as Curzon would tell visitors, in a phrase emphasising his flat Derbyshire *a*'s, 'While the pillars of Government House, Calcutta [modelled on Kedleston], were l*a*th and pl*a*ster, those of Kedleston were purest alab*a*ster.' There were huge chandeliers of Waterford crystal and wonderful views over the parkland and lake to the Derbyshire dales from the tall windows of this northern palace. Despite Robert Adam's heating system disguised in cast-iron altars, it was icy cold and none of Curzon's family, let alone Grace, felt about it as he did. In any case, it was far too far from London, where his presence was required in the War Cabinet (of which he had become a member when Lloyd George succeeded Asquith as Prime Minister on 6 December 1916), for him to live there for more than a few weeks of the year.

Soon after her father's engagement to Grace, Irene received her first proposal, from the entirely suitable Guy Benson. He went down on one knee and asked her to marry him. 'Yes!' she replied, whereupon he rose to his feet, kissed her chastely on the forehead and exclaimed, 'You are a brick, old thing!' This was so much at variance with Irene's ideal of romance that she broke it off at once. Curzon thought this displayed a greatness of soul. 'Such a woman deserves the best and some day she may attain it,' he wrote to Nancy Astor.

Curzon and Grace were married at Lambeth Palace on 2 February 1917 by Curzon's old Balliol friend Cosmo Lang, the Archbishop of York (the Archbishop of Canterbury had flu), Grace in a cream chiffon dress by Worth trimmed with Russian sable and a long sable cape. Curzon was so moved by the occasion that

Grace arrived at the altar to find tears pouring down the normally impassive face of her bridegroom.

After the wedding, they motored straight to Trent Park, together with their respective children. Irene brought her horses and accompanied the Duggan boys out hunting, often giving them leads over difficult fences. Nancy Astor kept closely in touch, frequently asking Irene and Cimmie over to Cliveden for the weekend or for parties ('we will have a dance and every sort of lark').

The Curzons' first party at Trent was Irene's coming-of-age dance, in January 1917. Irene, in the white that set off her dark looks so well, wore a wreath of green leaves in her hair, waltzing with closed eyes the better to enjoy the music. The war, with its terrible slaughter, had been dragging on for several years so the party, a comparatively quiet affair for 150, had none of the lavishness of her coming-out ball. Even so, when the Curzons motored to London the following day they were deeply upset to see a newspaper placard with the words: 'Curzons dance while Europe burns'. After this, they confined themselves to small dinner parties, chiefly for Curzon's Soul friends like Harry Cust, Arthur Balfour, Evan Charteris and Lady Desborough.

Because of the war Cimmie, eighteen that year, did not have the usual coming-out season and ball. Instead, after leaving her Eastbourne school, she began work at the War Office when the Curzons returned to Carlton House Terrace.

Grace was good at making men comfortable and she quickly learned Curzon's idiosyncrasies. He could not sleep unless every chink of light was shut out of the room, he liked simple, nursery food – seedcake, home-made jam, queen of puddings with meringue on top and jam inside – but was extremely fussy. 'Look, Gracie,' he would say, appearing in her bedroom at breakfast while she was drinking her coffee, reading letters, talking to her maid or having her nails done, and holding out his plate: 'This egg's far too hard.'

She ordered the boxes of chocolates from Rumpelmayer's, the fashionable teashop in St James's, through which he would munch when he sat up late at night dealing with papers. And she quickly realised that her arrival could do nothing to stop him taking his meticulous and detailed interest in the running of their houses. 'George works so hard and sits up so late,' she told Lady Cynthia

Asquith. 'He often doesn't come to bed till 2.30 but stays down writing out the menus for the servants in his different country houses.'

She was also well aware of Curzon's longing for a male child and, whatever her other faults in the marriage, never shirked her duty in this respect. Even during their engagement she had written: 'My beloved boy's child! Darling, this thought is already my biggest wish and my most earnest prayer. I am taking great care of myself – if ever we are blessed, he must be strong and all that your son should be.'

But there was no sign of an heir. With typical thoroughness, Curzon set about finding out why, and was soon assuring Grace – or, as he always now called her, Gracie – that a small operation would soon put things right. On 25 June 1917 he was telling her that this should be performed at Carlton House Terrace. 'The doctor only wants the carpets up in the bathroom.' It would, he assured her, be a mere nothing –

no cutting, no haemorrhage, no tests and no pain. No instruments even are used. It is merely putting in a series of little objects, each a little larger than the other, to distend the mouth of the womb. The whole thing will take but ten minutes. There would not even be any need for chloroform were it not that modesty requires it.

You will have to stay in bed for eight to ten days lying more or less flat on your back for the first few days but then sitting up in bed. All this is most gratifying, darling. They have told me that after the treatment and the operation the odds are greatly against a pregnancy in under six months but then it ought to be a certainty. It all appears to be plain sailing. It is such a relief to me.

After the operation Gracie, who had no intention of giving up her independent life and freedom of action, left for the villa at Reigate which she had bought at the same time as the lease of Trent. She had the perfect excuse: her children needed country air. She had no intention of hurrying back though Curzon longed for her return. 'Oh to think that in a couple of days Girlie will be in her Louis XV bed. Goodnight my darling Girl and I hope this long period of distress and pain is now coming to an end and that very soon all will be right. Your own loving Boy.'

*

Gracie had arrived in the Curzon family in the middle of worsening relations between Curzon and his two elder daughters. Both had inherited his powerful will, both had seen the independence that the war had brought to many of their contemporaries, both were young and longed for fun and excitement. Curzon's attitude to his daughters was as patriarchal as that of his own father and his views on decorum and propriety were – as with many who have indulged themselves sexually – stricter than the norm.

He felt himself entirely responsible for his motherless daughters and was determined to err on the side of precaution: young men who came to call were treated as assailants who had come to storm a fortress rather than potential friends or suitors. If he had had the chance, he would have chosen his daughters' husbands for them – and he certainly wanted to retain control of their money. To any suggestion otherwise he reacted in aggrieved and hostile fashion.

'If I felt I was in any way breaking away under-age or hurting you in that way your annoyance would be justified, but I am merely starting a three-month plan when my money will be my own,' wrote the 21-year-old Irene plaintively in the summer of 1917. 'Why could we not have talked it all peacefully out, without these unpleasant letters you always answer me with? Does it ever strike you that though you think yourself the badly treated father, that actions and decisions are only caused by your difficult and antagonistic attitudes to anything I ever say?'

Irene, as the eldest, found home life particularly trying. Having hunted since childhood, by now she regarded it as a way of life rather than a sport and she wished to build her life around it. She still rode her old favourite, Dandy, the solid, reliable grey cob, but she had also acquired larger, faster, better-bred animals more suited to the Beaufort and the famous Leicestershire packs that she visited whenever she got the chance, her handsome, rather mannish looks set off by a beautifully-cut dark blue habit and bowler hat.

In London both Irene and Cimmie went out constantly. As Curzon's daughters their circle was wide; as Astor protégées it was, if anything, wider. As Curzon remarked plaintively in June of that year, 'The girls are going out to one of their endless dinners so I shall be alone again.' Both girls had many admirers. Reggie

Winn, later to marry one of Nancy Astor's nieces, pined for Cimmie but as he was a year or two younger she did not take him seriously.

Baba, still only twelve and Curzon's favourite, led a docile schoolroom life at Hackwood, visited from time to time by her father. 'Poor little Sandra is alone at H, with the nice little governess. I had meant to go down to be with her but cannot stir. How many of those who see me in public realise, I wonder, how much pain and illness I have had or appreciate the misery of going through much that I have to undertake in the condition which I am compelled to accept,' he wrote to Gracie.

It was perfectly true: sometimes his physical wretchedness was such that after a day's work he would retire to his room and sob until worn out. Without laudanum, or other drugs, he often could not sleep.

For Irene and Cim, it was a different matter. Home was not the cosy refuge it was to so many of their contemporaries. An anguished letter from Irene, written to her father in September 1917 after one of his reproachful talks, explains why.

I know full well we were out a great deal but oh! Daddy! have you thought what my home life at Carlton House Terrace was like this summer? what untold misery you and Gracie have caused me until at moments I have felt I could bear it no longer. It was all so intolerable and we felt again and again you wanted Gracie to yourself and we sought our happiness elsewhere as life seemed one insurmountable obstacle after another at home. So I feel I must in justification explain why we were out so often. I must tell you I am beginning to feel I cannot bear all these burdens and quarrels much longer. At moments I feel desperate, and prepared to do anything. The uncertainties and eternal worries of my home life are too much for me. Daddy, *do, do* remember the incentive – your enjoyment – is not a one-sided case. Things might have been different if there had been warmth and understanding at home. . . .

All these difficult months have done for me, and I must tell you the truth, that I simply cannot face trying it all over again at Carlton House Terrace, as I cannot see how it is going to change. I must lead my own life, and I want a home of my own, where I can live in peace. You must forgive this. I have tried God knows how many times to go on but now I am driven to tell you what I feel is the only solution.

Also, for your own and Gracie's happiness, it would be far better if Cim and I could have a home to ourselves in London with someone near and dear to us. I have thought and thought in my misery about it all and it seems to me the only hope. Daddy, I want you to think it over and see what can be done. I am sure it would be the best and fairest for you as well as for us.

Your loving Irene.

In July 1918, Irene escaped by going to France to work for the YMCA. What was to become a lifetime of voluntary work had started the year before, when she first went to talk and sing to the boys of the Broad Street Club, to whom she gave a small billiard table and whom she visited weekly for the next forty years. Now she wrote to 'my Baba darling', on 29 August: 'I have written to Daddy asking if he will send me £50 so that we can get the men comfy chairs and tables as the YMCA are so slow and tiresome and one longs to get the hut really comfy and nice. I so wonder if he will. He does not give much to charity and would be doing such a good deed but less than that is not much good. Darling, grateful thanks for the gramophone which Sister has brought back safely.'

Cimmie had grown into a tall young woman with dark curly hair, an excellent complexion and a sweet-faced prettiness. If she had not been so attractive she might have been called strapping. Her chief charm was her nature: a genuine, unsophisticated sweetness that combined intelligence and warmth – all her life, wherever she went, she was immensely popular. On Armistice night, 11 November, her happy, uninhibited exuberance took the form of wrapping herself in a Union Jack, climbing on to one of the lions in Trafalgar Square, and leading those near her in a chorus of 'Land of Hope and Glory'.

Watching her in the crowd was a young army officer, his mood sombre. When she climbed down afterwards, he was standing near by.

'The war is over! Isn't it wonderful?' she exclaimed, her face alight.

'Is it?' he replied. 'Do any of you think for one moment of the loss of life, the devastation and misery?'

The young man was Oswald Ernald Mosley, known to everyone

as Tom. On that November day, he was just six days short of his twenty-second birthday. He was tall, dark and pale-skinned, with a powerful and athletic physique. With his flashing eyes, fitness and high spirits, there was something of the healthy young animal about him; later, his preferred style of oratory would be equally physical, prowling around the platform as he spoke and gesticulated with broad, sweeping gestures, a stabbing finger or fist thumped on a lectern.

His war in France had been brief: he had arrived there at the end of January 1915, leaving his regiment to serve as a Royal Flying Corps observer for three months before returning to England again that May. He had rejoined the 16th Lancers in November and three months later had been granted special leave to see a specialist with a view to an operation on his right ankle – injured, the Army was quick to point out, at home, 'not in nor by the Service'.

The injury and operation had resulted in his right leg becoming one-and-a-half inches shorter than the left. Thenceforth, he had stayed in England, first on spells of sick leave granted continuously for a year, then, after a month with the first reserve of Lancers, at the Curragh in Ireland. Here, after a fortnight, a Medical Board found him unfit to march. At the end of February 1918 he began work at the Ministry of Munitions and five months later moved to the Foreign Office.

Mosley, the eldest of the three sons of a womanising father whose wife had left him on account of his constant unfaithfulness, was the heir to a Staffordshire baronetcy. He had been educated at Winchester, which he hated, not so much for the academic side – he had an excellent brain – but for its emphasis on 'team spirit'. He was above all an individualist: he had excelled at boxing, and in particular, fencing, winning the Public Schools Championship at fifteen.

After school he went to Sandhurst to train as a regular soldier. During the last two years of the war, working in London, he had begun what was to be a staggeringly successful career as a seducer. One of these love affairs was with the older actress Maxine Elliott, through whom he met eminent politicians such as Winston Churchill, Lloyd George and F. E. Smith; encounters which decided him to turn to politics himself. When Cimmie came across him in Trafalgar Square he was about to stand as a Coalition candidate for the safe Conservative seat of the Harrow division of Middlesex in the general election of 14 December 1918.

With the war over, Grace plunged into the redecoration of No. 1 Carlton House Terrace. She brought a lavishness to all the rooms she occupied and used that was entirely feminine. Her bedroom at Hackwood had a Chippendale four-poster with blue silk canopy and curtains embellished with ostrich plumes, gilt mirrors, trinkets and an immense number of silver candlesticks scattered over the mauve damask dressing-table and her Chinese lacquer secretaire. In her boudoir there were *chaises longues* covered in blue silk, little side tables with more knick-knacks, Sheraton satinwood furniture and Adam bookcases in white and gilt.

Since Curzon first took over the lease of the London house, much had been done to it. Telephone lines had been laid in 1907 and the water-powered passenger and goods lifts put back in order; by 1915 there were six water closets as well as one bathroom.

Gracie tackled the house room by room. It was an ideal place for the parties she and Curzon planned to give. The ballroom, which had four long windows giving on to the balcony, was used for all the large official dinners for sixty or more that Curzon gave after his appointment as Foreign Secretary in January 1919 (following the resignation of Arthur Balfour). Guests sat at a series of smaller tables, identified by the colour of the roses in silver bowls at the centre, as a hired orchestra played outside. Flowers were sent up from Hackwood; sometimes, if Grace was planning a party soon after her return from the Riviera, she would bring back boxes of mimosa from Cannes. In the warmth of the hall, with its gold damask curtains and furniture, the tight yellow balls would soon uncurl and fill the air with their delicate scent.

For 'small' parties – of fewer than twenty-four – they used the ground-floor dining-room, hung with black-and-white velvet curtains from Italy. The footmen, inspected by Curzon before being taken on for posture, gait and cleanliness of fingernails, wore knee-breeches if there were more than fourteen guests and trousers if there were fewer: Curzon felt that a dinner party of twelve was almost a domestic occasion. When the Prince of Wales once attended a large formal dinner without wearing his Garter ribbon

Curzon (who did) wrote to him afterwards pointing out the discourtesy. The Prince replied with a charming note of apology.

As they turned into adults Curzon grew more distant than ever from his older daughters, to whom he was little more than a disapproving presence. Past the age when they could be treated as adoring pets who came in to watch him shaving, they shared a secret world of their own, with friends of whom he knew little. 'Where Cim is I have no idea,' ran one note. 'I never see her and do not even know if she is in the house.' Baba, now at Heathfield School in Berkshire, also seldom saw her father. The three sisters were close, writing to each other constantly, Irene in particular fulfilling a semi-maternal role to her youngest sister.

For their father, there was another crushing disappointment in the spring of 1919 when Gracie suffered a second miscarriage. 'What a blow! Poor Girly, poor Husband,' he wrote on 16 April. 'We must bear our disappointment, as so often before, and console ourselves thinking that it was too soon after these two months to expect anything so good. I wonder why Providence plagues us with all these false alarms and misplaced hopes. Will he ever relent and give us our own child? Never mind, Girly, you are more important than any child or a million children, so we will bow our heads and not cease to hope.'

When one of their friends conceived after five years of marriage he was pathetically excited. ('What a challenge – and what an encouragement.') He had, however, become extremely fond of Grace's children, with whom he got on far better than with his own. In particular, he adored her small daughter. 'Little Marcella is, as usual, the greatest angel.' His own children, he felt, were far less appreciative.

Grace flung herself into the preparations for Cimmie's coming-out Season, delayed because of the war. It was a task after Grace's own heart; for her, social life was a constant delight.

London was gradually emerging from the aftermath of war. Wounded soldiers in their blue suits and red ties were disappearing from the squares and gardens, ballrooms that for four years had been turned into hospital wards echoed again to the sound of dance music. The great houses reopened: Londonderry House in

Park Lane with its famous staircase up which four could walk abreast; Brook House, also in Park Lane, with its white marble hall (nicknamed the Giant's Lavatory); Devonshire House with its garden stretching from Piccadilly to Berkeley Square; Holland House, in Kensington, with its $\frac{3}{4}$-mile-long drive winding through trees. Many male faces were missing but the rules of chaperonage were still intact, and mothers, aunts or sometimes fathers sat on the familiar small gilt chairs ranged round the room, its brilliant lights deterring their offspring from anything even vaguely improper.

Most of the time Curzon kept well away from Grace's frenzied social activity – which, however, was not too all-consuming to prevent one of the fits of hysterical jealousy that had become a feature of their married life. For Grace affected to believe that Curzon still hankered after Elinor Glyn.

'How glad I am that you are having so gay a time but why do you say "As you of course know, Mrs G is in London!" ' wrote Curzon on 13 May 1919. 'Really, Girly, you are incorrigible. I have not now and I never have had any communication with Mrs G since we married. I have kept my word. I have not the slightest idea whether she is in London or in Paris or either do I care. You ought not to say such a thing, for there is not a word of truth in the suggestion. After two and a half years *do begin to believe*, oh Girly, please.'

Curzon's ideas on the sort of man his daughters should marry were so definite that at the ball he gave for Cimmie in July 1919 he suggested a match with one of them to the young Oliver Lyttelton (later Lord Chandos) as he shook hands with him at the top of the stairs. 'Ah, Oliver, good evening. It is my dearest wish, as I know it would have been that of your dear father, that you should become affianced to one of my daughters.' When Lyttelton, taken aback, reported this later to Irene and Cimmie, they were much amused.

For Cimmie, her father's suggestion would have been too late: she had become involved with a much more determined suitor. Tom Mosley had duly won his Harrow seat with a majority of 10,000, becoming the youngest MP in the House, and he had met Cimmie again briefly at Trent Park. She had forgotten him and looked puzzled when he said: 'We meet again, Lady Cynthia. Don't you remember Armistice Night?'

His pursuit of her began in earnest a year later, on the hustings at Plymouth at the end of 1919. Both were campaigning for Nancy Astor in the by-election at Plymouth caused by her husband Waldorf's elevation to the House of Lords on the death of his father. Cimmie, as a great friend and Cliveden habituée, spent much of her time with Nancy ('Cimmie is reported to be at Plymouth but as usual I am never told,' complained Curzon). Mosley had been brought into Nancy's orbit by her sister Phyllis Brand, who found him immensely attractive and invited him to canvass. Unfortunately for Phyllis, he only had eyes for Cimmie.

Curzon had little idea of Cimmie's incipient romance. He was much more perturbed by Irene's doings, and her growing desire for independence – and the use of her own money. He had written to her on 21 January 1917 (the day after she came of age) to explain that she was entitled to her share of the income coming from the Leiter estate and from the marriage settlements paid to him for his daughters' benefit. On this last he said: 'Probably the best thing would be to pay it into the joint account which I administer under the Court for the two other girls who are still minors, as your contribution to our joint homes.' That arrangement, he added, would only be until she married.

But Irene did not see why she should contribute a large sum for the upkeep of a number of houses that she seldom used when what she wanted was a home of her own. For this, she would need more than the 'allowance' suggested by her father. When appeals to him failed, she consulted the family lawyers, Humbert and Taylor, who wrote to Curzon in October 1919:

> Lady Irene insisted that she is getting no benefit from the maintenance of your various houses because she said there was no staff of servants kept up at them and if she wanted to stay temporarily at either of the houses she would have to take her own servants with her. She also denied that she wished to spend the whole of her income on herself but claimed that the margin between her income and expenditure should be invested by herself in her own way.
>
> We discussed the position very fully and in the result, Lady Irene

said she is willing for the present to agree to your suggestion that you should receive her income from America and pay her such a sum as would bring up her net income after deducting income tax to £4,000 a year.

The solicitors, who also acted for Curzon, added a warning note: 'I think it is probable that, later on, Lady Irene will ask exactly what is the income received from America in respect of the Settlement funds and the Leiter estate.'

Two months later Irene wrote an affectionate letter to her father to say that she had managed to find the 'only house left' in the Bicester and Whaddon Chase countries, at Bletchley.

It is a tiny little house, but with very good stabling for 11 and a coachman's cottage. It is only eight guineas a week and I have taken on the three servants. The cottage is unfurnished so Fox [her groom] and his wife must bring their things and I shall hire the rest for the extra grooms and chauffeur.

Can I have the linen I had at Bletchingley – you remember it, worn out remnants of Hackwood linen – and could I have the same silver set teapot, or is that in use? As to a car, are you willing to let me have the Fiat? or as it gobbles up petrol, would it be cheaper to hire one that uses less? What are your views?

A second letter, two days later, showed how much she felt herself a stranger in her father's life. 'I am going down to Heathfield to see Baba's play. Might I stay the night at Carlton House Terrace? I will come up after hunting and arrive in time for dinner. Hoping that will not put you out.'

She was twenty-three and he treated her, she felt, as though she was a wayward seventeen-year-old for whom he did not particularly care. When she travelled to Geneva in a party with a man to whom she had mistakenly been linked, and his two sisters, Curzon wrote her a damning letter that hurt her badly. 'Darling Daddy,' she replied on 20 September 1920. 'I am quite sure I would have seen the force of your arguments regarding the likelihood of our activities being misconstrued if only you had put it another way. Your imputations of a mean love affair made me furious. As always, you take me the wrong way and make any understanding impossible by the offensive manner in which you put things and the ungrounded aspersions you lay at my door.'

From Curzon's point of view the real sting lay in what followed. Irene's letter concluded:

> As you continually tell me what a 'failure' I am and that you can have no 'filial affection' for me owing to my unbalanced actions, I suggest that I relieve you of all further responsibility in the following way: that I take all my money and pay my own taxes and make an arrangement with my bank allowing you so much which will enable me still to have the right to enter Hackwood as a house.
>
> You can let the world know exactly what action I have taken, so that the responsibility for any further action of mine cannot be laid at your door.

It was the beginning of an irreconcilable breach.

7

'She Must Do As She Pleases'

~

Curzon was aware that his relationship with his children was deteriorating. Writing to Gracie from Kedleston in August 1919, he described how even Baba had lost her sweet and affectionate ways and become silent and moody. 'I get very little consolation from their society. They have become so used to a purely selfish existence that they make no effort to please. Sandra is absolutely silent and I have to make conversation the whole time, while Cim is in her rather arrogant, defiant mood. I suppose they regard themselves as doing me a great favour by coming here at all but I own I shall be rather relieved when they go.' It did not seem to occur to him to wonder why they seemed to have changed so.

Cimmie was in truth nervous as to how her father might react to hearing that the young man who had been pursuing her so vigorously was slowly winning her. For Curzon had spent so little time with his daughters – and even less since he had married Grace – that they had come to regard him as a stranger. Nor did they make allowance for the debilitating effect of his constant pain – but then, they did not see their father after he had returned from a Cabinet at 2 a.m., reduced to sobs of anguish as he pored over the week's butcher's bill.

For Irene and Cimmie, the usual gulf between the generations was exacerbated by the effect of the war. Girls who had constantly read of the deaths of the young men they knew, who had worked in some capacity to help the war effort and who were in any case full of the exuberance of youth, could not force themselves back into the rigid mould of the disciplined Edwardian young. They also resented the lack of privacy over friendships: though they might not see their father for days, no one could ring them up without his being aware of it and often intercepting the call. Curzon always answered the telephone himself in his London house and even when in bed managed this by means of a receiver fitted with an extending arm.

With the much younger Baba, his relationship was still distant but serenely uncomplicated. He wrote to her often, sometimes a few lines twisted into a tiny package ('Darling Baba, you are a sweet girlie and I love you very much'), sometimes longer letters: 'Darling Sandra, Although I did not get to bed until three this morning I am writing this in bed before dawn as I awoke very early – about four hours sleep. Too little! I have been wondering how my little girl is getting on ...' But he seldom saw her.

All the sisters suffered from the lack of an older female confidante. Their mother had died when they were so young that any memory of the real person had been overlaid by an idealised image of her. They had become extremely fond of Elinor Glyn and then she had suddenly and dramatically vanished from their lives – although they did their best to keep in touch by writing to her frequently in Paris – and they undoubtedly realised that their father was responsible for ejecting this loved figure from their lives. They liked the kind-hearted Grace but she had begun to absent herself with increasing frequency, taking long holidays in Paris and refusing to go to Kedleston, which she complained had not enough lavatories and no telephone. Both Irene and, in particular, Cimmie were very fond of Nancy Astor but love – or rather, Love – was undoubtedly Elinor's subject. And Cimmie's feelings were confused about her new suitor.

Cimmie stayed with Elinor in Paris during the Peace Conference of 1919 where, the only woman in the Salle des Glaces, Elinor was reporting on the Treaty of Versailles for the Hearst newspapers. After an official dinner at Versailles to which Cimmie, who had lost her luggage, had to wear a sapphire-blue satin teagown of Elinor's, they sat up late talking and gazing at the stars through the windows of Elinor's apartment. 'God is up there watching us, and I know he will always bring me through,' Cimmie told Elinor confidently.

She had resisted Tom Mosley's advances for some time. Though she found him fascinating as a friend, she was frightened both of the intensity of his feelings and of his experience with women (one of her earlier boyfriends had written: 'There is a reason for knowing your Tom very thoroughly, and this is best discussed with a married woman'). Finally, after he had persuaded her to come to Leicestershire and hunt with him, she fell in love with him; it is likely that there, on his home territory, he succeeded in seducing her.

'I fear that side of me is very vital and strong,' he wrote to her after what he described as 'tonight's few moments', continuing, 'but I do love you with all the strength of the other side, which is the only side that matters and which I have never given to any other woman.' Poor Cimmie could not know what agonies 'that side' would soon cause her.

Theoretically, there was no reason for Curzon to refuse his consent to the marriage and, in any case, Cimmie at twenty-one did not need her father's approval. But she was aware that he wished his daughters to make grand matches and she longed for him to like the man she loved. Her apprehensions were justified. Curzon was quite prepared to send Mosley away if he did not think him suitable. He was always on his guard against fortune-hunters and he was also anxious for his daughters to be as happy in marriage as he had been with their mother. On 22 March 1920, he wrote to Gracie: 'Lady Salisbury has given me a good account of young Mosley. He is coming to see me this evening and I am making independent enquiries. I do hope he is all right. I shall soon find out, I hope, if he is really in love with Cim and what are his ideas and prospects. Don't send your congrats to Cim until you hear from me whether I find him all right.'

Mosley passed. The following day, Curzon wrote again to Gracie:

The young man Mosley came to see me yesterday evening. Very young, tall, slim, dark, rather big nose, little black moustache and rather a Jewish appearance. I put to him the whole case about a young man at 23 taking a young girl of 21 for life, and all that it meant. Was he sure of himself? of her? of both of them? were they prepared to join for the big things for a lifetime? She was strong, independent, original. Could he promise her fidelity? devotion? could they take the rough as well as the smooth?

It turns out he is quite independent, etc, and has practically severed himself from his father, who is a spendthrift and a ne'er do well. The estate is in the hands of trustees who will give him £8–10,000 a year straightaway and he will ultimately have a clear £20,000 per annum. He did not even know that Cim was an heiress.

Yesterday I had a satisfactory report about him from Edward Talbot, our whip in the House of Commons, and today Bob Cecil, for whom the young man has worked, came and told me he regarded him as a keen, able and promising warrior, with a good future before him. So I have done what I could and have no alternative but to give my consent.

Everyone was delighted by the engagement. Irene and Baba, already magnetised by Tom's dark good looks and aura of sexual power, felt a deep, vicarious involvement in his love affair with their sister. For the 24-year-old Irene, this marriage represented something almost magical. 'My thoughts will fly to you both tonight with all the prayers and wonder and sacredness that surround that little wedding ring,' she wrote on the evening of their marriage.

Baba, a sixteen-year-old schoolgirl, was affected more powerfully still. As her sister's future husband, Tom Mosley became the first man in her own generation to be on an intimate footing with her. This close relationship, charged with his powerfully masculine presence, was both intoxicating and overwhelming. Her hypnotised fascination was so noticeable that one day Grace remarked: 'I believe Baba is even more in love with Tom than Cimmie is.'

Nancy Astor, devoted to Cim, and impressed as well as grateful to Tom for his work on her behalf, wrote, 'I do love Tom too. You will be *just* the kind of wife he needs and wants. I feel he must have a great soul, or he would never have asked you to share it.' And from Elinor Glyn came the dramatic comment: 'You two will rule the world'. Curzon himself was pleased that his daughter was marrying a rising politician of whom his close friends spoke well and who was, into the bargain, rich and landed.

The original plan of a wedding in Westminster Abbey was abandoned as Cimmie wanted only a small number of guests. She would have liked Kedleston but it was too far away. Eventually the Chapel Royal in St James's was settled on and here they were married on 11 May 1920. Cimmie, noted several newspapers, defied superstition: first by marrying in May, and then because her Molyneux white silk crepe dress had a long train embroidered with lilies in silver and pearls (a symbol of tears) and with leaves of pale green (symbolising jealousy).

Curzon, as always, did everything *en prince*. There were lilies everywhere, seven bridesmaids in green chiffon dresses with petal skirts, King George, Queen Mary and the King and Queen of the Belgians in the front pew and Princess Alice and Lord Athlone behind (the last four had stayed at Hackwood beforehand). Afterwards there was a glittering reception at 1 Carlton House Terrace, where Gracie's boudoir, awash with carnations and lilies, was reserved for the royal party and twelve selected guests.

Curzon showered his daughter with presents: a long rope of pearls, a chinchilla cape, a fur coat, an emerald-and-diamond ring. The Mosleys' first home was at Guildford, after a honeymoon at Hackwood and then in the Italian coastal village of Portofino, en route to which they had to pass through Paris. Here they saw Elinor Glyn who emphasised to Cimmie the importance of loyalty, telling her: 'You will be Tom's Chief of Staff always.' Curzon predicted a desperate struggle between Cimmie and Irene over their joint lady's maid, Andrée, which he thought – correctly – that Cimmie would win.

Though Cimmie's marriage had brought a rush of family love and affection, this united domestic front soon splintered. Grace gave vent to one of her hormone-enhanced spasms of jealousy, causing Curzon to write to her bitterly at the beginning of August 1920, about her 'great wickedness' to him:

It springs in this case from a suspicion for which there is not the slightest foundation. I go down to Lympne for a Saturday afternoon conference. Only on my arrival do I find the remnants of a country house party which apparently you regard with jealousy ... what you mean I have no idea. All I realise is that, as usual, my one poor little holiday is sacrificed and I find you on the other hand having one of your monthly quarrels with me out of nothing. Surely after three and a half years of married life you might be a bit more trustful, a little less jealous and a little more kind.

The Curzons were soon reconciled; their mutual desire for an heir would alone see to that, and a few weeks later when Grace wired him with 'good news' their letters were as loving as ever. He responded delightedly when she told him what her gynaecologist had said. 'His report about womb and chance of child-bearing is very encouraging and you must feel much happier, as I do. My precious girl, it is most splendid news.'

In April 1921 he wrote to her of his eldest daughter in terms that suggest an undesirable hanger-on rather than a child. 'It is very good of you to allow Irene to come to you [in Paris]. I hope that she will not be a nuisance and that you will not allow her to sponge. Her suggestion of coming was rather a crafty one in her own interest. I trust you to be firm as regards my position. It is now regularised by her initiative and wish and I do not desire to alter it.'

For the disagreement between Irene and her father had rumbled on. Although she had threatened to remove all her money from his hands, she had agreed to continue with the old arrangement, whereby he paid her an allowance, for a further year.

It was seldom that Irene came home. During the hunting season she lived near Oakham, Rutland, where she had taken the Albert Street stableyard, which had a small house attached, on a three-year lease. With her went her groom, William Fox. Setting herself up in this new life cost more than Curzon seemed prepared to allow her and she was forced to write to him frequently for more money. A typical letter (in March 1920) makes clear how grudgingly Curzon dealt with his eldest daughter. 'Daddy, I don't quite understand about this motor bill. I thought that when you offered to lend me the Fiat you were setting it up ready for me. I never for one moment thought you expected me to repair it before using it. I had to pay £60 for six weeks for a hired car while waiting for it so that if I have to pay for it it will total about £200 and for that I might have bought a tiny car and had it for good.'

Even the lawyer hinted delicately that Curzon was trying to make his daughter pay too much. 'I cannot help thinking that a mistake has been made. It is quite clear that Lady Irene cannot carry on the arrangement agreed unless she receives the first quarterly payment of £500 at once.'

It was perfectly true: she had had to buy a cottage for Fox and though she started the season riding 'old Dandy, game as ever at

23', she needed new, fast horses for the great Leicestershire grass countries. With the ones she bought she acquitted herself so well that in December 1921 the Master of the Quorn, Algernon Burnaby, wrote to her asking if she would do himself and his joint Master, Mrs Paget, 'the honour of accepting the Quorn hunt button'.

Curzon put up resistance to every attempt to make him release the money that Irene needed for hay, oats and saddlery and to set up her stables. He had always complained of being short of money, chiding Grace for the amount she spent on flowers ('Stevens' minimum charge, even for a lunch, is £22'), complaining of a bill for linen of £100 and talking of the high cost of servants.

In April 1920 he wrote to his wife:

I lie awake at night worrying about money matters. I have nothing in the bank and don't know how to go on. On top of this, while Irene is sheltering beside you, comes a further demand from her lawyer for her super tax of last year, making altogether over £2,000 that I have been asked to pay over the past fortnight to her. Needless to say, I have not got it.

I must say, I feel rather hurt at her profiting by you in Paris while her lawyer continues to bombard me here and I don't think it ought to have been done. If she wants to have things on a legal basis, so be it. Let her exact her full legal claim and go. But she can't do that and at the same time claim your protection. I see that my daughters will be the end of me.

As usual, he saw things from his point of view only. The fact that he owned four main houses – Kedleston, 1 Carlton House Terrace, Hackwood and Montacute – as well as Bodiam and Tattershall Castles which he was restoring and repairing, seemed to him wholly proper and Irene's suggestions for economies that would benefit them both fell on deaf ears.

When you tell me you had to find £1,500 and you cannot continue to do so, ought we not to retrench in other ways, like others are forced to do? [Irene suggested in August 1920]. We never go near Broadstairs and is not our [his daughters'] share of these and other houses very remote? Montacute we never go inside, Baba occasionally lives at

Carlton House Terrace and Hackwood is only lived in for about two months. I know it is a sore point but I benefit little by these shares and can scarcely feel the places are homes. If things are so bad – forgive me for saying all this – ought not both sides to pull in?

As for the £545 and the £2,000 which was given for my dressing, hair, travel and charity, you know that £1,150 has gone on horses. You ask what has become of the other two thirds of my income, £1,332 approx. About £400 has gone on charity, as with that income I feel one ought to help others. £300 has gone on maids, travelling, hunting, stabling and all the extras in life. I spent over £100 on car and garage which ought not to be. My dressing this year comes to £400 as things are frightfully dear. I can meet these demands by so planning out my remaining moneys coming in but I cannot if I do not refund myself what I am owed.

If Grace had been at home, she might have persuaded Curzon that his daughter's pleas were understandable. She frequently mediated between the girls and their father and, an inveterate spender herself, would have sympathised with Irene's requests.

But Grace was again away, this time taking a mud-bath cure at Langenschwalbach in the Rhineland, on the advice of the Queen of the Belgians, as it was supposed to promote fertility. The cycle of pregnancy and miscarriage had continued for five years; Grace was now in her mid-forties and this was a last great effort to conceive an Earl of Kedleston. Her response to her husband's complaints was to say that she did not presume to advise him – 'I am full of confidence in my Boy' – and to ask him to find her a French maid who was a good hairdresser and a valet who 'understood' hunting clothes for her son.

The cumulative effect of constant efforts to make her father disburse what was really hers had the effect that the lawyers had foreseen: Irene finally decided she had to take complete charge of her own money – and terminated the 'allowance' arrangement.

By the beginning of 1921 Curzon's lawyers, Taylor and Humbert, had received a letter from Irene's solicitor explaining that Curzon still owed her nearly £3,000. Though this was backed up with statements from the Leiter Trust it drew forth a letter of rebuttal from Curzon, written with such emotion that it was almost indecipherable. In March, Irene's solicitor replied crisply that Irene was fully within her rights to end the agreement and that the words 'repudiated' and 'violated' were therefore unjustified.

> The fact remains [continued the lawyer] that for the first half of the current financial year Lord Curzon has received either £5,990 or £5,400 – let us say the latter – out of his daughter's income and out of it has paid her £1,000, leaving £4,000 clear in his hands.
>
> Even after providing for the taxes on the £5,400, amounting in round figures on the rate of the whole year's income to £2,700, there would still be a clear credit left in his hands for the six months only of £1,700.
>
> Lady Irene states therefore that upon every ground, whether legal, equitable or moral, she cannot believe that her father will not carry out his agreement and obligation and pay to her the sum necessary to pay the taxes from the money received and retained by him between April and October 1920, for which taxes the Inland Revenue look to her primarily.
>
> In that connection she would like me to point out that for the year for which the arrangement existed, the total remittances which her father received are as follows, from the Leiter estate, a total of £11,698 17s 6d, out of which his Lordship says he gave back £589 16s 3d.
>
> Thus the total received by Lord Curzon amounts as you will see to a very large sum indeed – much larger than was ever contemplated when Lady Irene made the arrangement in October 1919.

Irene hoped that there would be an opportunity for reconciliation when her father was created a marquess (an expensive honour at £630 2s in fees and stamp duties, payable to the Home Office) in the King's Birthday Honours on 26 May 1921. This elevation had first been mooted six months earlier when Bonar Law, leader of the Conservative opposition, told Curzon that the Prime Minister Lloyd George proposed it as recognition of Curzon's four years as Leader of the House of Lords, member of the War Cabinet and then Foreign Secretary. Telegrams and letters poured in, from Indian maharajas, from Belgium, from friends, from the Foreign Office – and from Irene, who wrote almost as a timid stranger.

'A timely line of congratulation and pleasure at your great honour. I would like you to think that as your daughter I was delighted for your sake and that you deserved it for all the work you do for England.' She signed it simply 'Irene'.

This did not diminish Curzon's hostility towards his eldest daughter. He now did his best to denude Irene of her share of the settlement income. He still had Cimmie's; on her majority she had received her Leiter Trust money and when she married she had left her share of the settlement income with her father because she did not want to deprive him too suddenly of what he had been used to.

In June a long letter from Curzon's lawyers went to the leading KC, Dighton Pollock. After setting out the position, it said: 'Lord Curzon considers that Lady Irene has behaved badly to him and in the exercise of the power given in the Settlement he has directed that the income of the Trust Funds over which he has power of appointment shall be applied to Lady Cynthia and Lady Alexandra. The effect of this direction is to increase the incomes of Lady Cynthia and Lady Alexandra and, according to the arrangements made, incidentally that of Lord Curzon.'

Cimmie had no intention of benefiting at the expense of her sister. Instead, at the urging of her husband, she too asked for the share of the settlement income that was rightfully hers – Tom had bought a newspaper in his constituency, Harrow, to publicise his speeches on Ireland (he deplored the use of the Black and Tans) and it had failed, incurring debts.

On 21 September 1921, Curzon reported to Grace that he had received an extraordinarily offensive letter from Cimmie:

> She described my attitude, heaven knows why, as mean, petty, unwarrantable, unaccountable and incomprehensible. My daughters seem to go mad when a question of money is concerned and Cim is heading straight towards the same result as Irene, which indeed I suppose she desires.
>
> That any daughter of mine should have written in such a vein I should have deemed incredible were it not that I have previously had the same from Irene. Humbert tells me they are hard up. They paid £8,000 for their Guildford home taking it out of settlement. I do not think there is any force in her legal claim but am going to take the lawyers' advice, also whether I can make another redistribution to her detriment. I certainly would if I could.

Curzon was so anxious to do this that he requested his lawyers that same day to ask for Counsel's immediate opinion on whether he could redirect his elder daughters' share of the settlement income in favour of Baba – which would, of course, leave it in her father's hands.

Counsel's opinion was that he could not. Curzon's reaction was immediate, and icy. 'My dear Irene,' he wrote on 21 September 1921. 'I will deal just as you did over the unjust bargain. You will then see what you deserve and be able to devote whatever sums you please to your pleasures, your charities and your hunting. Above all, you will be free from any interference from your father.'

A week later he received a letter from Irene written straight from the heart:

> I wish to God the faults on both sides had not inevitably come to this ending but I want to try and hold on to the hope that now the cause of all our unhappiness has been removed the better things and the links we have between us may be able to appear and the love which I know at the bottom is there may cover up all the hurts and pains that have gone before.
>
> I loathe quarrels and rows and their horrid consequences and my actions may seem to you those of one who does not care and that I have none of the feelings of what home and my father are and ought to be. Deep down no one realises them more than me and I desperately want peace and friendship to reign between us in the future. May we forget all the things that have been said and my prayer is that out of this action of mine good may come and you will not feel that it is the severance of two people who can never get on together. No one wants that less than your Irene.

There was no reply. For a young woman of twenty-five to realise that she would never see her father again was a devastating psychological blow, especially in an era when single young women living on their own were virtually unknown. Irene was effectively orphaned, at an age when most of her contemporaries were either married or still had the secure emotional background of home.

Cim was to receive the same treatment. 'The thing is certain,' wrote Curzon to Grace in October 1921. 'The excellent Tom Mosley has been to see Humbert and in the same breath talks about the value he and Cim attach to paternal and filial relations. They mean to take the whole money and I think the best thing to do is to say Take it. I cannot stand the perpetual torrent of threats and abuse and insinuation.

'But I am going to write an account of my adumbration of what they call their money since their mother died and of what they have done to me. And there I will leave it.' Curzon, given to setting every aspect of his life down on paper, now wrote a note justifying his conduct, which he put among his papers, sending a copy to Cim. It is dated 1 November 1921.

When Irene took away the whole of her fortune I made no concealment of the fact that I intended to take advantage of a change in the Marriage Settlement which permitted of my altering the distribution of a portion of the income. This clause had been in the settlement the day before I married in 1895 on the intercession of my first wife in order to provide for the exact situation that has now arisen. Viz, the contingency of one or more of my future children of the marriage acting in the event of her death in a manner that would injuriously affect the position of the interests of their father.

When Cynthia married, I consulted my lawyer as to the propriety of asking her to leave a portion of the entire fortune now hers to assist her father, already embarrassed by the sudden withdrawal of the entire income of his eldest daughter. We made these arrangements with Cynthia and her lawyer that she should leave with me that portion of her income which had accrued from the Marriage Settlement, which was expected to amount to about £3,000 a year.

She even hinted at legal proceedings to be instituted by her sister or herself while protesting at any suspension of the affectionate relations that ought to reign between father and daughter. At the same time, although declaring her intention to carry out the obligations which she had accepted upon marriage, she indicated that circumstances might compel her to modify or terminate it, as in the present situation.

I am unwilling to continue any controversy on the matter. I would not willingly be again addressed in the language which Cynthia employed to me in her last letter and which I cannot forget. She must do as she pleases. A father does not with pleasure in any circumstance accept 'an allowance' – the phrase she habitually employs – from his daughter, but he would sooner not accept it at all than know it is found grudgingly and with obvious regret.

It was the end of his relationship with his two eldest daughters.

8

Baba Comes Out

~

The year Baba came out, 1922, saw Curzon suffer one of his bitterest blows. On 1 May the new Prime Minister, Bonar Law, a sick man, set off on a sea voyage, leaving Curzon to deputise for him. It soon became clear that Bonar Law would not recover (cancer of the throat was diagnosed) and on Whit Sunday, 20 May, he resigned.

Curzon appeared the obvious choice as successor. He was Foreign Secretary, an international figure and a much-respected statesman of superb intellect, with a bottomless capacity for work and flawless public integrity. Stanley Baldwin, although Chancellor of the Exchequer and Leader of the House, appeared to have little chance against Curzon. But Bonar Law gave no advice on his successor and the King turned to a former Prime Minister, Arthur (now Lord) Balfour.

Just as he had done fourteen years earlier when Curzon was seeking support for his election to a parliamentary constituency,* Balfour refused to support his old friend. This time he went further still, actively advising the King not to send for Curzon. For the first time, Labour was now the largest Opposition party and there were no Labour peers. Balfour added that his uncle, Lord Salisbury, had found the greatest difficulty in governing from the House of Lords even though in his time the Opposition party of Liberals had just as many peers as the Conservatives.

While the debating was going on, Curzon and Grace were

---

*As a member of the Irish peerage, Curzon had been (then) entitled to sit in the House of Commons.

spending the Bank Holiday weekend at Montacute (still without a telephone). It was one of their rare moments together: Grace had just returned from another of her numerous Paris visits. Late on the evening of Whit Monday the village policeman bicycled to the house with a telegram from the King's Private Secretary, Lord Stamfordham, saying that he wanted to see Curzon the following day.

Curzon, like almost everyone including the press, was convinced that Stamfordham's summons was to tell him that he would be sent for by the King to form the next government. But when Lord Stamfordham entered the drawing-room at Carlton House Terrace, where Curzon and Grace were waiting amid the tapestries and tigers' heads, it was to say that the King had sent for Stanley Baldwin.

For Curzon it was the final crushing of his lifelong ambition. He could not restrain his sobs, and he felt unable to dine with Lord Farquhar the following night to meet the King. He wanted Grace to refuse too but she told him they could not appear to sulk or seem resentful. The King sent for her to talk to after dinner and said at once: 'I suppose Curzon wouldn't come tonight because he didn't want to meet me?' Grace answered truthfully that while Curzon was very hurt and disappointed, he was genuinely unwell. The King said he would send for him and tell him personally the reasons for the decision. This thoughtful gesture so mollified Curzon that within two days he had agreed to continue as Foreign Secretary and made a generous speech pledging loyalty to Baldwin.

Nevertheless, it was a deep and grievous wound that may well have contributed to his illness that spring – and which meant that he played no part in the coming out of his youngest and favourite daughter. He felt wretched and wrote pathetically to Gracie on 15 May:

Went to your room and slept with my head at the foot of the bed so as to escape the early morning light through the shutter chinks, awake 11.30–2.30, took a mild chloral then for about two hours light sleep, the first for ten days.

Poor me. I have had a miserable morning. Leg spinning, back aching, involuntary bursts of tears. The chef gets worse daily and I will give him notice before the end of week. He has given us one ice three times in five days and chicken five days running ... the doctor came this morning and I enquired eagerly what I had in my leg and the reply was thrombosis, phlebitis and lymphangitis! The right leg is more than two inches longer than the left. I have seen nobody so far as I have not felt up to it.

That Season saw the return of the full-scale evening court for the first time since before the war. A ruling from Buckingham Palace stated that the trains of gowns were to be no more than two yards long instead of three so that they would trail at most eighteen inches along the ground. But the Prince of Wales feathers, the embroideries, the veils, the deep curtseys in front of a King and Queen blazing with orders and diamonds, were back with a flourish.

At court balls men still wore knee-breeches and black silk stockings (with thick black cotton ones underneath to hide their hairy legs) and left their swords in a pile outside the ballroom; at formal dinner parties they took women in to dinner, offering their right arms to do so. At the Curzons' enormous dinner parties their butler stood just inside the drawing-room door holding a silver tray on which were little folded cards bearing the names of the male guests: inside each was the name of the lady to be escorted to the table.

Grace took charge of her stepdaughter's Season with enthusiasm and skill. She suggested that Curzon should give Baba a sum of £200–£250 to cover her clothes, and she offered to take her to buy them in Paris (where Baba had been at school for the previous year). It was the perfect pretext for one of Grace's increasingly frequent visits to the French capital. For what Curzon did not know was that she had taken a lover, General Sir Matthew 'Scatters' Wilson, and would often meet him at the Paris Ritz.

Scatters Wilson was a brave, genial, philandering Yorkshire baronet for whom any pretty woman was automatically a challenge. Robust, energetic, clubbable and fond of a joke, he was a sportsman who enjoyed hunting, big-game shooting, cricket and, especially, racing. When Gracie met him he was the Unionist MP for Bethnal Green – a seat he held, ironically, until the change of Government that so shattered the man he had cuckolded. He himself was married to the eldest daughter of Lord Ribblesdale, the husband of Margot Asquith's younger sister Charlotte (Charty) Tennant.

Scatters, born in 1875, had been educated at Harrow and served with the 10th Royal Hussars. In the South African War of 1899 he won the King's Medal with three clasps and the Queen's Medal, also with three clasps, before being invalided home with enteric fever just before the war ended in 1902, after which his service continued first in India and then in England. He was exactly the sort of gallant, dashing, free-spending scamp who appealed to Gracie and he soon established a strong and ultimately disastrous influence over her.

Baba was presented by Grace at an evening court on 7 June to a King in the uniform of Colonel-in-Chief of the Life Guards and a Queen in silver brocade, in a ceremony which began when the Royal Family entered the Throne Room at 9.30 p.m. precisely. A few weeks later, on Tuesday 18 July, Grace gave a dance for Baba at 1 Carlton House Terrace. It was a grand ball, with powdered, liveried footmen in attendance, lilies, roses, carnations and azaleas sent up from Hackwood and arranged in gilt baskets, women in tiaras and men in white waistcoats and black tailcoats – many of the more energetic dancers with a spare collar or two in their pocket.

As always when royalty was being entertained, the Robert Adam silver was brought up from Kedleston, for the dinner party for thirty beforehand. There were two tables, a large round green malachite one for the royal party – the Duke of York, his sister Princess Mary and Lord and Lady Lascelles – presided over by Grace, her luscious Gaiety Girl looks set off by a pale pink Vionnet dress worn with pearls and one of Mary Leiter's tiaras. (To ensure that Gracie always got the seating exactly right, Curzon had thoughtfully provided his wife with a table of precedence.) Baba looked slender and beautiful in a dress of white silk and tulle embroidered with tiny crystals. After dinner a further four hundred guests, including the Prince of Wales, arrived to dance. The number of each dance was propped up on the band's piano and every girl carried a small dance card with a tiny pencil attached to write down the names of her partners under the number of the dance they had requested.

Curzon, who was recuperating at Broadstairs, had to miss the party. Also absent from Baba's ball were her sisters. Nancy Astor, who loved the Curzon daughters, may not have been conscious of the schism between Curzon and Irene since the latter already led a fairly peripatetic life. But she would certainly have discovered that Cimmie, her own favourite and married to a young man whom she also knew well, was no longer seeing her father.

Mistakenly, she attributed it to Gracie's influence. A month before the dance she went up to Grace at a dinner given by the American Ambassador and tactlessly asked: 'Why have you turned your stepdaughter out of doors?' As no one else had heard of the breach and Grace complained to her neighbour, Mrs Lloyd George, at this public rebuke for something that was not of her doing, the result was that everyone thought Nancy had once again gone too far.

Irene was not her father's daughter for nothing: she had inherited much of his strong will, and she was determined to take control of her own life, a difficult goal in an era when, despite their brief foray into wartime freedom, women were still regarded as dependent upon, and subordinate to, men. Hunting was her ruling passion and she was able to devote most of the year to it but late spring and summer also had to be filled. Anxious not to cause awkwardness during her sister's Season, she turned to another of her loves, travelling, then an altogether more leisurely affair. In Jerusalem she had met Ronald Storrs who had been appointed Governor of Jerusalem and Judaea two years earlier (when the League of Nations granted the British Government a mandate to govern Palestine, Jordan and Iraq).

Storrs, then forty, was the first of a number of men to recognise Irene's potential as wife to a governor or ambassador. Handsome, dignified, with an air of confidence and authority that would later make her into an admirable public speaker and head of committees, she was a strong presence in any room she entered – and she was very rich. Storrs proposed to her so frequently that, worried, she wrote to her father.

Curzon was alarmed: he considered Storrs an undesirable, though more on social than professional grounds ('Did you know he went to the Revelstokes uninvited and had to leave?' he wrote to Gracie). As he still would not communicate directly with Irene he got Baba to write to her and after a few days enquired casually what had happened. Baba told him that Storrs had proposed to her sister repeatedly, the first time a few days after she had arrived. 'But she had already found out he was a bounder and refused. The next morning she got my letter and felt entirely justified.'

Irene seized this opportunity to extend the olive branch yet again. From the Hotel Britannia in Venice she wrote to her father on 26 August. So conscious was she of his enmity that she dared neither salutation nor affectionate ending.

I want you to know that I was greatly touched by your care and thought for me in getting Baba to write to me over Ronald Storrs in Jerusalem. My inner repulsion to him anyhow prevented anything happening after his proposal but Baba's letter reached me the morning after and I took it as a guidance, and I have treasured the thought that you got her to write it. Thank you, Daddy.

Cim and Tom come here next week. I expect you were proud Baba was such a success in London this summer and stood out in every way, in distinction, poise and charm. Gracie was marvellous to her and she realises it profoundly. Those two years of mine abroad before the war have been the background and basis of all this travelling interest I now have for seeing the world. My German has come back quite easily. I wish Cim and Baba could have had it. I am grateful to you for it.

Baba was an immediate success when she came out. Acclaimed as the prettiest debutante of the 1922 Season and 'the most beautiful brunette in London', from the first she was noted for her chic and an individual style that led rather than followed fashion. Where the vogue was for hair cut short and waved at the sides with the rest tied up in a small bun at the back, Baba enhanced the proportions of her oval face with long hair drawn back and knotted in a loose bun on the nape of her neck and instead of the long, loose dresses that embraced the new freedom, her silhouette was crisp and exquisite. 'Lady Alexandra, in dark blue, emphasised the attractions of the perfectly tailored suit,' recorded *The Lady* and when she began to wear dresses of soft, peppermint-green chiffon that fitted close to her slim figure yet floated as if in a breeze, it was a fashion quickly copied.

It was also observed that the royal princes greatly admired this new young beauty. The Prince of Wales, several years older and deeply in love with Mrs Dudley Ward, the pretty wife of a Liberal MP, thought of her affectionately as a glamorous golfing or dancing partner for his youngest brother Prince George. Another link was her friendship with Lady Elizabeth Bowes-Lyon, the beloved of the Duke of York.

Prince George soon became deeply smitten, sending her little notes and presents from the Palace ('Baba dear, here is the bag I promised but you'll probably think it is *too* awful. If so let me know and I'll try and get another'). Baba taught him to drive in her little two-seater – for a young man to take a girl 'motoring' was a favourite courtship ploy in those days when cars were still comparatively new, roads empty, narrow and twisting, and most people were driven by their chauffeurs. With no driving licences to pass, learning to drive was considered the work of an afternoon and the tutoring took place on the way back from a morning's golf at Swinley.

'I did so enjoy Saturday and we did have fun even tho' your poor nerves must have been terribly shaken from my driving,' wrote Prince George on his return to HMS *Excellent* in Portsmouth. Both of them had been startled, as they stood up to change seats on arriving at the main road, to see a Daimler pass with the stately figure of Queen Mary in the back – the Prince was already overdue at Osborne House on the Isle of Wight. 'We must have some more golf and I hope so much to see you again soon and you are so sweet to me. Please don't forget the wee photie, will you? ... I'll write again soon. Much love. G'

But Baba's affections were not engaged. She was very young and she had plenty of other suitors. Most, like Lord Westmorland, could be invited to lunch or dinner at 1 Carlton House Terrace but one, she knew instinctively, had better not be mentioned just yet.

The Prince of Wales – always called by his fourth name, David, by his family – had arrived back a month earlier from an extraordinarily successful tour of India, whither he had been sent to still the disaffection felt after a war in which Indian troops had fought gallantly, laying down their lives for a country which was not their own. 'He has brought back from India a young Indian

Army officer named "Fruity" Metcalfe,' wrote Frances Stevenson (later Lady Lloyd George) in her diary for 22 June 1922. 'The two are inseparable and his family are furious about it.'

Captain Edward Dudley Metcalfe – who had acquired his nickname in his university days – was an Indian cavalry officer who had been attached to the Prince's staff on his Indian visit and who had become the Prince's best male friend. He was tall and good-looking, with reddish hair, blue eyes and a soft brogue he kept until the end of his life. He was completely outside the small network of people who made up what was called 'Society' ('Who is this "Juicy" Metcalfe?' enquired the elderly, deaf Queen Alexandra) but he was high-spirited, good-natured and a superb horseman. Although always perfectly respectful and efficient, he treated the Prince exactly as he would have treated any other man friend and the Prince loved him for his charm, gaiety and naturalness.

Fruity, born on 16 January 1887, was the son of the Head of Industries in the Irish prison service. His parents led a busy social life, centred round the racing for which Dublin was famous. He was educated privately and, after leaving Trinity College, had entered Sandhurst in 1907 and joined his regiment, the 3rd Skinner's Horse, in November 1909 as one of nine squadron officers of whom four, like himself, were subalterns.

In 1914 he sailed with his regiment for France, where they were moved about as reserves and, like most cavalry, saw little fighting. On 1 September 1915 he was promoted captain and in June 1916 sent back with his regiment to India. Told that they would remain there, Fruity and a friend volunteered to serve with the 7th Meerut Cavalry Brigade in Mesopotamia; here they fought the Turks on the Tigris front. In August 1917 he won a Military Cross and shortly afterwards was Mentioned in Dispatches. By May 1919 he was back with the regiment, now involved in the Third Afghan War. When the Armistice was signed in September 1919 the regiment returned to Quetta and in 1920 he was seconded to serve successively in three princely states. When the hunting-mad Prince arrived in India Fruity, with his personal friendships with many of the maharajas, encyclopaedic knowledge of horses and perfect manners, was a natural choice as an ADC.

The Prince had not wanted to go to India: he was madly in love with Mrs Dudley Ward, wife of a Liberal MP, and the tour promised only hard work and unpopularity. He went out on the *Renown*, which dropped anchor in Bombay early on the morning of 17 November 1921, nervously aware of his responsibilities. With him as companion was his friend and cousin, Lord Louis ('Dickie') Mountbatten; also in the Prince's suite was Admiral Sir Lionel Halsey, at forty-nine a much older man, sent by the King to keep an eye on his son and act as ballast. To the Prince and Mountbatten Halsey was known as the Old Salt.

Almost immediately, Fruity and the Prince became fast friends; Lord Louis, too, like him immensely. 'Fruity Metcalfe, the nicest fellow we have. Poor, honest, a typical Indian cavalryman,' he wrote to his fiancée Edwina Ashley, the beautiful heiress grand-daughter of Edward VII's friend Sir Ernest Cassel.

Admiral Halsey disapproved of Fruity thoroughly while unwill-ingly falling victim to his charm. 'He is an excellent fellow, always cheery and full of fun but far, far too weak and hopelessly irre-sponsible. He is a wild, wild Irishman and no one knows anything about his family.' Fruity had entered the Prince's bedroom one afternoon while he was having a siesta and asked him if he would like to play polo because, if so, several of his maharaja friends would like to lend ponies. Twenty-five polo ponies subsequently arrived, necessitating an extra train to transport them.

Fruity provided much-needed relief and relaxation for the Prince after the strain of being 'on duty' so often. With Mountbatten, they soon became known as a trio. Mountbatten's diaries of the trip are full of references to things 'we three' have done, from early-morning polo practices to paperchases. Nor was Mount-batten jealous of Fruity's superlative riding ('In the finals I was up against Fruity who of course beat me'); when Fruity took a crashing fall in a polo match Mountbatten was first out on the field to help carry his unconscious body back. After the Prince, Fruity was the first person that Mountbatten and Edwina, who had come out to stay in India, told of their engagement.

The Prince could not bear to part with his new friend. When he came home he brought Fruity with him. In August 1922 Fruity was gazetted major and awarded the MVO; in September he was made an extra equerry to the Prince but he was already an integral part of the Prince's life and circle. With the Prince, he was the only other guest at the first dinner party given by the Mountbattens after their marriage in July; with the Prince, he went evening after evening to the nightclubs that were springing up all over Mayfair.

These temples to the new religion, dancing, were frowned on by the older generation, led by the King and Queen, who deeply disapproved of cocktails, jazz and dancing cheek to cheek. But for the Prince of Wales and anyone of his generation, dancing was as much part of life as cinema-going would be in the next decade. The Prince's favourite restaurant-nightclub was the Embassy, at the Piccadilly end of Bond Street, where he could be seen every Thursday night and quite often other nights as well at his own sofa table by the wall.

Here he would take Mrs Dudley Ward in a party of his intimates – one or other of his brothers, Fruity, Lord and Lady Brecknock, the Mountbattens and Mountbatten's older brother Lord Milford Haven and his wife. In Mountbatten's absence at sea, Fruity would act as Edwina's escort when the Prince arranged a party for the Co-Optimists Revue, the Cabaret Girl or the Midnight Follies, always followed, of course, by dancing, at the Embassy, Kit-Cat Club or the Grafton Galleries, where Fruity and Mountbatten were honorary members.

It was after an evening at the Grafton Galleries that the Prince of Wales, his brothers, his friend Fruity and Baba decided that they could not bear to stop dancing – especially as it was the first time Paul Whiteman's band had played there. The solution, decided Baba, was for them all to go to 1 Carlton House Terrace. Curzon and Grace were away and the only remaining servants slept in the basement, so there was little chance of them being discovered. The Prince of Wales collected some champagne from York House while Baba and Prince George went ahead to the silent, shuttered house. In the dining room they pushed the long table aside and pulled dust-sheets from the furniture. Baba fetched tooth-mugs from all the bathrooms – the only glasses she could find – and when the Prince of Wales, the band, and the rest of their friends arrived the impromptu party began. It ended at six in the morning. Baba and Prince George, due to stay with Philip Sassoon at Trent, changed in their respective houses into the tweeds suitable for a country weekend and set off at 7 a.m. for the Trent golf course.

All would have gone unnoticed except that Prince Harry, the heaviest of the four royal brothers, sat on Curzon's superb dining-room table and cracked it badly. Baba was so terrified that she told Gracie, who smoothed it over with Curzon. If anyone else had committed such a crime – or anyone else had told him of it – Curzon would have been furious.

9

The Absentee Wife

~

For Christmas 1922, Gracie and Baba were at Hackwood, Cim and Tom in the South of France, Irene at Melton Mowbray and Curzon in Lausanne for the Peace Conference. With Lloyd George now out of the picture, his decision to stay on as Foreign Secretary was ratified by Baldwin's recognition of his powers. 'I have suddenly been discovered at the age of 63,' he wrote to Gracie. 'I was discovered when I was Viceroy of India from 99–06. Then I was forgotten, traduced, buried, ignored. Now I have been dug up and people have found life and even merit in the corpse.'

Unhappily, the creature comforts in Lausanne were not up to those in any of Curzon's houses. 'Having no valet I now have to dress myself,' he wrote plaintively, requesting Gracie to bring or send brandy, soda, a box of cigarettes and a bottle of his favourite hairwash. His back was causing him more trouble than ever. 'My new cage is broken and the fractured pieces of steel cut into me and tear my skin and clothes.'

Though Grace wrote her husband letters breathing misery at his absence ('it almost breaks my heart, the thought of Christmas there without you') she spent as much time away from him as she could. After a series of balls in November she had made one of her regular visits to Paris where she was feted ('flowers as usual from the Aga Khan, Mme de Castellane and Charles Mendl [First Secretary at the British Embassy in Paris]'), with dinner parties and luncheons galore.

Immediately after Christmas she set off for the smart resort of St Moritz, giving as her reason fun for Baba, who was joining her there on 9 January. 'I am so sad not to be able to spend our anniversary with you,' she wrote from the Palace Hotel. Many might have wondered why, with cars, private coaches on trains, servants to pack for her and accompany her and endless time at her disposal, she could not manage it. But Curzon recognised resignedly that the St Moritz whirl had priority, though he wrote wistfully: 'It is nice to think that we are in the same country.'

In St Moritz, where the Season was at its height, Grace was a noticeable figure, wrapped in opulent and becoming furs as she drove about in a scarlet sleigh. To Curzon's alarm, one of Baba's suitors, Lord Westmorland, had also arrived in St Moritz. When Gracie suggested that Baba, suitably chaperoned, remain there after she herself left, Curzon would have none of it. He was becoming disenchanted even with Baba, the only one of his daughters he still considered loyal. He believed that she was incapable of affection and he constantly complained that she never kept in touch with him ('No good expecting Baba to write'). Nevertheless, he sent her a Christmas cheque.

According to his lights, he had tried to be a good father but was uneasily conscious that he had failed. From his women friends among the Souls he received attention, flattery and warm affection; from his stepdaughter, little Marcella, a happy, unquestioning devotion. Why could not his daughters be more like these templates of desirable female behaviour? He was far fonder of Marcella than of any of his own children. 'To me, the happiest moment in the 24 hours is when darling little Marcella comes in.' It was more, though, a question of Marcella's personality than her age (she was fifteen): she was gentle, serene and so intuitive that they were always in sympathy. Her undemanding presence was a contrast to the girls who had inherited his own strong will.

He did not soften towards Irene, for instance, when at her instigation he allowed her to visit him briefly in the spring of 1923, which she followed by a humble letter of thanks: 'Dear Daddy, I came away profoundly grateful for having seen you for those few minutes. It has made such an immense difference to me. I take things that touch you so deeply to heart that it would make all the difference if you felt I might see you from time to time and so hold on to ties that deep down mean everything to me. Thank you again for those minutes which, though short, meant the world to Your grateful daughter.'

By contrast, his attitude to Grace was subservient, with constant pleas that she might spare some time to come and see him, requests that she would write more often, demands that she should rest and free herself from cares ('your holiday seems to be one long course of self-sacrifice,' he wrote without the slightest trace of sarcasm). These expressions of devotion only varied when he was forced to defend himself against Gracie's jealous accusations.

Occasionally he was able to dismiss some baseless charge ('Ever since that fatal evening when we dined with Maud and I committed the seemingly unpardonable error of talking after dinner to Diana Cooper you have been different'); more often than not he did not know why she was attacking him. 'You say I will understand why your feelings towards me have so changed. I have read those words and I have not the faintest inkling to what they refer. I am not conscious of having failed in the smallest respect in loyalty to you. I am not capable of that. I have not the slightest idea what I am supposed to have done or not done.' Sadly he concluded: 'You show affection to almost everyone else until I almost feel I am the person who comes last and counts least.'

Gracie's self-chosen role as absentee wife did not prevent her from doing what she could for Baba. She took her to balls and parties; she took both Irene and Baba to the Buckingham Palace Garden Party that concluded the Season on 29 July 1923 – Grace in white lace with amber feathers in her white hat, Irene in a champagne-coloured frock and Baba in white.

Baba, like Irene and Cimmie before her, was treating Cliveden more and more like a second home. For her there was another attraction: Nancy Astor's 25-year-old son (by her first marriage), Bobbie Shaw. A glamorous young officer in the Blues (the Royal Horse Guards), he was an ornament of the Cliveden circle, known for his wit as much as for his good nature. He was the only person who could stand up to his mother in full flood, stopping a stream of argument or direction with a single dry remark that reduced her to a helpless gust of laughter.

He was very attracted to Baba and she, at nineteen, equally drawn to him. They made a striking couple; with their looks, slim, elegant figures and chic, they seemed, said one of the Langhorne uncles, like the two juvenile leads in a musical comedy, ready to glide effortlessly into a stylish dance number. It was assumed by everyone that one day in the near future they would announce their engagement.

But Bobbie had a secret. He was homosexual. It was not something Baba could possibly have known or even guessed. No one would have dreamed of discussing such a subject in front of a young unmarried girl and homosexuals themselves were extremely careful not to betray their sexual orientation – it was, after all, a criminal offence – so much so that many married and fathered children. Bobbie, however, was an extremely honourable man who had no intention of marrying Baba in order to provide himself with a 'blind' and who was far too fond of her to deprive her of the chance of real sexual happiness in the future. Gently he made it clear that marriage was not on the cards, so tactfully that he always remained one of her best friends.

She had many other admirers. Prince George was still pursuing her, to the displeasure of the King and Queen when they were linked publicly in the press. 'Another row about you, my dear, which was trying, however it is all right and I had it out with them, and it was only the papers,' he wrote from Balmoral in September 1923. On another occasion, after playing in a golf foursome Prince George, the Prince of Wales and Fruity Metcalfe playfully signed a pledge promising to pay Baba £100 (about £2,500 in today's money) if they smoked too much.

We the undersigned swear, on oath, that we abide by the following compact.
(1) P of W two cigarettes before five o'clock, plus pipes
(2) P.G. four camel cigarettes before five
(3) E.D.M. four cigarettes before five o'clock.
This agreement to commence May 23rd and to expire June 25 *or* we agree to pay £100 in default to be equally divided.
Signed: Edward P, George, E. D. Metcalfe.

(They kept their pledge, as a note in Baba's handwriting shows.)

It is an interesting document, if only because it shows the Prince's signature on the same piece of paper as his brother George and Fruity – the two men of whom he was fondest (years later, Lloyd George told his equerry Dudley Forwood that these were the only two men in his life whom the Prince really loved).

For Fruity, since their return from India, the Prince had come to feel an affection so deep and all-embracing that it could have been called love, as a letter written the previous autumn (19 September 1922) from Balmoral shows. It is worth quoting in full, if only because, if addressed to a woman, one could be forgiven for mistaking it for a love letter:

My dear old Fruity,
I am so sorry I have not written before. I have been meaning to but I'm too *bloody* (£50 to you) sleepy after dinner, which is the only time I get for letters as I'm out all day after the stags. I *loathed* having to come north on Tuesday and leave you behind, the first time in nearly a year, that's all. I'm missing you *a whole lot*. I most certainly am!

But I'll be back south in a fortnight and it's my duty to come here for a bit, not only to see my family but also to see all the keepers and ghillies and servants, some of whom I've known for 20 years. It's desperately cold and I feel much as I would in the Antarctic, all tucked up, and it's my first taste of real cold for two years and I hate it worse than ever!! I missed two stags yesterday but shot well today and got *four* so I'm quite pleased with myself for once and they were all long downhill shots. But stalking seems very tame after riding, as everything else does, and I'm missing my riding terribly, and hope to God I won't loose (*sic*) the very little I feel I've picked up in the last six weeks! And what about all my lovely boots? I feel that every step I take on the hill is making my chances of getting into them again smaller and smaller!! This feeling haunts me.

But enough balls and nagging. Honestly, and you must know it by now, I miss you terribly when you are away, and somehow I want to say I'm ever so grateful to you for being the marvellous friend to me you have been ever since we left India; I don't count so much *before* March, do you? as we saw so very little of each other as compared to now. Oh! I can't write what I want to say but I am oh! *so very* grateful to you for *everything*. Your marvellous friendship first and then all your help with the horses and ponies and the running of my stables. But I'm not going to write a soppy letter though I *insist* on your *driving* out of your silly old head any ideas or thoughts of returning to India when your year's leave is up. As a matter of fact there's been no mention of your name up here as yet but that don't make a scrap of difference. I'm just not going to let you go back to that Godforsaken country and life and insist on you staying with me (officially) to run my stables etc but actually, to … well, carry on being what you've always been to me and are now, my greatest man friend. I can't just explain why you hold that 'position' and mean so much to me, right here on paper, it's just YOU!! But now I'm getting sloppy again and you'll hate me if I get like this and besides I must dress for dinner, for which it is a far greater crime to be late than at Badminton. But you know what I mean!!

I hope you will get this before you go west on Sunday and I enclose a letter for old Wilder. I can't bear not to be going to Easton Grey with you next week and mind you don't jump the horses over the schooling fences.* You can do anything you like in the closed school and may jump out cubbing if Master lets hounds go. But no more as I want to be there for the dirty work even if I'm not capable of doing it myself!! I know you'll say I've been vocalising and put me in 1st or 2nd Div. But I only want to try and tell you how grateful I am to you for all you've been and are to me and how much I'm missing you and how I want you to chuck any ideas of leaving me unless you want to for your own private and personal reasons then of course you are free now as you've always been but I've gotten an idea that you don't want to leave me for either private or personal reasons. So 'cut it all right out' *now* and for all time. Must stop now.

Be good tho' I bet you aren't. Be careful of that little bitch from Peshawar but give my love to Mrs Belleville. What a shame to rag you but the latter is the goods while the other isn't *your* affair at all. Please write to me.

Yrs ever EP

PS I miss all the fun and jokes we have together so terribly. I've written pages to the old Admiral!

Curzon had spent the late summer taking a cure at the French spa of Bagnolles. He was worried, as always, by his financial affairs. Grace, who had agreed to pay him £200 a month, seldom did so. Rent, rates, taxes, living expenses, repairs, wages and entertainment for the two principal houses, 1 Carlton House Terrace

*The Prince had been hunting with the Beaufort, from Easton Grey House near Malmesbury, where he kept a string of ten hunters.

and Hackwood, came to £20,389 15s 3d a year; Montacute House cost £1,589 10s 10d; Naldera, the house in Broadstairs, £299 13s 7d; income tax and supertax £6,067 5s; Baba £1,025 7s 3d. 'A total of £32,371 15s!'

He came back from France on 5 September 1923, when he reproached Gracie for not taking the slightest interest in him, his health or his doings. 'You have never once asked me how was my leg. Not one word have you ever said about my office or Foreign Affairs – you who once rebuked me for not keeping you au fait with everything that passed. For five weeks I have lived in absolute solitude.'

Grace was now pursuing her own life with unblushing selfishness, spending as much time away from her husband as she could while simultaneously trying to offload on to him as much of the responsibility for her children as possible. It was Curzon who had to find a tutor for Hubert; Curzon who arranged a party as a treat for Marcella's sixteenth birthday on 24 November, first lunching with her and then taking them all to the theatre afterwards; Curzon who wrote several times (fruitlessly) to Marcella's older brother Alfred to remind him of his sister's birthday; Curzon who mopped Marcella's tears afterwards when Alfred made no responses, failing even to turn up for the luncheon.

It was Curzon, too, who had to deal with the boy's drunkenness at Balliol, who had to make arrangements to extricate him from his 'decadent set' by sending him abroad. 'Unless we save him now, Gracie, it will be too late,' wrote Curzon to his wife. As a first step, Alfred was sent to stay with Irene for a week, then returned to Carlton House Terrace, giving his word of honour that he would always be in by midnight. Instead, he stayed out all night, letting himself in by the area door when it was unlocked in the morning and, as Curzon put it, 'drinking and cavorting with women, with whom he had on most occasions been home'. He still had gambling debts from Balliol and to keep afloat he had sold his car and pawned his jewellery. Curzon bought back the car, tried to find the jewellery and spent hours talking to Alfred. He begged Gracie not to go on giving Alfred money and above all to understand the seriousness of her son's behaviour. Finally, in February 1924, Curzon decreed that no bill would be honoured unless it was from a tradesman or a debt of honour. 'The Randolph

Hotel, the tarts and the night club will not be paid.'

Grace was not particularly grateful. After the desperate attempts of the previous years to conceive and carry an heir, she had virtually given up all pretence of married life. Curzon did not make it easy for her: she was a woman who needed attention and, apart from the life of the bedroom, she received little from her husband. By his own account, he had no time for recreation and had only dined out once that year; instead, he sat up until two or three in the morning working on papers. Lord D'Abernon, to whom he confided this, notes in his diary: 'This regime almost compels him to relegate to the morning hours the lighter amenities of conjugal life'. Not surprisingly, Gracie described herself in one letter as 'only your wife in name'.

She seldom saw her husband. Though always protesting her longing to be with him, she managed to arrive in London when he was in Kedleston, to be in Scotland when he was in London, and then to depart in October for Switzerland ('I long to return as I no longer care for this place but the children seem to love it'). Nor had she been at home when the Mary Curzon Hostel for Women was established as a charity on 6 October 1922, at 170 King's Cross Road, with Curzon's great friend Consuelo Balsan (the former Duchess of Marlborough) as trustee.

Curzon, who devotedly sent Grace flowers, chickens, rabbits and fruits whenever she was in England, felt her indifference badly. He wrote sadly from Kedleston, where many of his plans were going awry: '... all these worries and never one to turn to or speak to. I think you must try, Girlie, to be a little more nice to me in the future. It is telling on me badly ...'

His unhappiness was exacerbated by a frightful row with Baba, who wanted to go to America. No doubt she felt she would like a change of scene since she had turned down Prince George and Bobbie Shaw had made it plain that their future was not together. But she was only nineteen and, although Nancy Astor had issued a blanket invitation to the houses of her Langhorne relations in Virginia, she knew that her father would not let her go without a carefully-planned itinerary of visits to approved houses. One after another, these planned visits fell through, but not Baba's determination. Curzon anguished over her plans, asking Lady Salisbury to visit him – he had to come down in his dressing-gown, so painful was his back – so that he could ask her advice.

Lady Salisbury consulted Nancy Astor, and both agreed that on no account should Baba be allowed to go unless every day and week of her time in America was mapped out with bona fide invitations in advance. 'When Baba comes back from Irene on Tuesday I shall probably have a fierce encounter,' Curzon wrote to Gracie. Two days later, he did. 'This morning I had it out with Baba and went through a rather terrible scene. I implored her not to live for pleasure and excitement only but to do or attempt something serious but I fear it is not in the child.' To make allowances for a nineteen-year-old's need for fun was not in Curzon's nature.

His sole source of love and affection was Marcella, who travelled with her nurse to whatever house he was staying in. He loved her sunny nature, her originality, her frankness and her trusting delight in his company, all of which seemed to compare so unfavourably with his own daughters. He gave her little presents like Georgian paste shoe buckles; he reported gleefully that he had done a very difficult crossword puzzle in the *Westminster Gazette*, sent it in in Marcella's name and won a prize. 'Marcella is very pleased with the little terrier Chips Channon gave her, which capers about her school room,' he wrote to Grace in St Moritz at the end of November. 'I see next to nothing of Sandra who is out all day. Where she goes I have no idea as she never leaves word with anybody.'

One of the places to which she went during that winter of 1923 was to her sister Irene, in Melton Mowbray, the small Leicestershire town at the heart of the best hunting country in England. Here Tom Mosley had successfully courted Cimmie, here Irene was now well established, settled in Sandy Lodge, the hunting-box that would become her home. From it, she hunted regularly with the Quorn, the Belvoir and the Cottesmore, with occasional days with the Pytchley and the Fernie. Here, too, was the Prince of Wales, hunting as often as he could manage with the Melton packs. With him, in charge of his horses, came Fruity Metcalfe.

10

Melton Mowbray:
Life at the Gallop

~

When the Prince of Wales began to hunt with the Leicestershire packs during the season of 1923/4, the small market town of Melton Mowbray became as important socially as it had traditionally been for its closeness to three of the best hunts in England, the Quorn, the Belvoir and the Cottesmore.

Melton revolved around hunting. The wide grass fields of Leicestershire gave such good galloping that two horses a day were needed; for those who hunted five days a week this meant maintaining a dozen or so horses and their grooms from October to late March or early April each year. In Melton hunting boots were made, and polished to mirror-like gloss with spit, polish and a deer bone; here hunting ale was brewed; here there were saddlers, breeches-makers, purveyors of straw, fodder and oats, horse dealers and grooms. Here too were numerous large or small hunting-boxes, owned or rented by those who hunted regularly. From 1923 onwards, the most famous was Craven Lodge, where the Prince of Wales stayed.

Craven Lodge, originally called Craven Cottage, was one of several noted hunting-boxes at Melton which offered accommodation – others were Wicklow Lodge, Sysonby Lodge, Staveley Lodge, Hamilton Lodge and Warwick Lodge (where one American tycoon stabled fifty horses). On a small hill overlooking Melton, it had acquired its name when rebuilt the previous century by a nephew of the first Earl of Craven. In 1922 it was bought by one of Tom Mosley's best friends, the 28-year-old Captain Michael

Wardell of the 10th Hussars. A great sportsman and an enterprising businessman (he later became general manager of the *Evening Standard*), Wardell converted Craven Lodge, run by his mother and stepfather, General John Vaughan, into a kind of 'hunting club' for those who did not want the trouble of their own establishment.

The house with its twenty-four principal bedrooms was divided up into several sizeable apartments and the stabling extended to provide sixty-two loose boxes and six saddle rooms for the use of the occupants. The large main rooms of the former house, furnished with comfortable sofas and chairs, became the club drawing- and dining-rooms. There were seven acres of grounds and courts for squash, then becoming a favourite pastime on non-hunting days, were soon added. The Prince enjoyed his first stay at Craven Lodge so much that he decided he wanted something more permanent, and the Urban District Council quickly approved plans for a private flat for him overlooking the Craven Lodge stabling. He took formal possession of this in the autumn of 1924.

All the Prince's intimates poured down, from his brothers to the Earls of Dudley, Kimberley, Rosebery, Derby, Sefton, Westmorland and Londesborough. Most came to hunt, the men immaculate in white buckskin breeches and glossy top hats, the women in beautifully tailored blue or black habits (women invariably rode side-saddle with these shire packs), with white linen waistcoats or stocks and bowler hats.

Others, like Baba, came simply to enjoy the social life – during the winter months Melton became a microcosm of smart Mayfair society. There were balls, like the one given by Lady Ancaster just after Christmas 1923, to which Baba went, and innumerable dinner parties. Marquises, counts, earls and rajas attended the annual performance of Gilbert and Sullivan by the operatic society or danced with the public at British Legion dances in the Corn Exchange. On several occasions there were three royal princes at dinners organised by the local branch of the National Farmers' Union. One was the Prince of Wales, who said in proposing a toast to the farmers: 'I am trying to pay off a debt, or I should say a fraction of the debt, that I owe for many happy days of riding over your land.' As the Prince said in one of his letters to Fruity, you could jump one of these Leicestershire cut-and-laid fences six abreast. There were social events every evening, including a weekly dance at Craven Lodge; after dinner, poker was a favourite amusement, with sums the equivalent of thousands today being won and lost nightly.

So chic did Melton Mowbray become when the Prince of Wales made it his winter headquarters that the Prince's favourite Embassy Club opened a branch there above a shop in the Market Place – the Prince's passion for dancing was almost as great as for hunting. The first dance, held at the King's Theatre in November 1923, with the Prince as guest of honour, was comparatively makeshift, with the footlights given coloured shades, the sides of the stage banked with orchids and ferns, and curtains instead of the London Embassy's mirrored walls, but like the later, more sophisticated dances it was packed. The Curzon sisters were both there, Irene in gold tissue, Baba – one of the Prince's partners – in green and silver brocade.

That winter, Baba often visited Irene. When the bitter quarrel between Curzon and his two elder daughters over their inheritance had taken place Baba, still at home, had heard the story from her father's point of view. At first she believed that it was her sisters who had behaved badly and there was a temporary coolness. But good relations soon resumed. Like everyone else, she adored Cimmie, and she was fascinated by Tom. His powerfully male aura and the immediate assumption of intimacy natural with a sister-in-law who was only a schoolgirl when they first met had flattered and bewitched her. She was still young enough to find Irene's semi-maternal attitude comforting and reassuring, and staying with this older sister, so well established at Melton, provided a welcome escape from the difficulties of life at home. Although she did not hunt, she loved the diversions of Melton. Everywhere the Prince went, Fruity Metcalfe went too, so she and Fruity met constantly. It was during these visits that Fruity fell deeply in love with her.

Baba was used to male admiration. She was also conscious of her youth and inexperience, and well aware that this was not a match that would please her father. Fruity was seventeen years older than she was, only of her world by the freak of chance, and the violence of his emotions scared her. She wrote to him in December 1923 to tell him that she loved him – she thought – but on the other hand she might easily meet someone else. What she made absolutely clear was that she did not want any kind of commitment at that moment.

Fruity, a generous-spirited man, responded with impassioned declarations of love and a promise to give her all the time she needed. 'Dearest Love, God is not kind to allow me who worship you to be the cause of hurting you. It is not right that my love for you, and your love for me, should be the cause of making your life, which is a far from happy one in some ways, even more difficult that it at present is. Forgive me, sweet woman that I love – forgive me.

'I want you, I need you, I want to see you, look at you, be near you. You say you want a year, or is it a day. *Yes, Yes*, my love, take what you want and all you want.'

In February 1924 the Prince of Wales had an accident that aggravated his family's worry about the dangers to which his passion for riding was exposing him. While riding one of his hunters round a jumping circuit he took a fall and broke his right collar-bone. Fruity, who was with him, tied up his arm and took him to the nearest surgery. Later on that month the Prince, his arm in a sling, went to Paris under his favourite incognito, Lord Chester, taking Fruity with him. They went stag-hunting, to the Folies Bergère and to a dinner at the British Embassy.

At the same time, Baba was recuperating from an operation for appendicitis and was whisked off by Irene for a long weekend in the bracing air of Brighton. Before she left she scribbled a short letter to the Prince of Wales apologising for being on such bad form at their last evening out in a party. He replied immediately with a charming note that shows the depth of their friendship: 'Surely you know me well enough not even to say you've been rude and that night of all times when you weren't really fit to go out and dance so soon after the operation. I know you did it so as not to cart me which was sweet of you and much appreciated by me. You must take care of yourself. Yours, E.P.'

Only weeks later, in March 1924, Fruity was the one injured, while trying out a new horse for the Prince at the Aldershot Command drag hunt near Long Sutton in Hampshire. The horse fell at the third jump, a high fence with a ditch, and Fruity was hit in the face by the hoof of the horse following. This time it was the Prince who dashed to get help and, with his brother Henry, visited him in the Cambridge Military Hospital. Fruity's jaw was broken, his face needed twenty-seven stitches, his lips were torn and several teeth knocked out.

Treatment by the noted plastic surgeon Harold Gillies restored his looks though his nose, said one columnist, was now more that of Caesar than Apollo. The Prince, said Fruity, was kindness itself, especially given his attitude to illness. 'When the P is well he doesn't want anyone near him who is not well too,' wrote Fruity to Baba. 'He's a funny lad, but very lovable and has always been wonderful to me.'

The King and those around him had become worried by Fruity's influence on the heir to the Throne. The two were inseparable, confiding everything to each other and sharing jokes and code words inexplicable to others. Both had an obsession with clothes and would spend hours discussing cuffs or the placing of buttons (Fruity almost invariably wore check suits, the Prince often favoured grey).

Even before Fruity's advent the Prince's love of horsy sports, in particular hunting, had made his family fearful. It was natural that Fruity, a brilliant horseman who had been employed by the Prince to manage his horses, would encourage the Prince in what was rapidly becoming an obsession. Like many Irishmen, Fruity had an excellent eye for a horse and he was determined to see that his royal master was mounted on the sort of animal that would take him to the front of the hunt.

As the Prince was a rider of almost desperate recklessness who did not care what risks he took, inevitably he often came to grief and it seemed quite possible that one day he would suffer serious injury, even death. At least one serious accident or fatality every season is recorded in Irene's hunting journal: 'Mike Wardell larking about on the way home from hunting over a little fence got a thorn in his left eye and had to have it out.' 'Lord Derby's only daughter Lady Victoria Bullock never regained consciousness after a bad fall. All the royal brothers out as usual this season.' 'While the Prince of Wales was out, a former Master of the Pytchley was killed when his horse fell and rolled on him.'

The Prince fought to keep Fruity, the King to have him sent

away or at least no longer in his son's household. The question was shelved for a while when the Prince decided he would visit his ranch in Pekisko, Canada, in the early autumn of 1924, stopping off en route for a few days in New York to watch the international polo. He managed to avoid being accompanied by Admiral Halsey, instead taking Fruity and Brigadier Gerald ('G') Trotter.

G Trotter, who had lost his right arm in the Boer War and wore his uniform sleeve pinned across the front of his tunic, was a genial man whose main pursuit was pleasure. His official post was Assistant Comptroller of the Prince's Household. Although more than twenty years older than the Prince, he was his constant companion, deplored almost as much as Fruity.

Fruity went on ahead, in August, with the Prince's polo ponies. By now deeply in love with Baba, he could hardly bear to leave her. 'It's only six hours since I left you, my dear Love, wet-eyed but *oh so* brave, for my sake I know. You were just grand my darling and I thank you for it and know how much of a strain it was for you to bear up, and smile. I realise well how you felt in that taxi, with the wee dog, returning to Carlton House Terrace (that strange house that has given me some such wonderful moments and yet I dislike it; mainly because I know you do, but also because it seems to stand solid and massive between me and you my beloved).'

Fruity's intuition was correct. The last thing Curzon would have wanted for his youngest and most beautiful daughter, who could have married literally anyone she chose, was a man with no money, no title, no land or no compensatory position in politics. Indeed, once, told by the butler that the hat and gloves in the hall belonged to 'Major Metcalfe', he had stormed upstairs to Baba's sitting-room and almost thrown Fruity out – though this was in part due to his stringent belief that tea and cucumber sandwiches, brought in by a footman, were not an adequate chaperone for any unmarried daughter of his.

The lovesick Fruity wrote to Baba constantly. 'I've not talked to you for such a long time but you've never left my thoughts – never. I've been comparing you with others (I am honest) and you've won, without a race. They just don't come up to you in any way. You have them beaten before the start. I've seen a few lovely women and girls but your beauty, Pansy darling, overwhelms them.'

He was leading his usual active life, playing tennis and golf on Long Island, swimming and dancing as well as getting the ponies fit for the Prince's arrival from Canada. When the party did arrive, in mid-September, there was a jolting shock in store.

The Prince seemed to have turned away from Fruity – his sudden abandonment of those he professed to love was to remain a feature of his character – in favour of G Trotter. Although Fruity did not know it, it was an eerie foretaste of what was to come; then, he was quite simply wretched. 'It just cannot go on unless there is a big change very soon,' he wrote unhappily to Baba. 'I feel it so terribly. I have *never* let him down, *never*. I have done every possible thing for him, and now this. No wonder I feel miserable. There is d——d little left for me.

'You, my love, are not for me either. I know it and feel it (and hide it even from myself).'

Baba wrote to him often ('you have no idea how much your letters mean to me') and the princely party was feted constantly – there were balls, parties, race meetings, polo matches and, as Fruity put it, 'one bathes in champagne'.

The Prince's defection rankled. Fruity was loyal to the core of his being; and the Prince's arbitrary, casual replacement of himself as chosen companion by G Trotter hurt him badly. 'The P seems very happy, he's enjoying himself a good deal,' he wrote to Baba. He and old G never leave one another, it's almost uncanny. The P refers every single thing to G now, G is the only person who knows anything of HRH's movements or ideas...

'I wonder where you are and what your thoughts are and if you are making someone love you. I fear it's only too easy and too probable. No one is kissing you, is there darling? Tell me. No – don't.'

In September he was writing to her: 'You see, all the love I gave him before is yours now, and it matters so little to me what he thinks or cares about me. I'll do my job with him but the personal thing I once gave him is gone forever. If *he* wants me, I'll respond – but that's all I can ever do now. I loved that young man with the very best God put into me but I can't feel ever again the same as I did. *You* have all my thoughts, my best feelings. One can't divide things – I can't, anyway.'

In Fruity's mind, he had lost the two people he loved most –

and was to love most in all his life. This mood may have accounted for an episode that could have had embarrassing consequences. One night Fruity had visited a house of ill repute and, finding himself unable to pay, was chased out of it by the prostitute to whom he owed money – minus his trousers, which she had stolen. Worse still, in them was his wallet, which held several letters from the Prince. Fortunately, no harm was done. After the tour Tommy Lascelles, the Prince's Private Secretary, told this story to his neighbour at a dinner party, without realising she was a friend of Baba's. Next day Fruity arrived at his house unannounced before dinner and knocked him down in his drawing-room (they made up their quarrel a few months later).

The Prince's seeming rebuff did not last long. Once back in England, hunting with Fruity from Craven Lodge as often as possible, the old intimacy was quickly re-established – to the King's annoyance. 'Had a talk with D on getting home about Metcalfe. I found him very obstinate,' reads the King's diary for 6 November 1924.

Fruity was far less certain of Baba's feelings. The coolest-headed of Curzon's daughters, she was also the most *mondaine*. As she grew older, her friends and family came to believe that, as the saying goes, her head invariably ruled her heart. In fact, it was the other way round. In addition, she was only twenty, and she was in love. The arguments for and against marriage to Fruity raged in her mind, a torment often confided to his sister Muriel Russell.

As for Fruity, the high hopes and idealistic enthusiasm with which he had accompanied the Prince of Wales back from India soon evaporated. He did not have a place on the Prince's permanent staff. Worst of all, it seemed as if there was no future for him with the girl he loved. If his army career were not to suffer irreparably, he had to rejoin his regiment. Late that autumn, he wrote Baba what must have been one of the most difficult letters of his life:

Dear Love, It is not easy for me to write. I've thought out letters to you during this last six weeks, I've written letters and burnt them. I've spoken to you, in my mind, hundreds of times. You have been with me, in my poor thoughts, day and night since you left me. You can disappear from St Moritz and I just hear vague rumours of your movements from people whom I hate to hear them from. You return suddenly without any warning – you are in London when I am there. I hear from my sister of your arrival, then you walk with her and she tells me of your troubles. My poor darling child, I feel *deeply* for you in your worry and uncertainty. May God help you in your trial. I only wish I could.

I would do all in my power to make you happy. All – all – all. Dearest one, it does hurt me so to know you to be wasting any of the hours of your life unhappy and in trouble. If you have felt this period as Muriel tells me you told her you had and you are still undecided whether you really love me or not, then dear one I am afraid that unknown to yourself (perhaps because you do not like to think it true) you have not yet really loved. You have yet to feel all the happiness (and sorrows I fear) that only true love can bring to you.

Now Pansy my love I will keep out of your way. If we *do* meet do not fear of my manner to you. I will appear just the same to those who look on. You may come here to stay with Nancy Tree, well, I'll go to London if you wish it. I will do all I can to let any wounds caused through me heal, as indeed time does very quickly. You are through the worst, darling. The big thing is you have proved you can do without me. If you had felt otherwise – well, I'd not be writing this letter. Now, sweetheart, I leave for India for certain. Maybe I sail next month, or there is a *faint* chance I may not leave until after the hot weather. Anyhow, I leave England and all in it for certain, and then your worries are greatly over.

I write this letter hoping it will help you. Remember also that I will *always* help you in any way that I feel is *really for your eventual happiness*. You can always call on me because I just love you with all my heart and soul. There is no need to answer this as it will hurt you to do so.

For Fruity, the future looked bleak.

11

The Passing of the Viceroy

~

Fruity was well aware that he was not the kind of man that the world – and Baba herself – expected her to marry. Even though she said she returned his feelings, he felt that he should point out his unsuitability from a worldly point of view. Just after Christmas 1924 he wrote to tell her so. 'All the love and adoration that God has made me capable of is all I offer you. It's been yours for some long time now. Do with it as you will – I will understand.

'. . . I am not worthy of you. Things are against us. Age, position, money, brain. I mean *you* want a lover with ambition, with big ideas, a man to make a name for himself in this so cruel world. I am not blaming – I understand. But I love as you will never (I think) be loved again. Remember – I love you terribly – and I'll never change.' He was to be proved right on every count.

Fruity had an unexpected ally in the Curzon camp. Grace was anxious for him to bring his suit to a successful conclusion. She did not enjoy seeing Baba unhappy, torn between love and the knowledge that marriage with Fruity would distress Curzon; even more, she wanted to get Baba safely off her hands before launching her own daughter, Marcella (then at finishing school in Paris). Marcella, though extremely pretty, was a shy girl and the last thing Grace wanted during her daughter's first Season was the constant presence of a beautiful stepdaughter distracting possible suitors. 'I must say I *do* like your stepmother,' wrote Fruity to Baba. 'She is perfectly sweet to me.' Better still from his point of view, Grace accustomed Curzon to the presence of Fruity in Baba's life and, more gradually, to the idea that Baba's feelings were engaged.

Then came other welcome news. The Prince of Wales had fought long and hard to take Fruity with him on his forthcoming tour of British Africa and South America in March 1925 but had not been able to persuade his father to allow this. What Fruity had not realised was that the Prince was also doing his best to see that his friend was not left stranded. 'I got this [an extract from a letter from the King] by a letter from the P. sent to me early this morning,' Fruity told Baba. 'Oh dear, I felt so ashamed of myself this morning having doubted him.' The Prince had written: 'I hope this will make you less sunk. Look in and *wake me* before you go to Liverpool, no matter how early. EP'

The extract from the King's letter of 18 January, read: 'I am glad to hear that you hope now that you have a billet for Metcalfe *in England* under the W[ar] O[ffice] when you start in March for S.A. I shall of course be ready to help him to get it when you let me know what you wish me to do.'

From Fruity's point of view, Curzon was not such a terrifying obstacle as he would once have been. As 1925 opened, his health and morale were in steep decline. When the first Labour Government gained office in January 1924 he had, of course, lost the Foreign Secretaryship but when, ten months later, Labour was overturned by a huge Conservative majority he confidently expected his old job back. When the Prince Minister, Stanley Baldwin, had told him that he was not to return to the Foreign Office it was an appalling disappointment. Although he did not wish to take up a lesser appointment he was chivvied by Grace into accepting the figurehead positions of Lord President of the Council, Leader of the House of Lords and Chairman of the Committee of Imperial Defence. 'As you know,' he wrote to her, on 8 November 1924, three days after the fateful Baldwin interview, 'I would not have swallowed what I have done or consented to take office again were it not that you so strongly wished me to do so, and that I am always urged to do the big thing though with equal regularity it is always forgotten as soon as done.'

He felt miserable, frustrated ('a new Government formed and I with no boxes coming in and nothing to do'), disillusioned and lonely. He had perforce accepted that he was to have no heir; two out of his three children were estranged and the third appeared to be in love with a nobody. His country did not seem to want his knowledge and experience yet lack of Departmental responsibility did not mean that he saw more of Gracie – indeed, she may have pressed him to accept the lesser Governmental posts against his wishes to keep him as much as possible out of her way.

To console himself, he went to stay with one of his oldest women friends, Consuelo, the former Duchess of Marlborough, now Madame Jacques Balsan, at the Balsans' house on the French Riviera. 'They have 350 acres, bought from nearly 80 persons, a huge property running right down to the sea. The upper part is terraces, the lower is a pinewood. It is wonderful what they have done and with what taste,' he wrote to Gracie, who had also been invited but had found reasons not to come.

Even with the Balsans, he felt the need to work and spent much of his time in his room writing his book on India ('I hope I am not being an inordinate bore. I kept to my room most of the morning and again later and do not think that I interfere with their domestic life'). It was also a way of keeping disappointment at bay. Both the Balsans found him much changed, Consuelo telling her next visitor, Winston Churchill, that although he was a charming guest, full of anecdotes and wit, he was 'sad and humble. The Fairy Queen [Grace] flouts him and laughs at him and now he is no longer the All Highest.'

Gradually Curzon emerged from his shell, remarking approvingly that Jacques Balsan (whom he had not met before) was much better than he expected. 'They are an extraordinarily well suited couple, he is very intelligent and well informed, she is, as always, very sympathetic and sunny and sweet.' Grace, he hoped, would arrive soon; she had promised to come for the last three days of his visit – but yet again there was a cancellation. He went back to London in February, shedding tears when he left the Balsans and telling Consuelo that he had not had such a happy holiday since he was a young man.

On 5 March, while dressing for dinner at Christ's College, Cambridge, where he was due to speak to the university's Conservative Association, he suffered a severe haemorrhage from the bladder. The following morning before breakfast Grace arrived to bring him home to Carlton House Terrace.

It was quickly apparent that he was gravely ill. It is possible that he had had some inkling he might not live much longer: during the holiday with Consuelo he had told her that he constantly thought of Mary and had suddenly remarked, 'I know that Mary will be the first to greet me in heaven' ('I hope that she will have got a comfortable and noble Mansion ready for him and precedence all arranged with the Authorities,' Churchill wrote to his wife when he heard this).

At Carlton House Terrace, Curzon lay in bed discussing and amending his will and compiling a long handwritten memorandum of forty-four clauses, detailing everything from the whereabouts of his papers to a defensive note about his expenditure of Leiter money. 'Should the plea ever be put forward that the pictures [in his various houses] were purchased with the funds that would ultimately fall to my daughters, the reply is that I bought nearly the whole from funds belonging to me personally which I saved up for the purpose; and that if I had bought them with Leiter money, I had a perfect right to do so under the orders of the Court out of the allowance made to me personally by the Court.' The final result, together with a codicil, he signed on 8 March with his butler and nurse as witnesses.

He was operated on the same day. Afterwards he lay in Grace's big comfortable bed in her big comfortable bedroom, attended by Sir Thomas Horder, the King's doctor. There was no disguising the seriousness of his condition and Grace and Baba spent most of their time with him.

When Irene, who had been in bed with flu and a temperature of 102 two days earlier, heard that he was desperately ill, she motored up from Melton Mowbray. At the door of Carlton House Terrace she was turned away by a footman. She was so shattered by this final rebuff that she went straight to the Carlton Hotel where she retired to bed for two days. In her autobiography, Grace gave as her reason for refusing Irene entry to the house that the arrival of a daughter so deeply estranged would lead Curzon to believe he was dying (that her own presence was so rare that ten days of constant attention might not give him the same idea seems not to have entered Grace's head).

Baba, with no mother and separated from both her sisters, miserable at seeing her father suffer and at the thought that she might soon be orphaned, was under intense strain. Apart from Grace, the only person she could really talk to, albeit by letter only, was Fruity, who kept in daily touch by note. Although she did not tell her father of this, Curzon had become aware of their growing closeness, for during these last days he told Grace: 'I think Baba may marry Major Metcalfe.'

Fruity's steady, constant sympathy and understanding must have reassured Baba that here was a man who would always protect and care for her. 'I just can't go to bed without letting you know how well I understand what you've been through today, my poor sweetheart', runs one typical letter. 'The uncertainty, the gloom, the shock of seeing your father worn out, fighting for his life – it has been just terrible. My dear one, I feel for you deeply.'

A week after the operation Curzon developed congestion of the right lung. As he fought painfully for breath it was obvious to the doctors and those around him that the end could not be far off. As he got worse, he asked to see the woman he had once loved so deeply, Elinor Glyn. The message (recounted later by Baba to Cimmie and from her to Elinor Glyn's daughter Juliet) was never passed on; Gracie's jealousy endured until the end. On 18 March he wrote a last letter – this final missive from the vast pile of his lifetime's correspondence an almost illegible protestation of loyalty to the King, who was about to set off on a Mediterranean cruise.

That day the doctors told Grace there was no hope and Sir Thomas advised her to tell her husband he was dying. 'He is a very great man, and it would be wrong to deceive him any longer. He should be told the truth so that he may prepare his mind in his own way.' When Curzon asked Gracie what the doctors had said when she returned to his room she replied gently: 'Darling, I'm afraid you are very bad.' Closing his eyes, he repeated the Lord's Prayer. They were the last words he spoke. The next day, 19 March, he lapsed into unconsciousness and the following morning, at 5.30 a.m., he died, with Grace, his brother Francis and Baba at his side. It was Baba's twenty-first birthday.

'Beloved Pansy,' reads a scrawled note from Fruity. 'My poor child. I feel deeply for you, especially on such a day. What a birthday for you! My poor darling, every happiness should be yours on this day. But one thing, my love, there is, I feel sure, for each and all of us, only a certain amount of happiness that is to be our portion in this life and as now you are not being granted your natural share then it is *yet* to come to you and you will get it, I promise you.'

Irene, who had inherited her father's barony of Ravensdale, did not comment at all on his death. Instead, a note in her journal merely says: 'Old Dandy sent to the Kennels, to my great grief.'

The funeral service was at Westminster Abbey on 25 March. Curzon's coffin, made from a 200-year-old oak from Kedleston, was covered with an antique red velvet pall embroidered with the Curzon arms in gold and studded with gold nails. His Order of the Garter, Star of India, the Order of the Indian Empire and the Victorian Order lay on purple cushions at the foot; the pall-bearers were the Prime Minister Stanley Baldwin, the Lord Chancellor, the Speaker, the Chancellor of the Exchequer, Lords Salisbury and Birkenhead, Asquith and Ramsay MacDonald.

There was a second, family service at Kedleston the following day when Curzon's coffin, like the coffins of past generations of Curzons, was placed in the white marble vault of the chapel he had restored, on a white marble shelf, beside the white marble effigy of himself that he had commissioned during his lifetime. Next to it was a space holding a postcard with the words 'Reserved for the second Lady Curzon' in Curzon's handwriting in the thick blue pencil he always used. Two carriages and a dining car were engaged for the family and friends who travelled up. 'Scatters Wilson who has come partly because he is in love with Lady Curzon and partly because it is on the way to the Grand National, Fruity Metcalfe who has come because he is in love with Baba Curzon,' wrote the author and diplomat Harold Nicolson in his diary. 'They talk racing all the way up.' After the interment, the party returned to the house, where Nicolson noted seeing Baba and Cimmie. 'Very upset. Very sweet.' Irene was not present.

Curzon's will, thanks to the emendations and alterations he had made just before his death, was an extraordinarily badly-drafted document. Nevertheless, it made one thing perfectly plain: Gracie was to inherit virtually everything. To her went the remaining twelve months of the lease of 1 Carlton House Terrace and those contents not destined for Kedleston; to her went Hackwood (which had another eighteen months of lease to run) and all its contents, from horses, carriages, cars and chandeliers to pictures, tapestries and furniture; to her went Montacute House and its contents; she also received a jointure of £1,000 a year from the Kedleston rents. His daughters and his stepchildren, as Curzon pointed out, were amply provided for by their respective Leiter and Duggan inheritances; nevertheless, to his Duggan stepchildren he left £500 each 'as proof of my affection'. His beloved Marcella inherited in addition the villa Naldera at Broadstairs, together with all its contents. The two castles, Bodiam and Tattershall, went to the National Trust, together with generous bequests for their upkeep.

To his own daughters he left only their mother's clothes, carefully stored for almost twenty years. His will also allotted them those few pieces of their mother's jewellery particularly specified by her in her own will when she first went out to India but, with the exception of Cim who had been given her mother's pearls when she married, none of the three girls received any of these items. Nor, as their mother would surely have intended, did their father leave them any of the rest of her splendid collection, much of which had come from their grandfather (though some was acquired after the making of her will). All of it had been given or was left to Grace.

At the time, Baba was barely concerned, her mind occupied far more by the trauma of her father's death, her growing love for Fruity and, perhaps, a realisation that she too, like her sisters, would now have to make her own way in the world. The idea of marriage – the only 'career' open to the young women of her circle – seemed ever more alluring.

Fruity's pursuit of her had seemed to many of his friends bound to end in failure. Paradoxically, his own realisation of this had much to do with his ultimate success. He behaved towards Baba with the strictest honour, never attempting to 'push' her into anything and always making sure she understood how little he had to offer in worldly terms. But his looks, his charm, his deep loyalty and his popularity with their friends spoke for him. By the time he was living with the Mountbattens he had begun to hope.

Fruity had gone to live with them after the Prince left for South Africa on 30 March. He could not have had more opulent lodgings. Brook House, their Park Lane palace, built in the 1850s by Thomas Wyatt, had been inherited by Edwina from her grandfather, the immensely rich Sir Edward Cassel. The hall, grand staircase and first-floor gallery were lined with white marble, there were twelve bathrooms, several lifts, a stream bubbling among mulberry trees in the garden and a dining room in a two-storey pavilion. With the Prince away, Mountbatten was Fruity's closest friend and he had become as devoted to Edwina as he was to Mountbatten. Soon he and Baba, with the Mountbattens, made up a foursome who often lunched together in London, went to watch Mountbatten play polo, religiously saw every new revue from the Midnight Follies to the Co-Optimists or dined together before going to a play followed by dancing. At weekends they would often go and stay at the Mountbattens' country house, Adsdean, in Sussex.

Without Curzon's overwhelming presence and with Grace's active encouragement, the relationship between Fruity and Baba was thriving. On 25 May 1925, Edwina's diary reads: '... later to the Embassy and the Kitkat Club, Fruity told me of his engagement to Baba.' The next day: 'Shopped with Fruity and Baba and tried to find an engagement ring.' The announcement of the engagement, on 26 May, sent a shock wave through much of society. Though they were each other's equals in looks, style and chic, the Viceroy's daughter and the handsome cavalryman had little else in common. It was an era in which, despite the upheavals of the war, worldly considerations still counted, and the engagement of this slender, aristocratic heiress and intimate of princes to a poor Irishman of no particular background who was seventeen years her senior was, in the eyes of the stuffier members of society, a *mésalliance*. For others, Fruity's charm and his closeness to the Prince of Wales, which gave him the entrée everywhere, made him the most glamorous single man around.

But the answer was much simpler. Baba was deeply, passionately and physically in love for the first time in her life – so much so that she simply did not notice that Fruity had hardly read a book and that his good nature, gaiety and charm hid an intellectual void. Her own character and personality were still to a large extent unformed and she was bowled over by this attractive man who adored her.

Fruity himself could not believe his luck. His nature was sweet, loyal – once he had given his devotion, nothing would shake it – simple and modest. 'I don't know why my Bobs married me,' he would say in his rich brogue. 'I have no money and I've got no brain'. (This last was untrue: his letters show a sharp-eyed, humorous and perceptive intelligence.)

He sent a cable to the Prince at once, who wrote from the royal train in South Africa on 27 May: 'My dear Baba, This is only a scrawl to make this mail to say how delighted I was to get Fruity's cable last night to tell me you were both engaged – it's the best news I've had in a long time and you know how much happiness I wish for both of you.'

To Fruity he wrote somewhat less formally:

So you've pulled it off at last. I *was* pleased to get your cable last night and you should get mine today. No news could cheer me more. I'm absolutely delighted for you 'cos you do deserve a bit of good luck if anyone does and that's the best luck anyone could have – shabash [well done]; and you know how much happiness I wish for you both. My God, if the King could win the Derby today – I got my usual on at I hope at least twenties three weeks ago ... This tour is hell and v. little fun tho' funny – few good lookers or amusing people. I'll leave it to you both to get yourselves a *naice* wedding present. Must stop – write again soon.

A week later, the Prince wrote a long letter from Durban. Delight at his friend's happiness was complicated by other, less easily articulated emotions. When the Prince loved, he loved with abandon and his friendship with Fruity, the closest he would ever have with another man, was intimate and exclusive. Marriage would inevitably loosen this charmed bond.

Thank you for your last *wild* letter. I guess I know the mood you wrote it in – rather like mine after two or three more cocktails. But I'm keeping the deadly booze well under this trip and the cigs too so that I really am d——d fit considering. No drinks before 6.00 and only two cigs before tea. It was a strain at first but it's easy now and so well worth it. I played polo once last week and rain did in another game but I'll play here and tell you all about it. I believe it's going to be fun here and I'm glad I'm stopping two extra days 'cos I spotted some d——d good lookers at the races this afternoon and am going to some good parties ... I'm glad you miss me sometimes and I miss you too, often. But you won't miss me any more though ... Damn it Fruity, why in hell didn't you pull it off before I left? It would have helped *us* *both* so much wouldn't it? you from being so sunk and me from feeling such a shit.

But all's well that ends well and I'm every bit as pleased and excited over your engagement as I was a week ago. It really is *marvellous* and despite what I've said it must be nicer for you that you pulled it off *after* you'd left me officially. But I know you'll never leave me really, not as a friend – but no more sob stuff and I must dress for a public dinner tho there's a good party arranged for later. I hope the one in the white hat will be there!

To Mountbatten he wrote: 'It is splendid about Fruity and Baba – I rather despaired of his pulling it off. You must tell me all about it when I get back.'

A fortnight later the Prince wrote again, this time from the train to Southern Rhodesia, asking Fruity to look out for a couple of point-to-point horses for him before the newly-wed Metcalfes set off for India in September and also to arrange to sell some of his horses at Melton so that other, better ones could be bought. 'Then I'll be able to start hunting in October with, so to speak, a clean sheet and free of all debris ... it's too bad you'll be gone to India. I would have liked to have seen you again, and married, and it'll be another year at least. Must stop now for a stunt [the Prince's name for the public duties he had to perform]; and the mail goes next station too.'

In the hectic months before the wedding Fruity escorted Edwina to parties while Baba was staying at Hackwood or dined with both Mountbattens and their friends. 'Dined with Peter, Mary, Dickie and Fruity and we went to see Mixed Doubles,' reads the entry for 20 July, the night before Fruity and Baba's wedding.

They were married on 21 July 1925 at the Chapel Royal. Baba was given away by Grace, though escorted to the church by her stepbrother Hubert Duggan. She had half-a-dozen child attendants, including the two little Mosley children, Vivien and Nicholas, four and two respectively. Also present were the couple's dogs: Baba's wire-haired terrier puppy John Willie held on a ribbon by a footman a few yards away from the bride, Fruity's more obedient terrier, John, near by. Though it was a small, ostensibly quiet wedding there was a crowd of two thousand outside St James's

Palace and magnificent presents. Fruity gave Baba a gold-and-tortoiseshell dressing-case, a diamond ring and a diamond-and-sapphire ring. The bride bought herself the tiara deemed necessary by all married women of her social standing: although Mary Leiter had had three diamond tiaras, Curzon had left all these to Grace.

From Grace came a sable wrap for Baba and a walnut dining table for Fruity. Cim and Tom gave Baba long ruby-and-diamond earrings; Irene gave Baba a diamond corsage ornament and a large pearl pin to Fruity; from the Queen of the Belgians there was a pearl-and-diamond bracelet set, in the latest fashion, in platinum; from the Mountbattens came a gold cigarette-case for Fruity and an ivory one with a sapphire-and-diamond clasp for Baba (all, of course, from Cartier). From Sir William and Lady Birdwood there was a handsome Persian carpet – Fruity was going to join Sir William's staff in India as his ADC.

The Metcalfes left for India at the end of September, setting off overland, accompanied by Irene as far as Marseilles. Here they took ship on the 30th. With them went a mountain of luggage and Baba's beloved car, a unique, cream-coloured custom-built Baby Rolls which she had bought from the Mountbattens. Irene returned home the following day.

12

Cimmie and Tom:
Early Married Life

~

Cimmie Mosley's early married life had begun blissfully. Ahead of
her stretched a future filled with promise. She was passionately in
love with her husband, who constantly told her of his adoration.
She believed, moreover, that he was destined for great things and
that her part was to help him. Their daily life, filled with ease and
friends, was happy; Tom was a charming, witty companion and
his expert, experienced lovemaking after any quarrels – for Cimmie
could not help noticing his open approaches to other women –
quickly smoothed over disagreements or hurts. Constantly, he
reassured her that she was the only one who mattered to him. The
Mosleys' large house, 8 Smith Square, was within easy reach of
Parliament while for weekends and holidays they rented houses in
the country or abroad.

Their first child, Vivien, was born on 25 February 1921. The
following year, during the winter of 1922–3, they took a house on
Cap Ferrat, inviting Baba to stay with them. Tom had to return
early to speak in Parliament; it was the first time they had been
apart for more than two nights in their marriage. 'I am so terribly
unhappy at leaving you – nothing would have made me go if I had
realised what it meant and nothing will again,' he wrote to Cimmie,
now five months pregnant with their second child, on 12 February
1923. 'Please please do not be too sad and look after your wonderful darling self for your T who adores you.'

He did love her – but at the same time he was having an affair
with a mutual friend with whom they had been in Venice the

previous summer. For Cimmie, who found out before long, this was to become a familiar pattern. So, too, would be her forgiveness. Unable to arm herself with the cynicism that would allow her to play the same game or the indifference that would prevent hurt, she could not reconcile herself to her husband's unfaithfulness. It was always Cimmie who ended up apologising. 'Dear heart, I am so sorry for the way I harry and worry you – have made too high a mountain out of the molehills of your faults ... No one has ever had a sweeter man and I do appreciate everything, all you give me.'

The Mosleys' second child, Nicholas, was born on 25 June 1923. Within weeks, they had set off for their annual summer holiday in Venice, leaving Vivien and the new baby, who had been ill almost from the moment he was born, in the care of their nanny, Nanny Hyslop, who had been Cim and Baba's nurserymaid when they were children in India. Tom's belief was that the upbringing of children should be left to 'professionals', and Cimmie's total allegiance was to Tom. For the children, Nanny Hyslop would be their lifesaver.

Politically, Tom was shifting direction. He disagreed violently with the Government's policy in Ireland. To counter the Irish Republican Army's guerrilla warfare, with its accompanying atrocities, the Government had covertly formed groups of mercenaries, known as the Black and Tans from the colour of their uniforms. These men, neither police nor army, fought back in similarly ruthless style, matching savagery with savagery. In the House of Commons, Tom spoke out forcefully against this policy, and was greeted by boos and jeers from his own side.

His response was to leave the Conservative benches and in the general election of 1922 he stood as an Independent – though backed by the local Conservative Party. Steadily, he was moving leftward. His feeling for the working man was genuine – but beneath it lay a far more powerful emotion: ambition. As he had told Archie Sinclair,* he was determined to be Prime Minister in twelve years' time. The Labour Party seemed to offer the greatest opportunities both for high office and for social improvement.

*Sir Archibald Sinclair, Bt, the Liberal MP for Caithness and Sutherland, later Viscount Thurso.

Cimmie, whose belief that her husband was destined for great things never wavered, encouraged this new direction. She entertained the Labour leader, Ramsay MacDonald; he was charmed by her and they formed an easy friendship. When Baldwin called another general election at the end of 1923, Tom's majority at Harrow fell to 4,600 as his old Conservative supporters dropped away. Labour emerged from the election as the strongest party, with 191 seats, and a Labour Government was formed. It was time for Tom to declare himself.

In March 1924, three months into the first Labour Government, he made a formal application to join the Labour Party. Ramsay MacDonald, now Prime Minister, welcomed him warmly; his mother wrote a letter praising his 'amazing courage and self-sacrifice' in this radical step. In 1924 the Labour and Conservative Parties were divided almost entirely on class lines and a member of one who crossed the floor of the House to join the other was regarded as a class traitor and renegade. 'He is the most accomplished speaker in the House,' noted the social reformer Beatrice Webb in her diary that month, 'and hated with a quite furious hatred by the Tories whom he has left.'

As for the party itself, though many regarded Mosley as a 'catch', especially for his powers of oratory, others mistrusted the arrival of someone from his background. How could anyone brought up with money, servants, foreign travel and a Winchester education understand the problems of working men and women?

The first Labour Government lasted less than a year. Doubts about Tom Mosley's suitability did not stop Labour Associations all over the country from offering him the chance to stand in the general election to be held in October 1924. Of the seventy constituencies he could choose from, he settled on Ladywood, in Birmingham, then a fief of the Chamberlain family and the seat of the future Prime Minister, Neville Chamberlain, asking its voters to 'overthrow the false gods of reaction which have dominated the city for the last generation at the cost of so much suffering'. It was in Birmingham, too, that he met two of the men who would for a time become his most ardent followers: Allan Young, the Borough organiser of the Labour Party in Birmingham, and John Strachey, son of St Loe Strachey, the editor of the *Spectator*, and a cousin of the writer Lytton Strachey.

Again, Cimmie did all she could to promote Tom's cause. She became a member of the Labour Party herself, she made a speech on behalf of John Strachey when he was readopted as Labour candidate in December 1924, and she appeared on platforms with her charismatic husband. A contemporary account of a meeting at the Empire Hall in London records: 'Suddenly there was a movement in the crowd and a young man with the face of the ruling class of Great Britain but with the gait of a Douglas Fairbanks thrust himself forward through the throng on to the platform followed by a lady in heavy, costly furs.' The writer notes Tom's emotional appeal, then continues: 'Suddenly the elegant lady in furs got up from her seat and said a few sympathetic words ... she spoke simply and almost shyly, but yet like one who is accustomed to be acclaimed and, without stagefright, to open a bazaar or a meeting for charitable purposes.'

Tom Mosley's brilliant oratory, the sense of idealism and purpose that he conveyed to the Ladywood audiences while speaking passionately and fluently without notes, almost won him the seat – he was beaten by a mere seventy-seven votes. It was a staggering achievement in the heart of Chamberlain country and he felt deservedly pleased and confident that a by-election would soon give him another chance.

In the meantime, he went with Cimmie on a trip to India and, with John Strachey, began to write a book to be called *Revolution by Reason* (published in 1925). When Tom's great friend, Robert Boothby, the newly elected Conservative MP for East Aberdeenshire, visited the Mosleys in Venice at the end of the summer of 1925, he found the two co-authors discussing their opus on the Lido every morning. Often Tom, a powerful swimmer, would swim far out into the lagoon to think and brood by himself.

At home, 1925 saw Irene embarking on the love affair that would distort her life for a decade. In the close-knit hunting society to which she belonged, adulterous liaisons were common. Fit, healthy, emotions heightened by the adrenalin of excitement and danger and with no preoccupation in the world save to enjoy themselves, the members of the smart hunts were known to lead lives as racy off the hunting field as on it. A wealthy, titled young woman living an independent life with no visible family protector was soon a focus of masculine attention. Irene's dark good looks and figure set off to perfection in one of her well-cut side-saddle riding habits in dark blue or black, drew many admirers. Warmly emotional herself, it was not long before she was deeply in love. Unfortunately, her passion was for a married man.

He was Gordon Leith, a dashing, good-looking hunting man married to a pretty wife nicknamed 'Cuckoo'. Irene, well aware that such a liaison ran counter to her own deep religious and moral scruples, struggled against her feelings. It was partly to escape from Gordon and, simultaneously, to distract herself that she set off on a world cruise soon after Baba and Fruity had left for India.

She was met in Colombo on 9 January 1926, by the newly-weds. From then on, their progress was viceregal: staying in Government House in Madras, fetched by Rolls-Royce for dinner at various palaces, polo, shooting, the Horse Show and Delhi Week, tennis, lunches, bridge, dinners. Fruity, as a good ADC should, partnered Lady Birdwood in a tennis tournament; Irene watched an investiture in Viceregal Lodge, Delhi, before she and Baba went to hear the outgoing Viceroy make his final speech on 9 February.

Her relationship with Baba, a girl of twenty-two to Irene's more worldly thirty, was still fond and indulgent. 'Baba looked marvellous in lace with orange flowers over her ears,' she noted in her journal. 'Baba looked divine in blue velvet pyjamas and a wreath on her head.' When she left them on 28 March she was seen off with roses 'as if I were the Ex', there was 'a last delicious talk with Baba', and in Calcutta 'sweet letters from Baba' await. There she was shown round the Victoria Memorial. 'Everything breathed Daddy.' For one who had been so decisively thrust away by her father it must have been poignant indeed.

The tour continued by ship to Rangoon, Mandalay and Penang, then on to Hong Kong, Shanghai and Tokyo, where Irene changed to the *Empress of Asia* to sail to Vancouver and then travelled by train to Los Angeles to stay with Elinor Glyn, arriving on 1 September. Here Hollywood high society was at her disposal: 'Elinor, John Wyman and I dined at the Chaplins.' 'Elinor and I dined with the Laskys in their Early American beach house. Mary and Doug came. Also there were the Harold Lloyds and Adolphe Menjou and his brother. We saw a ghastly film after and all the husbands and wives sat side by side!!' She went to Cecil B. De-Mille's studios, as a dog-lover she fell for Rin Tin Tin, she dined with the Sam Goldwyns, watched Walter Pidgeon dancing the Charleston and took advantage of American dentistry to have her teeth crowned and capped.

But there was plenty to remind her of the absent Gordon – it was the same story of unrequited love everywhere: Bea Lillie silent, white and wretched when John Gilbert failed to arrive at a party, Charlie Chaplin confiding in her about his coming divorce from Lita, Pola Negri dressed in black and screaming like a banshee at Valentino's funeral, of which Irene wrote: 'Thousands lined the streets. We got to the cemetery and over the mausoleum an aeroplane plunged and whizzed dropping roses. It filled me with horror – all the plaques and cubicles and vases of flowers, wicker chairs and settees made of it a lounge for a garden party. The pall bearers, all the great directors and Charlie Chaplin, carried the coffin in to the shrine where poor Pola kissed it for the last time and wept and screamed and swooned. The coffin slid into a marble cupboard and the door closed and we all dispersed. Pola was carried out into her car, overcome.'

For Baba in India, there was the first meeting with a man who would later assume such importance in her own life. This was the incoming Viceroy, Lord Irwin (better known later as the first Earl of Halifax) who arrived in Bombay in April 1926. Born in 1881, he had been happily married to Lady Dorothy Onslow, daughter of the Earl of Onslow, since 1909.

The new Viceroy was a tall, imposing figure with a high domed forehead over an ascetic face and an imperturbable manner (during the whole of his Viceroyalty he is said to have lost his temper only once: when a favourite, disreputable hat was thrown away by a member of his staff). As Baba was the daughter of a former Viceroy and Fruity the friend of a prince, the Metcalfes were quickly invited to lunch at Viceregal Lodge. Another bond was the affection in which the Irwins held Naldera, the small encampment after which Baba was named. They would escape here from Viceregal Lodge in Simla as often as they could.

As for Fruity, the Prince's friendship showed no sign of dimin-

ishing, with a regular correspondence on both sides. The Prince
had just given up polo and now he flung himself with his usual
ardour into golf. One letter from him (on 25 August 1926), written
from Sandwich Bay in Kent where he was staying near Mrs Dudley
Ward, described this new passion. 'I must say I do like this golf
game – am just crazy about it. I'm improving, only very slowly,
but surely. It is difficult and of course not a quarter the fun polo
is.'

For Fruity it was warming to realise the strength of the Prince's
affection – and reassuring when he concluded with a hint that the
life they both loved at Melton would resume. 'I'll hunt full out
just as long as I still want to jump fences in front of other people,'
wrote the Prince. 'The moment I don't I'll stop and take to big
game hunting and more intensive golf, and indoors sports!! But I
hope that won't happen in years and that you'll be hunting season
after next. Love to you both from EP.'

Irene, back from her world tour, found a world even more
frenetically gay than when she had left it in November. Fashion
followed fashion – ostrich feather fans, headache bands, bangs,
pearl chokers, Venetian glass lamps, painted furniture and, that
November, the first bottle party. In tune with the *Zeitgeist*, Maud,
wife of Sir Bache Cunard, rechristened herself Emerald and launched into three decades of entertaining – endless lunch, dinner and
supper parties and, later, gatherings in her opera box and after-
performance entertainments.

A year's absence had not achieved the break from Gordon Leith
that Irene had intended. He came straight away to see her at
Claridge's, where she was staying. Her first full day in London, 16
November, gives a flavour of her London life at that time. She had
a reunion lunch with Cim, saw Gordon at three thirty, the hostess
and decorator Sibyl Colefax at four thirty, and accepted an invitation to Cliveden from Nancy Astor. Cim brought her children
to tea at five and at seven Gordon came again to see her before
she left for Tom Mosley's birthday dinner at Smith Square. After
it she, Cim, Tom and his agent went to Charlot's Revue and on to
the Gargoyle nightclub, where they met Bob Boothby, Amabel and
Clough Williams-Ellis, John Strachey and others.

Two days later, Irene cancelled the Cliveden visit in order to
lunch with Gordon at the Embassy Club. The following day, she

saw another admirer, Artur Rubinstein, the pianist whom she had met so many years earlier at Hackwood. After attending his concert, she dined with him and the Jowetts, talked until midnight and then went on with Rubinstein to a party given by Sibyl Colefax in his honour. 'We disbanded at 2.45 after a perfect time. Arthur had left Paola de Medici behind and was just as stimulating and vital as ever.'

By the end of November she was back in Melton, straight into the heart of that rich, hard-riding set whose recreations were drinking, gambling, dancing and discreet or not-so-discreet love affairs. The pace was set by the Prince of Wales, famously brave and mounted on superb hunters, ready to dance all night with whichever beautiful woman he fancied.

His relationship with the woman he adored, Freda Dudley Ward, was by now (unwillingly on his side) platonic. He was showing signs of interest in the beautiful Lady Furness, who had married the hugely rich Lord Furness, chairman of the Furness shipbuilding company, coal-owner and industrialist, only eighteen months earlier as his second wife. Lord Furness, a noted hunting man who was a former Master of the York and Anstey, owned Burrough Court, near Melton. Since meeting the Prince, Thelma, who did not hunt, had suddenly discovered the attractions of life in the country. Night after night she could be seen dancing with him at the Melton Embassy, exquisite in fuschia, black or a rose-painted Lanvin dress. Two other additions to the Craven Lodge 'set' were the wealthy polo-playing young Americans, Laddie Sanford and Jock Whitney.

Jock Whitney was already known as one of the most eligible young men in the Western world. His father was among the wealthiest men in America, both sides of his family had held important posts in the US Government; President Theodore Roosevelt and his entire cabinet had attended the wedding of his parents. Born in 1904, Jock was the same age as Baba, and after graduating at Yale University had come up to Oxford that autumn. He had been brought up in a horsy milieu: his mother, Helen Hay Whitney, ran the famous Greentree racing stables near Lexington, in the Kentucky bluegrass country, and almost his first action on arrival in England was to buy a couple of hunters. He and Laddie (later to become the lover of Edwina Mountbatten) quickly blended into the Melton life.

Days at Melton had a routine. The keen – and most were very keen – could hunt four or five days a week. Meets were at ten thirty or eleven, with a change of horse at around one thirty – no single animal could keep up the pace across those huge grass fields if it was a good day. When the light went around teatime the second horse was handed to a groom and its owner went to tea with the nearest friend, often playing a rubber or two of bridge afterwards, generally for shillings rather than pounds. Then it was home to change and out to dinner, often for fifty or more people, where extroverts like the two young Americans danced the Black Bottom to the strumming of a ukelele.

If there were no dinner parties, evenings were spent at Craven Lodge, usually ending in poker for high stakes – Irene's diary notes constantly that she has lost £40 – or they might catch the train to London for a special party. And all the time, either galloping across a field beside her, meeting her for lunch in London, invited to the same dinner party, or escorting her home, there was Gordon Leith. 'Dined for Olga Lynne's concert, crammed with all my friends. To the Charleston Ball at the Albert Hall then at 11.45 to Alice Wimborne's marvellous party till 1.45 then Gordon Leith brought me back to the Charleston Ball where we remained till 3.45, seeing wonderful exhibitions from men women and children and the Cabaret shows and the Blackbirds. Gracie very gushing to me. Always with Scatters.'

Next day it was back by the early train in time to hunt again. Sometimes Cim and Tom, who both enjoyed hunting, came to stay with her; she would mount them and all three would go out together. It was during these weekends that the Mosleys must have realised the depth of Irene's feelings for Gordon – and hoped that it would simply blow itself out.

It was a life that left little time for outside interests. Tom Mosley had realised this a few years earlier when he sold his hunters to concentrate on politics. That autumn, he and Cim were campaigning hard. Earlier in 1926 they had visited America; on their return Tom was invited to stand in a by-election in the Birmingham constituency of Smethwick. Cim did all she could to help her husband. 'Cim in throws [sic] of a Labour election for Tom, making silly speeches and painful references to her title', records Irene's diary.

Smethwick was adjacent to Tom's former constituency of Lady-wood and the goodwill and following he had built up there stood him in good stead. Despite vicious personal attacks on both him and Cimmie he won the seat, increasing Labour's majority to 6,582. Cimmie wrote at once to Nancy Astor, so supportive of them both and one of the few who understood the realities of political infighting: 'Thanks darling and I'm glad to know there are a few who know that I never could say the things or behave in the way the utterly unspeakable capitalist press allege I do. It's all grand up here and Tom will be back in the house before Xmas!'

Irene spent the Christmas of 1926 at Cliveden. Nancy Astor, who had assumed the role of older sister/godmother to all the Curzon girls, was glad for all or any of them to come to Cliveden on such family occasions as well as virtually any weekend they wanted. She was also as free with her opinions as any close relative. 'Criticism of my lips and nails from Nancy and abuse of all my friends,' wrote Irene in her diary two days before Christmas. On Christmas Eve the Astor boys charlestoned all day to Irene's new gramophone; on Christmas Day there was a huge lunch followed by tennis on the indoor court and Cim and Tom came to dinner.

Nancy, who had greatly disapproved of what she thought of as Tom's defection to Labour, was nevertheless warmly welcoming. 'Everyone was very decent to him though Geoffrey Dawson and Bob Brand hate him,' noted Irene. 'They were both very pathetic, Tom even looking lonely and lost for once, tho' Cim was utterly at her ease.' There was bridge, more tennis, charades – 'Nancy Astor inimitable as a rich Jew, a fat girl with that bulging mask, and an invalid with spots all over her face and a bandaged leg'. Back at Melton, Irene gave a dinner party followed by poker ('won £60!'), dropped everything when Gordon telephoned her to dine with him, tried to stifle her irritation when she found herself playing poker with Prince Henry, the youngest of the royal princes ('*maddeningly* slow at poker!') and, like everyone else, charles-toned all evening at the Craven Lodge New Year's Eve party. 'The Prince there with Freda. Got to bed at 5.30.'

By the end of that spring, all Curzon's daughters had acquired new houses. Cimmie and Tom Mosley, who had wanted a family home in the country, found it in Savehay Farm, an old and beautiful red-brick building in the village of Denham, in Buckinghamshire. Surrounded by fields, with lawns running down to the River Colne, it was a peaceful rural retreat that was easily accessible from London. It was soon expanded to fit their needs, modernised and redesigned inside by the architect Clough Williams-Ellis, husband of John Strachey's sister Amabel.

Irene, tired of staying at Claridge's whenever she came up to London, wanted her own establishment with her own servants, where her little Sealyham terrier, Winks, could run freely and which would, no doubt, be more discreet when Gordon wished to call on her. With the aid of her solicitor, she found a house at 3 Deanery Street in Mayfair. It needed complete refurbishment, which would take several months.

She soon had to look for another house. Baba was anxious to come home. For Fruity, their time in India had been, as he wrote to Baba during one of his brief absences, the happiest of his life, in the career he loved, with the woman he loved by his side. 'I've lived all these 12 months as I did not think it possible for humans to be allowed to do,' he wrote to Baba on 21 July 1926. 'I never thought it would be allowed for one to be so happy as I have been.'

Baba disliked Simla and the rain, she was not too keen on the other army wives and she wanted to return to the life she knew. She persuaded Fruity to leave the Army – after all, with her money, there was no financial incentive for him to remain a serving officer. The Prince of Wales was delighted with the news. 'I am very very glad to hear that you are not stopping on with Birdy, because that means you will be returning early next year.'

In order to avoid paying a sizeable chunk of income tax, the Metcalfes could not return until the late spring of 1927. 'I've been wondering all these weeks why you never answered my cable to the ship, sent a day or two after you'd sailed from Bombay, or told me when you'd be back in England,' wrote the Prince of Wales.

'Now I hear from Irene – who I saw hunting today and a bloody bad day too – that you arrive in Cannes tonight and can't make England till April 'cos of income tax. Oh! Gawd, what a country, what a life. I'm disappointed 'cos I'm longing to see you *both* again, especially you. A whole month more is a long time. *Listen!* You can't or you don't care to shoot back for two or three days only soon do you? But I guess I shouldn't say that or even suggest it!'

The house Irene rented for Baba was near Coombe Hill golf course, in Surrey. She also employed servants for her and lent her sister her own cook until she had found one she liked. On 6 April she went to meet Fruity and Baba at Victoria Station. 'The train was 40 minutes late. Found Baba looking lovely and well and felt choked and silly with tears,' she wrote of that day. 'We dined at York house and talked and chatted. The Prince was overjoyed at seeing Fruity again.' The next night she and the Metcalfes again dined with the Prince and went to Blackbirds, the Café de Paris and Uncle's. 'The P. was in great form and he and Fruity got utterly giggly and inane. I for the first time charlestoned with the Prince.'

Baba did not dance that evening. She was pregnant with her first child, one of the factors that had decided her and Fruity that they needed a house in London as well as in the country. They bought the lease of 19 Cowley Street, Westminster. It was registered in Fruity's name, but Baba's money had paid for it. It was her first real appreciation of the power conferred by wealth. The pattern of their respective roles was emerging; soon there would be no doubt who was the dominant partner.

13

Irene: In Love with
Married Men

~

With Baba's return, the lives of the three sisters began to intertwine once more. For just over a year, they were closer to each other emotionally, physically, socially and even politically than at any other time in their lives. There was in any case considerable overlap between their circles: Irene knew 'everyone' in the smart hunting world of Melton, where Tom had hunted until he sold his horses to devote himself to politics. The focal point of that world was the Prince of Wales – and the Prince's best friend was Fruity.

The sisters visited each other's houses to stay the night, for hunting, for a dinner party, sometimes just to change for dinner or dress for a wedding. In March 1927 Cim went to Paris to see Baba, then returned to Leicestershire for more hunting. At Melton Irene was in a whirl of gaiety, playing poker at Craven Lodge and dashing up to London after hunting to a dinner party at Nancy Astor's ('sat between Bobbie Shaw and Ronnie Tree') and constantly dining with Gordon Leith, either at her house or his.

On 18 May the Curzon sisters' nineteen-year-old stepsister Marcella was married to a young barrister, Edward Rice, in a packed St Margaret's, Westminster, with Thomas Beecham conducting his orchestra, little Nicky Mosley as one of her pages and Gracie glamorous in pale grey with a pink toque. Gracie, who felt that other suitors of Marcella were preferable, had done her best to prevent the match, only giving in when Marcella had climbed out of her window one night and hidden with friends for twenty-four hours. All the Curzon daughters were on Marcella's side: Cim, the

1. George Curzon in his vice-regal robes

2. Kedleston Hall

3. Curzon and Mary in 1903, with their daughters Irene (left) and Cynthia

4. Hackwood

5. Elinor Glyn
in 1905

6. Irene, Cimmie and
   Baba at Hackwood
   in the First World War

7. Grace Curzon
   at Hackwood

8. *(facing page)* Cimmie and Tom Mosley, shortly after their wedding in 1920

11. Curzon with his first grandchild, Vivien, at Hackwood in March 1921

12. Cimmie

(facing page)

9. Vivien's christening, April 1921: Nanny Sibley is holding Vivien

10. The christening party: Tom Mosley, Marcella, Alfred and Hubert Duggan; front row: Cim, Gracie, Irene and Baba

13. Irene hunting at Melton Mowbray in the Twenties

14. Melton Mowbray: fancy dress party. Irene is in the centre of the front row.

sister with whom she felt a special bond, had written to her delightedly from Smith Square: 'The only thing Marcella darling that matters is marrying the fellow one loves – all that *is* so important and I am sure that is what you are doing.'

A week after Marcella's wedding Irene was at Artur Rubinstein's concert. 'He played gloriously. To see Arthur again was a real breath of life.' So much so that the next day she put off a luncheon party when Rubinstein telephoned her. She was fascinated by his musical talent, his extraordinary energy and the sex appeal that had already netted him numerous conquests. For his part, ever since their first meeting in the grandeur of Hackwood, when he, as a young, impoverished musician, had played before Irene as daughter of the house, she had appeared to him not only as a desirable woman but as a challenge.

Irene left him only to go to the best party of the season, a cabaret dinner given by the immensely rich Laura Corrigan, an American widow whose avowed aim was to conquer London society and most of whose parties involved not only the best of food and drink but expensive presents for the guests – especially those with titles. Next day, though, there was a disappointment: Artur had invited her to Paris but once there 'I found him with the Polish lady'. Sad and disillusioned, her spirits rose when Artur, never one to let a lady go off the boil, invited her to a luncheon *à quatre* in his tiny flat by the Sacré-Coeur. 'He was like a child with it and had been out to buy flowers, glasses and cheese for us,' she noted fondly.

The Season rattled on, with dinner parties, cabarets, dances, parties when everyone sank too many cocktails ('The Prince arrived – blind!' noted Irene's diary. 'Fred and Adele Astaire were drunk and leaning over the sofa throwing cushions at everyone'), supper parties for the opera, luncheons with Elinor Glyn at the Ritz, dinners with Artur Rubinstein. Irene, with her warmth, her interest in people, the funny or intriguing stories she told, in her low, rather 'Curzon' voice that emphasised certain words, of the people she had met on her cruises or in America, was in demand everywhere. Rich, independent and quite prepared to indulge in the common Melton sport of late-night bed-hopping, she was nevertheless too seemingly formidable for many men, who could not detect the vulnerable creature beneath the sophisticated carapace. When Gordon failed to come and see her during a whole week when she was ill while staying with Cim in Smith Square she was miserable – though it did not seem to strike her that if he had come it might have been a cause for gossip.

Her strange double standard came into operation once more when she refused to come to Savehay Farm one weekend because Sylvia Ashley would also be there. When Cim questioned her, Irene let slip that Sylvia appeared to be eyeing Tom; next day Cim telephoned in a fury, telling Irene angrily that she had 'ruined everything' and was idiotic to think such a thing.

But Irene was not being 'idiotic'. Tom Mosley's infidelities were already the subject of gossip. Irene herself had been to bed with him during the course of one romping, drink-fuelled Melton evening but, as everyone there understood, such escapades were not to be taken seriously and were tacitly forgotten by all parties the next morning.

Thus Irene, protective of both her younger sisters, could with complete sincerity castigate anyone – Tom or paramour – who hurt her beloved Cim. She was in fact staying with Baba when they heard that Tom Mosley was away in Paris, returning that night; both knew he had a mistress in Paris, called Maria. He was at the same time pursuing the actress Blanche Barrymore, wife of John Barrymore.

But all this paled to nothing beside the arrival of Baba's first baby on 8 July 1927, to whom the Prince of Wales had promised to stand godfather. Baba's son David was born at 6.15, in his grandfather's house, 1 Carlton House Terrace (the Metcalfes' house in Cowley Street was not yet ready for occupation). Gracie, although she had offered her own house, neither appeared nor asked after Baba until some time after the birth when she sent a message to say that all her servants were shortly leaving for Hackwood.

For Grace was still leading life on the grandest scale, as Irene was to see when invited down to Hackwood the following day. It was the first time she had been there for almost eight years and to return to the house from which she had been virtually banned by her father aroused a mixture of emotions. All the flowerbeds had gone, to be replaced by lawn, there was a new golf course, and indoors the panelling had been stripped away and the dining room returned to its original Regency pillars and lighting.

Inevitably, Scatters was one of the house party. When Irene walked with him round the bluebell woods in the hot sun she noticed that Gracie had let the place get very overgrown. It proved to be an unhappy homecoming: Grace seemed constantly cross with Scatters and later, talking to her stepmother in her bedroom, Irene found her miserable, depressed and discouraged. What Irene did not know was that Gracie, led on by Scatters, had been speculating and had invested heavily in an oil company that had gone bankrupt. Scatters was a gambler who had so far been lucky and becoming a stockbroker was a natural progression for him. Unfortunately he knew much less about stocks and shares than he did about hands of cards – his bridge was so good that his winnings formed a large part of his income – and had induced Gracie to invest in some 'sure things' that had drastically lost value. She had also sunk a lot of money into a stud owned jointly with Scatters.

At the end of the summer the Mosleys, in common with many of the smart, rather louche set in which they moved, went first to the South of France and later to Venice. The Riviera, newly popular and still unspoilt, was dotted with small fishing villages, idyllic little pine-fringed bays and small rocky promontories seemingly made for the erection of elegant, secluded villas. Here the Mosleys and their friends would congregate, to swim, sip cocktails, dine under the stars and pursue their various *amours*.

Irene had begun a love affair with one of her hunting friends, Bobby Digby. It quickly ran into trouble when he began to succumb to the noted beauty Mrs Richard Norton. It was all too reminiscent of Gordon Leith's constant assurances that 'one day' he would leave his wife for her.

Still pining for Gordon, unable to distract herself with Bobby, she set off on one of her curative travels, this time to New York on the *Mauretania*; when she returned in November, Bobby came back to her. But again it ended, literally, in tears. 'B made me cry and said my determined spirit broke any man. I sobbed and sobbed and felt it about true.' Next night at the Embassy, in a large party with Fruity, Baba, Cim and Tom, Jean Norton was again 'eyeing

Bobby'. But there was always hunting. When foot and mouth,* followed by a hard frost, stopped it, parties took over.

The London 'sets' of the Curzon sisters were beginning to diverge. With a husband in the House of Commons, Cimmie's was necessarily becoming more and more political. She had thrown herself so fervently into Labour Party doctrine that she did not hesitate to proselytise the virtues of socialism whenever she got the chance. 'Cim gave us a long socialist dissertation after dinner,' records Irene's diary of 13 May 1928. 'She was so certain and heartwhole one could not argue with her.'

Irene, passionate about music and the theatre, knew many in the arts world. During that summer, luncheons with Gerald du Maurier, Anita Loos, the Irish tenor John McCormack, Paul Robeson, Beatrice Lillie, Ivor Novello, Oliver Messel, Noël Coward, Maurice Baring and Syrie Maugham alternated with dinners with the Marlboroughs and the Salisburys.

There was also a new admirer. All through the spring of 1928, Irene lunched, dined and walked her sealyham Winks with one of her hunting friends, 'Flash' Kellett. It was a relationship complicated by the fact that his wife Myrtie was having an open flirtation with the Prince of Wales, which made Flash miserable and earned Irene's usual disapproval of anyone who publicly broke the rules. Her outings with Flash continued until August, when Myrtie began to reel her husband in. 'He left me at 10 in a very shattered, broken frame of mind', records Irene's diary of 11 August after a gloomy dinner at the Berkeley, 'and I had uttered a few grim home truths about Myrtie.'

It was back to Gordon again. They went together to Paris for a week before Irene went on to join the Mosleys and their party – Bob Boothby, John Strachey, Baba and Fruity – in their villa at Antibes. It was almost as social as London, with luncheon parties in beach pyjamas with the Douglas Fairbanks, Elsie Mendl or Somerset Maugham, bathing off rafts or the rocks and candelight dinners where Tom flirted with another of his conquests, Georgia Sitwell, the pretty young wife of Sacheverell Sitwell, youngest of the three famous literary Sitwells.

*A highly infectious disease of cattle, which could be carried from one field to another by horses' hoofs, hence the ban on hunting.

But beneath the sparkling surface, glittering like the Mediterranean sea in the sun, the darker currents of their lives were swirling. Irene listened to Cim and Tom rowing upstairs – rows usually ended by Tom flinging out as Cim sobbed – or heard him speak rudely to her sister in public. 'Felt badly the strained atmosphere', runs her diary for 28 August. 'Tom went to the casino and I talked for the first time in my life for two hours to Cim over the misery of her present life and Tom's insulting behaviour to her.' In turn, Irene poured out her heart to Cim, telling her every detail of 'the Gordon mess'.

That summer Tom's father died and he inherited the baronetcy. Georgia Sitwell, going to tea with Cim and Tom, found Cim surrounded by the Mosley diamonds. 'She was planning what to do with them, that is how to have them reset,' wrote Georgia in her diary. 'Tom actually says she will need the tiara one day as it is, to wear – as Queen of the Communists I suppose!'

Georgia also noted her first meeting with Baba, later to become a close friend. 'Alexandra Metcalfe was there, very pretty, chic, hardfaced and oh! so conventional and ordinary.' It was a small and in many ways strangely incestuous circle: Georgia was at the height of her affair with Tom Mosley – one of his notes to her, written from his bachelor flat, simply says 'Come!' – and there were numerous luncheons à deux, yet at the same time she was pursuing her friendship with the unsuspecting Cimmie.

Sach was less complaisant. 'We went to Jean Fleming's for cocktails,' wrote Georgia on 8 November. 'On the way back Sach began as usual about the Mosleys and we had an awful time. I decided it was time to put a stop to the more tiresome aspect of his attitude and get really angry so he may give less trouble for a while. He hates all people who may give one a good time.'

In the autumn Gracie and Scatters Wilson won the Caesarewitch Handicap at Newmarket with Arctic Star by three lengths – they had bought the horse in Ireland as an unbroken two-year-old for £800. Scatters led him in, a dashing figure in the black-and-white check coat that made him so easily recognisable at winter race meetings. It seemed a pattern that would stretch ahead for years.

But change was imminent. The common front that had formed between Cim and Irene when both had the same difficulties with their father had fallen away as they became established in their new lives. Cim, with her children, her anguished, adoring love for her husband and her growing involvement in his political life, now had more in common with her younger sister, also a mother – and perfectly able to hold her own with Tom.

Irene, with her work for East End clubs and for charities, her strong religious faith, the emotionalism that burst through a somewhat formidable exterior, the loud, rather flamboyant colours she preferred and the good looks that were handsome rather than pretty, did not fit into the category of women Tom liked as guests or mistresses. Baba, slim, beautiful, clever, amusing, always perfectly dressed and still fascinated by him, was much more his cup of tea.

As for Baba, the year in India, Fruity's devotion, the open admiration of other men, her success in London and her own powerful personality had given her a new perspective. She loved her husband but she knew she was the dominant partner in the marriage; hers was the money and what she said went – not only because she held the purse-strings but because Fruity, who could not get over his luck in marrying her, could not bear to say no to her. At the core of the Prince of Wales's circle, she saw the power that royalty confers; with the Mosleys, she began to glimpse the fascination of political power – that sense of being at the heart of things that grips like a vice. Irene was eight years older, but Baba no longer felt like the little sister.

In 1928, for the first time, the Curzon sisters spent Christmas apart. Baba and Fruity had sailed for America on the *Olympic*, after Nancy Astor had given a huge farewell lunch for them. Irene was at Melton, lonely and miserable despite the parties: 'barring Flash no one in the room caring if I looked lovely or hideous, and I fled home in a black fog, alone and on my feet and in a sudden fear of utter loneliness. All the years here have never made me walk home alone before in utter horror of everyone only wanting bed.' But she gave a dinner party on Christmas Eve, won £35 at poker on Christmas Day and drank port with the Prince of Wales at the Quorn's Boxing Day meet – his first day's hunting that season.

The Mosleys spent Christmas with their children at Denham, returning there on Boxing Day after a visit to the fount of socialism in its purest form – the house of Sidney and Beatrice Webb. After they left, Beatrice wrote in her diary: 'It struck us both that he and she had changed – partly from his long illness last autumn and winter,* partly from the ups and downs of electoral failure and success; also from social boycott by their own set and an uneasy position in the Labour Party. He is disillusioned. Labour politics for an aristocrat are not attractive – current and cross-current from left and right and very little real comradeship.'

In Mosley, the Webbs believed that they saw a possible future leader of the party to which they had given their lives. 'With his money, his personal charm and political gifts, his good-looking and agreeable wife,' wrote Beatrice, 'he is dead certain of Cabinet office and possibly has a chance of eventual premiership.'

*After his wartime injury, Mosley suffered from recurrent phlebitis, particularly in the affected leg.

14

Lady Cynthia Mosley, MP

~

Accidents in the hunting field did nothing to check the sport's popularity. Everyone who could, hunted; even politicians came to Melton to pick up a little of its glamour by association. Stanley Baldwin, brushing up his image of the bluff, warm-hearted countryman, stayed with the Master of the Quorn during the season of 1928/9, following hounds in a phaeton drawn by a white cob. The equipage plunged over the Leicestershire grass, Baldwin's familiar cherrywood pipe gripped between his teeth all the while.

The King and Queen did not share Baldwin's enthusiasm. For years they had been worried that the Prince of Wales, a bold and reckless rider, might kill or maim himself in the hunting field. When the King fell ill in the autumn of 1928, the thought that his heir might soon succeed him must have given this anxiety a sharper edge. The Prince, who had returned from South Africa because of his father's health, did not begin his hunting that season until Boxing Day. Almost immediately, there were three fatalities with his favourite pack, the Quorn, that would have reached the ears of the King and Queen.

The Royal couple began to put pressure on their son. Although the Prince attended the Melton Ball in January 1929, gay as ever, with the foxtrot all the rage, two dramatic changes were about to take place in his life, bringing 'the Melton years' to a close.

The first was a new mistress. That January, while his longtime beloved, Freda Dudley Ward, was away in Palm Beach with her husband, the Prince ran into the voluptuous Thelma Furness again and immediately invited her out to dinner. She accepted equally promptly. Very soon, they began a highly charged and passionate affair. The Prince would arrive for his regular Thursday nights at the Embassy Club with Thelma, and sometimes also her twin sister Gloria Vanderbilt, both in chiffon dresses with row upon row of narrow diamond bangles on their wrists which they called their 'service stripes'. On other nights they could be seen at the Kit-Cat Restaurant with Prince George, bringing with them most of the Melton set.

The second change affected Fruity and Baba. The Prince finally yielded to parental pressure and gave up hunting. On Saturday 23 February, 1929, all his hunters, with the exception of one old horse, were sold by auction at the Repository in Leicester. 'HRH The Prince of Wales is not hunting any more, or riding in any point-to-point races this season,' the auctioneers, Warner, Sheppard & Wade announced in their catalogues and posters.

At once the Prince's life became much more London-based. He had his own apartments in London, at York House in St James's Palace, and turned some of his furious energy into renovating them, chiefly by removing some of the warren of bedrooms and replacing them with bathrooms, a ballroom and a new dining room where a hundred people could be seated. The chintz sofas and portrait of Queen Mary remained over the drawing-room chimneypiece.

St James's was a royal palace and the Prince had always wanted somewhere he could think of as his own, preferably in the country, where he could have complete privacy. He asked his father for Fort Belvedere, a battlemented semi-derelict royal property, half small castle and half house, six miles from Windsor. The King agreed at once.

To the Prince, 'the Fort', as he always called it, became home; and he loved it, as he always loved, passionately. He gutted its interior, installed central heating and, following the American custom he so approved of, bathrooms for almost every one of the bedrooms – a rarity when many large country houses still existed on just one or two. He planned a ballroom and a basement gymnasium holding a practice golf tee and net, and a steam bath. The lily pond beneath the battlements was replaced with a swimming pool and a tennis court was laid out. He chopped down the yew trees growing close to the house, which kept every room on that side in perpetual shadow, replaced the Victorian laurel

shrubbery with rhododendrons, and cut paths through the woodland of fir and birch.

It was not a particularly large house – the walnut table in the
dining room hung with Stubbs paintings seated only ten. The best
furniture, Queen Anne, was in the library. His bedroom, with its
Chippendale bed, had tall windows hung with dark red chintz
curtains that looked out on the terrace. Family photographs stood
about and there was a miniature stairway at the foot of the bed
so that his favourite Cairn terrier, Cora, could climb up. Thelma
slept in a bedroom that could have been designed for one of the
grandes horizontales of the Belle Epoque – walls of pink satin, an
enormous four-poster hung with the same material, flounced,
looped and gathered to each bedpost by pink ostrich feathers.

Although the hard labour of chopping down trees and hacking
away years of undergrowth mopped up the Prince's physical energy
it did not supply the adrenalin high of hunting. He began flying
lessons, buying himself a De Havilland Gypsy Moth. A road was
made from the front door of the Fort to Smith's Lawn in Windsor
Great Park, where a private royal aerodrome was built. The King,
determined to keep his heir safely on the ground, countered by
forbidding the issue of a flying licence.

Emotional crisis rather than change dominated Irene's life. Men
seemed to float in and out of her orbit, a number of them becoming
lovers – in January 1929, for instance, she saw Artur Rubinstein
again, dining at the Embassy with him in a party for four. 'He
drove me home and we had a long talk. Whenever I see him he
breathes life and humour and vitality into me.' It was, perhaps,
that evening that their long-drawn-out and sporadic affair began,
although Arthur was anything but reliable – the next day she
waited in vain for him for half an hour with John McCormack
and his wife until they eventually gave him up and went to the
cinema without him.

She had several other admirers. Though Myrtie had put her foot
down and Flash was seldom allowed to see her, another, Paul
Duhamel, was besottedly in love. Unfortunately, he chose to
propose to her the night after she had had dinner with the man
she loved, Gordon Leith, and had gone on to spend the rest of the

night dancing with him at the Embassy. 'G. took me home and was adorable but I told him I could not face dinner at his house with Cuckoo. It nearly drove me mad.' After this, Paul Duhamel's declaration that, for him, she had all he wanted in a woman 'of sex, charm, wit, taste and brains' fell flat. 'I told him I had only loved one person for six years and he [Paul] was wonderful and asked nothing of me but to see me and give me of his friendship – just another tragedy in my life.'

The lunches, the dinners, the parties, the hunting, the poker, the charity work, the cocktails, the concerts, the presidency of the Melton Mowbray Amateur Dramatic Society and the Leicester Symphony Orchestra (with its concerts conducted by the up-and-coming young conductor Malcolm Sargent) and the late-night suppers continued. A determined champion of women, Irene was also Chairman of the British Women's Symphony Orchestra, for whom she collected money: it was, as she correctly said, the only medium through which women students could learn the art of orchestral playing – impossible in the male-dominated orchestras of the day.

Outwardly, she seemed to have everything; inside she was gnawed by loneliness. Men who had professed undying devotion, like Bobby Digby, had married other women. Both her sisters were married, with the children she longed for. Worst of all, her affair with Gordon Leith seemed to be no nearer fulfilment. To be kept on the end of a string for six long years – for that is what it amounted to – would make any woman despair. For Curzon's daughter, it was intolerable. Though humble at heart, Irene was sophisticated enough to know that her advantages in worldly terms amounted to a full hand – she was good-looking, independent, titled and possessed of a fortune enough to be a magnet in its own right.

And yet, at thirty-three, she was emotionally caught in a net from which she could not seem to break free, waiting for the love of her life finally to leave his wife and claim her. Every time the proud spirit she had inherited from her father revolted at this humiliating position and she attempted to put distance and time between them, as with her cruises, Gordon would seek her out and renew his promises and the affair would start up again.

Affectionate lectures from her old family doctor, roses from other men, counsel and comfort from Elinor Glyn, could not stop the sleepless nights and tumultuous thoughts. 'All day I had a sob in my throat and the ache of wanting someone to take me into the sun for a month and forget everything, but every one I love has a wife or is tied,' she wrote on 23 April. Eventually, she broke down, bursting into tears while lunching with Baba. It was a complete reversal of roles. From then on the balance of their relationship shifted. Baba comforted her sister and told her she would talk to Gordon.

One opinion, however, was never enough for Irene. When a friend advised her to consult her brother-in-law Tom Mosley, she did so, rather nervously. To her surprise, he was kind and understanding. He would, he said, speak to Gordon and find out his intentions.

At last the nightmare of waiting was over. Tom's intervention had cut the Gordian knot. He was able, as one man to another – and as a man known for his own extramarital affairs to another man indulging in one – to ask Gordon the direct question: 'Do you intend to marry my sister-in-law?'

The reply was equally direct. 'I'm afraid not, old boy.'

Tom did not feel he could tell Irene this himself and deputed Baba to do so. On 6 May went to Baba who gave me my doom,' records Irene's diary. Baba told the weeping Irene that Gordon had seemed staggered at the thought that anyone would expect him to leave Cuckoo. 'So I must never see him again', the day's entry ends dolefully.

Irene had turned to Baba rather than Cimmie not so much from choice but because all Cimmie's time was taken up with politics. She was not only speaking on Tom's behalf in Smethwick as well as appearing up and down the country with Ramsay MacDonald and giving garden parties for Labour Party workers at Savehay Farm, she had decided to stand for Parliament herself in the general election of 30 May 1929. She was extremely popular in the party. The tough trade-union leaders were flattered when she asked them to dinner and her all-round niceness made the coterie of MPs surrounding Tom her devoted friends.

Her constituency was the safely Conservative Stoke-on-Trent

where her opponent, Colonel Ward, had achieved a 4,500 majority at the previous election. She spent much of her time there, speaking constantly, doing her best to meet as many people as she could and expressing Labour policy with a heartfelt sincerity. Because of Cimmie's looks and style, her opponents immediately dubbed it 'the mannequin election'; she tried hard to dress down, usually campaigning in a beige coat and skirt and brogues, though she enlivened these with a chic scarlet hat and gloves 'just to show which side I am on'.

The straightforwardness of political campaigning was a contrast to the emotional turmoil of her private life. Tom's infidelities tortured her but as long as she could believe that (in his phrase) they were no more than his 'tiresome ways' and that no one could take her central place at the core of his life, she was able to keep some sort of equilibrium. Even when he acquired a bachelor flat in Pimlico, 22b Ebury Street, which was little more than one huge, elegant bedroom, even when he had a brief affair with the wife of a Conservative MP who acquired a photograph of him naked – passed round the Tory front benches while he was making a speech from the Labour front bench – she forgave him, though often not until there had been blistering rows and scalding tears.

From early on in their marriage Cimmie had determined to do more than simply fill the role of wife and mother. When Tom crossed the floor of the House, she had abandoned her Tory heritage without a qualm, cutting herself off from many of her friends – though neither Mosley thought for a moment of adjusting their lavish and hedonistic way of life to the more puritan Labour ethic. Instead, they simply carried on with the same social calendar, encouraging like-minded friends to join them; soon, their favourite summer resort, Antibes, was described (in *The Times*) as 'a summer club for the socialist intelligentsia'.

Cimmie's appearance, too, exuded glamour rather than socialist earnestness. When she and Tom accompanied Ramsay MacDonald to Berlin, where he was lecturing to the Committee for International Discussion on 16 October 1928, it was Cimmie who entered the Reichstag first, Cimmie whose clothes – grey silk dress, grey velvet cloak, ermine cape and string of pearls – which were lovingly described rather than the MacDonald lecture. She had embraced socialism with the fervour of the convert, yet it was hard to equate her persona with Harold Nicolson's description of her as 'profoundly working class at heart'.

But her zeal and dedication were genuine. For Cimmie, politics was not something one picked up and put down, or an occupation chosen to please her husband, and she resented Tom's slight air of patronage. When Irene and two other friends were staying with them at Savehay Farm a fortnight before the general election, these strains erupted shatteringly. 'A most tragic and painful row took place between Cim and Tom at dinner over the cars for the Election and he was vilely rude to her,' recorded Irene. 'She is so exquisite and faithful in her love and he so ruthless of her. I wish at times he could disappear off the face of the earth as he only brings her endless agony.' Next morning Tom took the Mosleys' Bentley and Irene had to telephone for her own car to come and take her sister to London.

Many of those close to the Mosleys thought that Tom exploited his wife's willingness too freely, often persuading her to speak when she was exhausted or under the weather. Harold Nicolson in particular believed that this often amounted to cruelty – but then, a streak of cruelty often underlay what Tom described as 'teasing'.

When his devoted friend and closest lieutenant John Strachey married (in April 1929) and rice was produced to throw at the bride – an American woman all his friends disliked – Tom, his best man, whispered to the bridesmaids, 'Throw it upwards. It hurts more.' Yet his charismatic presence, brilliance and oratory won back those with reservations, like Irene, when she heard him speak at Birmingham town hall.

Cim campaigned for her husband as well as herself. In a red dress with a buttonhole of white heather, she addressed a gathering of three thousand at Stoke after an introduction by Ramsay Mac-Donald; next day Cim spoke several times in Tom's constituency of Smethwick, before leaving for a day of speeches, open-air meetings and talks in schools as well as canvassing in Stoke.

Her hard work paid off: most of the people she spoke to said they would vote for her. All her life she had had the ability to get on with all sorts and kinds of people, and to make herself loved by anyone who knew her well. When she knocked at the poorest doors she evoked not resentment at her obvious wealth and her title but admiration and liking.

Her growing popularity caused her opponent Colonel Ward to start a rumour that despite the Leiter millions she had a brother whom she callously allowed to remain in the workhouse. When Irene heard this slander she went to Colonel Ward's meeting and heckled him from the floor, yelling that he was telling a lie, she was the candidate's sister and knew more about the Leiter fortune than he did.

'Ward was as white as a sheet, the Chairwoman called for the police and I left the room taking three quarters of the clapping, shrieking women with me. I was cheered all the way down the streets to Longton.' There, buoyed up with triumph, she spoke to the two thousand people waiting for Cim (who was delayed and did not arrive), telling them of her sister's sincerity and capability. The excitement and stress of her unexpected intervention took its toll and after being violently sick Irene spent a sleepless night wondering if she had done the right thing.

More strenuous canvassing followed, knocking on door after door of mean streets, Cim in a red suit, a red toque on her dark hair, and a car bedecked with red and yellow ribbons to take her to the larger meetings. By now she was well known and acclaimed, and the large square in Stoke-on-Trent was packed with a yelling, cheering throng for her final meetings. On Polling Day her supporters encouraged voters out and Irene took a number to the booths in her car. The excitement was intense. After a quick dinner, Irene took Cim in her car to Smethwick, to hear Tom's result. He achieved a majority of 7,340. 'His and Cim's reception was tremendous when he came out and spoke to them,' recorded Irene. 'We then went to the Labour Club where he was carried round the room and Cim was rushed round it too.'

Then it was Cim's turn. Back they all went to Stoke for the count. At 3.30 a.m. it was announced: Cim had not only beaten Colonel Ward by 7,850 – an unheard-of result in that safe Conservative seat – but had polled over 26,000 votes as against 13,000 Labour votes in the previous election.

As Cim, shaking with emotion, was given a rapturous reception, Irene was aware of the elation around her as more and more Conservative seats in Birmingham fell to Labour. 'Everyone murmured that night that Cim and Tom had broken the great Chamberlain backbone in Brum,' she wrote joyously. 'Seldom have I taken part in such a frenzy of thrill and nervous tension. The huge crowds watching the twelve white placards coming out and being hung on the side of the Town Hall throughout the night was a most dramatic picture.'

The morning confirmed victory: this first election in which there was universal adult suffrage brought Labour back to power with the first majority Labour Government. Irene gave Cim the present she had bought for her, so sure was she of her sister's victory: a gold bracelet with 'Stoke 1929' on it in diamonds.

As the Mosleys left to meet Ramsay MacDonald and celebrate, Irene returned to London. Still elated, she went to see Baba. It was like a douche of cold water: Baba did not approve of Irene's new political allegiance – or, as she put it, 'turning Labour'. It was, said Baba, a traitorous act; what would all their friends say? She herself had helped Nancy Astor, who had just scraped in with a majority of 250. Besides, Labour children were so badly behaved.

Six days after the election, the exhausted Cim had a miscarriage.

When the new Government was formed Tom, though not in the Cabinet, was asked to be Chancellor of the Duchy of Lancaster and to co-ordinate the Government's policy on the most serious problem facing them: unemployment. This now stood at 1,164,000 and was increasing by the month. Very quickly, it became obvious that Tom was the party's rising star and many of its younger members gravitated to him. John Strachey, elected as member for Aston, became his Parliamentary Private Secretary.

However, until the Parliamentary recess was over, the summer was for playing. That year, all the sisters flung themselves into the Season. But though the Mosleys were as social as ever, not everyone had forgiven them for what was still seen as a kind of treachery. Irene walked out of Georgia Sitwell's party, where she had been talking to Harold Acton and William Walton, when Lady Eleanor Smith arrived, 'because of all the filthy things she said about Cim and her election in sables and pearls. I told Georgia to tell her why I had left.'

Irene's literary and theatrical friendships increased: she was on terms of intimacy with the Lunts, Paul Robeson and his wife, the John McCormacks – and Artur Rubinstein, who accompanied her home on several evenings. She was trying her best to forget Gordon but it was difficult.

The Metcalfes' lives remained as intertwined with the Prince of Wales and his circle as before. They shared a house at Sandwich with the Prince for golfing tournaments, they holidayed in Biarritz with him and Thelma Furness, accompanied also by Lord Ednam and G Trotter. With Edwina Mountbatten, Baba opened a club called Master's, at 7 Savile Row, intended as a counterpart to Buck's, the men's club next door. It only lasted a year, although Captain Buckmaster, owner and founder of Buck's, advised them on the running of it and allowed them to use the last part of his name: its lady members preferred lunching with men and men who did lunch with them felt intensely uncomfortable when their hostesses, as members, had to do the paying.

Like Irene, the Metcalfes stayed with the Mosleys in Antibes (though it was the last year they would do so: Fruity hated the Riviera life). Also there were Bobby Casa Maury and his beautiful blonde, green-eyed wife Paula, a former model and Tom's long-standing mistress; and staying at the Eden Roc Hotel were the film star John Gilbert and his wife. Everyone wanted a crack at John Gilbert, from Daisy Fellowes, hoping to be asked to the Gilberts' moonlight party on the top balcony of the Eden Roc, to Baba, who successfully pounced for the seat beside him at dinner.

Next day it was Irene's turn, trying to make sparkling con-versation while Tom, opposite, whispered almost under his breath the whole time to Paula Casa Maury about which of the three Curzon sisters was ahead in the Gilbert stakes, 'the heavyweight, the light or the middle'. As Irene was classed as the heavyweight she was justifiably annoyed.

At such close quarters it was impossible to conceal the difficulties in the Mosley marriage. Tom, who alternated between cutting Cimmie dead and making sarcastic remarks, was so unpleasant to his wife when she asked him about plans for her birthday that Irene lost her temper and called him a cad. When the holiday ended, after a brief detour to Marienbad where she managed to lose six pounds – Irene saw Gracie in Paris, staying at the Ritz. 'She was as ever when alone disarmingly sweet and loving. I had an hour of delightful chat with her over myself – and Scatters.'

For the long affair between Gracie and Scatters had finally

frayed and disintegrated. By ill-judged financial advice, by encouraging her to pour more and more money into their joint racing venture, he had ruined her. Gracie, who had never had to think about money and who had always lived the life of an exceptionally wealthy woman, did not at first notice the gradual diminution of her fortune. As it dwindled, so the pace of her losses increased. Although Arctic Star, far and away the best horse in their jointly-owned stud, ran in the 1929 Caesarewitch in Gracie's colours – brown and pink halved, with pink cap – it was the last fling. Arctic Star, Arctic Light, Irish Moor, Okanagan and Economy (a sad misnomer) were put up for sale during Cambridgeshire Week at the end of October.

A few days later, on 31 October, Cimmie made her maiden speech in the House of Commons, on the Second Reading of the bill to amend the Widows, Orphans and Old Age Pensions Act. Again her appearance made its way into the Parliamentary reporters' accounts; described as 'the bright star of the debate', she cut 'an aristocratic figure dressed in black and with a white fichu ornamented with red and white carnations'. She expressed herself with great freedom and frankness against her opponents' contention that increasing pensions and thereby giving people something for nothing would weaken the moral fibre of the nation. 'Demoralisation is something I know a great deal about,' she declared. 'All my life I have got something for nothing. That is entirely due to luck and I think a great many members opposite' – here she pointed to the Conservatives – 'are in the same position. We have all got something for nothing. The question is: are we demoralised? *I* am not demoralised.'

Although she had to be reminded to address her remarks to the Speaker rather than the benches opposite, it was considered an excellent performance.

15

The Mosley Memorandum

~

For the Mosleys, the autumn of 1929 was taken up by politics. The Wall Street Crash of October 1929 had brought the question of unemployment into sharp focus; Tom, for whom the subject was all-consuming, had written and spoken about it to such effect that he was asked to work out a practical policy for dealing with it.

Unfortunately, he was under the overall direction of J. H. Thomas, the former General Secretary of the National Union of Railwaymen, Lord Privy Seal to Tom's Chancellor of the Duchy of Lancaster. Thomas was old, set in his ways, unable to grasp economic theory – especially when (as often) fuddled by drink – and as a Labour politician of the old sort, he was in any case suspicious of Tom. He believed that Tom was an adventurer, using the Labour Party for what he could get out of it; Tom thought Thomas a dinosaur. It did not help that the Prime Minister, already frowned on by many in his party for preferring to spend his leisure with aristocrats rather then trade unionists, was clearly taken with both the Mosleys.

As Beatrice Webb wrote in her diary at the time: 'Mosley, whom I met at lunch, is contemptuous of Thomas's incapacity, of the infirmity of manual working Cabinet Ministers generally and very complacent about his own qualifications for the leadership of the Labour Party. That young man has too much aristocratic insolence in his make-up.'

Cimmie, she added, had charmed the House. The subjects on which she had chosen to speak were those about which many felt strongly but which had not always had much of a public airing.

In February 1930 Cimmie asked Parliament to consider some form of what is now known as planning control. 'Powers should be given to the local authority to decide whether a house is suitable to the surroundings, whether it is wisely and properly placed and is the right colouring,' she said.

Tom was well aware of the undercurrents in the Labour Party. Knowing that any radical new theory he submitted to Thomas would automatically elicit a negative response, he worked on his own. With his friend John Strachey, Allan Young (now his PPS), the veteran politician George Lansbury and the Scottish Labour leader Tom Johnston, he evolved what came to be known as the Mosley Memorandum. It was largely based on the economic principles of his friend John Maynard Keynes; and proposed a large-scale programme of public works and the mobilisation of national resources to fight unemployment. It also embodied a principle that instinctively scared his party: the focusing of power in the hands of a small inner group.

Tom, never a team player, would soon refine this ethos still further to its ultimate principle: personal power. But at that moment, with unemployment the major issue in the western hemisphere – in the US it had risen to over seven million, in Germany to over five million – ambition and idealism had coalesced into a single strand and his anxiety was simply to get things gone. Among his intimates, he bewailed the 'crass stupidity' of the Labour Ministers with whom he had to deal.

He was a young man in a hurry – but from Thomas's point of view, Tom was seriously at fault in showing his work to outside helpers without so much as consulting him, Thomas. There was further acrimony when Tom sent his Memorandum to the Prime Minister on 23 January 1930, asking him to place it before the Cabinet – again without consulting Thomas. This time, Thomas offered his resignation to the Prime Minister, which was refused, and Ramsay MacDonald delivered a private rebuke to Tom.

After discussing the Mosley Memorandum, the Cabinet appointed a sub-committee chaired by Philip Snowden to consider it in depth. As the sub-committee procrastinated there was an atmosphere of crisis within the Mosley household. 'Will Tom resign?' wondered Georgia Sitwell on 22 February.

Gradually it became clear that the Government would reject the

Mosley Memorandum; and on 9 May it did so. Accepting it would have meant abandoning free trade and the gold standard, measures which would have caused disruption and disunity within the entire party. Conscious that the economic blizzard was about to commence, conscious that the new and untried party must be seen to hang together, the Government closed ranks.

'Oswald and Cynthia Mosley here for the night, at a critical moment in his career,' wrote Beatrice Webb on 19 May. 'Is he or is he not going to resign?'

By the next day Tom had made up his mind. He went to see the Prime Minister and, though MacDonald tried to dissuade him, resigned his government office (the other two Ministers concerned with combating unemployment, Lansbury and Johnston, remained). In his letter of resignation of 20 May Tom said he found it inconsistent with honour to remain in a government that would not discuss its election pledges. MacDonald, who regarded the tone of his letter as one of 'graceless pompousness', wrote in his diary that night: 'Test of a man's personality is his behaviour in disagreement. In every test he failed.'

In the House Tom began to attack what he saw as the Government's apathy and lack of constructive action. Then, no longer bound by Cabinet rules, he put the Mosley Memorandum to a meeting of the Parliamentary Labour Party on 22 May. It evoked sympathy and interest but provoked a general feeling that Tom should not be seen to attack his own Government at this crucial moment. The experienced politician Arthur Henderson asked Tom to take the 'noble line' of withdrawing his censure motion against the Government to allow them to consider his plan more fully. This attempt to shift him from his intransigent stance failed: Tom insisted that his proposals be put to the vote. Despite an eloquent speech, he achieved only 29 votes against 210. Although his courage was admired, forcing the issue in this way was widely considered a tactical mistake – or, as Irene put it, 'a stupid egotistical error', though she was thankful that Cim was wholeheartedly in agreement with Tom over his stance. 'That is all that matters to them both.'

On 28 May Tom made his resignation speech as a Minister in the House of Commons. It was a tour de force. 'Mosley's speech in the second attack on Thomas is acclaimed as that of a distinguished parliamentary orator, wholly admirable in manner and style,' wrote Beatrice Webb. She went on to ask the question at the back of many minds.

Has MacDonald found his superseder in Oswald Mosley? MacDonald owes his pre-eminence largely to the fact that he is the only artist, the only aristocrat by temperament and talent, in a party of plebeians and plain men. Hitherto he has had no competitor in personal charm and good looks, delightful voice and the gift of oratory. But Mosley has all these with the élan of youth, wealth and social position added to them.

Mosley still has a young man's zeal. He lacks MacDonald's strongest point – genuine puritanism. He is entangled in the smart set and luxurious habits; he is reputed to be loose with women; he rouses suspicion, he knows little or nothing about trade unionism or Co-operation, he cannot get on terms of intimacy with working men or with the lower middle-class brainworker. He is, in fact, an intruder, a foreign substance in the labour movement, not easily assimilated.

In Melton, Irene was finding the life she had chosen for herself increasingly hollow. The most noticeable difference made by the Prince of Wales's departure was an increase in the wildness of the parties. Drunkenness that would have been frowned upon in his presence was becoming commonplace – 'Charlie took off his trousers and did fearful dances in white pants', 'Peter Ackroyd was found drunk in a spare room in the morning, stark naked in bed'. At the Melton Ball Irene ran out of the building to escape the harassing advances of one man only to have another, whom she did not care for, propose to her on the way home.

Everything seemed to conspire to depress her. She was losing money constantly at bridge and, though this was not a financial worry, it made her feel stupid and incompetent. She saw the same old faces at all the parties; one evening, with a similarly disillusioned woman friend, she worked out what it was about them that so irked her. 'Diagnosed our disgust and antipathy to 90 per cent of the hunting people as their being really common, no breeding – tho' I hate that word – and so having no rare sensitiveness or exquisite feeling which jars so badly on one day after day.'

Yet 'breeding' was not really the problem: Irene made friends delightedly with writers, artists and musicians, black, white or Jewish, without a thought as to their lineage. She sent roses to Mrs Paul Robeson, she went constantly to the Polish Embassy with her friend Jan Masaryk (the future Foreign Minister of Czechoslovakia), she was half in love with Artur Rubinstein.

The underlying cause of her unhappiness was the knowledge that her love for Gordon had no future. She should, she knew, avoid seeing him – but this would mean giving up hunting. As it was, every sight of him was a pang. Unable to cut him out of her life completely, she saw him occasionally, with disastrous results. 'G dined with me. Had a ghastly breakdown of weeping and misery after and had to get Lena [Lena Sibley, her lady's maid] down or else I should have gone mad. Devotedly Lena held my hand with hankies on my aching brow till I fell asleep at about three.'

She was less unhappy when she returned to London in the late spring. Although her future looked barren the present, with its wider circle of friends, its plays, concerts and galleries, and its physical proximity to her sisters, was more agreeable. There were teas with Cim at Smith Square, where politicians and housemaids would pass one another on the single staircase, and a chance to play with the children in their nursery or watch them being bathed.

In default of the motherhood for which she longed, she was a devoted aunt. When seven-year-old Nicky had appendicitis she was a constant visitor; when she went to Baba's house there was two-and-a-half-year-old David toddling across the nursery floor towards her ready for the games and romps he did not always get from his mother. 'I seem to understand my sisters' children so much better than they do,' she reflected with a touch of complacency.

Although Ascot was rained off, the social round scarcely faltered. Every hour of the day seemed packed with concerts, plays, dances, private views, fancy-dress parties, cocktail parties followed by dinner, followed by bridge followed by supper at the Hungaria or the Savoy. The Mosleys gave enormous weekend house parties, or invited friends for the day to Denham, where they played tennis, lay on the lawn, bathed in the river, or unwillingly listened to a sparring match between Cim and Tom.

After one of these episodes, perhaps because Irene had witnessed it, Cim was unpleasant to her at that evening's ball (on 8 July). 'You do not look your best. I think you had better go home.' Irene fled in tears, to be consoled by the faithful Lena. A few days later Cim rubbed in the message that Irene should acquire a husband before it was too late by telling her how Bendor [the Duke of Westminster] adored Loelia Ponsonby and how Irene should be in that position – but wasn't.

It was a rare display of nastiness from the normally sweet-natured Cim. Tom's unfaithfulnesses brought out qualities alien to her happy, carefree nature. Despite the urging of Baba and Irene, who wanted her to give Tom a fright, she had always refused to visit the bachelor flat in Ebury Street that Tom had taken; it would have smacked of snooping and spying and she could well imagine his jibes about such activities but she could hardly stop herself imagining what went on there.

Meanwhile the arguments went on. When Irene returned to her house in Deanery Street one evening at eleven thirty it was to find Cim and Tom there having a row. 'It was just about some stupid bill and he rushed off in the car in a rage and poor dazed Cim still could not see how it had all arisen.' That night, Cimmie stayed on at Irene's house and wrote miserably to Tom:

> I am entirely bewildered. I just don't understand – why have you been so horrid to me not only tonight but ever since I got up from chick-enpox. As the sound of my voice and my presence (and you've seen so little of me) seem to drive you demented I resort to poor Irene's method of putting pen to paper.
>
> You leave me *alone* in London for the weekend to look after Nicky [their son Nicholas, aged seven, had just been operated on for appen-dicitis] and go away with another woman for the weekend. You never see Nicky from before his op. Saturday morning till Monday evening . . .'

It was little better in Cowley Street. Baba, when not disagreeable ('Of course she criticised my lovely black fur coat and said the collar was wrong') seemed always to be 'in the extremes of gloom'. Baba was pregnant again but what was causing her depression was a gradual disillusionment with her marriage. The truth was that she and Fruity were very different people and after the natural decline in the sexual excitement of the first years they had little in common. Fruity was charming, kind, delightful, funny and supremely loyal but even his best friends did not call him clever. 'Fruity is a sweet man but too stupid,' wrote Georgia Sitwell in her diary, after an evening in a party with him at the Kit-Cat Club.

Baba's shift in perspective had been brought about by several factors. Fruity running the Prince of Wales's horses, trying hunters for him, managing his stables, was a man doing a job at which he was expert, and like all professionals actively exercising a supreme skill, commanded respect. But now that the Prince had given up hunting, Fruity's job had disappeared. He was still the Prince's best friend and the Metcalfes still moved constantly in the Prince's circle, but there was a great difference in a husband active, occupied and full of plans to one often hanging round the house.

There was also the financial discrepancy. During the Melton years, when her husband filled a role that they and their circle considered important, the difference between Fruity's income and Baba's had not seemed important. In London, with a different way of life, friends with wider interests, and a house and nursery to run, the balance shifted. From the early days of their courtship the devoted Fruity had always tried to do what his 'Babs' wanted and the pattern, set in stone by the fact that Baba paid most of the bills, emphasised her dominance in the relationship.

She had so far indulged only in mild flirtations but she was conscious of her sexual power. She was beautiful, with high-cheek-boned, aristocratic looks, her witty remarks delivered in a languid drawl; her slim figure was always exquisitely dressed. The sophisticated assurance she exuded masked the powerful libido she had inherited from her father. It was a combination many men found challenging – and irresistible.

More crucially, at twenty-six Baba was not the same person as the dazzled girl who had fallen so headlong in love with a man whom no dispassionate observer would have picked as her husband. She had grown up and her mind was expanding. She had just begun, also, to take an interest in the charity that would occupy so much of her time in later life – the Save the Children Fund. She wanted occupation, conversation and company that was intelligent as well as fun.

*

The Mosleys went off as usual to Antibes on 2 August 1930. Irene, still hankering after Gordon, decided once again to put the sea between them. Before she left on a tour of Norway, the Baltic and Russia, she went to one of the last house parties given by Grace at Hackwood. It was dominated by Margot Asquith, more eccentric and outspoken than ever. 'Margot tyrannical over her bridge. I had her both evenings with Chips [Channon] and Alfred [Duggan]. She got me so rattled I was paralysed. I lost £43 and the old girl won £38 and Chips £56. The tennis was poor. Margot played golf with Chips in black shoes, red socks and white silk stockings, a baby's shetland and a black and white spotted skirt, the ball ricocheting off every mole hill.'

Irene returned in September but even the consolation of an old admirer and a happy dinner with Fruity, Baba, Cim and Tom at Smith Square was not enough to blot out thoughts of Gordon and she set off again in October, this time for the Middle East. She was called home from her travels when Baba gave birth to twin daughters on 14 November 1930, after a long and hard labour, and became so ill that it was feared she might not live.

Irene's anxiety over Baba was such that she did not leave London to hunt until the New Year. Even Cliveden was depressing. 'A dark autumnal day,' wrote Harold Nicolson, visiting it in late November. 'Thirty two people in the house. Cold and draughty. Great sofas in vast cathedrals. Duff and Diana Cooper, Tom and Cimmie, Oliver and Lady Maureen Stanley, Harold Macmillan and Lady Dorothy, Brendan Bracken, Bob Boothby, Malcolm Bullock and Garvin [the editor of the *Observer*]. After dinner Nancy, fearful that her party was falling apart, whisked out her false teeth and put on a Victorian hat to make the party go. It did not.'

When Georgia Sitwell went to tea with Cim and Tom at Smith Square the talk was of politics and Baba's poor health. Baba stayed with Cim and Tom at Savehay Farm to recuperate from the birth of the twins, refusing to allow Fruity to leave her side. When Cim took him off to Hackwood one day there were scenes: Baba, accustomed to having her own way, had a full-scale temper tantrum. Irene, there to keep her company in the intervals of looking after her maid Lena who had just been diagnosed with cancer, listened crossly as Baba yelled that she had been left alone and no one loved her. A few days later, back in Cowley Street, she was cheerful again.

Irene was dividing her time between dashing back to London to see Baba and Lena, whose tumour was so large it was inoperable, hunting – often with Fruity – and the inevitable games of poker. There was one notable absentee, she recorded. 'Thelma, due to join Duke in Africa, produced mysterious appendicitis in Paris, returned after ten days there and is now off again!!! What is the "Princess of Wales" up to? I lost £8.'

In February 1931 Fruity, worried by Baba's continuing pallor and thinness, took her to Torquay for a fortnight in the hope that the sea air would restore her health. It was not until 4 March that the twins, Davina and Linda, were christened at the Chapel Royal, Baba exquisite in a broad-tail coat with sable collar and cuffs, tight black hat and orchids pinned on her collar. Cimmie, in an eerie foreshadowing of her future, was dressed completely in black.

16

The New Party

~

'Tom is organising his new party,' wrote Harold Nicolson, staying at Savehay Farm for the weekend, in his diary for 15 February 1931. 'Poor Cimmie cannot follow his repudiation of all the things he has taught her to say previously. She was not made for politics. She was made for society and the home.'

For Tom had decided that the only way to achieve what he wanted was to strike out on his own. He was disillusioned with what he saw as the apathy of the Government, he lacked the patience necessary to make the political machinery work for, rather than against, him, he believed that something had to be done quickly – and he very much wanted personal power. He decided to found a new political party, which he called, quite simply, the New Party.

He planned his resignation from the Labour Party for 20 February; after him would go, one after the other to ensure maximum publicity, the five other members of the group who had signed the Mosley Manifesto – Cimmie, John Strachey, W. J. Brown, Oliver Baldwin and Robert Forgan. He also hoped eventually to draw into the New Party other young and restless MPs sympathetic to his ideas, including some of the younger Conservatives such as Harold Macmillan, Bob Boothby, Oliver Stanley and Walter Elliot.

'An amazing act of arrogance,' Beatrice Webb commented in her diary on 25 February 1931. 'Oswald Mosley's melodramatic defection from the Labour Party, slamming the door with a bang to resound through the political world ... Mosley's sensational exit will matter supremely to himself and his half-dozen followers but very little to the Labour Party ... except that it means the loss of five seats, the other resignations are of no importance to the Labour movement. The New Party will never get born alive; it will be a political abortion.'

The first to hand in their resignations were Strachey and Baldwin. Then, on 3 March, Cimmie resigned. Her letter to the Prime Minister said:

I have been forced to the conclusion that the present Labour Government differs little from the preceding Tory and Liberal Governments.

Every attempt to make the Front Bench face up to the situation and put through an adequate and comprehensive policy to deal with unemployment has met with complete failure.

The Government has pursued a policy which leaves the electorate tragically disillusioned, as I confess I am myself.

The speech of the Chancellor of the Exchequer the other day finally confirms my opinion that the Government has abdicated to a complete acceptance of the philosophy of their most reactionary opponents.

Ramsay MacDonald replied privately in a vein that mixed the regretful with the savagely ironic.

When you came in a year or two ago we gave you a very hearty welcome and assumed that you knew what was the policy of the predominant socialist party in this country and that, with that knowledge, you asked us to accept you as a candidate and to go to your constituency and assist you in your fight.

You are disappointed with us; you have been mistaken in your choice of political companions, and you are re-selecting them so as to surround yourself with a sturdier, more courageous and more intelligent socialism for your encouragement and strength. You remain true, while all the rest of us are false. Whoever examines manifestos and schemes and rejects them, partly because they are not the sort of socialism that any socialist has ever devised, or because they amount to nothing but words, is regarded by you as inept or incompetent.

We must just tolerate your censure and even contempt; and, in the spare moments we have, cast occasional glances at you pursuing your heroic role with exemplary rectitude and stiff straightness to a disastrous futility and an empty sound. We have experienced so much of this in the building up of the Party that we must not become too cynical when the experience is repeated in the new phase of its existence. Perhaps before the end roads may cross again and we shall wonder why we ever diverged.

The reaction to Cimmie's resignation by her outraged constituents was immediate. The same day the political council of the Burslem and District Industrial Co-operative Society sent her a resolution expressing 'great dissatisfaction' at her reported attitude and requesting her to reconsider the proposed policy of resignation and breaking away from the party. The chairman of her constituency committee wrote reproachfully: 'While I have always felt you were sincere in your desire to improve the lot of the people, I think your secession from the Labour Party is a bad let-down for all those who worked so wholeheartedly for you in your contest.'

Tom's behaviour also caused much ill feeling in his Smethwick constituency, especially as Allan Young was approaching members of the Labour organisation there, offering those known for their platform qualities £5 a week to speak for the New Party.

We of the Birmingham Labour movement feel that you have let us down badly and justified all that your critics said when you came over to us [wrote the editor of the local Birmingham Labour newspaper]. Had you devoted your ability and eloquence to the task of converting a majority of the people to the socialist policy of the Labour party, thus ensuring the return of a majority Labour Government at the next election, you would have been a great figure in our Movement – honoured for your service and well rewarded with office. But you could not wait. And now you are being likened to Winston Churchill. I am sorry.

Tom had planned the New Party carefully. His devoted lieutenant, John Strachey, would provide much of the intellectual firepower, the able Allan Young was the organiser and Cyril Joad, from the Independent Labour Party, became Director of Propaganda. Tom had secured some financial backing from the car magnate Sir William Morris, and was prepared to pour his own fortune, now largely liquid, into the New Party coffers.

Irene went with Tom's mother and brother to the inaugural

meeting of the New Party in the Memorial Hall, Farringdon Street, on 5 March 1931. So many people turned up that the overflow was put in another room and more than a thousand were turned away. The only person missing was the one for whom they were all waiting – Tom had developed raging pleurisy. W. J. Brown, another good orator, was also ill, and the burden of putting across Tom's message to a noisy and controversial audience fell upon Cimmie, backed up by Strachey and Forgan.

Irene recorded: 'Cim was magnificent and undaunted by two ghastly hecklers, a communist and a drunken Labourite. She dealt with them and the crowd finally got livid with them and wanted them evicted. She gave dramatic touches and Forgan drab stuff. Countless questions followed.'

The repercussions over Cimmie's resignation continued for some time. On the evening of 6 March a special meeting of the Stoke, Fenton and Longton Labour Party called upon her to resign her seat in Parliament: of the twenty-one delegates present, only three voted against this motion. The secretary for the Labour Party in the constituency, who had also been Cimmie's election agent, fell on his sword, and his resignation was instantly accepted.

Not so Cimmie. Three nights later, speaking to a meeting of three thousand at the King's Hall, Stoke, with queues outside the door, she made it plain that she did not intend to resign her seat. She plunged into the attack straight away.

'I want to say this as to the demand – of which I have received no notice – that I should resign my seat. I look upon it as the most tremendous cheek and humbug [cheers]. When I came to Stoke the Labour vote was 12,000. At the last election I brought it up to 26,000.'

'You won't get it again!' shouted a voice from the balcony. Swinging round, she shouted back indignantly: 'Well, give us a chance!'

There were such constant interruptions that at one point she shouted, 'Please, please, please give order!' before she made her final point.

'If it came to a break with the Socialist Party I would rather go on with my fight than stick to a Government that is not doing its job,' she said. 'I am just as much a socialist as I have ever been, and even more so.'

On 13 March the Stoke, Fenton and Longton Divisional Labour Party passed a resolution stating that in view of the resignation of Lady Cynthia Mosley, MP for Stoke-on-Trent, from the Parliamentary Labour Party, they confirmed the action of the executive committee in requesting her to resign her seat. Their anger was understandable, as was their feeling that she should either vacate the constituency or fight it as a member of the Labour Party. But neither Mosley wished to leave Parliament.

Immediately after her immense effort on behalf of Tom at the inaugural meeting Cimmie had gone down with a bad cough but, with the New Party to nurse, she had to get up to continue campaigning. Tom was still ill, his temperature spurting up to 105 at times; all through the spring of 1931 Cimmie, Strachey and Robert Forgan undertook a series of meetings up and down the country, all three making speeches that were constantly heckled. When Cimmie spoke in Birmingham to launch the New Party the first question from the audience was: 'Have you brought your money bags?' In Dundee the three of them joined arms and led the audience in singing 'The Red Flag'.

At the end of March Tom went with Cimmie and Baba – still recuperating after the birth of the twins – to convalesce at Lord Beaverbrook's villa in the South of France. While there, he heard of the first chance to test the New Party publicly: a by-election at Ashton-under-Lyme, a Lancashire cotton town with 4,690 unemployed, caused by the death of the sitting Labour member, whose majority was 3,407. The election was to take place on 31 April – yet Tom remained in Monte Carlo and perforce another candidate, Allan Young, was chosen.

The New Party needed all the help it could get. One of the most effective speakers it hired was the former miner, navvy and trade-union official Jack Jones, who used the back of a lorry as his platform. 'When I presented myself at the headquarters of the Party it was to find the political flotsam and jetsam of 1929 floating around,' he wrote. 'Ex-candidates of all parties, and to give the thing tone, one ex-Cabinet Minister in the person of Sir John Pratt [a former Liberal Junior Lord of the Treasury].'

Jones, a tough former agitator, had little time for the New Party toffs who stayed in comfort at the Midland Hotel, arriving by car for meetings. But he had a great admiration for Cimmie, who joined him on the road: 'The two most willing workers were Cynthia Mosley and Strachey's American wife. Mrs Strachey was by no means an effective speaker, but she could hold a crowd long enough to rest some of those whose throats were wearing [out].'

Most of the speaking took place in the large cobbled market-place. Here Jones and two ex-communist assistants tried to pull in the crowds in competition with the Conservative and Labour speakers. First to emerge from the hall would be Cimmie, to be helped on to the loudspeaker lorry by Jones, where she would take her turn speaking. Her fearlessness, and her readiness to face the noisy crowds – many of whom were Labour supporters angry with the Mosleys for splitting the vote – deeply impressed Jones.

> Cynthia Mosley was both able and willing. With me she must have addressed at least a score of very big outdoor crowds during the campaign and also scores of 'in our street' talks to women. Whilst her husband and Strachey and the others of the first flight were looking important in the presence of reporters or talking about the hooking of the floating Liberal vote, the cornering of the Catholic vote, and preparing their speeches for the well-stewarded big meetings indoors each evening, Cynthia Mosley was out getting the few votes that were got. It was her work that saved our deposit, for she worked like a Trojan. She always answered my SOS's for speakers.

Six days before the by-election Tom made his first appearance in front of a crowd of almost seven thousand at an indoor meeting but even the famed Mosley eloquence failed to win the seat. On the night of the poll the market square was filled with people waiting to hear the result. When it was announced: Conservatives 12,420 votes, Labour 11,005 and New Party 4,472, a howl went up from the furious Labour supporters who blamed the New Party for allowing the Conservatives into a safe Labour seat. When they caught a glimpse of Cimmie and Tom they booed and hissed.

So great was the crowd's anger that the police advised Tom to slip out through the back of the town hall. Never lacking in courage, he refused, though he told Cimmie to let the police smuggle her out to shelter in the house of a local supporter while he faced the angry crowd, described by Jack Jones as having all the appearance of an American lynch mob.

I looked at Mosley sideways [wrote Jones]. Certainly didn't have the wind up. More savage than frightened. White with rage, not fear; he showed his teeth as he smiled contemptuously out on to the crowd that was howling at him and calling him names – many of which I had been called in my time.

'Come on,' he said impatiently. We others packed around him and the police packed around us as we plunged into the crowd. Men cursed, women shrieked and spat at us. We got through to the shelter of the hotel and the first thing Mosley did when he got there was to rush to the phone to make inquiries about his wife's safety.

Few of Tom's friends cared much for his new associates. 'Lunched Tom and his not very nice satellite Allan at Carlton,' wrote Georgia Sitwell on 19 May. 'Talk of politics. Find Tom a little disappointing as a political figure. He is too preoccupied with Freud. It may be a joke but it goes too far.'

Baba, now taking an interest in politics, was torn between fascination and disapproval while Irene had rushed back to her own preoccupations. The sufferings of her maid Lena, perhaps her closest confidante, made her miserable, she was involved with various unsuitable men and Baba, in her direct way, had told her she was drinking too much. One May evening, when Irene had joined friends at the Savoy, she wrote: 'I got nervy and started to faint and Lefty [Flynn] took me home in a taxi. I know Baba thought I was drunk. It is now such a mania with me that I fear if I say anything dramatically they will say I have had a couple.'

In June 1931 came the news they had all expected. Grace was stony-broke and the bailiffs owned everything in Hackwood and Carlton House Terrace; her only hope was to live with her son Alfred on his £4,000 a year. Grace's other son, Hubert, had already bailed his mother out to the tune of £50,000 at which he drew the line, much to her annoyance. Gracie's abuse of her children for not helping her failed to enlist sympathy: her wild extravagance was all too well known.

Distraught though she was over Lena, Irene continued with her social life. Baba, her powerful personality emerging from the chrysalis of youth, did not hesitate to give Irene advice whether it was wanted or not. Confident in her own impeccable chic, she tried to tone down Irene's flamboyant, colourful, hit-and-miss style for the grand ball given by Lord and Lady Crewe on 14 June. 'I only had last year's black lace dress and was implored by the family not to wear my bohemian jewellery or sequin cap but Mummy's pearls and be enormously dignified.' Her efforts paid off: next day Baba rang Irene up in rare complimentary vein.

At the beginning of June 1931, Tom held a 'weekend school' at Savehay Farm. John Strachey, whose left-wing principles were drawing him more and more in the direction of communism, seized the moment to make a thoroughly Marxist speech, applauded loudly by Cyril Joad and Allan Young, who were furious at Tom's decision to create a 'youth movement' to keep order at meetings: a development which smacked uncomfortably of Germany's fastest-growing new party, the National Socialist German Workers Party. This had seen its 2.6 per cent share of the votes cast in the Reichstag in the election of 1928 rise dramatically to 18.3 per cent of the popular vote in 1930. The Strachey speech heralded an unbridgeable split in the New Party.

Two weeks later, Tom acquired a notable adherent. Harold Nicolson, whose popularity as a writer, historian and broadcaster was soaring, left his well-paid job editing the *Evening Standard*'s Londoner's Diary to edit the New Party paper, *Action*.

This gain was soon to be counterbalanced by a damaging loss. When Tom announced at a meeting in the Cannon Street Hotel on 30 June that his movement was trying to create a new political psychology, a concept of national renaissance, of new mankind and of vigour, his disciple John Strachey became so alarmed that he announced that he was against authoritarianism. Tom's response was a stinging public rebuke, describing Strachey as a 'pathological socialist', after which he left the meeting with some of the new and physically powerful friends who had been attracted to the New Party's brand of militant politics: the East End boxer Kid Lewis, the Oxford rugger player Peter Howard, and Peter Cheyney the crime novelist. This band of toughs had begun to follow Tom around like a kind of unofficial bodyguard. Though Tom never lacked courage, feeling against him in the Labour Party as a deserter and vote-splitter was bitter.

The New Party was in a state of flux. Some of its founder members were veering sharply to the left – Strachey later became a communist – and Tom himself believed that Liberals such as

Lloyd George and Winston Churchill might approach him for support if a national government were formed in response to the dire economic situation. However, his underlying belief that power should be concentrated in the hands of the few, and by implication himself, was so apparent that on 17 July Harold Nicolson was noting in his diary: 'I think Tom at the bottom of his heart really wants a fascist movement but Allan Young [the secretary to the New Party] and John Strachey think only of the British working man.'

The split was not long in coming. On 20 July Strachey produced his own memorandum, 'The New Party and Russia', which insisted that trade with Russia should be preferred to trade with the Dominions. Britain could afford to allow Russia long-term credit, Britain should make 'a progressive break with that group of powers (of which France and the USA are the leaders) which is attempting to restore the pre-war form of capitalism'.

Tom rejected Strachey's memorandum, since its thesis was contrary to his own programme. Strachey, Young and Joad resigned from the New Party in a blaze of publicity, declaring that 'Mosley is adopting a conservative or fascist attitude'. Joad added that he did not want to belong to a party that was about to 'subordinate intelligence to muscular bands of young men'.

At this time, the Curzon sisters' oldest, closest friend Nancy Astor was grappling with bitter news. Her son by her first marriage, Bobbie Shaw, Baba's old love, had been arrested for homosexual offences. For Nancy, ignorant of this form of sexual behaviour, it was a double blow: learning of 'beastliness' as well as the shattering knowledge that the being she loved best in the world was to go to prison (although homosexuality *per se* was not a criminal offence, proven homosexual acts were).

Bobbie's life had seemed glittering. A glamorous, witty, popular officer in the 'Blues' (the Royal Horse Guards), he was a natural leader and in that regiment of horsemen one of the best: he twice won the Grand Military Gold Cup as well as many other steeplechases. Although his closest friends must have guessed his sexual orientation such things were never discussed and, provided a homosexual was discreet, were never likely to be.

If Bobbie had formed a discreet liaison with someone of his own class few would have been any the wiser and the cardinal sin of scandal avoided. But in 1929 he was found guilty of a homosexual act with a soldier. To preserve his reputation and that of the regiment, he was reported drunk on duty. His commanding officer told him to resign his commission or face a court martial. It was given out that he had to leave the Army for drunkenness, socially a far more acceptable alternative.

His family believed the lie – especially as, demoralised by the loss of the life he loved, he began to drink more. Nancy agonised constantly over his behaviour but worse was to come. On 13 July 1931, five days before Nancy and Waldorf planned to visit Russia with the writer Bernard Shaw and Nancy's devoted admirer Lord Lothian, Bobbie was told by the police that he was about to be arrested for a homosexual offence.

He had already been warned twice about importuning guardsmen – naturally enough, he knew the pubs they frequented near the barracks. The police told him that they would not be issuing the warrant for his arrest for four days, which would give him plenty of time to leave the country. After a year or so, the charges would be dropped and he would be free to return. But Bobbie decided to go to jail, perhaps through some mistaken idea that this would 'purge' him of his 'sin'. When Nancy heard this she lost control completely, weeping hysterically and clutching the curtains. It was not long, though, before her iron will and talent for practicality reasserted themselves.

As the Astor family owned both *The Times* and the *Observer*, she and Waldorf were able to ensure complete silence in the press – even her enemy Lord Beaverbrook kept it out of his newspapers. Meanwhile, Nancy had to go to her constituency of Plymouth, first to open a big hospital fete and, the following day, to welcome the Prince of Wales there.

Baba – one of whose most salient qualities was loyalty to her friends – immediately sent a note to Bobbie. 'Bobbie dear, I hear you are in trouble. I have tried to find you everywhere but failed. If I can help in any way let me see you. I am in London tonight and tomorrow.' The Prince of Wales wrote a sympathetic letter to Nancy as soon as he heard what had happened. 'Baba and Fruity have told me you knew all about it at Plymouth, and so I should like to say how absolutely marvellously I think you behaved and bore up during that long day of presentations. It does seem a cruel shame that a minute's madness should be victimised when we know of so many who should have "done time" in prison years ago.'

Bobbie's case – again thanks to family influence – was heard quickly. The morning after his arrest he was tried in the Magistrates' Court while Baba, together with Waldorf, Nancy's niece Nancy Lancaster and Nancy, whimpering like an animal, waited in the Astor house in St James's Square for the verdict. Bobbie was given four months' imprisonment; next day Nancy went as planned to Russia.

Prison broke Bobbie. His mental collapse was such that he could not bear the idea of Nancy collecting him on his release. Baba, perfectly prepared to brave any publicity or scandal by association, met him at the prison gate at seven thirty in the morning and took him to the Basil Street Hotel for breakfast. From there, he went to the Astors' house at Sandwich, where he stayed for some weeks. Eventually, after trying several options – and being sent to Paris to avoid the threat of a new case – he settled in a house which Nancy had built for him in Kent.

Tom did not let the state of affairs in the New Party hinder him from his usual forms of enjoyment. The huge weekend parties at Denham continued, as did his pursuit of women, with Georgia Sitwell still in the lead. 'Lunched alone with Tom at the Ritz,' records her diary for 24 June. 'Enjoyed it. Talked politics and ourselves.'

Politics was the dominating subject everywhere. The economy was about to reach crisis point. On 31 July the Government received the report of the May Committee, set up to assess the economic situation, which was found to be far worse than originally thought. The budget deficit for 1932, expected to be around £20 million, would in fact be nearer £170 million. The Committee recommended that taxes should be raised, the pay of all State employees, from Ministers, judges and the Armed Services down to postmen, should be reduced and, crucially, unemployment benefit ('the dole') should be cut by 20 per cent.

For the families of working men who had lost their jobs, this meant malnutrition on a scale unknown since the worst horrors of the previous century; and for a Labour government to accede to it was unthinkable. This gloomy report caused a run on the pound and further unemployment.

Tom had come to believe ever more strongly in individual power through direct contact with the public in the fascist manner ('he conceives of great mass meetings with loudspeakers – 50,000 at a time, wrote Harold Nicolson in his diary). At the end of July 1931 he held a New Party rally at Renishaw Park, the home of his friend Osbert Sitwell. Forty thousand people were present to hear Tom declare: 'We invite you to something new, something dangerous.'

Then, as Britain teetered on the edge of the financial whirlpool, the leader of the New Party, which had so rousingly declared the need for urgent action, went on holiday with his wife.

17

High Life and Low Morals
on the Riviera

~

The Mosleys went as usual to Antibes, arriving on 2 August. When Irene joined them at their villa on the 4th she found them surrounded by a familiar crowd of the ultra-social – Cecil Beaton, Doris Castlerosse, Beatrice Guinness and her daughters Baby and Zita Jungman, Sylvia Ashley, the Michael Arlens. More swarmed in to bathe at Maxine Elliott's villa or sip cocktails, the women in beach pyjamas and pearls, the men in linen trousers and Aertex shirts.

One evening an incident occurred which might have inspired Somerset Maugham's story 'The High Divers' ('The lady climbed up her 8oft ladder and dived into a tiny tank 4 and a half foot deep with flaming petrol burning on the water'). Another evening could have been the inspiration for Noël Coward's song 'I Went to a Marvellous Party' ('Dear Cecil arrived wearing armour, some shells and a black feather boa ... Maureen disappeared and came back in a beard ...') That particular party was given by the couturier Captain Edward Molyneux and faithfully recorded by Irene. 'The nigger band from the Monte Carlo New Casino, a dance floor laid down, everyone in the world there – marvellous fireworks – Noël Coward singing and playing on the piano – Elsie Mendl did a shy-making performance on the dance floor of standing on her head – ring a ring a roses, we all fall down – Oliver Messel caught in an incriminating position with several men...'

And, alas for Irene's good resolutions, Gordon Leith was there too. They spent the evening together and he took her off to the Hôtel de Paris in Monte Carlo, where they got a room. 'Gordon still holds a world of enchantment for me,' she wrote and when Charles Mendl told her that his life had been warped by one woman she said sadly 'like mine by one man'.

She was not too preoccupied to notice Tom's new girlfriend, Lottsie, the wife of the immensely rich Alfred Fabré-Luce of the bank Crédit Lyonnais. Lottsie, petite, fair-haired, blue-eyed and full of merry chatter, was already linked to her new lover by one of the invisible network of liaisons that criss-crossed that tight, raffish little world. Her brother, Prince Jean-Louis de Faucigny-Lucinge, was married to the former Baba d'Erlanger, long-term mistress of Tom Mitford, brother of Diana Guinness, the woman who would soon overshadow Cim's life.

Tom brought his usual energy to the pursuit of Lottsie, who was a willing prey. He would whisk her off to Villefranche when Cim was busy with the children or pursue her to Monte Carlo, ostensibly to see Baba and Fruity who were staying there. Sometimes he would ask her to join the Mosley party and though Cim did her best to keep an eye on them the pair would slip away for hours.

The unhappy Cim was at a loss to know how to deal with the affair, happening in full view of everyone. She alternated between sticking to Tom like a leech whenever Lottsie was around and loftily ignoring her husband's behaviour. Almost invariably, though, rows ensued. Still deeply in love with her husband, she was deliriously happy when one evening he condescended – in Irene's words – to dine alone with her. Later they all went to a nightclub, where Irene weakened sufficiently to sit for a long time talking to Gordon 'and was fiercely eyed by the two Curzon sisters!'

At home the economic situation had reached crisis point. When Austria's biggest bank, Kredit Anstalt, had closed its doors on 18 June 1931 (the French had refused to cancel the punitive German reparations debt), this created a domino effect all over Europe. On 19 August the Cabinet had, after much heated debate, finally agreed the ratio of new taxation to cuts in the social services in a compromise economy package which included a 10 per cent cut in the dole. Then the Conservative and Liberal leaders told Mac-Donald that they would not stand for more than 25 per cent of these measures in the form of new taxation (the previous year, income tax had been raised from 4s in the pound to 4s 6d, and supertax increased also).

This, of course, threw the burden of raising the rest of the money on to cuts in public-service wages – and the dole. The TUC, led by Walter Citrine and Ernest Bevin, was adamant that neither the wages of the low-paid nor the dole should be touched. It was deadlock.

On 22 August, as the Mosley party flocked in a chattering mass around the cocktail bar of the Eden Roc, then drove to St Tropez to buy up everything from fishermen's jerseys to 'droll' hats, Harold Nicolson was leaving the offices of the *Evening Standard* to assume the editorship of the New Party magazine, *Action*. He could not have chosen a worse moment to start a political career. That same day the Cabinet was informed that America would not help with a loan unless the dole were further cut. Unanimously, the Cabinet refused: no Labour Government could pass such a measure. Just before 10 p.m. the following day MacDonald set off for Buckingham Palace intending to resign, and with the resignations of the entire Cabinet in his pocket. But the King had already ascertained from the other two Party leaders that they would be willing to serve in a government headed by MacDonald, and persuaded him to remain in office.

Next day, 24 August, MacDonald told his astonished Cabinet colleagues that he was staying on as Prime Minister of a National Government – a government that would in fact be largely Conservative. To his party, as to his Cabinet colleagues (all but three of whom refused to serve with him) MacDonald's action was seen as a bitter betrayal of all Labour stood for. Within a fortnight, he was expelled from the party.

In Antibes, Tom's pursuit of Lottsie was so blatant that at one moment Cimmie ran out of dinner and down the street in a blind rage. What neither Tom nor Cimmie could have known then was that she had just become pregnant with her third child.

The news of the sudden change of government at home in the following day's newspapers was a welcome diversion. Tom left that afternoon for London; his wife and family remained in Antibes. That night Irene and Cim went to Maxine Elliott's fancy-dress party, after which Cim, who drove herself home at 5.30 a.m., fell asleep at the wheel and, at a hairpin bend, hit the wall of the corniche road – fortunately on the landward side. Next day the round of lunch parties, dinners and nightclubs began again. For Irene, it had all suddenly become too much: the drunkenness, the endless cocktail chatter, the affairs, her sister's unhappiness and the torture of having the man she loved so close to her and yet so inaccessible. She decided to go to America, sent her maid to England for clothes and money – the banknotes were brought over cut in half for safety – and left on the *Augustuz* from Cannes on 4 September.

In London, Nicolson was briefly optimistic, thinking that the New Party might stand a good chance in the general election announced for 27 October 1931. 'Find that we have had orders for 110,000 copies of *Action*,' he wrote in his diary for 12 September. 'This of course is solely on a sale or return basis and does not mean a guaranteed circulation of even half that figure. But it does mean that the newsagents think a priori that there is a prospect of disposing of something like that number.'

Nicolson's elation soon disappeared as he began to realise that the New Party was changing shape. Tom was steadily moving away from the Parliamentary ethic of a Cabinet with the Prime Minister *primus inter pares* towards the concept of the Leader, in whom was vested autocratic powers. He was fascinated by the Italian leader, Mussolini, dictator of his country since 1922. Where most Britons saw Il Duce as a comic-opera figure posing and strutting ridiculously in a series of uniforms, Tom saw a single individual successfully running a country. Where the average Englishman viewed Mussolini's blackshirts as unpleasantly militaristic, Tom saw an escort of muscular young men as a Praetorian guard, allowing the Leader to put his message across in the face of often physical opposition.

When, on 20 September, he addressed an estimated 20,000 people in Glasgow – referring to the Labour Party as 'a Salvation Army that took to its heels on the Day of Judgement' – he was attacked by communists with razors, fought off by his personal bodyguard. 'Tom says this forces us to be fascist and that we no longer need hesitate to create our trained and disciplined force,' noted Harold Nicolson. They differed on the question of uniform: Nicolson, who was becoming more and more unhappy, suggested grey flannel trousers; Tom wanted, and got, black shirts on the *fascisti* lines.

The discussions with Harold Nicolson, the searches for suitable candidates, the plans for what would happen when New Party candidates were in the House of Commons went on apace. Georgia Sitwell's diary for 5 October notes tersely her lunch with Tom at the Ritz: 'Talked of politics'. Three days later, on 8 October, the first issue of *Action* was published – thirty-two tabloid pages selling for 2d.

Action did nothing to sway the voters towards the New Party although Tom's reputation for brilliance and oratory led to approaches to him personally from both Tory and Labour. But though his ideas for the future of the New Party were still inchoate, the appeal of personal power was too strong to resist. He refused all offers, though gloomy about the New Party's electoral chances.

The election of October 1931 was a disaster for the New Party. Its twenty-four candidates, none of whom was elected, were of an appallingly low standard – some barely literate, others disreputable. None, except for Tom, had Parliamentary experience, a lack not compensated for by the sight of boxer Kid Lewis campaigning in tandem with the aesthete Sacheverell Sitwell. In addition, the National Government was already putting into practice many of the Keynesian measures advocated by the New Party which – perhaps because of this – had campaigned on the unappealing premise that: 'We believe that within a measurable time this country will be exposed to the danger of a proletarian revolution. We believe that such a revolution will mean massacre, starvation and collapse. We believe that the one protection against such a disaster is the Corporate State. We shall not cease to proclaim that doctrine.'

A second National Government, Conservative in all but name (the Conservatives won 473 seats), was elected overwhelmingly. MacDonald's part in this was roundly denounced by Beatrice Webb: 'Within the new Ministry are the most prominent enemies of the Labour movement'. Tom, who had stood in Stoke-on-Trent, where Cimmie had made herself so popular, came bottom of the poll with 10,834 votes but managed to save his deposit (one of the only two New Party candidates who did).

Nicolson, who lost his deposit – he polled a mere 461 votes as New Party candidate for the Combined English Universities – found that this crushing defeat did not depress Tom, though he was worried by the amount of money *Action* was losing. His ideas, and his determination to mould his party into the increasingly unpleasant shape he wanted, were as strong as ever. 'Dined Tom at Boulestin's,' wrote Georgia Sitwell, with whom he was having an affair. 'Talked politics. T. at his worst.'

Yet his personal charisma gave his determination an irresistible momentum. 'I am loyal to Tom since I have an affection for him,' wrote Harold Nicolson in his diary on 2 November 1931. 'But I realise his ideas are divergent from my own. He has no political judgment. He believes in fascism. I don't. I loathe it. And I apprehend that the conflict between the intellectual and the physical side of the N.P. may develop into something rather acute.'

Nicolson's perspicacity was all too justified. The idea of a quasi-militaristic youth movement, whose members should be fit, tough and anxious to drill and march, was taking shape in Tom's mind, despite Nicolson's frequent warnings ('In England anything on those lines is doomed to failure and ridicule'). On 23 December, Nicolson had to give notice to the staff of *Action*: its circulation had dropped from an initial 160,000 to less than 20,000 and it was losing money at the rate of £340 a week. The last issue appeared on 31 December.

By the end of 1931 unemployment had reached 2.7 million and exports had halved in value. In Swansea, when Tom arrived to speak at a 3,000-seat cinema booked on a Sunday night by Jack Jones, hundreds of blackshirts had been drafted in from London, Bristol and Cardiff. Setting the future pattern, Tom arrived with a personal bodyguard and walked through lines of his uniformed cohorts to the platform.

The swing towards fascism was too much not only for Nicolson and the students of Glasgow University – when Tom stood for the Rectorship, he came last in a field of five – but also for Jack Jones. When Jones resigned, it was to Cimmie he wrote because of his admiration for her and her hard work in the Ashton-under-Lyne by-election campaign. 'I felt there was one person I'd like to help, and I knew that she would be in need of all the help she could get.'

He was right. Cimmie was finding it difficult to come to terms with the direction in which Tom was taking the rump of the New Party. 'Cimmie wants to put a notice in the Times to the effect that she disassociates herself from Tom's fascist tendencies,' noted Harold Nicolson that December. 'We pass it off as a joke.'

By January she was taking little interest in politics. Five months pregnant, her health poor and her relationship with her husband wretched, she was physically and emotionally low. Tom's sarcasm and bullying, often in public, rendered the vulnerable Cimmie miserable, angry and confused. There had also been an expensive lawsuit in the US over the Leiter millions, which she and Tom had lost.

She was, though, as social as ever, lunching at the Ritz with the Sitwells, unsuspectingly asking Georgia to tea and dining out. At the same time, Georgia was developing a friendship with Baba, whom she had met for the second time at a luncheon party given by Emerald Cunard on 3 February 1932. The next day the Sitwells and Metcalfes made up a party at the Embassy Club, where Georgia danced most of the evening with Fruity.

But it was still a peripheral friendship. The Metcalfes were as deeply involved as ever with the Prince of Wales and most hostesses who entertained him entertained them also. At the end of February 1932, for instance, Emerald Cunard's dinner party for the Prince included the reigning favourite, Mrs Dudley Ward, and Fruity and Baba as well as guests like Lady Londonderry; and when Georgia and Sachie Sitwell went to Quaglino's on 26 February they saw the Prince with Thelma Furness, Fruity and Baba.

Without the challenge and sheer hard work of Westminster life, Tom's superabundant energy needed more of an outlet than party-going and he took up fencing again. He had always loved it and, now that he no longer had the demands of Parliament as an excuse, it also provided the perfect cover for his illicit rendezvous. At the same time, with his days and evenings virtually free, he was able to pursue the promptings of his roving eye, scanning dinner parties and gatherings for likely young married women – the rules of the game stipulated that debutantes, whose reputations would have been ruined by an affair with a notorious philanderer, were strictly off-limits, while the women he chose were no more anxious than he to break up their marriages. The huge bedroom at 22b Ebury Street, with its gusts of warm air that played over the occupants of the large double bed at the touch of a button, was the setting for sex as recreation rather than grand passion.

Just after Christmas 1931, Georgia Sitwell's diary begins to mention the latest addition to London society, the 'golden Guinnesses'. Bryan Guinness was the son of Colonel Walter Guinness (later Lord Moyne), Minister for Agriculture until the previous Labour Government, and Lady Evelyn Guinness, a daughter of Lord Onslow. Besides being extremely rich, he was gentle, good-looking, sensitive, idealistic, a writer of poetry and extraordinarily sweet-natured.

His young wife Diana, the mother of the couple's two small boys, was, like her husband, blonde, but there the similarities ended. Tall and slim, with huge blue eyes, beautiful legs and small, graceful hands and feet, her physical presence was spectacular. She was also a far stronger character than her husband and, though charming, capable of ruthlessness. Brought up in a remote Cotswold village, Diana Mitford (as she then was) was the fourth child of seven, six sisters and one brother, born to Lord and Lady Redesdale. The powerful and unconventional personality of their father and the toughness needed to survive the bullying of the eldest sister, Nancy, had honed a personality with a core of steel.

Although not yet twenty-two, Diana Guinness had already made a great impact on the small, close-knit web of London society. The beauty of her generation, she was also clever and witty with an enormous appetite for life. Adolescent boredom had left her longing for the metropolitan pleasures of concerts, conversation and fun with amusing friends and she had flung herself whole-heartedly into the social life that marriage opened for her. She had a coterie of admirers, many of them her husband's intellectual and aesthetic Oxford friends, whom the Guinnesses entertained constantly in their house in Buckingham Street (now Buckingham Place) near St James's Park. London life, with its chat, its parties, its concerts, museums and art galleries, was still fascinatingly new to her, as were many of the people she met. Her charisma was such that Emerald Cunard had already declared that Mrs Guinness would be her successor as London's leading hostess. She was young and inexperienced – she had married at eighteen – but she was clearly a star.

Diana Guinness and Tom Mosley met at a dinner party on 28 February 1932. Diana, seated next to Tom, argued with him about politics all through dinner. Her convictions had been formed during the General Strike of 1926 when, as a schoolgirl of sixteen, she had felt furiously sympathetic towards the starving miners and their families while deploring any government that could allow such things to happen. After dinner she listened to Cimmie, hugely pregnant, loyally extolling the merits of fascism.

Diana thought little of that first meeting. To Tom, who had already noticed her earlier at a dance, she presented a challenge that he could not pass by.

18

Diana Guinness,
Trophy Mistress

~

After the collapse of the New Party in the 1931 election, Tom was courted by both major parties. The Tory Chief Whip David Margesson asked him to rejoin the Tory Party and, he told Harold Nicolson, he had been approached to lead the Labour Party. Neither of these prospects appealed to him. His mind was finally made up for fascism. As Nicolson wrote: 'He wishes to coordinate all the fascist groups with NUPE and thus form a central fascist body under his own leadership.'

It was a decision towards which Tom had been advancing for several months, reinforced by a visit to Rome three months earlier (in January 1932) with Nicolson and Christopher Hobhouse, one of the many unsuccessful New Party candidates in the election of the previous autumn. He admired the energy and efficiency of the Italian fascists, and he was also conscious of the growing youth movement in Germany.

When he returned to England, the New Party was formally disbanded (at a meeting on 5 April) although its youth section, NUPA, started seven months earlier, was kept on in a reduced form; and his political association with Harold Nicolson came to an end. As Nicolson had written to a friend: 'I do not believe in fascism for England, and cannot consent to be identified with anything of the sort.'

Tom flaunted such identification. Even though fascism, with its growing connotations of violence, was a word offputting to most English ears, he determined that there should be no ambiguity about the new movement he intended to lead. What if the name fascist deterred many? He only wanted true believers, dedicated to his view of Britain's future – and prepared to back him in his quest for personal power. The same motivation led him to brood on the question of a uniform – it eliminated physical expressions of class difference and would allow his 'stewards' to recognise each other. Not least, the quasi-militaristic appeal of a uniform would attract both the young and those happy to raise their fists in defence of his controversial policies.

Cimmie, though she found it difficult to follow Tom in his new enthusiasm, believed that her life was taking a happier turn. The wounding quarrels had subsided and Tom was once more a gay, loving, considerate and witty companion. Her pregnancy had made her depressed and irritable but ironically her ill-health had drawn them together. She had been unwell for months and suffered from fainting spells; now she was diagnosed with serious kidney trouble and a caesarean operation was recommended, which would have resulted in the loss of her baby, too young to survive. 'Tom is faced with the awful dilemma of sacrificing his wife or his child,' wrote Harold Nicolson on 8 March. Bravely, Cimmie took the decision not to have the operation.

What she did not know was that Tom's pursuit of Diana Guinness was proceeding apace. From that first dinner party where they had argued so strenuously, their paths had crossed constantly – at lunches, at dinners, at cocktail parties. It was not long before he had persuaded her to lunch with him – long lunches during which he elaborated on his theories, with all the intellectual clarity and vigour of which he was a master, and with all the animal magnetism that had drawn so many women to his bed.

Diana was a peach ripe for the picking. Desperate to escape the confines of her upbringing into the wider world, she had married, as she thought, for love. Fascinated by Bryan's circle of intellectual and aesthetic Oxford friends, feted by London society, she had found her feet in a world where she felt she belonged – smart, artistic, intelligent and fun-loving. Bryan, by contrast, would have liked nothing better than to lunch or dine every night with his beautiful young wife; Diana found such possessiveness stifling. 'Who ever heard of married couples lunching together?' she would say scornfully.

At the same time, she was conscious that her life lacked direction. She was enthralled by Tom's intellectual brilliance and soon convinced by the force and clarity of his arguments; and when he told her that she alone could help him achieve his objectives, she felt as though she had been enlisted in a crusade. She had found the cause and the man; together, they were irresistible.

Not that Diana Guinness was the sole focus of Tom's attention. He was writing a book, *The Greater Britain*, in which he expounded his ideas and philosophy; and there were also other women friends. Throughout March and much of April, Georgia Sitwell clung resolutely to her position as chief mistress – even if it meant hearing stories of her lover's liaisons over lunches at the Ritz or seeing him with someone else ('saw Tom with Miss Charles at Café de Paris'). Cimmie, near her time, waited quietly at home.

The Mosleys' third child was born on the morning of 25 April 1932, by caesarean section. Tom, his mother Maud Lady Mosley, Baba and Irene were all gathered in Smith Square by eight thirty. The operation was performed at nine fifteen and an hour later her delighted family were shown a healthy curly-haired boy weighing just over 7lb. It was the last real happiness Cimmie would enjoy.

After the birth of her baby, Micky, and blissfully conscious of Tom's attentiveness, she wrote to him – on 11 May, the twelfth anniversary of their wedding – to say what a happy day it had been and how much she wanted the next year to be happy 'for us two as private people and for you publicly. How I long for it to be better than beastly 1931 and how much I want above all else for loveliness and understanding and sympathy to be with us and between us.' A fortnight later, she left for the Villa d'Este to try and regain her health.

Irene, still pining after Gordon and battling against her tendency to seek solace in alcohol, was deeply depressed. To add to her misery, she was suffering from piles. She was worried, too, about the cracks that seemed to be appearing in her younger sister's marriage. Baba had complained of Fruity's 'insane jealousy'; the truth was that the obvious attraction she held for other men, and her response to them, roused all his underlying insecurities. As for Baba, her dominance over him was now well established: when Irene gave Fruity a lift to London one day, he let slip that Baba became angry if he lunched, however innocently, with another woman.

But these disturbances were mild compared with the months ahead. Artur Rubinstein, with whom Irene had been conducting a sporadic but passionate love affair for years, had been less than attentive recently, and at one party even rude and indifferent, though this blow to her pride was soon forgotten in concern over Cimmie, back from the Villa d'Este with a back so painful that she could scarcely sit up, or even lie down flat. At Denham that weekend of 19 June all Cimmie could do was lie and sunbathe though the house was full of friends as usual, and as usual Irene was shocked by the loucheness of the Mosleys' set. 'Georgia and Sachie came to dinner, the talk was nothing but gossip and "muck".'

Worse still, Irene had become aware that her brother-in-law's pursuit of Diana Guinness was serious – and that Cimmie did not know this. On 28 June Irene cancelled lunch with Tom as neither she nor Baba had decided what attitude to adopt.

Tom's affair with Diana was even more intense than Irene or Baba guessed. On 7 July, the Guinnesses gave a house-warming party at their new house in Chelsea, 96 Cheyne Walk, to which they asked all their friends, including the Mosleys. Diana was dazzling in grey chiffon and diamonds that set off her blonde, moon-goddess looks to perfection. At some point during the evening, she and Tom made a commitment to each other – not for marriage, as Tom had made it clear that his marriage to Cimmie was lifelong – but as lovers 'for ever'.

Diana, to whom furtiveness was unknown, made little attempt to conceal the fact that she was seeing Tom. Knowing that marriage was out of the question, she did not see herself as a threat to Cimmie; well aware of Tom's reputation as a philanderer, she assumed – when she thought about it at all – that Cimmie would regard her as just the latest in Tom's line of conquests.

Meanwhile, she was gloriously happy and the disapproval and growing unhappiness of her husband meant little to her, caught up as she was in the heady experience of a grand passion and the thrill of a political cause. In true Mitford fashion, she shared much of her idealism with the sister of whom she was seeing most at that time, the ardently pro-Nazi Unity.

To add to Irene's feeling of being unloved and unwanted, she now learned that the 45-year-old Artur Rubinstein was marrying a girl of twenty-three. Irene had always believed that he would never marry, preferring a life without commitment, and indeed on his wedding morning, after picking up the wedding rings from Asprey's and taking his future brother-in-law to lunch at Quaglino's, he recorded that he was 'suddenly panic-stricken at the thought of losing my freedom'. Generously, Irene bought the happy couple some green candlesticks from Fortnum and Mason's and sent the bride a ruby-and-diamond brooch of her own with a warm and charming letter. The couple's wedding reception on 27 July, given by Lady Cholmondeley, a friend of both Irene's and Rubinstein's, was at 4 p.m. It was a huge and lively affair, packed with ambassadors, writers, musicians, society figures and artists. Rubinstein's young bride Nela, who thought Irene looked 'biggish, handsome and sort of manly', thanked her profusely for her brooch and letter, little suspecting the tumult of emotion behind her gracious public face. When Nela was out of earshot, Rubinstein managed to whisper to Irene that he *must* see her that evening between seven thirty and eight. He was a man who was always deeply concerned about his ex-lovers but as a very wary letter-writer he preferred tête-à-têtes.

The newly-weds then went on to a dinner Rubinstein was giving at Quaglino's where, he later recorded: 'I got really drunk for the first and last time in my life.' But not too drunk to slip away on the pretext, whispered to one of his friends, that he must go and console one of his old flames, desperate that he was getting married. As his biographer points out, while his wedding dinner was actually taking place, Rubinstein was in bed with this unknown woman.

It was, of course, Irene. After the wedding reception she had gone home in a passion of tears, waiting in a state of nervous distress for Rubinstein. 'I got frantic at Arthur who only turned up at 7.50,' records her diary. 'Oh! the agony of that talk when it transpired he once thought of wanting to marry me and he had not the courage because of my name. I told him I would have gone anywhere with him and all the time I felt the urge to keep him, oh! keep him with that blasted dinner hanging over my head.' Later, Rubinstein eventually confessed to friends what had happened. 'I slept with my ex-girlfriend that afternoon. The reason I did it was to prove to myself that I wasn't trapped by my marriage.'

It was back to the bottle again. When she arrived at Cowes at the end of July, she found Cimmie and Baba waiting for her there. 'I had anguish for an hour as with utter sweetness they attacked me on my "trouble" and begged me to get cured. They were really marvellous.' Back in London, she dined with Cim and Tom at Quaglino's and after Tom had left for Paris Cim told her that Tom had been 'exquisite to her since the baby and she had not been so happy for years'.

Next day Irene went with Baba to see Dr Ironsides, a physician with a reputation for assisting patients with such problems. Baba managed to see him alone for half an hour before Irene came into the room and the doctor then tried to persuade her to enter a nursing home or have a nurse at home but Irene fought both these ideas vigorously. Her determination paid off – temporarily. Soon she was in the country, playing tennis and swimming and feeling 'as fit and well and happy as a two year old'.

She was also doing her best to help her brother-in-law. A number of years earlier she and Tom had had what would now be called a one-night stand after a hunt ball at Melton, and his personality and sexual magnetism still exerted a powerful tidal pull on her. His incipient fascism was not yet the brutal, racist affair it was to become, and he expounded his plans to alleviate the misery of the Depression and the wretchedness of the unemployed with idealistic vigour. So when her friend Israel Sieff told her that he was head of a group of fifty equally worried industrialists who were looking for a leader, she promised to put him in touch with Tom, although the meeting had to be postponed when she arrived back from the country to find she had been burgled. By the time the burglars were caught and most of the jewellery found, Cim and Tom had left for their annual European holiday.

In 1932, they took this in Venice instead of Antibes. As Cimmie was still not well enough to travel by car, it was agreed that Tom would drive and she and the children follow by train. What Cimmie did not know was that Tom had arranged to meet Diana Guinness, driving there with her husband and two friends, running into her as if by chance at Arles or Avignon.

But at Avignon Diana developed diphtheria. Terrified that a letter from Tom would arrive at the hotel, she managed to get a message to him through her friends that she would meet him in

Venice when she was well. Tom, who got her message in Arles, drove on to Cannes and, a week later, met the Guinnesses, again as if by chance, on the Venice Lido where all the fashionable world congregated to swim.

For Cimmie, it was a hideous awakening. It was impossible for her not to realise that her husband and Diana Guinness were conducting a passionate affair. They seized every pretext to disappear and, once round a corner, would slip into the nearest gondola to spend the afternoon in one of the little hotels with which Venice abounded, only reappearing, glowing, and with the flimsiest of excuses, at dinner-time. It was the end of the fool's paradise in which Cimmie had been living. Still in pain from her back and the kidney infection, ungainly with the weight she had put on during her pregnancy but not yet shed, and older than the dazzling, elegant Diana by twelve years, Cimmie must have realised that the comparison did not favour her.

She was in agony. 'If only you would be frank with me,' she wrote to Tom after they had returned home. 'If you had said you would like to take Diana out for the day Sunday I would have known where I was. Oh darling, darling, don't let it be like that. I will truly understand if you give me a chance, but I am so kept in the dark. That bloody damnable cursed Ebury [his flat in Ebury Street] – how often does she come there? Do you think I just forgot all about her between the Fortnum and Mason party and last night? I schooled myself the whole week never to even mention her in case I should say something I regret.'

Her misery was compounded by a full confession from Tom. In an effort to reassure her that his continual affairs were no more than diversions, he decided one evening to make a clean breast of them. Cimmie was shattered by his revelations. 'But they are all my best friends!' she wailed. She was so upset that she stayed at home instead of accompanying him to a dinner party; here Tom met his friend Bob Boothby, whom he asked to go and comfort Cim.

'What have you done to her now, Tom?' said Boothby, who loved Cimmie and had watched Tom's affair with Diana unfold in Venice.

'I have told her all the women I have slept with,' replied Tom.

'*All*, Tom?' asked Boothby incredulously.

'Yes, all,' replied Tom. 'Except, of course, for her sister and stepmother' – a reference to his early flings with Grace and Irene.

Ill and miserable, Cimmie went with her two elder children to a spa called Contrexeville in eastern France to try and regain her health and, if possible, her joie de vivre.

While she was away the promised meeting between Tom and Israel Sieff finally took place – an encounter that both found promising. Three weeks later, on 1 October, Tom's book *The Greater Britain* was published. The first edition of 5,000 sold out immediately. Simultaneously, Tom launched the British Union of Fascists, with a flag-unfurling ceremony in the old New Party offices in Great George Street, Westminster. Cimmie made designs for a fascist flag, and both the Mosleys discussed how to turn Sousa's 'Stars and Stripes' into a fascist anthem, with words by their friend Osbert Sitwell.

The British Union of Fascists held its first public meeting on 15 October, in Trafalgar Square, attended by a smallish crowd standing in a fine drizzle. Georgia Sitwell, who had driven back with Sachie after a long beach holiday in Europe, noted rather jealously in her diary for that day: 'Daddy and I went to hear Tom harangue crowd in Trafalgar Square. Few people – and of course Diana G. new girl.' Tom made his speech on the plinth at the bottom of Nelson's Column. He was soberly dressed in a dark suit and tie, with a white shirt, but around him were eight men in black shirts, worn with grey flannel trousers.

Though that first meeting was peaceful, few that followed were. There was shouting and heckling at the next one, on 25 October, in the Memorial Hall in Farringdon Street – and the first hint of a racially divisive policy. 'Fascist hostility to Jews was directed against those who financed communists or who were pursuing an anti-British policy,' said Tom, in his first public reference to Jews. Irene was worried even though Maud, Lady Mosley, who was also there, told her that the reports of trouble were greatly exaggerated.

Three days later, Irene recorded: 'Tom swaggers like a schoolboy ... throwing two lads down the stairs at Farringdon Street. All this swagger and vanity for Mrs Bryan Guinness and Doris Castlerosse. When he is such a magnificent orator and if he had vision could have carried the entire hall with him without descending to these blackshirt rows he seems to revel in. And none of his friends will tell him what a ridiculous figure he makes of himself.' When Israel

Sieff came to see her on 31 October she realised that, in spite of all her efforts at bringing them together, this source of support was now closed. 'I wished he could reclaim Tom and get him out of this awful musical comedyism. After his inane jibe to the heckler as coming from Jerusalem, Sieff told me he was now so bitter he will not give him money for his industrial investigations. Oh! how tactless Tom is. It makes me sick.'

At the end of October the Guinnesses gave a ball at their country house, Biddesden, in Wiltshire. No one, seeing the faces of Tom and Diana as they greeted each other, or the white, wretched countenance of Diana's husband Bryan, could have mistaken the relationship; and, as usual, the lovers disappeared during the evening.

Cimmie, now fitter, was making a determined effort to regain her former looks and style. She had spent time planning her new winter wardrobe, which she bought in Paris. The final touch was an impressive blue fox fur-coat from Bradleys. Whether it would enable her to compete with Diana Guinness was another matter. On 11 November, after lunching with Tom at the Ritz, Georgia Sitwell got a closer look at his new beloved. 'Went to see Diana Guinness, looking lovely. Sensible, human but youthfully arrogant.'

It was a perceptive judgement. Only a few days later, Diana came to a decision that would throw terror into the hearts of all three Curzon sisters. Her marriage, she had come to believe, was a mistake; and she intended to leave her husband. Only someone supremely confident in her ability to survive in a social world hostile to divorce, and uncaring of family and public opinion, would have abandoned a man so kind, good-looking, loving and rich and by whom she had two children.

The Mosleys, who planned a large family Christmas, with Irene, Baba, Fruity and the Metcalfe children, to be followed by a New Year house party, took a house in Yarlington, Somerset, for the holiday. Within two hours of Fruity's arrival at teatime on Christmas Eve, there was a falling-out between him and Baba, who disappeared to bed, refused to come down to dinner, and banished her husband to a dressing-room for the night.

The arrival of Brendan Bracken, Bob Boothby and the Sitwells restored the temperature, and on Christmas Day Fruity insisted on being Father Christmas. Almost at once, the children found his clothes hanging in the downstairs lavatory and the cry went up: 'Father Christmas has left his clothes behind!' Then, from behind his white cottonwool beard came Fruity's unmistakable voice as he sought to distribute the presents: 'Read the bloody names out, I can see nothing!'

Boxing Day afternoon was notable for its discussions and arguments over the New Year's Eve party planned by Cim: what to do and how to conceal it from the gossip columnists, who had already written it up and asked to come down and photograph the guests. Among them, invited by Cimmie – in a spirit of fatalism, bravado or altruistic love for Tom – was Diana Guinness.

19

'Goodbye My Buffy'

~

In January 1933 Diana Guinness took a small house in Eaton Square, just round the corner from Tom's bachelor flat. Although Tom had told both Cimmie and Diana that he did not intend to leave his wife, the Curzon sisters found this hard to believe. To them, the knowledge that this young woman had left her husband and virtually set herself up as a mistress within yards of her lover's pied-à-terre was a clear proof that she intended to lure him away from Cimmie. 'My heart is in my boots over the hell incarnate beloved Cim is going through over Diana Guinness bitching up her life,' wrote Irene. Diana called it 'nailing my colours to the mast'. What was perfectly clear to all of them was that the affair with Diana was different in kind and quality to any of Tom's previous liaisons.

All through that spring, for what remained of her short life, Cimmie suffered bitterly. She knew she was no longer as attractive as she had been and the presence in her husband's life of this young beauty, with her charm, ease of manner and joyous, uncomplicated approach to life, made her feel fearful and defeated. Diana was told by her family and friends that she was ruining her life – her three younger sisters were forbidden to visit her – but she cared not a whit. That Diana was prepared to court social ostracism and set herself up openly as Tom's mistress seemed to Cimmie evidence of the younger woman's implacability, while in Tom's eyes, it could hardly have been a greater compliment.

Cimmie might have worried less had she known that her husband was seeing Baba almost as frequently as he saw Diana. Baba had been fascinated by her brother-in-law ever since, as a schoolgirl of sixteen, she had seen her adored older sister and her glamorous bridegroom as the incarnation of romance. From the start, Tom had treated his sister-in-law with a teasing intimacy, often involving physical horseplay that sometimes went too far ('Baba furious when Tom dropped her in the bath,' wrote Irene on one of these occasions).

Baba's growing interest in matters political and her longing for intelligent company brought her even more under the sway of Tom's powerful personality. Family loyalty apart, she was genuinely fascinated by the political ideas he expounded with such vision and clarity and with Diana Guinness's arrival on the scene, she was able to justify her increasing pleasure in his company by telling herself that any influence other than Diana's was good for her sister's marriage.

As a result Tom, who saw Diana for lunch or dinner two or three times a week, saw Baba almost as frequently. Sometimes he saw both women as well as his wife on the same day, necessitating exactly the kind of emotional juggling he enjoyed. Often all three of them turned up at the fascist meetings he now held regularly, striding on to plinth or platform with a bodyguard of muscular young stewards 'to incite the faithful and intimidate the enemy'.

Fascism, it seemed, was on the march. In Germany the new Chancellor, Adolf Hitler, had been in power since the end of January, his carefully choreographed public meetings evoking a quasi-religious response from a disheartened and impoverished people. Although many older people had voted for the Nazis, the average age of Party members was thirty-two; and much of its message was to youth, a pattern followed by Tom with his call to British youth to throw over the 'tired old men' of the Government.

Not everyone believed that he was on the right track. 'We discussed Mosley's position and I said that his fatal miscalculation was in believing that you could create a youth consciousness in Britain,' wrote Robert Bernays, the Liberal MP for Bristol North, in his diary for 1 March. 'They said too that he had gambled on a course and had not realised how tremendous were the forces that made for stability. Archie Sinclair said his trouble was lack of patience. He had determined, in 1924, to be Prime Minister in 12 years. If he hadn't been in so much of a hurry about it, he could have been.'

Tom, however, saw his future as the powerful, charismatic leader of a political force that would sweep away the old, exhausted parties. After his second visit to Mussolini in April 1933 he wrote in his magazine *The Blackshirt*: 'Fascism is the greatest creed that western civilisation has ever given to the world.'

In the same month Irene also had a significant meeting. She had accepted an invitation from her friends Peter and Mary Hordern to stay at the villa they had taken on Lake Maggiore. The Horderns were already there, but Peter suggested that his brother Bill should drive her out to Italy, with Sheila Graham, a young girl whose father, Miles, was already there.

Miles Graham was a good-looking man of exactly Irene's age, divorced from his wife Evelyn, a daughter of the Earl of Lovelace. Their children, Sheila and Clyde, were largely brought up by Miles's mother Ellen, married to Lord Askwith. Miles was of medium height, his military bearing emphasised by an athletic figure. Good-looking, clever – he had been a scholar at Eton – and virile, he was extremely attractive to women and for years had pursued a successful affair with the society beauty Lady Portarlington. Only those who knew him well realised that he possessed a fiendish temper. He was once supposed to have chased Winnie Portarlington round his drawing-room with a knife.

He was also extremely ambitious. In that spring of 1933, the most important woman in his life was his mother, with whom he had an exceptionally close bond. This powerful personality, who had successfully brought up her own children through her writing, did her best to further Miles's interests in every way possible. Worldly and sophisticated, she regarded his liaison with Lady Portarlington as a feather in his cap rather than a moral blight. Recently, he had been suffering from a mysterious illness that today might have been diagnosed as ME: its main symptoms were exhaustion of mind and body. When he wrote to her on 12 March from his house in Little Stanhope Street that he hoped to go for a month to the Italian lakes 'for sunbathing, which the doctor strongly recommends', Ellen Askwith was delighted.

He added: 'I have been thinking a good deal about politics lately – if only the new businesses succeed and they get used to my absence it might be a good opportunity to find an opening. I am 37 and it's nearly time to begin.' Both of them were to bear this in mind in the months to come.

Irene set off on 12 April with Bill Hordern and Sheila, who had met neither of them before, a prospect her father seemed to think would be appealing rather than terrifying. 'It must be an exciting idea for her to motor across Europe with two unknown people,' he wrote to his mother. 'I know Bill Hordern will be nice to her. Lady Ravensdale I hardly know but they say she likes children. All my best love Mummy darling. I miss you very much sometimes. Your darling Manikin.' In the event, Sheila disliked Irene so much that she put a metal model of Frankfurt Cathedral on Irene's seat in the car, hoping that the spire would wound her in the bottom. Graciously, Irene overlooked it.

Miles soon realised that this hardly-known fellow guest could be one of the most helpful stepping-stones to his planned Westminster career. Irene's dark good looks were in full flower, her energetic tennis-playing appealed to his sporting side and her genuine kindness promised warmth in a stepmother. Above all, her wealth, title and the resonance of the Curzon name would add immense lustre to the pretensions of any would-be Conservative MP.

On 22 April he proposed to her. As her diary records ecstatically: 'Miles strolled in on me at 8.30 and we had our bubbly in Mary's room. Lying on our beds afterwards he whispered into my ear would I give him children and marry him, and of all amazing things in utter calm I said I might. I did not believe myself. He told me with amazing delicacy and loyalty of his plight with Winnie and we beat round how to deal with her.

'After tea I went shopping with Mary and Miles in the car, and I dropped in on Patrick and Loelia [Westminster] before dinner. I could not make out my complete peace after all my years of worry and pain.' Mary all unknowingly had said to her in the morning: 'I wish I could see you and Miles married.' What Irene did not know, and what Miles naturally did not tell her, was that he half-suspected his hostess was in love with him herself.

After a walk to see a pretty little church we talked of Winnie and the great quandary he was in on the way home. I entirely bouleversed Mary with our news. She was wondrous sweet to me in begging me to get married out here quick or else Winnie would come charging out. I shall never forget the beauty of Miles's speech to me in the dining room. He was crying and holding on to my breast and some time he told me I could still take it as a joke and call it all off.

For Irene, tied up for so long in a hopeless love affair, conscious of the passing of time and the dwindling hope of the children she so much longed for, engagement to the personable, sought-after Miles represented sanctuary as well as happiness. Now she would be part of the magic circle, no longer subject to the faint patronising of her younger sisters, no longer regarded as a worry, a burden or a useful stand-in.

At first all was rapture. Two days after they were engaged they became lovers. 'My Wedding Day' wrote Irene at the top of that day's page in her diary, describing how she and Miles had 'climbed the mountain to our little chapel and married each other before the altar' – a detail faithfully reported by Miles to his mother.

Miles, anxious to secure his prize and aware, as Irene was not, of the undercurrents in the villa, urged her to let him get a special licence in Turin and to marry him there. But when she realised the situation, she felt it her duty to stay with the distraught Mary. 'At breakfast Mary was in a bad state of nerves and jabbered at Peter and when she went out Peter, Miles and I knew it was because she was in love with Miles, and her behaviour in handing him over to me had been a fearful strain.'

But nothing dimmed Irene's happiness, though she could not help noticing her sisters' differing, and characteristic, reactions to the news of her engagement – the one all warmth and excitement, the other coolly analytical.

Beloved Cim rang up from Denham, hysterical with joy and said Nanny and Andrée [Cimmie's former lady's maid and now house-keeper at Denham] had cried for half an hour. She gave a heavenly joy in her talk and took it as a lovely fairy story.

Baba from Paris a few moments later was much more froide and comme il faut and said what was his business and his appearance and who or what was he. Not much of Cim's lovely warm thrill. Peter and Mary had dined upstairs which gave Miles and me a chance of peace alone downstairs.

Mary behaved like a jealous child, unwilling to give up its toy. A mere week after Irene's engagement she found her hostess hysterical, wild and screaming, refusing to allow her husband into the room. Irene managed to calm her eventually and tried to console the wretched Peter.

> Then we talked the matter over [she wrote that night]. We all knew the basis of it. She is madly in love with Miles. I felt she had staged the whole scene.
>
> My happiness was shattered when Miles took me to my room by him walking up and down in a frenzy and saying I had better call it off. Obviously I was only obsessed by him temporarily and I was doubtful of him. Mary had told him I was uncertain how good a mind he had got. Oh! the cruelty of it. Spent a nightmarish night, feeling desolate and wanting to chuck it all. I nearly went mad.

Next day everything was sunshine again, with Miles back on form, chat, giggling, games of backgammon, gaiety and fun and telegrams of congratulation from the two eldest Mosley children, and Tom 'who hoped for a lot of little barons'. There was even a 'marvellous' letter from his mother that brought tears to her eyes.

Mary was not done yet. She did everything she could to sabotage Irene's happiness, from telling her that Miles was making up to another female guest to running him down in every way. When Mary's husband Peter agreed with this judgement, calling Miles slick, a libertine and no companion for Irene at all, she was plunged in gloom but managed to dress for dinner in a devastating black dress and diamonds.

After dinner Miles, unable to guess what was wrong with her, came in to see her. 'I lay holding his hand in dumb crying agony. I asked him to lie in the other bed and hold my hand all night. When he went back to undress Mary charged in on him and slated him and called him a cad and a brute and if he would not be nice to her she would ruin him and me and never stop working against us.'

Mary continued to do her best to prise Miles away from Irene, bombarding him with letters and saying that Irene had told her he was 'no good sexually to her' – a canard she quickly disposed of. Irene would have been even happier had she seen the entry in Lady Askwith's diary: 'A perfectly delightful letter – the letter of my dreams – from Irene'.

15. Baba and Fruity's wedding, 21 July 1925, at the Chapel Royal, St James's Palace

16. Cimmie speaking on Tom's behalf in December 1926 in the Smethwick by-election

17. The successful Labour candidate at Smethwick and his wife, 22 December 1926

18. Fruity, Baba and Monica Sheriffe at a meet near Melton Mowbray

19.
Paula Casa Maury (one of Tom's many mistresses), Bobbie Shaw, Baba and Fruity in the grounds of Craven Lodge, Melton Mowbray, 1928

20.
Irene standing on the running board of her Rolls as she waits for her groom, Fox, to bring her horse to a meet at Sproxton, near Melton Mowbray, January 1927

21. *(facing page)* Prince George (later Duke of Kent, standing), the Prince of Wales and Fruity at breakfast on the balcony of the house at Sandwich taken for golf, summer 1929

22. Fruity and Baba at the Derby, 3 June 1931

23. Fort Belvedere

24. A poolside party at The Fort, in a photograph taken by Baba in summer 1933, including Dickie Mountbatten (second from left), sitting next to the Duke of York. Thelma Furness sits at the feet of the Duchess of York.

25. The Prince of Wales competing with Nancy Astor in the semi-final of a Parliamentary golf tournament in 1933. HRH won comfortably.

26. Count Dino Grandi

She and Miles decided that the only thing to do was to go away together. 'From then on the world – my world – seemed to expand in peace and beauty ... it was delicious dressing myself to look my best and going down to dinner with Miles. We got the band to play which got us all "woosy".' The only sore spot was a telegram from Lady Portarlington claiming that she had only heard of their engagement at a dinner party, to which Miles wired back tartly that he had written to her before anyone else and the letter must have gone astray. 'Yet another letter gone astray,' she responded equally crisply.

Irene, who thought that Win Portarlington was probably lying, tried to smooth matters over by persuading Miles to let her write a letter saying that every effort had been made to tell her before anyone, after what she had meant to him for years, and together they took the letter to the post. On the way back, hearing music they dropped in at a bar where people were dancing. 'They played Tauber again for us and the man crooned and oh! it was heaven, and the moon and the nightingales from our balcony before we went to bed were the Garden of Eden. The nightingales chortled all night.' It was to be their last uncomplicatedly happy evening.

Soon these dramatic events would pale into insignificance. At home, Cimmie, who had had kidney trouble for several months, had begun to feel other symptoms of illness. She was passing water all the time and had a severe pain in the lower part of her abdomen. Thinking it might be appendicitis, she went to her doctor.

It was an era when operations to remove the appendix were medically fashionable but riskier than today because there were as yet no antibiotics. Cimmie had had a presentiment that her condition might not be straightforward, telling Lady Mosley and Andrée that she was frightened. 'I don't think I'm going to get well,' she said. To Andrée she added: 'I have been fearfully unhappy.'

Her operation, performed on 9 May 1933, appeared to go well. After it, Tom went straight round to Diana's little house for lunch. One of the other guests – only six could fit in the dining room – was Unity Mitford.

The following day, Miles gave the house party on Lake Maggiore a shock by reading out of the *Continental Daily Mail* the news that Cim had been operated on for appendicitis the day before and was doing well. Irene, who wired Tom in a frenzy, got a reassuring response although she wept when she realised that it probably meant no Cimmie at her wedding. 'Baba and Fruity mean nothing to me at it,' she wrote that night.

Another telegram from Tom told her that Cim had had a bad night but that progress, though slow, was definite. Irene's worry was such that she could not sleep; the following morning she and Miles wired Tom to ask whether they should postpone their wedding or go ahead with it, as planned, either on 22 or 23 May. It crossed with a telegram from Tom that arrived in the early evening: 'Cim very seriously ill. Baba and doctors do not suggest your coming home. Will wire further developments.'

Irene, demented with worry, tried to ring Tom's mother's flat, a long-drawn-out performance in those days when every call had to go through an operator – several, in the case of a foreign country. As they spoke, Tom arrived from the nursing home near by and, taking the telephone from his mother, told Irene that Cimmie's appendix had perforated and peritonitis had set in. 'Her strength was poor but she was holding her own. He would not urge me to come home but I must do what I felt like,' records her diary.

Though terrified of flying Irene was determined to get home as quickly as possible; within minutes, Miles had found out the times of flights and connecting trains. Her maid Violet packed one small suitcase for them both; at seven the following morning, 15 May, they began the long journey by train and plane, with several changes, finally arriving at Croydon airfield at 9.05 p.m., to be met by 'sweet Baba, a little lone figure'. They went direct to Deanery Street. 'Miles seemed to like my house and old Winks,' wrote Irene, 'and we were so happy with each other that last evening before doom broke over us.'

At 7.30 next morning, 16 May, Lady Mosley telephoned. Cim was going downhill. After a better night she had had a relapse at 7 a.m. and was being given saline injections as she was too weak for a blood transfusion. Without disturbing Miles, Irene dressed quickly and rushed to Lady Mosley's flat where they ate a hurried breakfast. Tom, who dropped in for a quick wash, told them not to come to the nursing home. Then Baba appeared, icy cold in manner, and walked back there arm in arm with Tom. Fruity was the next arrival and for an hour Lady Mosley and Irene had to listen to him until they crammed on their hats and made their way to the nursing home, where they sat in the waiting room while telephones rang and nurses scurried in and out.

Tom appeared, to ask Irene wretchedly if she wanted to see Cim – or would Irene rather remember her as she had been, radiant and lovely? Breaking off suddenly, he asked Irene and Andrée to fetch the flowers that had been sent from Denham to Lady Mosley's flat, to put beside Cim's bed. Baba sat on a chair placed directly outside Cim's door. After a while Miles and Fruity turned up; Irene sent them to Lady Mosley's flat for lunch, going back there herself for a cup of coffee before sending the two men off for a walk round the Park and telephoning Nanny Hyslop that the outlook was bleak.

'Oh! that afternoon of horror,' wrote Irene in her diary. 'Ma [Lady Mosley], Andrée and I crouched outside that door while my angel breathed her last few hours. Poor Tom came out once or twice and said he could get nothing through to her. If only the doctors had warned him she was going he had so much to tell her and now he was trying to get through to her how magnificent her life had been in its splendour and fulfilment. She had said to him that morning: "I am going. Goodbye my Buffy," which she always said when he walked away through the garden at Denham.'

Even at this extreme moment the jealousies and antagonisms between oldest and youngest sister made themselves felt. 'Baba sat in broken solitude in the bathroom and try as I would to hold on to her hand she turned away from every advance.' What Irene wrote next in her diary explains this coldness. 'Ma told me, alas! alas! Cim had got her to read my last letter to her and so of course she read: "I only want you, not Baba at my wedding. Miles is a worker, thank God! not like Fruity. If Miles turns to Baba and not you to turn me out smartly I shall kill him."'

'My precious got weaker and weaker and oh! her stertorous breathing in the last half hour was torture to hear through the crack in the door where I could just see in the mirror Tom murmuring to her his last words of love.'

They learned from the doctor that from the start Cimmie had put up no sort of a fight. Both mentally and physically, he told them, she had never lifted a finger to live. All of them felt they knew why: Cimmie, who had fought for so long to keep her marriage going, believed that she had finally lost the battle and that Diana Guinness had taken her husband from her. From then on, those closest to Cimmie viewed Diana as directly responsible for her death.

Cimmie's body was taken to Smith Square, where lilies, roses and lilies-of-the-valley surrounded the coffin, with a garland of roses plaited by Lady Diana Cooper trailing from it. Lady Mosley, Miles, Nanny and Irene knelt to pray at the foot and Irene swore to her dead sister that she would never fail her.

That day Georgia Sitwell, Tom's former mistress and wife of the Mosleys' friend Sacheverell, who had spent a wretched night thinking of Cim, went to see Andrée. 'Despite her hatred of Tom she said no one knows how wonderful he has been. He spent every minute with her for a week. He talked to her for hours and hours as she lay dying and Andrée thinks she understood.'

Miles and Irene, who had been comforting the Mosley children, did their best to keep up the children's spirits through lunch. After it, Miles went to rest in the spare room. When he came down Irene could think of nothing to say to him. She sent him home and tried to get hold of Elinor Glyn, to whom she and Cimmie always turned in times of crisis, but she was out. Baba drove Tom down to lunch at Denham before they visited the Cliveden chapel together, where Cimmie's body now lay. Later Baba and Tom came to dine with Miles and Irene at Deanery Street, where they talked of Irene's trousseau, with Baba telling Irene how to improve her style.

So good was the rapport between them that evening that later, in the drawing-room, Irene poured out all her worries over her seeming inability to respond to Miles after their blissful time in Italy. 'Baba's sweetness, her understanding of marriage were a revelation to me and gave me back the balance and calm I was losing. I could not believe I had found such common sense and sympathy in her after all those years of coldness and before the men came in, we talked on Tom, the children, Diana Guinness in a barrierless spirit of understanding. I thanked God! When she phoned Tom was already in bed at Denham. With renewed peace in my heart, Miles and I got back to understanding and Italy, all barriers down and he said indelibly lovely things to my broken spirit.'

Next day she gave away to her maid Violet, her housekeeper Mrs Shaw and the other servants all the clothes in her wardrobe that Miles, determined to smarten up his future wife, had ruthlessly discarded at the villa on Lake Maggiore.

Baba's extreme closeness to her bereaved brother-in-law was already beginning to worry Fruity – Irene noticed how edgy they were with each other but supported her sister. Baba must go to Cliveden with Tom if he wanted her to, said Irene; they must stand by and patiently wait as she was the one person on whom Tom depended for everything.

On 19 May there was a short memorial service for Cimmie at St Margaret's, Westminster, Tom carrying gardenias and the children's posies of flowers laid on strips of brocade. 'Unbearably sad,' wrote Georgia Sitwell. 'I howled.' Miles, who had tactfully declined to be present, waited outside for Irene in his car and drove her home for lunch, where they were joined by Baba and Fruity. After getting her hair and nails done, Irene went to see Elinor Glyn, who had adored Cimmie. 'We had a heartbroken talk and she read me her article on Cim for the *Sunday Graphic*. Elinor is always a great and devoted soul to us children.'

Life gradually resumed its pattern. Baba did her best to find her sister appropriate clothes for the new married life ahead and Irene nervously met her future mother-in-law and sister-in-law, Betty, over tea. Then came a visit with Miles to Baba and Fruity at their country house at Coombe in Surrey, where Irene's nerves began to jangle yet again when she sensed that her sister and her fiancé were dissecting her together after dinner while she and Fruity were playing the gramophone in another room. When she tackled Miles, he told her that Baba, known for her chic, could give her good advice on clothes that would set off her beautiful face. 'I only say all this to you because I'm so proud of you,' he added. Irene melted, and allowed Baba to take her to Fortum & Mason to choose lingerie, and to Cartiers for a wedding ring on the pattern of her own.

However she could not suppress her anxieties. Miles's indifferent health and languidness worried her – and her deepest emotions were still for Gordon. Again, she poured her worries out to Baba, who became scared and miserable for her sister in her turn. But the practical Baba was determined to do more than wallow in

Irene's neuroses. She went to see Gordon, evoking from Irene the grateful diary entry: 'She has helped me marvellously. I was nearly out of my mind.'

What chiefly worried Irene was Miles's apparent coolness. He was often aloof and distrait, complaining of fatigue and treating her, she thought, more like a sister than a beloved. Lady Askwith also sensed problems, writing in her diary: 'Liked Irene immensely but felt anxious. She is very charming and easy to get on with and sensible. Pray God it goes right.'

The fatigue Miles complained of masked something more serious. Still in love with Lady Portarlington, he was finding it more and more difficult to sustain this engagement undertaken largely for the sake of his career. Slowly, it was beginning to unravel.

By the end of May 1933 Irene feared the worst. Their relationship seemed to be splintering against the rock of Miles's indifference. As it disintegrated, there were endless agonised discussions, icy kisses and quarrels that left Irene traumatised but Miles indifferent. 'Nothing ever remains or makes any impression on my mind or troubles me for any length of time,' he remarked after one such contretemps, bouncing off her bed and leaving the room. Again, it was Baba who resolved the situation, while Irene and Miles were staying with the Metcalfes. After another tortured talk Baba went in search of Miles and found him sunbathing by the tennis courts. She told him she thought he should leave.

It was the end. There was a painful talk with Irene in his room before lunch and another in the woods afterwards, where Miles apologised pitiably for hurting her, but saying that unless either party felt they could not get on without the other it was hopeless. Both wept bitterly and Irene fled in order not to say goodbye.

Baba tried to comfort her sister with the ambivalent remark that she must not be so miserable – after all, it was not as though Miles had been expressing undying love – but that they must strive to remain dear friends. As she pointed out to their luncheon guest, Lord Castlerosse, who had come to play golf with Fruity, there were many ways in which Miles was not right for her sister.

Irene's feelings for Miles remained strong for some time. When she heard Baba talking to him on the telephone she felt a terrible pang of misery. She had wasted years of her life in an unhappy and fruitless love affair with Gordon and the thought of what could be her last chance of happiness slipping away demoralised her. Lady Askwith too was sad when she received a letter from her son saying that the engagement was over. 'I am very disappointed and unhappy,' she wrote in her diary. 'I liked her so much – I thought Miles's happiness was secure and my anxieties over. Well, God's will be done.'

Soon, it was Irene's turn to help her sister. Staying with Fruity and Baba at Sandwich for gold in mid-June, she was startled when her sister returned unexpectedly to the house, weeping. Fruity had become furiously jealous over one of their golfing four, who had been invited to supper. Irene talked to Fruity, who would not listen, then she wrote to him, spelling out every point with a lucid clarity which she was incapable of bringing to her own affairs: Fruity's age compared with that of Baba, the unreasonableness of expecting such a beautiful and intelligent woman to go through life without being spoken to or made much of. He was lucky, she told him firmly, to have had such single-minded love for so long and he must not allow it to be crushed by a molehill. With Baba's approval, she pushed the note under Fruity's door.

Next morning he thanked her for her sweet letter and said that though he saw all her points, to him Baba's flirtation was more than a simple crush and ultimately it would hurt both of them. But Fruity stuck to his guns. 'Move him I could not,' commented Irene, adding that she had a feeling Miles would have been equally mulish in the same situation.

Soon Fruity would have much more reason for complaint.

20

Keeping It in the Family

~

When Irene and the Metcalfe family returned to London, plans began in earnest for their various holidays. When Tom, at his most charming, arrived for dinner one evening in June, Irene discovered that she was to be pressed into service looking after both Mosley and Metcalfe children. After he had gone, Baba came to Irene's bedroom for a chat.

Here she disclosed that Tom had asked her to accompany him on a motoring trip through Bavaria that August and that she was apprehensive of Fruity's reaction if she asked for a fortnight's 'leave' for the trip. The obvious solution was for one or two other people to join them but when she suggested this to Tom later that June evening, he made it perfectly clear that he wanted Baba on her own – or no one.

Anxious though everyone was to console Tom after his terrible loss, it seemed an extraordinary arrangement. Irene, remembering her own brief entanglement with him, was uneasy. Baba, she felt, was playing with fire. Thus she was astonished when Lady Mosley telephoned to beg Baba to go away with her son. Otherwise, said Lady Mosley ominously, a *third party* might go with him. The idea of Diana whisking him off was anathema to all three women and Irene came to the reluctant conclusion that better 'poor Baba' than 'the horror'. Anyway, could Tom even contemplate Baba as a sexual stopgap when he still appeared so grief-stricken over Cim?

Lady Mosley's fears seemed to be justified when Baba rang Tom up on a day when he was supposed to be at Denham and found he had gone to London. The sisters assumed, correctly, that there could be only one reason: Diana. Filled with foreboding, Irene rang Lady Mosley, who confided that she was 'terrified the horror had sent for Tom after her divorce was through and that she was doing everything to capture him'.

In fact, Diana was indifferent as to whether she married Tom or not but the sisters would not have believed this had they known the truth. For a well-brought-up young woman with two small children to be content to remain a mistress to a widower – and a notorious lecher – was something they could not comprehend.

Tom's visit to Diana gave Baba further justification for her determination to set off with him. She had been half in love with him for years and, without the taboo of her sister's marriage, her underlying obsession with him surfaced, fuelled by the powerful libido she had inherited from her father, the intense intimacy of the past few weeks and the sudden reliance on herself of Tom, normally so strong and self-sufficient.

But she was not accustomed to playing second fiddle, least of all to the hated Diana, and she was not prepared to embark on the longed-for trip without clearing this up. Her pretext for this was her well-developed sense of *comme il faut*: if Tom *was* seeing Diana, it was a flagrant gesture of brutal disrespect to the late wife he professed to love so deeply and she could not help him – or provide company on his trip – if he continued to do so. It was not hard to carry Irene with her on this.

Irene and Lady Mosley met to discuss the Diana question. Tom, said his mother, had asked her to tell his sisters-in-law that he did not contemplate seeing Diana after his trip with Baba. Lady Mosley added that she had reported to him what she had heard: that Diana had said she was out to get him and that those who knew her said she was the most determined minx and talked freely to everyone. Tom refused to believe any of these tales; Diana, he said, was dignified and sweet and would never chatter loosely like that. Hearing this, Lady Mosley wept and said Tom was so marvellous to his children that perhaps Cim had died to save his soul. 'I wondered!' wrote Irene, more cynical where Tom was concerned.

Tom, who found the idea of persuading the conventional Baba to come away with him on a such a risqué trip irresistible, had a ready answer for her doubts. With his usual facility, during one of their intimate dinners, he convinced Baba that seeing Diana was an obligation, like others he had had to take on after Cimmie's death, and that he could not shirk it. There was, he assured her, nothing in it; their relations were platonic. Baba could not make Tom see how cruel such meetings were to the memory of Cim.

Behind Baba's loathing of Diana lay an intense sexual and emotional jealousy. Her rationale for trying to make Tom, who was, after all, a widower, stop seeing Diana, newly divorced and equally free, was that 'people would not stand for it, and his future would be destroyed'.

On 27 June the Prince of Wales, bringing his brother Prince George with him, came to stay at the house the Metcalfes had taken at Sandwich, on the Kent coast, for golf. The princes, driving their own car, without either valet or equerry, arrived so much later than expected, at 2 a.m., that the Metcalfes and Irene had already gone to bed. A few days after the royal brothers left, the party, augmented by Tom, broke up, setting off in two cars for London.

Once again, Baba and Tom drove together, followed in the Metcalfe Rolls by Irene and a highly disgruntled Fruity. His wife, he felt, was becoming far too close to Tom. All the way to London he muttered angrily about 'this Tom hysteria', and Baba's 'sacrifice' to Tom in watching and guarding him. Fruity thought this was rubbish and Tom's behaviour hypocritical – Tom himself was responsible for Cim's death by his cruelty. At the house, Irene's thoughts ran on a different track: Baba told her that during the drive up Tom had promised over and over again to put Diana Guinness right out of his life. 'I wonder for how long?' thought Irene dubiously. 'Oh! if only for ever!'

Baba's plans for the rest of the summer did not include her children. Returning from a brief visit to Scotland on 10 July, her first engagement was a meeting to organise the day nursery to be set up in Cimmie's memory in Kennington. Both she and Irene looked 'illish', noted Georgia Sitwell, one of the friends co-opted for the project (the nursery eventually cost £5,000 to build; except for £1,990 from Lambeth Council, all the money was raised by Cimmie's friends). This decided, Baba began to prepare for a pleasurable summer ahead, flinging herself into beauty treatments, making telephone calls, seeing friends and finally, tactlessly, asking the childless Irene how she could get the new nanny trained. After her trip with Tom she must go to Scotland and also to America! 'Must?' wrote Irene bitterly. 'Why? and her children to be seen to!'

As the summer passed Tom and Baba's increasing intimacy was unmistakable. Tom walked with Baba on the Savehay lawn in the warm evenings, his arm around her waist, whispering into her ear. When together, they had attention for no one else. After one occasion, dining with Lady Mosley, Tom and Baba, Irene wrote: 'Ma and I were embarrassed to a degree as Baba and he gabbled in each other's faces and occasionally flung us a perfunctory remark.' When they were alone together, Lady Mosley reported that after much arguing Tom had finally told Diana Guinness there was no place for her in his life and refused to see her again for a while.

At Denham the following weekend, 15 July, Irene began to wonder if Cimmie's death really had changed her brother-in-law. His attitude to his children was certainly different: at lunch he talked to Vivien about her school, afterwards he played with the eighteen-month-old Micky on the lawn. What struck her most forcibly was that he showed to Baba a consideration and kindness she had never seen him employ towards Cim. Perhaps a close relationship with Baba, even if it seemed temporarily to go a bit too far, was the lesser of two evils. 'I pray this obsession for Baba will utterly oust Diana Guinness,' she wrote before driving up to London to watch Tom massing his followers in Eaton Square before setting out on a march.

Baba's excitement at the coming trip with Tom had not altered either her dominating nature or her belief that her household should be run like clockwork even on a seaside holiday. Just before Irene left on a three-week Mediterranean cruise on the White Star liner *Homeric*, she was upset by 'a rude and peremptory letter from Baba' forbidding her to take her beloved old Sealyham Winks to the house at Angmering, on the Sussex coast, where she was to look after Baba's children.

Baba, setting off alone with Tom across France in early August, plunged almost at once into a passionate love affair. For Tom, seducing this beautiful, sophisticated woman was part game, part challenge. Domination and sexuality were an intrinsic part of his being. Even his politics were sexualised, with their macho symbols of uniform, marching and insistence on virile youth. The conquest of a woman who herself was a charismatic, dominating figure – whether of her husband, her household, or a dinner table – was especially sweet. Then, too, there was the link with her dead sister, whom he had loved deeply despite his constant betrayals. To this unremitting sexual adventurer, the thought that he was sleeping with his wife's sister must have added an agreeable touch of forbidden fruit, with its *frisson* of incest. Then, too, it embodied a full-blown tease of the malicious kind he so enjoyed: poor Fruity, despite his anger, could do nothing to prevent it.

Baba tried to rationalise her behaviour by telling herself that going to bed with Tom would get him away from the hated Diana Guinness. But she was too clear-sighted not to realise that to sleep with her dead sister's husband within three months of her funeral, abandoning her own husband and children to do so, could hardly be justified morally. Internally, she must have been torn apart. The principles of her upbringing had been firmly rooted. Loyalty – which of course extended to her husband – was one of the strongest strands of her nature. Later, she was to exhibit not only guilt but a sense of shame: she was too wordly-wise not to realise that most people were horrified that she should fall precipitously into the arms of the man who had caused her sister such terrible suffering.

Tom had told Cimmie (truthfully) that his endless affairs meant little: such sexual flings, he confided to his new love, Diana Guinness, were tremendous fun, to be treated almost as a joke. What was not a joke was if somebody, somebody of calibre, fell for him seriously. Diana's own open commitment had not only flattered him enormously but brought him to a degree of commitment himself. Now here was Baba, lovely, clever, desired, deeply in love with him and a constant reminder of the dead wife he had treated so badly. Keeping Baba happy, he could tell himself, was a form of recompense to Cimmie. Besides, there was the sheer delight of enjoying two such trophy mistresses simultaneously.

Irene spent most of September in Angmering while Baba was in Scotland, with her nephews and nieces. The children thought their 'Auntie Ni' wonderful: she let them play wild games, took David shrimping and unlike their mother showed them much overt affection. When they looked for hermit crabs David remarked thoughtfully: 'Mummy would never carry this seaweed for me.' Irene wrote her sister an eight-page letter about her children's doings, also noting: 'How can Baba go and leave those priceless children when they are so profoundly interesting in their development?'

Tom was now in high favour with Irene, thanks to his apparent change of persona. She supported him in his political efforts, visiting the new headquarters of his British Union of Fascists, which she had promised to spruce up. It was at 243 Battersea Park Road, formerly the Whitelands Teachers' Training College but now known as the Black House; in it lived the top echelon of the BUF and about fifty young rank-and-file Blackshirts, who drilled and trained under military-style discipline. She was delighted when Tom came to dinner at the end of September and described two successful meetings at Ashford and Aylesbury at which a number of farmers had been enrolled. 'We had a wonderful evening of talk but he broke my heart when he said life was over, he wanted to put fascism on the map and he did not mind if a bullet met him,' she wrote in her diary that night. 'He says Cim talks to him and is always by his side. We had great talks on Baba and Fruity and their future.'

Somehow, Irene had managed to convince herself that 'sweet Tom' and her sister were the injured parties in the emotional triangle of the two Metcalfes and Mosley, and that poor jealous Fruity was the one who should see reason. She told her brother-in-law that, Tom or no Tom, it was his tantrums that were damaging their marriage. For eight years, she said, warming to her theme, Baba had been sweet to him and spoilt him but her intellect was starved, so no wonder she blossomed with Tom. If Fruity did not accept their friendship, it would cause a deep rift.

When, in early October, Irene went with twelve-year-old Viv to Smith Square to pack up Cim's treasures, her heart was further wrung. The flood of misery when she looked at the photographs of her sister, so fresh and young and alive, turned to sympathy for Tom when he had to lie flat on his back in his Ebury Street flat with lumbago, and for several days she sent him all his meals. (She herself was having back trouble at the time, visiting the famous Dr Cyriax almost daily.)

Harold Nicolson also thought Tom had changed, writing in his diary for 11 October 1933: 'Whenever anything happens to remind him of Cimmie, a spasm of pain twitches across his face. He looked ill and pasty. He has become an excellent father and plays with the children. Cimmie's body is still in the chapel at Cliveden and he visits it once a week. It is to be buried at Denham in a high sarcophagus in a wood. Irene said that the children said to her: "We don't cry when you talk to us about Mummy, but we always cry when we talk about her among ourselves." '

By the 15th, however, Tom had recovered sufficiently to lead the fascist march past the Cenotaph in Manchester, watched by Irene, though because of his bad back he only walked a short distance. At 8 p.m. there was a big meeting at the Free Trade Hall for which Prince Paul of Greece and the Mosleys' friend Zita James arrived to stay at the Midland Hotel. Outside the hall stood a huge crowd, some of whom were communists. Inside were about nine thousand people, hedged about with two thousand Blackshirts. Tom entered in his usual dramatic fashion, marching down the main aisle with a powerful floodlight on him and mounting the rostrum amidst tremendous cheering. The meeting, save for two fights in the middle when five people were ejected, went smoothly.

Irene's public work and good causes continued. She was the first woman to speak at the Annual Gala in commemoration of Magna Carta at Runnymede, she had been the only white woman to attend the Emperor of Abyssinia's coronation in November 1930, and she was as active as ever in her East End club work. She was also involved with the Shilling Theatre Company, which aimed to bring good plays and performances within reach of the poor – a growing number in that era of unemployment. Seats cost only 1s 3d (the 3d was entertainment tax), there were two performances a night and a new play was put on every week with well-known actors. The company played in the Fulham Theatre by Putney Bridge, where Irene, who subsidised it heavily, organised the painting of the interior in a bright grass green to set off the heavy gilt ceiling, ready for its opening date on the 23rd.

Her main concern was Tom's children. She was the one to drive Nick back to school – lunching afterwards with her old beau Artur Rubinstein – who took Micky and Viv to the Metcalfe twins' birthday party, who sympathised with Tom when he had a return of his old enemy, phlebitis. She herself was suffering from the rheumatism that had attacked so many of her hunting friends after their numerous falls, but recovered in time to spend the following weekend at Cliveden. It would bring Fruity further cause for jealousy, and Baba another lover – Mussolini's Ambassador to London, Count Dino Grandi.

Ironically, it was Irene who met him first, sitting between the count and Walter Elliot at dinner. On Signor Grandi's other side was Nancy Astor's sister Irene Gibson, famed for her beauty twenty years earlier but extraordinarily irritating to Irene for the 'garrulous Langhorne fluffy stuff' that she talked to Grandi while Irene longed for some serious political discussion. When she and Grandi did began to talk he found him full of charm and distinction. 'He was thrilling on Tom. He watches every move of Tom's and as the press gives no fair verdict of his speeches, writes home himself the truth. He predicted the spread of fascism here after a Labour government. He spoke reverently of Cim and asked to go to the chapel.'

Grandi had that quality essential in a successful diplomat: the gift of saying exactly what all those to whom he wished to appeal wanted to hear. At thirty-eight he was young for an ambassador; he had joined Mussolini early on in his career and was one of the four fascist leaders who had led the march on Rome in 1923. Two years later he became a Minister in the Italian Foreign Office, where he showed great skill as a diplomat, communicating Italy's keenness on disarmament to the League of Nations while at home convincing Mussolini of the need to build up her military strength. His success brought him a title and Italy's highest decoration, the Order of the Annunciata. When, in 1932, he became Ambassador in London, he saw his job mainly as a propagandist for fascism.

Grandi was intensely social, full of charm, and a convinced anglophile (his first thought on arriving in England was that he was in the country which had beaten Napoleon). He quickly became London's most popular Ambassador and the darling of what became known as 'the Cliveden Set'. He entertained frequently at his sumptuous Embassy in Grosvenor Square, the former home of the Fitzwilliam family, where guests marvelled at the eighty-two rare museum pieces – tapestries and mirrors from the court of the Medicis, six of them from the Uffizi Gallery, silver candelabra made for the Bourbon kings of Naples. The fifty pictures included two Titians and some rare works of the primitive school; in the entrance hall stood an agate and lapis lazuli table from the Barberini Palace flanked by a 2,000-year-old statue of a boy riding a seahorse.

Women loved Grandi. He was tall and good-looking, with a pointed beard and dark flashing eyes that lit up with pleasure at the sight of a pretty woman. His approach to his marriage was Latin rather than the model of domesticity favoured by the Duce's fascisti: his petite, elegant wife Antonietta and his children were at the centre of his life but, like a traditional Italian male, he took it for granted that he could play away from home. He marked Baba down from the start and took the first opportunity to make her acquaintance. Fruity, who quickly spotted that Grandi found his wife attractive and that Baba appeared to be responding, would not settle down but played the gramophone most of the evening 'and nearly drove us mad', commented Irene.

Next day when Irene came down for tea, Baba and Grandi were nose to nose on the sofa again and Nancy and Phyllis (another of Nancy's sisters), for whom he had been asked as a beau, were angry. Irene stood up for her sister. 'Leave them alone,' she said. 'It is the first time she has talked to a good brain in years.'

Grandi's effect on the women of the party was pronounced. 'Nancy foamed over dinner as Baba had her teeth into him and Nancy had to talk over Baba and Grandi to Eddie on Baba's right and they were quite oblivious,' recorded Irene jubilantly. After dinner, while the men were downstairs drinking port, the women vied with each other over the intimacy of their conversations with him. Baba won easily when she reported that he had confided in her that he and his wife were so exhausted after the summer diplomatic season that they had had to give up their double bed for a while. Her status as Grandi's favourite was confirmed when the men came in after dinner and he made straight for her, sitting with her all evening.

Later, playing bridge, Irene and her four got the giggles when this time Fruity's retaliation took the form of reading a hunting novel aloud to Mrs Pakenham (later Lady Longford) until, recorded Irene, 'he started that awful gramophone again with Mrs Eden'.

It was clear that Baba was drawing away from her husband. A week later she worried even the loyal Irene by saying that Tom looked so wretched that he ought to go on a cruise. As he refused to go alone she suggested taking him halfway to Kenya. For Fruity, who by now detested Tom, this would be the last straw, thought Irene. Fortunately, Baba dropped the idea. She herself was still depressed after the break-up with Miles, though she cheered up a bit when Signor Grandi called to see her on 14 December.

Tactfully he praised Irene's bravery over a recent small operation and then, with equal tact, managed to slip into the conversation a reassuring phrase or two about how much he loved his wife – perhaps because he knew that 'lovely Baba' would arrive to whisk him away at six thirty before they both went to the same dinner party an hour later. The same thing happened the following week, only this time the nature of the relationship was more apparent: when Grandi called on Irene for a cocktail Baba turned up and demanded to know how long he had been there. At a quarter to seven she looked at her watch and said imperiously: 'Come on, give me a lift to Lancaster Gate.' Grandi stood up, Irene quickly handed him some books she had promised to lend him and the couple departed.

Irene did her best to see that the Mosley children had a happy Christmas, spending most of the holidays with them. For part of the time, Cimmie's friend Zita James came down to help in the absence of Nanny, whose father had died. Just before the festival itself Tom and Baba arrived. Irene, though conscious that her duty lay with her bereaved nephews and niece, was unhappily aware that the people doing least well were her own servants, who could not have the usual day off after receiving their presents from her because they were needed at Denham. She was in no doubt who had caused all this. 'It is Baba and her affairs that have ruined and corrupted the last weeks at Deanery Street and she never seems to mind,' she wrote bitterly on Christmas Eve 1933.

21

The Blackshirt Phenomenon

~

Irene took her duties towards Cim's children very seriously. Instead of returning to Melton and her hunting life there, she stayed on at Denham into the New Year, spending much of the day with them. This usually ended with hearing the prayers of the youngest, Micky, as he sat on her lap, when she did her best to keep his memory of his mother alive by showing him her photograph.

To add to Irene's unhappiness her little dog Winks was, at fifteen, clearly at the end of his life. Even a new suitor, the 51-year-old diplomat Nevile Henderson, was no solace. Telling him about Winks, whom she had loved almost like a child, she had to put the telephone down and run to her room because she could not stop crying. By 13 January she could postpone Winks's end no longer. Irene's diary entry that day reads: 'My love lay with his paws and head dozing on my lap and he looked up at me and pressed his wet nose up against me and I kissed him and kissed him goodbye in Audley Street.' Thoughtfully, Nevile took her out to lunch at the Dorchester but neither this nor knowing that Winks was going to his final rest unsuspectingly in his own basket was any comfort.

Nevile's quiet but persistent pursuit of Irene continued. He was eminently suitable: good-looking, tall and slim, with fine features. He was head of the Mission in Belgrade,* from which he was home on leave, and no doubt he was another who thought Irene was cut out to be the wife of a future ambassador. The problem was that she found him boring ('How minds like Tom's, Grandi's,

---

*Later to become Ambassador to Berlin from 1937 until the outbreak of war.

Stokowski's, Israel's ruin one for slower ones'). Eventually, one day, she lashed out at him and told him how his slowness maddened her. He replied by calling her selfish, to which she responded tartly: 'Why not?'

Nevile stood her angry denunciations quietly. 'He ended by saying that although he would want to murder me ten times a day he still would want to live with me – it certainly would be stimulating. Oh dear! oh dear!' Fortunately, the drama with Nevile, and discussing it later with her niece Viv, distracted her a little from the loneliness of her bedroom without the comforting presence of Winks in his basket.

Once again, Irene decided that the only way forward was a cruise. This time it would last for three months – time to make up her mind about Nevile and get over Winks. The faithful Nevile went down in the train with her to Southampton ('In those last moments his company was charming') and on 17 January she set off on the *Stella Polaris* first for the Americas and then the Far East.

In Colombo a letter arrived from Baba to tell her that 'Tom was livid that she [Baba] went to Ireland for Easter and deliberately asked Diana Guinness to Denham. Ugh!' Clearly, the danger from the dreaded Diana was not yet over. She also heard that her theatre had gone broke and had had to be closed for three months and, finally, Nevile Henderson wrote to say that he was coming to think she would not make him a good wife – a ploy that fell completely flat with Irene.

The *Stella Polaris* returned by way of Suez before finally docking at Monte Carlo, from where Irene went by train to Paris. While she was there, on 21 April 1934, Tom held a huge fascist meeting at the Albert Hall. It was in every way a triumph; even those whose political views nowhere coincided with Tom's acknowledged his brilliance, as this entry from the diary of the MP Robert Bernays makes clear:

It was horribly impressive – the banners, the processional, the atmosphere of virility and enthusiasm and the cheers that greeted Mosley's ridicule of the democratic system. He has perfect foils in Ramsay and Baldwin. His imitation of Ramsay at the Disarmament Conference and his description of Baldwin as the perfect representative of Britain asleep, with the Blackshirts as the incarnation of Britain awake, was perfectly done. He spoke for one hour and 45 minutes and the audience was riveted to him. It was nothing more than extreme Toryism, the curbing of the power of democracy through the so-called reform of Parliament, the strong hand in India, parity in the air, extreme economic nationalism, etc. But it was put across in a way that I have never heard Toryism put across before. It was political argument of a very high order, dignified, restrained, and expressed in superb language. The audience consisted of young toughs from the shops and the banks and that type of ageing ex-serviceman who has pathetically retained his military rank from the war. It was the people of England who, in Chesterton's poem, have not yet spoken. God help England if they ever do, for they are a mass of prejudice, ignorance, intolerance and cruelty.

Two days later, Irene was back in London, where she plunged with hardly a breath back into her social life, going the following night to Lady Portarlington's party, where she came upon her friend Sir Charles Mendl. He had heard that Nevile Henderson was pursuing her and immediately began to pay him glowing tributes, which Irene received coldly. There too was her former fiancé Miles Graham 'who never left me and who was delightful and highly flirtatious' – altogether an evening to restore her confidence.

She went down to Denham straight away, with presents for her nephews and niece, and lunched in the nursery where little Micky so enchanted her that she wished his mother could have seen him. The only discordant note was the relationship between Baba and Tom; after three months away she saw it with a fresh, more objective eye. She discussed it with Nanny – treated as a family friend and confidante rather than a servant – who was infuriated by Baba's behaviour and who told her that the Metcalfe children would be arriving for the summer holidays.

The days followed one another. Irene played poker with the older children and spent all the time she could in the nursery. Tom and Baba walked and embraced on the lawns in the May sunshine, talking softly together. Baba, thought Irene, appeared quite besotted.

The problem was that Baba had become generally bored with

the pattern of her life. She was not, like Irene, a person who naturally adored children and the customary upper-class practice of putting them in the charge of a nanny suited her very well. She enjoyed clothes, the business of making herself look beautiful and the tributes it elicited. Like others in her set, she did a little charity work, largely for the new Save the Children Fund.

This 'set' was that of the Prince of Wales, with its regular outings to the same places with the same group of people. Though she enjoyed golf, she did not share Fruity's other sporting interests and in any case the great bond of hunting, which had tied him so closely to the Prince and caused him to give up his career in the Indian Army, had been snapped – and Fruity without a purpose in life was very different from Fruity excelling at the job he loved.

The Metcalfes argued constantly about the sameness of their life and Baba's relationship with Tom Mosley, whose meetings she attended as regularly as she could (earning herself the nickname Baba Blackshirt from the diarist Chips Channon). The years of semi-sexual teasing had fed the passion she now felt for her brother-in-law; hypnotised by his physicality, sexual expertise and the charm he could bring into play at will, Baba was hopelessly in love. Thus the advent of a powerful newcomer on the Metcalfes' social landscape went almost unremarked. When Thelma Furness had left on a trip to America in January 1934 she had asked her friend and fellow American, Wallis Simpson, to help entertain the Prince. By the time Thelma returned in March, Wallis was in an impregnable position, though it took the Prince's circle many months to realise the extent of her influence.

For Baba and Fruity, she merely replaced Freda Dudley Ward and Thelma Furness as dancing partners for the Prince on the regular Thursday evenings at the Embassy. Neither of them knew that Freda's dismissal after seventeen years of close affection and, on the Prince's side, devotion, was as cruel as it was unexpected: one day when she telephoned the Prince she was told by the weeping telephonist: 'Madam, I have something so terrible to tell you I do not know how to say it. I have orders not to put you through.' If they had heard of this, they might have wondered how secure their own position was in the Prince's life – and whether the job that he had promised Fruity on his eventual accession would materialise.

Sympathetic as Irene was to Baba's dissatisfaction with her life, she put the interest of her late sister's children first. More and more, she was becoming their surrogate mother rather than a devoted aunt. When Baba wanted her to entertain Fruity one night so that she herself could go out to dinner with Tom, Irene firmly refused, saying that it was near the anniversary of their sister's illness and death, and she was determined to go to Denham to support Viv through this sad time.

Tom won back a few good points by turning up – with Baba – at the nursing home where Micky was to have his tonsils out. The four of them sat in the waiting room with Nanny, who was struggling to hold back her tears during her precious baby's operation. 'The beloved one went in so gallantly, giving the nurses the fascist salute,' wrote Irene that night. The operation was a complete success.

Baba's obsession with Tom had made her careless of her reputation. When she slipped away from one of Irene's dinner parties to go down and see him at Denham, Irene feared that such conduct would make people talk – if they were not already doing so. 'I think it unnecessarily provocative and stupid on her part,' she wrote. Georgia Sitwell, one of Cim's closest friends and Tom's former mistress, was already aware of the situation and seized the opportunity to stir the pot. 'Went to see Baba, made mischief, deliberately, with her about Diana Guinness,' runs her diary entry for 1 March 1934. Tom and Baba seemed to be becoming a couple, with Baba adopting Tom's views and both subtly patronising Irene as not really understanding what fascism stood for.

On 7 June both sisters went to Tom's great meeting at Olympia. The BUF was now at the height of its popularity, with somewhere between 30,000 and 40,000 members, many of them tough young men drawn to it by its aura of aggression. These trained at Blackshirt House, practising judo, marching, drill and boxing and, when needed, were taken to meetings in large vans with protective plating at the sides and wire mesh at the windows. Although the earlier meeting at the Albert Hall had passed off peacefully, trouble was expected on this occasion. The fascists' great claim was that they stood for law and order, while the communists were determined to expose them as thugs and bully-boys.

The meeting started half an hour late as those who tried to enter

the hall were obstructed but the fascist band played on brightly –
Blackshirt songs to the music of the Giovinezza and the Horst
Wessel Song. A new one had recently been added, called simply
'Mosley!' It began:

> Mosley, Leader of thousands!
> Hope of our manhood, we proudly hail thee!
> Raise we the song of allegiance
> For we are sworn and shall not fail thee.

The BUF's use of banners, spotlights, music and uniforms was
reminiscent of a Nuremberg Rally in miniature. First, down the
centre aisle of the huge auditorium, packed with around 15,000
people, came Blackshirts carrying the banners of the various
London districts, with their names in brass on top. After a sufficient
pause to build up expectations came Tom, all in black – boots,
breeches, shirt – his arm raised in the fascist salute with four of
his lieutenants just behind him. With spotlights focused on him he
mounted the platform and stood with the banners grouped below
and his uniformed bodyguards to each side as thunderous roars
of 'Hail Mosley!' swept the hall. 'I felt that Cim must be there,'
wrote Irene, 'and seeing all that she would be glad.'

Trouble came quickly, with constant heckling interruptions from
communist opponents followed by, in Irene's phrase, 'screaming,
surging evictions', with hand-to-hand fighting and weapons
ranging from chair-legs to spiked instruments and stockings filled
with broken glass used as flails. 'Very unpleasant,' wrote Georgia
Sitwell, there with Baba and Irene, 'terrifying crowd of roughs,
dozens of fights, casualties, broken heads and glass. Left in middle
feeling ill.'

Two days later the Blackshirts camped at Denham in one of the
big barns at the side of the drive. Irene, who had driven down
largely to see Micky, left quickly and drove over to Cliveden but
she could not escape discussion of her brother-in-law. Nancy Astor
brought up the subject of Tom and his philandering yet again as
they listened to him on the nine o'clock news. He was followed
by Gerald Barry condemning the brutal bullying of the Blackshirt
stewards which he said was worse than during the Irish Troubles,

and Brendan Bracken told Baba, when she eventually appeared indoors after hours spent walking the terrace with Grandi, that the Conservatives were so frightened of the BUF that they might rush a bill through forbidding the wearing of black shirts.

The rest of the house party also roundly condemned the Blackshirts' behaviour. Irene, apart from Baba the only one who had actually attended the meeting, felt indignant: she believed it was the communists rather than the fascists who had initiated the rioting and disturbances. Soon afterwards Baba left, to return to Fruity's bedside – he had pneumonia, a serious illness then. 'I wish he would either die or recover,' said Nancy characteristically, 'and not spoil Baba's happiness.'

On 14 June 1934 Cimmie's will was published. She had left property valued for probate at £20,951, with the whole of her residuary estate to be held in trust for her children and her jewellery, personal ornaments and watches to go to Viv as soon as she was eighteen. She left Savehay Farm to Tom, who was appointed executor along with the Public Trustee; with this official's agreement, the children's Leiter Trust money could be used for the upkeep of the family home.

As the Season gathered momentum both sisters moved from party to party. Irene's pleasure in such gaiety was rudely shaken when one of her friends told her that all her Jewish friends were turning against her because she was to be hostess at a fascist ball. The event in question was a dance arranged by Lady Mosley to raise money for the BUF which took place at Prince's Galleries on 27 June.

The ball drew an attendance of about seven hundred; Irene, Tom, Baba, Lady Mosley and the writer Francis Yeats-Brown shared a table. Tom spoke briefly in an appeal for funds to build an election machine, telling his listeners: 'Within the last twenty months a flame has been lit in this land which time will not extinguish or destroy'. At midnight Irene, elegant and distinguished-looking in tiara and a sapphire blue dress that made the most of her dark colouring, presented programme prizes.

She had played her part loyally at the ball but she was finding herself more disenchanted than ever with the behaviour of Tom and Baba. Her sister now told her to prepare herself for another English seaside holiday with Nanny and the younger children, as she had organised a rented villa in Toulon for Tom, herself and the older Mosley children.

On and on went the summer balls. At the Astors ('ultra grand,' wrote Robert Bernays, 'with the American Ambassador, the Elliots, Anthony Eden and Lothian') the party took place against the background of disturbing news from Germany. One of Hitler's closest colleagues, Ernst Rohm, the brutal, homosexual and over-ambitious head of Hitler's Brownshirts, had been 'liquidated' on 30 June in what became known as 'the Night of the Long Knives'. At least eighty-four others whom Hitler believed were implicated in a counter-revolutionary plot also lost their lives.

A few days later, a ball at the Hurlingham Club was made memorable for Irene when she sat at a table with Miles Graham's former mistress, Winnie Portarlington, who remarked to her: 'I am going to Le Touquet to see Miles play in the Bucks Handicap Golf Tournament.' Irene was so disturbed that she left at twelve thirty. 'What vile taste to show me she still owned him,' she scrawled in her diary.

There was no comfort at Savehay Farm. Tom and Baba seemed, she thought, to take her absolutely for granted. 'I resent the way I am looked on as a sort of governess, no thanks, no love, and Baba and Tom arm-in-arm all over the place and Ma and I looking like two waiting housemaids. Tom's fighting bull terrier came and slept on my chest. It was lonely too.' But Tom, who realised that without Irene to play a central role at Denham his own life would be immeasurably more difficult, was not going to push her too far. The first time he saw her alone, at the end of July, he set himself to win her round, deploying all his charm and gift for intimacy; Irene, who still found him fascinating, melted completely.

At the beginning of August she and Nanny set off for the seaside with Micky and the twins, where she would also have a chance to think over the Nevile Henderson question in peace. She realised that she would soon have to give him a definite answer one way or the other. She was fond of him, but she was not in love. After a week, she left Nanny and the children and motored to Padstow, where she had arranged to meet Nevile. They swam in a tinglingly cold sea and Irene noted with faint scorn that he shivered for half an hour afterwards. His good qualities were legion, she knew; he was a clever man with an interesting life still ahead of him in which she could share and he was endlessly patient – so much so that his acquiescence in her moods and whims irritated her.

She could not put her feelings into words, so she wrote her suitor a letter, begging him to understand that she wanted to leave. 'Oh, oh dear! Why do I feel so violently that if he touched me or kissed me I would shudder and yet he is so sweet with all his conceits and tics and would make some less strong-minded woman blissful. I walked to and fro with him beating around the marriage question. When we sat on the lawn before tea he was touching, calling me My Sweet and kissing my fingers and saying how he loved me being with him and it does not move a tremor in me. Oh dear!'

Next morning at breakfast she told him she had meant what she had said in her note; then, leaving a speechless Nevile, she went upstairs to pack. But when she felt his arm around her shivering with tension as if, she thought, he were about to explode, her soft heart got the better of her for the time being.

It was all too much. When Nancy Astor, who always tried to run her friends' lives, wrote telling her to accept Nevile – a protégé of Nancy's and a popular guest at Cliveden – Irene asked Nancy to leave her alone. 'The very attempts of people tend to drive me in the opposite direction, as I resent being dictated to like a child when I *must* know my own mind as a woman of 39, though I am fully aware you all do it in love and friendship. Can you see that, dearest Nancy, and understand? Your always loving Irene.' When another friend lectured her at length on Nevile's merits and why she should marry him, Irene recorded that she felt like a cornered, snarling vixen.

At the beginning of September she went to stay with other friends, who had also invited Nevile. They talked on the terrace from six until it was time to change for dinner and for the first time ever Irene felt truly relaxed with him. After dinner another talk, warm and understanding, made her feel that perhaps there was a flicker between them. But when he woke her at eight the following morning for a walk in the sun it had gone. 'I was cold, grumpy and unforthcoming and really wanted none of him or any male at that hour.' At breakfast, her host held forth spiritedly against independent selfish spinsters, with frequent nods of the head towards Irene, reducing her and her hostess to hysterical giggles. Although she received an endearing letter from Neville, written in the train on the return journey, at last her mind was finally made up. She would not marry him.

After the Albert Hall meeting, it seemed that Tom's fascists were a viable political force. 'Baldwin is convinced that his main job is to keep his party together,' wrote Bernays that autumn. 'I think he is probably right. A split in the Conservative party is Mosley's hope. Without the aid of the Rothermere press he was able to fill the Albert Hall last month. No other politician could come within measure of that but of course London is peculiarly susceptible to stunt politics. Still, it was a great achievement. It seems to indicate that Hitlerism is not nearly as unpopular as we would like to imagine.'

As for the communists, they were more determined than ever to demonstrate against what they saw as the fascist threat. On 9 September, they held an enormous counter-Mosley rally in Hyde Park, in which Tom's former lieutenant, John Strachey, played a prominent role.

By mid-September the Mosley family was back at Denham. While Tom and Nick were occupying a rainy afternoon by shooting rats in the barns, Irene crept to Cim's pink marble sarcophagus, now installed in its memorial garden and prayed to God and her sister's spirit to guide her in her dealings with Cim's children – and husband. 'I was nervously worried at the dim future of all those children and the babe and wished to God they were my own. Tom is such an undependable quantity.' This anxiety was dispelled when Tom – who must have been delighted at Irene's ready assumption of domestic responsibilities – agreed without hesitation to all her plans and suggestions for the future.

But this halcyon period did not last. Tom soon reverted to his former ways with the children, in particular his malicious teasing of his daughter. He was quick-tempered, brutal and sarcastic, suddenly rounding on her – as he had done with Cimmie – in public. Irene was an unwilling spectator and did her best to redress this by teaching Viv bridge and spending as much time with her as she could manage, though after one particularly cruel jibe all she could write in her diary was 'Ugh!'

Though Baba was so deeply involved with Tom, she was still anxious to keep her other admirer, Count Dino Grandi, on a string. When she returned from a visit or the country she would wire to Tom, and if he was at Denham he would rush up to meet her; if he could not, she would arrange an assignation with Grandi by note. 'Naldera darling,' he wrote from the Italian Embassy in September 1934, 'I get your letter just now, coming back from Virginia Water. I had in mind to ask you to come, one of the next days. I cannot today. I will try to ring you tomorrow evening and have a quiet hour with you.' On another occasion Irene, calling on her sister for an impromptu cup of tea, found Grandi there. 'Gulped tea and bolted,' she wrote. 'He stayed till 7.30!!'

Irene was under no illusions about their relationship. Going to lunch with her sister she often found Grandi there and Baba 'gay as a cricket'. When Grandi wrote, as he often did, to Irene – who as a rich, good-looking woman and a peeress in her own right was exactly the sort of distinguished social figure he wished to cultivate and persuade of Italy's friendliness – Baba became extremely jealous. She would demand to know what was in such letters and once, when Irene did not open a letter from him that had just arrived but took it upstairs to read, flung furious accusations at her of trying to steal him from her.

Irene, who was finding it more and more difficult to cope with her sister's dominating ways and influence over Tom, was nevertheless unselfishly pleased when she thought she had done them both some good. She knew that for Tom the link with Grandi was important (how important would only emerge after the war) and when she found herself at a party at the Savoy Hotel with Grandi in early October she made a point of eating supper with him and talking until two thirty. When she got home she woke Baba, to tell her all Grandi had said about her. Grandi had managed, in Irene's words, to convey 'his adoration of Baba tempered with huge tenderness and the yearning to control this love and not to mar it all. Very remarkable in a Latin!' She felt, she concluded, that through this talk she had perhaps been able to help all three of them.

22

Baba and Diana:
Sharing Mosley

~

In November 1934 Tom brought a successful libel case against the *Star* and was awarded £5,000 in damages. Sir Patrick Hastings summed up for him, cunningly manipulating Norman Birkett's reference to a denunciation by Tom of the Jews into a point in his client's favour. Afterwards, Tom and his two sisters-in-law, who had attended the court every day, celebrated his victory with a sumptuous lunch at the Savoy.

Irene's health had been pulled down by her operation and back pain. When she went up to her house near Melton for some hunting with the Quorn her groom, Fox, told her that she was so changed and thin he had hardly recognised her. But nothing prevented her from her usual busy round of charity committees, work for her East End clubs, luncheon parties, plays, concerts and dinners, though these were now fitted in with seeing as much as possible of the Mosley children. Often, they stayed with her in London; she went to their school plays and prize-givings and 'the blessed one', two-year-old Micky, came to her bed in the morning and played.

Now that the initial flush of grief was past, Tom had reverted to seeing less of his children. They had been looking forward to a family Christmas but on Christmas Eve Tom announced that his friends Paula and Bill Allen were coming to spend Christmas with them. The children were so upset that when the Allens arrived Nick refused to dine downstairs with them, Viv stayed upstairs with him in sympathy, and Nanny was in tears. Irene remained chatting politely until half past eleven, then she and Ma Mosley went upstairs to console Nanny and help with the Christmas stockings and the presents, which were put in a pile for each child under the tree.

Again, Irene melted when Tom came in just before going to bed to look at Micky in his cot. He looked, she thought, sad and lonely as he left the room; this, her adoration of her little nephew and her abiding feelings for Tom, combined to dissipate her annoyance. She told Baba about this later on the telephone but Baba, jealous, listened in icy silence.

On Christmas Day Irene breakfasted with the children in the nursery and was thrilled with Viv's delight at her present – Irene had turned Cim's old Persian lamb coat into a cape for Viv. At teatime Tom did his celebrated Father Christmas routine for Micky's benefit.

This followed the same pattern as always. At the sound of bells in the garden Nanny would exhort them: 'There's Father Christmas!' They would rush outside and Tom, dressed in his Father Christmas robes, face largely covered by fluffy white beard and whiskers, would quickly climb a stepladder to a ledge in the wide Garden Room chimney. When the children returned, saying they had just missed seeing him climb through the chimneypot, they would see him descending from the chimney inside with a sackful of presents. When he had finished distributing them, he would reverse the process when they ran outside to watch in vain for him. Rushing in excitedly with their presents, they would find Tom in his study and exclaim: 'Oh Daddy, you missed him *again*!'

This was the last spasm of Tom's apparent change of heart over his children. He returned to being an absentee father, who took little or no part in their lives, so much so that to his youngest son he would be simply an amiable stranger. His overriding interest in his political plans was so apparent that the Curzon family solicitor felt convinced that he would subordinate the children's interests to his own and sell Savehay Farm. Irene was particularly worried about Micky, whom she had come to regard as the son she had never had. Her diary entries frequently started with phrases like 'The blessed one sat on my bed with his books.' 'That angel sat on my bed with his motor cars.'

Halfway through January 1935 she decided to tackle the

problem head on. She took the family solicitor down to Denham and showed him over Savehay Farm. He, recognising at once Irene's sense of responsibility towards her sister's children, said that as she gave so much time to them, and as the head of the Curzon family, she had a right to decide what would be a fitting home for Micky. He also suggested that if the Official Solicitor thought otherwise, she should consider proposing to the Leiter Trustees in America that they should form a Trust under which Irene as guardian could distribute the money for the children. With such a Trust, he pointed out, Tom could not touch a penny of it.

On 26 January, just as Irene arrived for tea with Baba and Fruity, Baba was leaving to go to a film with Tom. Fruity seized the opportunity to unburden himself. 'I had two hours of poor Fruity on the disruption of his married life and Tom's influence over Baba,' she noted. 'His real love for her was deep and touching and he would give her anything for her happiness except hand her over to Tom.' She returned home to find Tom, this time with Nick, standing at the front door in the snow.

When Nick had gone to bed she tackled Tom about his disruptive influence on the Metcalfe marriage but after half an hour's unhelpful discussion he made an excuse to leave. On Sunday after church Fruity called round for another hour's inconclusive talk. He took her back to lunch with him and Baba at Cowley Street – a sticky lunch with awkward silences – then all three went to a concert in the Albert Hall. Halfway through the concert, Fruity got up and left.

The miserable situation hung over them all. Irene could not face a planned visit to Grandi and cancelled it; when she telephoned Baba she was told that Fruity had disappeared. Irene tracked him down to his sister Muriel's; when she told Baba of his misery, Baba in her turn broke down and cried. A few minutes later, as Irene was playing a last game of poker with the children, Baba and Fruity rang in turn, Fruity saying he had to see her that evening.

Irene returned from her dinner party at eleven to find Fruity waiting in her drawing-room and they talked for a further hour. 'It is pitiful and paralysing the fix they are all in,' she wrote that night. 'I cried myself to sleep in an agony that *someone* was creating such horror. Oh! that *he* had never been born.'

The triangular drama dragged on, with Irene cast in the role of negotiator. One sleepless night she wrote a letter to Fruity but under the stress of emotion her writing, always appalling, was indecipherable so she had to repeat everything she had written over the telephone. Immediately afterwards it was Baba's turn ('two hours of tortured talk. My brain will break').

Next day she felt so exhausted and overwrought that she put off her luncheon engagement on the pretext of a temperature and got her maid to telephone Fruity to say she was going away. There were more letters, telephone calls, meetings with Lady Mosley, talks with Baba and Fruity's sister Muriel.

At the beginning of February, Fruity came to see Irene yet again. He was resigned, dignified and miserable. 'How sad I felt when he left, that rare thing smashed, [himself] not wanted and having to face the inevitable. I tried to make him see I knew what he was feeling as I gave seven years of my best time, 26 to 33, to someone who tossed me aside in the end,' she wrote.

Later the same day, Baba telephoned, to say that Denham would be let for the months of May, June, July and August (in the event it was not), and that Irene must find a house by the sea for Nanny and Micky. Her tone was aloofly authoritative. As always when she felt guilty and ashamed, she was stricter with her children, sending them coldly about their business and snubbing Irene with a cutting indifference.

To add to the difficulties, Tom's lack of interest in his children had extended to the one member of the household who was indispensable. Nanny Hyslop had been a central figure in the children's lives since their birth, valued by Cimmie for the total love and loyalty she gave the Mosley family. At the very least, Nanny would have expected to hear of any changes that might affect her from her employer himself. Yet Tom had not spoken to her since the previous November – almost three months ago.

Irene was shocked to learn that Nanny had heard from Micky that a governess had been hired, and from Nick that Diana Guinness's children were coming to live at Denham. The children had told Nanny that Tom planned to get rid of her in the autumn when Micky started school and she was terrified of being turned into a glorified housemaid and waitress to the Guinness nanny until her departure. It was all that awful Diana, thought Irene (wrongly).

The quarrels with Baba went on. Baba, infuriated that Irene

27. The hall at Cliveden

28. Irene in 1930

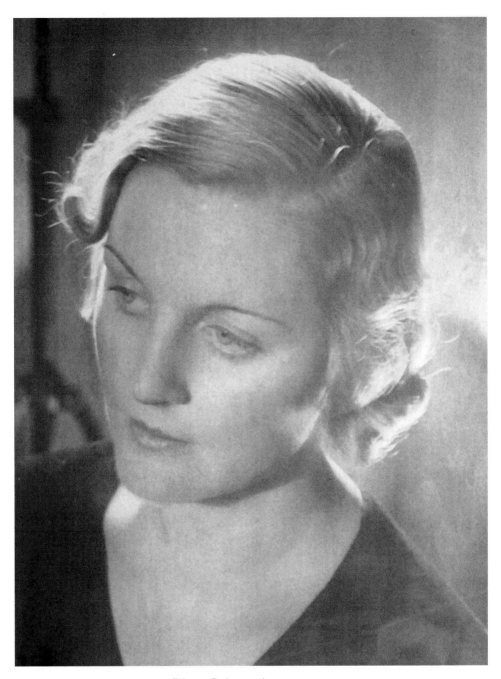

31. Diana Guinness in 1933

32. Miles Graham

33. Baba and Jock Whitney
at Phoenix Park, Dublin,
Easter 1934

34. Tom Mosley with his children Vivien and Nick on holiday in the south of France, August 1934

35. Tom Mosley addressing a rally in Hyde Park on 10 September 1934

36. The opening of the Cynthia Mosley Day Nursery on 1 July 1935. From the left: Baba, Irene, the Archbishop of Canterbury and the Mayor of Lambeth.

37. Baba on holiday, summer 1936

38. Château de Candé

39. The Windsor wedding, 3 June 1937. From the left: Baba, Kitty and Eugene Rothschild, Mrs Rogers, Walter Monckton, Lady Selby, Mrs Merriman, Wallis, Fruity, HRH and Randolph Churchill.

40. Tom Mosley acknowledging the greetings of his followers at Millbank, West-minster, before the start of a march through south-east London in October 1937

41. Fruity with the Windsors at La Cröe, south of France, in July 1938

should involve herself and forgetting her own confidences to the ever-sympathetic Irene, was often so rude that Irene would put down the receiver. There would be more calls from Fruity, telling Irene that she was the only sane person among them and that he was sticking to her advice despite the rows.

As always when things became too much for her, Irene went away, this time returning to Melton for some hunting before setting off on yet another cruise. She had done what she could; now it was up to the three people concerned. Her main feeling was one of anger; she felt that, once again, she had been 'put upon', the more so since Baba had not bothered to thank her for all her help with the children and the arrangements for the Mosley and Metcalfe summer holidays.

Baba in fact had plenty to occupy her. She was seeing Dino Grandi constantly and he was confiding both his political and personal worries to her, from finding the right specialist to remove his tonsils to the worsening situation in Africa (Mussolini had long wanted to expand his colonial empire and his troops were massing along the border between Italian Somaliland and Abyssinia).

Darling, thank you so much for having rung me up – it has been a beastly day today [he wrote on 18 March]. 'I don't know what I can possibly do tomorrow. The whole world is *really* going mad. The most unreasonable things are done everywhere...

We shall have a date tomorrow if I do not go to the sea? [to convalesce]. Thank you so much, darling.

You looked so beautiful the day before yesterday! Your eyes and complexion reminded me of Watteau or Fragonard.

G.

Back in Italy for Easter, he wrote to her just as assiduously:

I have thought of you so often here. Everything is going well, so far at least. Everybody [i.e. the Duce] satisfied and happy.

You looked so lovely at the tea party but, so much pale, darling. You spend too much of yourself, I know that. Will my letter find you somewhere in the country? I hope so. When I shall be back I will come for a quiet talk and a cup of tea. So many things to tell you, darling! I would see you happy, that's all. Au revoir, darling.

G.

If Baba hoped to make Tom jealous, the friendship with Grandi was a vain ploy. As Tom's mistresses were invariably married, he was used to sharing his women; and his attitude to sex was so frivolous as to preclude jealousy – how could you be jealous of another player in what was no more than a game?

In any case, Baba's friendship with Grandi, Mussolini's representative in Britain, suited his purposes. As recently discovered archives reveal, Mussolini had been subsidising the BUF for the past two years, with Grandi as the conduit, and Tom was anxious for this to continue. The organisation's running costs were high, membership was falling – and at only 1s a month brought in little at the best of times – and rich supporters had been put off by Tom's public declaration of anti-Semitism. Grandi had the ear of Il Duce; Baba, he knew, would always sing his praises to Grandi and the latter's *tendresse* for her might just tip the scales.

Baba preferred not to think about the strange financial link between her lovers, and its implications in terms of political behaviour – or even possible treachery. Neither Tom nor Grandi ever spoke about it and it was not a subject she wished to bring up. Years later, she was asked whether she knew what was going on. For some time she remained silent, finally replying, 'Of course, I thought I knew what was going on. But if you ask me "Had I got evidence?" the answer is "No".'

That spring there was an indication of the hostility Tom had generated even in traditionally apolitical circles. When Irene wrote to Princess Alice to ask if she would open the children's day nursery founded in Cimmie's memory her lady-in-waiting, Lady Katharine Meade, telephoned to say that Princess Alice would be delighted to do so – provided Tom were not present. Irene, after an argument with Baba, who said that they must bow to the Princess's wishes, sent back a note to Lady Katharine to say she could not accept those terms as Cimmie had loved Tom to her dying day. For good measure she added that politics and propaganda should not enter into such an occasion. The Princess agreed to come.

The rows between the Metcalfes intensified. One even took place in the august surroundings of a court ball on 13 June 1935 while

Irene, in topaz parure and tiara from Cartier, was admiring the gold plate as she and the Metcalfes drank coffee after the Royal Procession.

This event was remarkable in that it signalled unmistakably to his family and friends the Prince's growing obsession with Wallis Simpson. The King had banned Mrs Simpson's appearance at court but the Prince was determined that she should attend the ball. When he tackled his father directly the King said he could not invite his son's mistress on such an occasion. The Prince swore that she was not his mistress and the King accepted his word. His staff was more sceptical. His former Private Secretary, Alan ('Tommy') Lascelles, declared that he would find it as easy to believe in the innocence of their relationship as in 'a herd of unicorns grazing in Hyde Park'.

The signs had been there for some time. Lady Loughborough, a great friend of the Prince of Wales since the time fifteen years earlier when his brother the Duke of York had been in love with her, had been Chairman of the Derby Ball, held annually on the even of the Derby in aid of the Royal Northern Hospital. On the first occasion the Prince of Wales promised to come and bring a party. He did this for ten years, until 1935, when a friend warned Sheila Loughborough that if she wanted the Prince at her ball that year, she had better write and ask Mrs Simpson to take tickets.

'Why should I write to Mrs Simpson, whom I have never met?' she asked. Instead, she telephoned the Prince on 3 June, the day before the ball, and told him there was a rumour he might not come. He assured her it was unfounded. But at the dinner beforehand, the Duke of Kent, sitting next to her, handed her a note under the table. It was from the Prince, contained a cheque for £100, and simply said: 'Cannot be at the ball tonight as am going to the country.' He was with Mrs Simpson at Fort Belvedere.

A week later, the MP Victor Cazalet, brother of Irene's great friend Thelma Cazalet, was noting in his diary: 'Long talk with Prince of Wales. Mrs Simpson has complete control. He never leaves her. King and Queen very worried.'

In August the Prince wrote to his cousin, Louis Mountbatten, regretting that he had to abandon the idea of a cruise on a destroyer that they had planned for the summer. The reason was not far to seek: he could not conceive of a holiday without Wallis Simpson – and as this was a private trip in an all-male environment she would be unable to accompany them.

Denham and the company of the Mosley children was an uncomplicated relief to Irene after the emotional maelstrom of her sister's household. The welcome she received from her beloved Micky was a joy. 'When that blessed Babe hugged me and said he wanted to say his prayers to me it was pure happiness and made up for all meanness and pain during the week.'

Baba, who came down with Tom but without her husband, was in a better mood. Both made a point of being nice to Irene, so that when Tom asked her to approach her friend Lady Rennell to find out if she would rent her villa at Posilippo on the Italian Riviera for the month of August, she agreed. Once again, Baba intended to go on holiday with Tom but without her husband, ostensibly to help Tom with the children. The rows, the tears, the discussions, the pleas of the wretched Fruity, the advice of her sister, the disapproval of those in their circle, weighed nothing against Baba's passion for her glamorous brother-in-law. Nor did the fact that when she herself left after a fortnight, she would be replaced for the rest of the month by Diana Guinness.

Somehow she had managed to make herself believe Tom when he explained that his relationship with Diana was now platonic and that he could not abandon a young woman who had invested so much in him emotionally: she was also aware that he always did exactly what he wanted where women were concerned. When Irene dined with Baba and Fruity on their terrace, bringing with her all the information about the Posilippo villa, Fruity's misery was tangible but it touched Baba not a whit. 'I got all the Naples stuff out. Poor Fruity on seeing it seemed downcast and tragic,' wrote Irene. Quietly she told him she thought it would only make matters worse if he went too.

The opening of the Kennington Day Nursery on 1 July 1935 provided a welcome respite from the emotional storms of the past few weeks. Irene had been indefatigable, organising everything, writing personal notes to thank helpers, sending out the invitations and arranging the flowers on the day – huge vases of blue delphiniums, rambler roses in pots in the entrance passage. She bought the matron a jewelled lapel pin, sent with a special letter of thanks, and could well congratulate herself that everything looked 'too perfect for my Love'. Just before lunch she collected Vivien from Ma Mosley's flat while Andrée met Nick, up from Eton, at Waterloo. At the nursery, she showed round a reporter from the *Daily Mail* and a man from the new Gaumont British News.

The forty-strong audience at the opening ceremony included not only Lambeth Council workers and subscribers but luminaries like Winston Churchill, Brendan Bracken and the Noel Bakers. At three o'clock the Archbishop of Canterbury arrived, to be photographed in the big playroom, introduced briefly by Irene and then to make a speech about Cim and her great qualities so touching that Irene could not see for tears and Churchill also wept. A meandering oration about Lambeth by the mayor brought the audience down to earth and a vote of thanks to him was ably seconded by Baba in an elegant little speech. Tom, white and sad, was silent.

A few days later, the première of the first three-dimensional Technicolor film, *Becky Sharp*, at the New Gallery cinema, was held in aid of the Kennington Day Nursery. The major shareholder in this new process was an old friend of Baba's, the American Jock Whitney, who had begun to visit the newly-important British market regularly.

The emotions engendered by the opening of the day nursery were soon dissipated and the relationships between Tom and Baba, Tom and Diana, and Baba and Fruity once more a constant theme. Even at the Eton and Harrow match on 13 July Tom's mother seized the opportunity to discuss her son with Irene.

'I got very weary of the tirade on Tom's misdemeanours, she has gone dippy, poor dear, on the subject,' wrote Irene, forgetting that she herself was just as vehement in refusing to accept Diana Guinness's presence in his life. 'I sent my car for Viv and Nick as that fright Mrs Guinness was at Denham with Tom, to fetch them to Baba's.'

Unsurprisingly, with Tom entertaining Diana, Baba's other admirer, Count Grandi, arrived; naïvely, Irene thought of this as a 'lovely surprise'. After dining out, she and Grandi drove back to her London house together, where he further won her affection and approval by having a long, sympathetic conversation about her woes.

On 28 July Tom, Baba and the two elder Mosley children set off for their Posilippo holiday. As the mail plane to Rome took off from Croydon airfield at 6 a.m. in a dense mist Irene and Nanny returned to London, to prepare for their less exotic holiday with Micky and the twins in Cornwall.

While at Holywell Bay, Irene heard Baba's version of a near miss between Tom's two mistresses. Diana Guinness had suffered a devastating car crash in which her face was cut so badly that her looks were only saved by the brilliant plastic surgeon Sir Harold Gillies, whose skill was such that she was left without a mark. While she was lying in the London Clinic Tom wrote to her lovingly, urging her to 'hurry up and get better' so that she could come out and join them as planned for the last part of the holiday. Unable to bear the idea of lying in bed for another few days, Diana sent a telegram to Tom, persuaded her father to smuggle her out and caught the plane to Rome. She arrived before her telegram – and therefore quite unexpectedly – while a dinner party was in full swing at Posilippo.

'James came and whispered Mrs Guinness has arrived. Tom had wired her not to come till Thursday and she said she had not got it. Lie!!' wrote Baba on 9 August. Tom, adept at explanations, had slipped out of the dining room to see Diana, who had gone straight to bed, exhausted after her escape from the nursing home and the long journey. 'I didn't realise you were coming,' he said to her, but without rancour. 'I'm so sorry,' she replied 'but I did send a wire.' Five minutes later it arrived.

After their dinner guests had gone, Tom managed to assuage Baba's jealous fury by assuring her that he had not known Diana was coming and was furious with her for doing so. He told Baba that he had ordered Diana to stay in her room and not appear while she, Baba, was there and that he, Tom, did not wish to speak to her. Diana, he pointed out, as Baba simmered down, was simply there to convalesce. His master stroke, which convinced Baba that he really did not care whether Diana was there or not, was to whisk Baba off for a romantic three-day 'honeymoon' on his motor yacht *Vivien* to Sorrento and Amalfi, where they stayed each night in the best hotel, leaving the children and Andrée on board the boat.

Placated, Baba left for Tunis in a happier frame of mind, after which she set off on a trip that took her through the Kiel Canal on to Leningrad, Moscow, Teheran, India, Petra, Amman, Tripoli, Venice, Milan and Paris before finally returning to London at the beginning of December.

Awaiting her return was a letter from Dino Grandi. Britain had withdrawn the sanctions imposed on Italy after the invasion of Abyssinia. The *Daily Express* published a picture of Grandi leaving the House of Commons and captioned it 'The Winner'. When the paper reached Rome Mussolini, who regarded only himself as meriting this title, became so explosively angry that Grandi was recalled at once. Grandi, who had realised for some time the threat posed to his relationship with Baba by the return of her old flame Jock Whitney, seized the opportunity offered by his recall to try and sever their physical liaison. He left a note explaining his abrupt departure:

I thought the best thing was to let you think the worst of me and I do not pretend or ask this letter will change anything. The only thing I cannot help doing is just to tell you goodbye – we leave today at 2 pm. I will not be so far from you – we go to Sicily at Agrigento for a fortnight of crocodile life in the most splendid solitude, just in front of Tunis – namely, of you.

This will suggest lots of thoughts to me but I sincerely hope it will not suggest anything to you, darling!

I have *not* come to see you. I do know that you will *not* forgive me. But, believe me, *this is the best*.

There are things which one finds so difficult to explain – and you know me enough to realise how difficult for me is to say things which is so sad to talk about.

Please understand. I am sure that time will come soon, old things will come again, as they were. I feel just the same now *as I have always felt*. But I know that by then your friendship will be gone, perhaps for ever. My risk is great but I have no other choice.

Tom's affair with Baba, on the other hand, continued as if nothing had happened. Politically, however, he was at a low ebb. Not a single BUF candidate had gained a parliamentary seat in the general election of June 1935 which had swept Stanley Baldwin into power and given the Conservatives a massive majority in the new National Government. The financial contributions from Mussolini had ceased abruptly. Grandi, as shrewd as he was socially adept, now believed that the BUF would never be a force to reckon with in British politics. He told Mussolini that 'with a tenth of what you give Mosley, I feel I could produce a result ten times better'.

With help from Italy at an end, Tom turned to Germany. It was a path smoothed for him by his other mistress, Diana Guinness who, though only twenty-five, had already met all the Nazi leaders. She had first gone to Germany in 1933 almost on a whim. That August, alone and depressed in London, with the recently-widowed Tom on his motoring holiday with Baba, Diana had wanted to distract herself. She persuaded her sister Unity to accompany her to Munich; Hitler's press secretary, whom she had met at a party in the spring, had told her he could introduce her to the new Chancellor, adding that the music, museums and architecture of Munich would be a joy to them both.

The Mitford family had always had strong cultural links with Germany. Austen Chamberlain, the great friend of Diana's grandfather, the first Lord Redesdale, had written Wagner's biography, to which Lord Redesdale had contributed the foreword. Diana's brother Tom, a year older than her, with whom she felt a twin-like affinity, had won the Music Prize at Eton and considered music as a career: for this reason he had visited Germany several times and come back extolling its beauty and the renaissance of its people under the new Chancellor.

Hitler, with his dark deeds then in the future, was the man everyone wanted to meet. As Victor Cazalet wrote that autumn, 'One must admit Hitler has done a great deal with the Germans and many of his social reforms are excellent.' Although neither of the sisters managed to meet Hitler on that first visit, both were overwhelmed by the drama and excitement of the first Party Rally (in September 1933), with its blood-red banners, use of floodlighting and ecstatic, roaring crowds focused on the solitary figure of the Führer.

Diana began to learn German at once while Unity, obsessed with the desire to meet her hero, persuaded her parents to let her return to Germany and, by dint of placing herself constantly in

Hitler's path, was finally introduced to him at the Munich café he frequented for a late lunch. Once the longed-for meeting had been achieved (on 9 February 1925), she wrote joyously to Diana, who returned to Germany and was introduced to him in her turn. Quickly, Diana established an entente with the Nazi leader.

Apart from the fact that she wore make-up (frowned on in the Third Reich), she conformed exactly to the tall, blonde, beautiful Aryan looks that Hitler favoured. In those early days he had a penchant for aristocrats – he would often entertain the Kaiser's relations – and he credited English ones with far more political influence than they actually had. Above all, surrounded by yes-men as he was, he enjoyed the frankness of the two Mitford girls. Though they clearly admired him greatly, they were not at all overawed and their refreshing high spirits made a welcome change from nervous Party officials at the end of the day. With Diana, the more stable and intelligent of the two, he would discuss anything from films to the relationship between their two countries.

Baba recognised that Diana's star was now in the ascendant. 'Baba saddened me deeply by tales of Mrs Guinness' increased wriggling her way into Tom and the children and that she goes everywhere with him in a black shirt and has the entrée to Hitler and Goebbels for him,' wrote Irene. The realisation that she was now in second place may have prompted Baba to an unexpected decision: she told Irene in the course of a 'wonderful talk' that she had broken with Tom. 'I find her fearfully sad and "thrill-less" now she and T have "bust" and she is only 30,' wrote Irene.

It would not be long before a new 'thrill' would fill this emotional vacuum.

23

Mrs Simpson Rules

~

At the beginning of 1936, society was thrown into chaos by the death of King George V. It was clear that much was about to change, not least the image of impeccable moral probity that had characterised the previous reign. Queen Mary's first action after her husband's death was to take her son's hand and kiss it but this was one of the last acts in the new reign where tradition was to rule.

Immediately after his father's death, at five minutes to midnight on 20 January, the new King went downstairs and – in a thoughtless act which was to cause much offence – ordered all the clocks to be set at the correct time (they had always been kept at 'Sandringham time': half an hour fast, in order to give more time for shooting during the dark winter months of that sporting season).

'The scene in the House yesterday was a memorable one,' wrote the MP Robert Bernays on 24 January. 'Row upon row of black, and the Cabinet in frock coats and Mr Baldwin waiting shyly at the Speaker's Chair like some new member to deliver the message from the new King.' Of the King's appearance at Westminster Hall when its door opened to receive George V's coffin he wrote: 'The new King looked really like a boy overpowered by the weight of sudden responsibility.'

Others viewed it differently. J. H. Thomas, the railwaymen's leader, a great favourite of George V who stayed at Balmoral for a fortnight every year and was equally fond of the king, gave his verdict to Harold Nicolson: ''e was like that, you know, 'Arold, not afraid of people, if you know what I mean. And now 'ere we 'ave this little obstinate man with 'is Mrs Simpson. Hit won't do,

'Arold, I tell you that straight. I know the people of this country. I know them. They 'ate 'aving no family life at Court.'

Baba and Fruity expected a change in their own lives. The new King had always promised that when he acceded he would 'do something' for Fruity; now, they hoped, he would make him an equerry, or an extra equerry – something that would, at any rate, give him not only a certain standing but validate his decision to leave the Army and stay in England at the behest of the Prince. Such a post, they quite understood, might not happen immediately: the King obviously had much else to think about.

What they, in common with the rest of the country, did not know was that most of his thoughts were focused on the question of marriage to Wallis Simpson. According to the account later written by the lawyer Walter Monckton for the Royal Archives, the King had told Ernest Simpson in February that he wished to marry Wallis.

In any case, that spring Baba was deeply preoccupied with Jock Whitney. They had first met when Jock was at Oxford, hunting at Melton whenever he could. He was charming, generous, aesthetic, cultivated, with an alluring touch of recklessness. As well as hunting, he played golf and tennis whenever he got the chance. He loved flying and owned a series of small planes (surviving crashes in some of them), and divided his time between the family's sumptuous house on New York's Fifth Avenue, built in Italian Renaissance style, and their estate at Greentree, thirty miles from the city on Long Island's North Shore. Above all, he was fabulously wealthy. The family fortune was founded on oil and tobacco and his father's net worth at the time of his death in 1927 was estimated at $179 million – the largest estate ever in the United States.

Whitney did all the things a rich young man could be expected to do – with gusto, style and flair. By 1928 he had his own aeroplane; he played polo; and after he came into his inheritance he raced: through the Royal Family's trainer, Cecil Boyd Rochfort, he bought Royal Minstrel; through another trainer, he acquired Easter Hero, which won the Cheltenham Gold Cup (in 1929) and would have won the Grand National but for twisting a plate and cutting itself at one of the last fences.

Tall and with an athletic build – though bespectacled – Whitney had no difficulty attracting girls and in 1930 had married the year's most glamorous US debutante, Liz Altemus. As a wedding present he gave her a cheque for $1 million, a 2,000-acre estate called Llangollen in Virginia, with beautifully equipped stables and grooms to go with them, a gym, a swimming pool and a fuschia-coloured coach drawn by four white mules in which Liz could drive around its perimeters.

Soon after Whitney had invested in the new film process, Technicolor in 1933, he insisted on buying the film rights to an unpublished first novel by an unknown author. It was called *Gone With the Wind*. Since Britain was an important market for Hollywood films, this necessitated frequent visits to London. His marriage had become shaky, largely owing to Liz's refusal to have children, and when he met Baba again, he was soon deeply in love with her.

With his usual generosity, he showered her with presents, notably jewellery. Much of it was by Fulco di Verdura, the Sicilian duke who had become a jewellery designer. To Baba, Whitney gave di Verdura's famous clips and brooches; several represented elephants, their bodies a huge baroque pearl, legs and curling trunk of diamonds tipped with gold, surmounted by a crystal howdah and trappings of rubies and sapphires.

Jock Whitney was a man accustomed to getting what he wanted; he wanted to marry Baba and he knew that the Metcalfe marriage had unravelled. Baba herself felt so strongly about him that she went as far as planning to return to America with him, sending Irene a cable on 13 March saying: 'Sailing on the Ile de France. Fruity remaining behind.'

But Fruity did not want a divorce and Baba had no grounds on which to divorce him. He was the father of her children and, although mothers were almost invariably awarded custody of children in divorce cases, there would be a question mark over one who planned to take hers out of the country. Nor did she wish to land Fruity with a divorce case which would deeply prejudice his chances of getting a job at court just at the moment when, they hoped, he was about to be offered one.

She also shrank from the very idea of divorce: it was something one just 'did not do'. Retrospectively, as she often told her children years later, she came to regret not having married Whitney.

And, of course, there was Tom – with his intoxicating lovemaking, his constant changes of plan, his maddening determination to keep Diana Guinness in his life, his sudden bouts of dependence on her and equally sudden offhandedness, his stimulating, provocative political ideas, the sharp-edged wit that made poor Fruity seem plodding beside him, and the sheer, inexplicable magnetism of his physical presence that worked as powerfully on an individual as on a crowd.

This charisma was in evidence again on 22 March, when Tom again addressed a meeting of the British Union of Fascists in the Albert Hall to rousing effect. Outside, demonstrating against him as close as the police would allow, were the communists, headed by Tom's former friend and close associate, John Strachey. As always, Tom was careful to keep on the right side of the law but his extreme views were beginning to tell heavily against him: a second libel case he brought in February 1936 turned out to be a Pyrrhic victory when he was awarded damages of one farthing and had to pay his own costs.

Some days later Baba called on Irene after an evening with Tom, with whom she had resumed her affair. It appeared that he was now carrying anti-Semitism into private life, and had been furious when he learned that Irene had invited her friends the Sieffs to one of her musical soirées. 'He said he would never come near me if this continued and he would take Micky away from me,' wrote Irene in her diary that night. 'I was quite shattered by it.'

It was a sign of how far away Tom's focus had shifted from his family, to whom he was paying less and less attention. All his energy, and all the cash he could lay hands on, was being poured into the BUF (now known simply as the BU, since it had absorbed or wiped out other small British fascist groups). He had even begun to think of asking his children to refund him any money he spent on Denham when they came of age.

This did not stop him making any use he chose of the house and its servants, sending for Andrée, the Denham housekeeper, if he had given his own servants time off. The children too were increasingly feeling the effect of their father's unpredictable moods and his sudden ferocious teasing, usually with Viv as his target, had a devastating effect on their peace of mind. Nick's stammer had grown worse – Nanny, in a misguided attempt to help him and ease the embarrassment of the others, tried to make him look at his contorted face in a mirror – and Granny Mosley added to the general feeling of chaos by reporting that Cim had sent a psychic message saying she did not want the children to be much with Mrs Guinness.

Irene was glad to get away in April, on another cruise, this time organised by the Hellenic Travellers Club on the ship *Letitia*. She went with her friends Vita and Harold Nicolson, their younger son Nigel and Hugh Walpole. They visited most of the main sites of classical Greece, learning about them from the notable scholars on board as lecturers. Irene's dark, dramatic looks made a deep impression on the young Nigel, who thought her extraordinarily beautiful and – unsurprisingly, given her penchant for, and understanding manner with, the young – liked her very much.

Plans for the summer began, on her return, in an atmosphere of uncertainty and recrimination. Tom had not been, Baba told Irene, in an easy mood. 'He never is after he has been with that vile Mrs G,' thought Irene. But they did not see much of him, as he only visited Denham occasionally.

That spring of 1936, he had driven up to Staffordshire with Diana Guinness, who felt that her two sons needed more space than the confines of her tiny London house, to look at a large, beautiful and icy cold house called Wootton Lodge. Both of them had fallen in love with it instantly and Tom had rented it, Diana paying the wages of most of the servants and the indoor expenses. As it was close to Manchester, where he frequently spoke, Tom was able to spend a great deal of time with Diana. The Curzon sisters, who did not always know where his sudden absences on speaking engagements took him, felt erroneously that Diana tucked away in the depths of the country was much less of a danger than Diana as an ever-present temptation in London. Nevertheless Tom, through Baba, tried to persuade Irene to take his children up to Wootton ('absolute torture to me') while he and Baba went to the Ile de Porquerolles, just off the French Riviera.

Soon this plan was in the melting pot. When Baba heard that Tom intended to invite Diana Guinness to Porquerolles also, she refused to go. It was deadlock. Temporarily, their relationship was off.

Tom, anxious not to alienate Irene as well, invited her to lunch for a chat and to see his new flat at 129 Grosvenor Road, a converted nightclub on the Chelsea river-front, decorated by Diana in blue with the dramatic pillars in its main room painted white. 'Diana Guinness's taste is lovely,' recorded Irene. 'The drawing room is Greek, Tom's bedroom is Greek à la Caesar. By dexterous manipulation and the help of my cross I talked to him for an hour and a quarter on the whole Baba/Guinness/children situation and he was amazingly simple and sweet and clarified so much that eased my poor heart. He said I had been a help and I left at 3.45 praising God.'

Though Irene was spending virtually every weekend at Denham, often giving up visits to friends, during the week she allowed herself to enjoy the concerts, dances, dinners and luncheons of the Season. At one of these occasions Lord Willingdon, the former Viceroy whom she and Baba had met in India, told her how when he lunched with Lord Granard in the Royal Box at Ascot Mrs Simpson was put on his right. 'Though I laughed I think it is an *outrage*,' wrote Irene fiercely.

Mrs Simpson's influence was now paramount. The King, as all close observers noted, was her slave, and the more harshly she treated him, the more he worshipped her. His obsequious adoration meant that a new court formed round her, of those who flattered and toadied to her or whom she liked. If she did not like someone, the King would ruthlessly cut out even old friends.

Her style mentor Elsie de Wolfe, who had introduced her to the young American designer Mainbocher whose clothes she wore for the rest of her life, of course found favour with the King. His private plane, maintained at the expense of the Air Ministry but nonchalantly used to smuggle back lobsters, champagne or the Mainbocher dresses Mrs Simpson bought at half-price from Paris (on all of which duty should have been paid), was now sent there to fetch Elsie for consultation on the redecoration of Fort Belvedere, where for some time Mrs Simpson had given orders and acted as hostess.

The outward and visible sign of Wallis Simpson's position was the extraordinary and amazing jewellery the King gave her, jewels so huge and ostentatious that at least one sophisticated onlooker mistook them for costume jewellery. For Christmas and the New Year she had received from him gems worth £50,000 and £60,000 respectively; and every significant date was marked with at least a charm of gold and precious stones for her bracelet. He also financed her to the tune of £6,000 a year; at her behest he sacked long-standing employees and sold property to make savings or amass cash that would benefit her.

One of those privy to a plan of Mrs Simpson's known to few others was Walter Monckton. Monckton was an old and trusted friend of the King, who was godfather to his second son; they had met at Oxford, where they had both been in the mounted cavalry squadron of the Officers' Training Corps, and they had immediately established a rapport. By early April 1936, when the Royal Standard was raised over Buckingham Palace for the first time since the death of George V, Monckton knew that Mrs Simpson's lawyers had begun divorce proceedings, although at this stage he regarded this as a matter purely personal to the Simpsons.

What seemed much more serious, though known only to those behind the scenes, was that the King's passion for Mrs Simpson was causing him to neglect his kingly duties. By the beginning of April he was spending most of his time in his private sanctum, Fort Belvedere – with, of course, Mrs Simpson.

Where Freda Dudley Ward would have gently pushed him towards his work, Mrs Simpson did not. The red boxes that he had scrutinised so punctiliously at the beginning of his reign now lay unopened, or opened and with their papers scattered carelessly around the house. Since officials could only go there by invitation and often had to wait for hours, their chances of getting the King's initials on all the papers sent were low. Both the negligent approach to business and the lack of security horrified those in his office.

On 27 May the King gave a dinner party at York House, ostensibly in honour of Mr and Mrs Stanley Baldwin, at which Mrs Simpson was given precedence over the Prime Minister's wife. This unheard-of breach of protocol was construed by many as insulting to the dignity of both monarch and Prime Minister. Queen Mary, sixty-nine the previous day, was deeply upset. From the King's point of view, Mrs Simpson was to become his future wife and therefore the precedence was indisputably hers. His order that the Simpsons' names be published in the Court Circular (a similarly unprecedented move) was another attempt to make clear publicly the nature of their relationship.

Gossip about the King and Mrs Simpson had now become rife. When Churchill suggested to the King, at a private dinner party, that such gossip would increase exponentially if Mrs Simpson were free, the King answered disingenuously that he did not see why Wallis should remain bound in an unhappy marriage merely because of her friendship with him, an answer that he was to repeat again and again. 'By the end of June,' wrote Monckton later, 'I was seriously worried not about the prospect of the King marrying Mrs Simpson but about the damage that would be done to the King if he continued to make his friendship with her even more conspicuous.'

Mrs Simpson's sway over the King may have been responsible for the latest blow, as unexpected as it was dismaying, which the Metcalfes were dealt. The expected Household post for Fruity did not materialise; instead, on 23 June 1936, Mountbatten received a letter from the King asking him to be his personal ADC.

Baba was bitterly resentful at what she saw as a betrayal of Fruity by the King. She knew that if he had been given a job in the Royal Household their life together would seem less pointless. 'I had a most agonising hour with Baba in the Park and oh! How she cried,' wrote Irene as Baba gave way to her despair over the combination of her love for Tom and their rupture, her inability to escape with Jock Whitney to a new life in America and the massive blow to Fruity's hopes and expectations. Irene sent her footman to the Grosvenor Road apartment with a note to Tom about Baba's wretchedness and drove Nick to Denham.

Her letter drew blood: Tom rang up at midnight asking to see her the next day. They met for lunch and Tom agreed to climb down over his insistence that Diana Guinness came out to Porquerolles that summer. Triumphant, Irene went off to Baba's house in Cowley Street to wait for her there and tell her the good news. 'In she came at four, exquisite and perfect, and after all I had done for her she merely said it was all too late and she was not going. What a woman!'

The rows between Baba and Fruity, the outpourings of the unhappy Fruity to Irene, the depression over the King's failure to give Fruity a job, the stand-offs between Baba and Tom, both equally obdurate, fill pages of Irene's diary. The unhappy Fruity, who had been drinking too much, was despatched to Freiburg for a cure; he complained bitterly that Baba was not coming with him. 'She should be beside me now when I am ill,' he told Irene.

When Tom telephoned to say that he was being operated on for appendicitis at nine thirty on the morning of 29 July, at 31 Queen's Gate, it must have held macabre undertones for them all of Cimmie's last days, and his mother promised to stay in the nursing home and telegraph Irene with the result. Yet again, she was to be despatched with Nanny and Mick to Newquay while the older children would enjoy a more sophisticated holiday with Tom and his mother at Sorrento. Baba, after a visit to friends, would be in Berlin for the opening of the Olympic Games.

On 20 August, Irene received a letter from Lady Mosley to say that as they had all boarded the little local boat at Naples, out of the blue appeared the dreaded Diana Guinness – fetched by Tom's servant Dundas.

Only someone with Tom's powerful personality could have controlled such a diverse household: the children, subliminally aware of their father's relationship with Mrs Guinness and their grandmother's loathing for her, the two women as different as possible. Lady Mosley, who seldom opened a book and lacked any interest in the arts, seemed hopelessly philistine and uneducated to the cultivated Diana, who took refuge in a politeness made all the more excessive by the Mitford habit of loading their drawled sentences with superlatives ('unutterably awful and affected', reported Lady Mosley later).

In September, Irene was excited to learn that she was to be invited to Berlin for the Nazi Party Congress at Nuremberg though when told that she would be the Government's guest in Nuremberg, she had reservations. 'I am not sure I want to be obligated to the Führer.'

All the same, she went and, along with other visiting dignitaries, was taken in one of a fleet of large red buses to the Zeppelin Field where the parade and rally was to take place. Her diary comments on the great stands all round the field, the main block hung with red flags along the back wall, the flags on the skyline surmounted by eagles, seeming to float in the light breeze.

'Punctually at 10 the Fuehrer arrived at the head of a string of motor cars, standing erect in a brown uniform,' she wrote. 'The car stopped at the foot of the steps and standing erect in it he reviewed 45,000 land troops. Each camp passed him headed by its band and silver emblem. They were all clad in buff uniforms and carried spades over their shoulders. These men have to train in a camp for six months before their two years in the army and they do great land reclaimment and afforestation. Why don't we use our unemployed like that?'

After the review, Hitler mounted the rostrum. 'Then for the first time I heard the great man speak,' noted Irene, a fluent German speaker thanks to her year in Dresden before coming out. 'He replied with a fine fighting oration stoking up to a great height of emotion that National Socialism must live in the hearts of the people and not in parades and colour shows.' It must have brought back many an echo of her brother-in-law but when she later described the stirring scene to Baba and Fruity all her sister would talk about by way of response was her autumn wardrobe.

Clothes were a major preoccupation with both Metcalfes. Fruity, tall, handsome in perfectly cut riding clothes or tweeds set off by the upright carriage of the soldier, was a perfect foil for Baba's slender, immaculate elegance. But whereas Baba would spend hours at her dressmaker to ensure that every detail was right, Fruity would often ask her opinion over the daily minutiae of dress. 'Which tie shall it be this morning, Babs darling?' he would demand. 'D'ye think it should be the blue? Or would you say the red?' The constant flow of questions drove Baba to distraction and, according to Nanny, accounted for much of Baba's bad behaviour and rudeness, often to Irene, whose taste she characterised as simultaneously both over-flamboyant and dowdy.

Unsurprisingly, when Baba asked if the Metcalfes could use her house as a London base for the middle of every week the following summer, Irene hardly hesitated before writing to tell her sister that she did not think it would work.

Soon these family squabbles were eclipsed by the royal romance. In August the King, instead of going to Balmoral, had taken Wallis Simpson on a cruise along the Dalmatian coast in the yacht *Nahlin*, with a party of friends but without her husband. They were photographed everywhere, their liaison openly discussed in the American newspapers, and the buzz of gossip in the small world of English society rose to crescendo pitch.

On 23 September an incident occurred that caused widespread anger and disgust. As the King, following the usual royal custom, was staying at Balmoral during September, he had been asked to open the new Aberdeen Infirmary. He had declined to do so on the grounds that he was still in mourning for his father and in his place had sent the Duke of York. Although those on Deeside considered themselves to have a special claim to royal favour, this shirking of a royal duty might have been forgiven had the King not driven to Ballater station to meet Mrs Simpson and back to Balmoral with her sitting openly beside him in the car. 'That night, on the dour granite walls "Down with the American whore" was chalked up,' recorded a book of the period.* The King had, of course, ignored Churchill's suggestion that Mrs Simpson should not stay at Balmoral but somewhere near by.

She seemed to be everywhere, always smothered in jewels. 'My eyes were dazed at Mrs Simpson's emeralds!' reads Irene's diary after a party at the American Embassy on 2 October 1936. Harold Nicolson commented in his diary: 'It irritates me that that silly little man should destroy a great monarchy by giggling into a flirtation with a third-rate American.' Or as Ramsay MacDonald had more bluntly put it after seeing Mrs Simpson swept to Ascot in a royal carriage: 'The people of this country do not mind fornication but they loathe adultery'.

On 4 October Tom led his fascists in a parade and march in the East End of London, where there was a large Jewish community and a sizeable group of communist voters. Although, as usual, he obeyed the commands of the police to the letter, halting the parade and changing the direction of the march at their command, it was a needlessly provocative action and stirred up trouble as effectively as a stone lobbed into a bees' nest. The resultant mêlée – overturned lorries, the hurling of bricks, stones and glass, the charges with any handy blunt instrument – became known as the Battle of Cable Street. One of its repercussions was the passing of the Public Order Act which, among other clauses, forbade the wearing of uniforms for such marches.

Irene and Baba viewed the affray entirely from Tom's perspective ('It was the Jews and communists who created the disorder') – but

*Coronation Commentary by Geoffrey Dennis.

their reaction might have been different had they known what transpired two days afterwards.

On 6 October 1936, Tom Mosley married Diana Guinness, in the Berlin drawing-room of Dr Josef Goebbels and his wife Magda. Both knew that a register office marriage in England or France would not escape the notice of the press, and Diana used her friendship with Hitler to achieve the secrecy they desired. After the wedding, Hitler simply ordered the registrar to put their marriage certificate away in a drawer.

Tom, who did not inform even his mother of his marriage, had insisted on this secrecy. He told Diana it was to protect her from attack by his political opponents; its hidden agenda was so that he could continue his affair with Baba. Diana told her immediate family: she knew that her parents would view both her and Tom more kindly if they were married and she wanted the freedom to see her youngest sister, Debo, who had been barred from seeing her because she was 'living in sin'.

Baba was still torn between desire to break out of what she saw as her stultifying life and loyalty towards Fruity. The guilt she felt about her treatment of her husband and her betrayal of him with, of all people, her sister's husband found its expression in behaviour best described as a kind of poisonous gloom. Sometimes the hus-bandless, childless Irene, watching her, longed to tell her to be thankful for what she had got, otherwise she would 'miss every-thing warm and lovely in life'.

The King's love affair was now the sole topic of conversation at every luncheon or dinner party. 'Lunched with Baba and Fruity and Bobby Sweeney and we discussed the outrageous Cavalcade and Time with several awful things about Mrs Simpson and the gloomy danger of criticism of the King,' wrote Irene that October, before going with the Metcalfes to look at a house, Wilton Place, in Bel-gravia they were thinking of buying. What they did not of course know was that a few days earlier, on 27 October, the King had had his first interview with the Prime Minister. Baldwin had asked if it would be possible to halt the Simpson divorce proceedings – about to be heard at Ipswich – as, with Mrs Simpson free, there would be no stopping any gossip. The King gave Baldwin the same answer as he had given Churchill four months earlier.

The Metcalfes did not spend much time speculating about the

King's intentions. Fruity was too miserable and Baba too pre-occupied. Her infatuation with Tom Mosley was as strong as ever: in mid-November she tried to persuade Irene to come with her to Italy for a week, purely to act as a smokescreen as she had 'some important secret service work to do for T'. Fortunately, the scheme came to nothing; instead, Baba and Fruity settled on the house in Wilton Place, although it was the only thing they did agree on that bitter autumn. Soon, history itself would cause a change in their circumstances.

24

Abdication

~

At the end of October 1936 Wallis Simpson was granted a decree nisi in the Assize Court at Ipswich. Shortly after this, the King told Walter Monckton that he intended to marry her. Although Monckton had realised the depth of the King's passion, he had not expected this. 'I did not before November 1936 think that marriage between the King and Mrs Simpson was contemplated,' he noted at the time. 'The King told me that he had often wished to tell me but refrained for my own sake lest I should be embarrassed. It must have been difficult to him since I had always and honestly assumed in my conversations with him that such an idea (which was suggested in some other quarters) was out of the question.'

Shortly afterwards the King's Private Secretary, Sir Alex Hardinge, wrote the King a forceful letter in which he suggested that to quell some of the lurid speculation Mrs Simpson should go abroad for a time. The King then decided to inform Baldwin of his intention to marry, adding that he was prepared to leave the Throne if necessary (he told his family the same day). To Walter Monckton, the Prime Minister said that he did not think either the country or the Dominions would stand for the marriage.

From then on, things moved swiftly. On Sunday 15 November, Monckton lunched with the press baron Esmond Rothermere, who put forward the proposal of a morganatic marriage (one in which the wife does not take the rank or title of her husband), suggesting the same thing that evening to Baldwin. The King, desperate to gain his objective, preferably with Wallis as Queen, sent for the Prime Minister and asked him to ascertain the feelings of the Dominions and the Cabinet, thus forcing Baldwin to take up the matter on an official basis.

Telegrams were sent to the Dominions, setting out three possible options: that Wallis should become Queen; that it should be a morganatic marriage; or that the King should abdicate. The Prime Minister concluded: 'I feel convinced that neither the Parliament nor the great majority of the public here should or would accept such a plan'. To which the Cabinet added their own cadenza: 'any more than they would accept the proposal that Mrs Simpson should become Queen.'

A fourth possibility – that he should give up Mrs Simpson and remain on the Throne – had been decisively ruled out by the King, although privately Walter Monckton believed, like the Royal Family, that 'if and when the stark choice faced them between their love and his obligations as King Emperor they would in the end each make the sacrifice, devastating though it would be'.

The Dominions plumped for Abdication – Canada somewhat half-heartedly, South Africa and Australia categorically. New Zealand was less emphatic: Mrs Simpson would be impossible as queen but there was something to be said for a morganatic marriage. By now she had left the house in Regent's Park, which the King had rented her, for the safety of Fort Belvedere; soon after she went, a booing, jeering mob congregated outside and stones were thrown through the windows. From the Fort, with her faithful Aunt Bessie in attendance, she wrote a somewhat disingenuous letter to Edwina Mountbatten on 30 November:

Edwina dear,
I am lying here making all sorts of wise decisions, schemes, etc for leaving England for a while. I am really worn out with all the talk and all the furore the US press has caused here, and I know how happy my departure would make England. I think I shall have to use the story of Paris for hats, and then be hard to find, and then those charming people, the man in the street and the lunatics, will forget me, and all will be well once more.
Love Wallis

Edwina must have received it the day before the event that finally brought the affair into the open. On Sunday 2 December the Bishop of Bradford, concerned at the King's lack of regular churchgoing, preached a sermon on the sovereign's duties as Head of the Church of England. With what they saw as an attack by a cleric on the King's morality, the press felt free to unleash the flood of stories hitherto held back by the newspaper proprietors.

The following day, 3 December, the King had another audience with Baldwin. He now wished to get Wallis out of the country as quickly as possible. It was decided that she would stay with her old friends Herman and Katharine Rogers at their villa Lou Viei near Cannes, escorted thither by Lord Brownlow. The King, Wallis and his old friend Perry Brownlow dined at the Fort that night, after which Wallis set off with £100,000-worth of jewellery, without saying goodbye to any of the staff.

The news of Wallis's departure and of the King's intentions was round London in a flash. Most people felt like Irene, who wrote on 4 December: 'I feel so hideously angry that the King should have carted his people and England by asking to marry her. Mrs Simpson has apparently vanished to the South of France. Went to bed raging at this woman and the appalling catastrophe whatever the result she has brought on the King.'

On the same day the King had another interview with Baldwin and asked to see Churchill. As he was not in the Cabinet, and Baldwin had no objection, that night Churchill dined at the Fort. His advice was to play for time, largely to see what measure of support the King would gain. Later, Churchill gave an account of that meeting to Robert Bernays, who wrote in his diary on 9 December:

Winston told me that the King was in an extraordinary mental state when he visited him and that once or twice he seemed to be seized with a mental anaesthesia.

Where I do sympathise with the King is in his appalling loneliness. Winston found him quite alone. He hasn't one real friend to lean upon in this frightful emergency. His case seems to be arrested development. He has never passed the stage from boyhood to manhood. He is the spoiled child of success with the film star mentality. He sees his job only in terms of cheering crowds. He has never thought the matter out. He imagined that he could quietly retire into private life, leaving his brother to perform the dreary ceremonial functions while he spent a tranquil life gardening at Fort Belvedere and holidaying on the Riviera, occasionally emerging to open a hospital or review the Fleet and receive the cheers that mean so much to him.

For the first time he has been brought up against the fact that abdication means exile and that for the rest of his life he can serve no useful purpose.

As the terrible week rolled on, the two men who had spent so many of the early, carefree years with the King sent him supportive notes:

My dear David [wrote Mountbatten to his friend and cousin],
I can't bear sitting here doing nothing to help you in your terrible trouble.

Do you realise how many loyal supporters of all classes you have?

If you want me to help you, to do any service for you, or even to feel you have a friend of Wallis's to keep you company, you have only to telephone.

I don't want to be a nuisance but I don't want to feel there is nothing I can do except bite people's heads off who have the temerity to say anything disloyal about their king – though practically none do so – at any rate in my presence.

Your ever loyal devoted dutiful Dickie

Fruity, whose devotion had never wavered, wrote a heartfelt letter from Wilton Place.

Your Majesty,
Words cannot express how deeply I feel for you during these terrible days of anxiety. When I was in trouble you stood by me, and I wish to God that I could be of some service to you now.

Please always remember, Sir, that I am ready to do anything for you at any time.

Monckton, clever, practical and as a lawyer aware of all the constitutional and legal implications of the various courses of action mooted to the King, put forward the idea that Parliament should pass two bills immediately: one in which the King renounced the Throne and the other granting Wallis's decree absolute* (without this, Wallis would not gain her divorce and the King would have abdicated in vain), but most of the Cabinet rejected this as it smacked of a bargain. Everyone, including the King, felt that the matter should be decided quickly, as the general uncertainty was destabilising.

The King's own wish was to broadcast his intentions to the nation and then to go abroad for a while to give the people time to come to a measured decision. 'I have read the broadcast he wished to make,' wrote Monckton. 'In it he asks for the happiness of marriage, etc, and says neither he nor Wallis would insist on her being made Queen but that a title suitable for his wife should be given her.' This broadcast, with its appeal to the emotions of his listeners, was disallowed as being unconstitutional.

By now the King had virtually decided to abdicate, though on 8 December Baldwin went once more to the Fort to plead with him for a reversal of his decision. Again, the King refused, as he did a last-ditch appeal from the Cabinet the following day. Though utterly steadfast, he was exhausted, both from the tension of awaiting the outcome and by the constant telephone calls from Cannes in which Wallis alternately threatened to give him up or demanded that he obtain as much as he could get financially from the royal coffers.

'George [the Duke of Kent] came in to see us at six in despair,' wrote Edwina Mountbatten in her diary. 'He had just returned from the Fort where the King has definitely made up his mind to abdicate in favour of the Duke of York. Everything these days is too depressing for words.' That night there was the famous last dinner at which were present two of the King's brothers, the Dukes of York and Kent, Walter Monckton and several others. 'The King exhausted but puts up magnificent show,' wrote Monckton.

By the end of Thursday 10 December Monckton was equally exhausted. He arrived at Fort Belvedere at 1 a.m. with the draft Instrument of Abdication (to come into effect on Friday 11 December) and at 2.40 a.m. was caught by the King for a talk before he could retire to bed. At 9.30 a.m. the Duke of York

---

*A decree absolute was not granted until six months after a decree nisi. An official called the King's Proctor kept an eye on petitioners and if there was any hint of collusion the decree nisi could be overturned.

arrived at the Fort to be followed a few minutes later by the Duke of Gloucester, with the Duke of Kent arriving at ten.

Within minutes, the signing and witnessing of six copies of the Instrument of Abdication and seven of the Address for the House of Commons had begun, the sheets of paper spread over a simple mahogany table, with the King alone unaffected by the atmosphere of despondency. 'Dickie down at the Fort all day,' runs Edwina Mountbatten's diary. 'Chaos reigns. Final preparations for the King's Abdication being made. Everyone completely sunk except the King, who remains fairly calm and cheerful, and completely determined.'

Monckton returned to London with two notes from the King to Baldwin for inclusion in the Prime Minister's statement to the House of Commons that afternoon. Later that day Baldwin joined the King, the Duke of York and their financial advisers at Fort Belvedere to work out a settlement.

Here the King, no doubt under tremendous pressure from Mrs Simpson, made an uncharacteristic but fatal mistake: he lied to his brother about the size of his fortune, estimated by most authorities at around £1.1 million, inclusive of a settlement on Mrs Simpson of £300,000. Instead, he told the Duke that he only had £90,000. He made the same statement to Winston Churchill, with the result that neither trusted him again – to the immense detriment of future relations.

Baldwin's statement to Parliament that afternoon was described by Harold Nicolson as 'Sophoclean and almost unbearable'. It affected Robert Bernays equally, who wrote:

> I suppose none of us who were present will forget as long as they live the scene in the House of Commons on the day of the Abdication.
>
> Baldwin's speech was an amazing performance. Its material was little pieces of paper with ideas on them contributed obviously by his colleagues. When he came in with the despatch box he found he had lost his key. He desperately searched his pockets for it and then found it under Neville Chamberlain's legs. Then he tried to sort his papers, upset them and had to retrieve them from the floor. Then Hoare had to answer a question and put his papers on top of Baldwin's notes with the result that they were upset again and had to be retrieved from the floor once more.

At Denham, Irene went into Micky's nursery at 6 p.m., where she found him cutting pictures of Mrs Simpson out of the *Daily Sketch* and saying, 'Nasty Mrs Simpson', 'Horrid Mrs Simpson', before chopping them into pieces. 'I gather he had overheard Nanny saying something in the nursery,' wrote Irene. 'Tears ran down our faces, both Nanny and I, as we listened to the six o'clock news and Mr Baldwin's statement.'

That night the King worked late on his broadcast, getting up early the following morning to finish it. He had invited Churchill to luncheon, to give a final polish, and it was while they were together that he ceased to be King. As Churchill left, he quoted Marvell's famous lines on the beheading of Charles I: 'He nothing common did or mean, upon that memorable scene.' The ex-King's servants did not share that view; none of them would accompany him into his new life.

That evening the ex-King left the Fort at eight thirty, with his brothers, to dine at Royal Lodge. After dinner Walter Monckton fetched him and drove him to Windsor Castle, from where, at 10 p.m., he was to make his broadcast to the nation under his new title of HRH the Duke of Windsor. 'You must believe me when I tell you that I have found it impossible to carry the heavy burden of responsibility and to discharge my duty as King as I would wish to do, without the help and support of the woman I love', was the sentence that best sums up his attitude – and his failure.

All over London, audiences trickled out of theatres, where the Duke's speech was broadcast, as they could not bear to stay for the rest of the play. In Wilton Place Irene listened to it with the Metcalfes:

Louis Greig* had told me not to cry as the King had wanted this through and through and I was not to dramatise his agony of heart. I could wish he had left Mr Baldwin's fine eulogy of himself as the last picture as his little melodramatic epilogue of seven minutes had no greatness and was rather 'hot'-making and mingy. But it made me howl all the same. His voice sounded thick and muddled too. I said it

---

*A great friend and confidant of George VI.

was emotion. Baba said the King was a tortured demented soul, quite different from Louis's view.

Monckton then drove the Duke of Windsor back to Royal Lodge to say goodbye to his family. As it was midnight by then, Queen Mary and his sister Princess Mary soon left for London; the Duke and his three brothers 'chatted about everything except that which was in their minds,' according to Monckton. 'We kissed, parted as freemasons, and he bowed to me as King,' wrote the new king, George VI. Then the Duke and Monckton left for Portsmouth, the Duke talking easily and cheerfully all the way: it had been arranged that he would leave for France that night on the destroyer HMS *Fury*, accompanied by Ulick Alexander and Piers ('Joey') Legh.

So last-minute were the orders to the destroyer's captain, Cecil Howe, that he was obliged to borrow bedlinen, crockery, glasses and an experienced steward from the Royal Yacht. The *Fury* left Portsmouth at 2 a.m. and because the weather was poor lay off the Isle of Wight for some hours so that the ex-King could get some sleep. But his nervous tension was such that he sat up in the wardroom until 4 a.m., drinking brandy and talking of recent events. The *Fury* reached Boulogne at 3.40 the following afternoon, 12 December, tying up at a berth sealed from public view, and the party set off by special Pullman for Austria, where the Baron Eugene de Rothschild had put one of his houses, Schloss Enzesfeld, near Vienna, at the Duke's disposal.

A few days later, the diarist Chips Channon made a perceptive comment. 'I heard that garrulous gossip, Malcolm Bullock, with an expertise of felinity, remark for me to overhear: "I don't know what the Archbishop meant, as the late King had no friends". It is terribly true; only Fruity Metcalfe with his checks and his brogue. No other man friend did the King ever have.'

A young man called Dudley Forwood, an attaché at the British Legation in Vienna, was staying with the Rothschilds for a visit planned to include Christmas when his Ambassador, Sir Wolford Selby, rang him from the Embassy to tell him that the Abdication had taken place and that he must return at once. Forwood drove through the night and when he arrived learned that the Duke of Windsor was already on his way and that he, Forwood, was to be seconded as his equerry.

With the Ambassador, he met the Duke on his arrival in Vienna and they drove to Schloss Enzesfeld, set among low wooded hills and with golf and skiing near by to provide the energetic diversions which the Duke loved. Kitty Rothschild, who regarded the Duke's visit as a great social coup, was waiting to welcome him but her hopes of gaining a foothold in the Duke's circle were to be disappointed, thanks to Wallis's paranoid jealousy.

There were misunderstandings from the start. The Duke, depressed and frustrated at his separation from Wallis, was not an easy guest. It was not so much his habit of consoling himself by playing his drums loudly to a gramophone record until late at night while drinking too much brandy that worried the exhausted Legh as his attitude to his hostess.

While the former King expected everyone to conform to his wishes, Kitty, as a great beauty, was accustomed to have men fall in with hers. Out of courtesy he would go for a drive with her if she suggested it, hoping to entertain him, but these expeditions would irritate him intensely since all he really wanted to do was wait by the telephone for a call from Wallis Simpson.

Wallis, out of her depth, scared and angry, was not bearing up well. During hours of hysterical telephone conversations she berated her lover over virtually every detail of her life and his (in the three months the Duke stayed at the Schloss, he spent over £800* on telephone calls).

Christmas at Denham was also characterised by tensions and misery. There were thirteen for lunch, with only one servant to cope, and as Tom had given his manservant the day off Irene had to summon a housemaid from London to help out. Only after church did Tom appear, followed by Baba, Fruity and their children for lunch. Tom's Father Christmas performance at four o'clock went off as brilliantly as usual and tea, with Christmas cake and

*£24,000 as at March 2000 (Bank of England figures).

crackers, followed by dancing round the tree and presents, was a great success.

From then on, things went steadily downhill. At six o'clock Fruity was delegated to drive Nanny and the twins back to London. Miserable at leaving his wife with the man he so detested, he said goodbye to Irene with tears in his eyes. Boxing Day was marked by a flaming row at dinner, instigated by Tom, in a foul temper at being away from his new bride and the more adult delights of Wootton. Since none of them knew that he was now married to Diana, they could not understand such an outburst of vitriol, triggered by so trivial a cause – the cook's not sending in a green vegetable at dinner. Working himself up, he swore that he would sack the entire staff, adding that Irene and Baba could get out too. Viv became scarlet in the face, tears sprang from Baba's eyes, Nick's spectacles misted up, Granny Mosley talked wildly to get to the end of dinner and Irene, who could take no more, ran out of the room.

Two days later Fruity returned and the season of goodwill ended with another monumental row, this time between him and Baba. Almost at once, Fruity left to ski in Kitzbühel. Baba concentrated on settling into the new house in Wilton Place, dumping her children on Nancy Astor whom she managed to annoy by her casualness. 'I do think you might have the decency to drop me a line when I am looking after your children,' wrote Nancy on 12 January 1937. Baba also heard from the irrepressible Dino Grandi:

Your letter has given me much pleasure and I thank you, darling. I enclose the photo you wish and I hope you will not forget entirely your 'impossible' friend, who is and will remain – in his own way – nearer, much nearer, to you than you can possibly believe.

You ask me why I told you of being 'dead'. I did it only because I felt, after everything which has happened, that that was the only decent way through which I could ask your forgiveness. The dead are easily forgiven and forgotten...

How is Irene? And your children? I am missing London so much, much more than you may imagine. But the future is open and I have many hopes in many ways ... Naldera, darling, my sweet friend, I am yours.

Ge

At Schloss Enzesfeld, Dudley Forwood was finding the cross-currents of emotion a desperate strain.

> It was a very bad time [he recalled later]. The Duke was in a great great state. I was only 24 and not very capable of dealing with a 42-year-old ex-King. I knew he had this curious devotion to Fruity so I telephoned him in his house in Wilton Place and said: 'We really need you badly. Joey Legh has left and I'm not coping very well.' And Fruity in a typical Fruity way said: 'I'll be on that aeroplane first thing tomorrow morning, boy.' And he was.

Before flying, Fruity telephoned the Duke to ask him if he would like him to come for a short stay. 'Would I like you to!' responded the Duke enthusiastically.

Wallis thought otherwise. She now wrote to the Duke: 'Darling, I have just read in the paper that Lambe [a young naval officer appointed equerry in July 1936] is to return to London on the 19th [January]. Who is coming out in his place? You cannot be alone with Fruity. In the first place, he is not capable of handling the post and dealing with servants etc. In the second place, it is necessary that you have an equerry at all times. Surely you have some friends or your family for you to send someone to you. You must not be alone with Fruity: I won't have it.'

She may have genuinely felt that Fruity could not deal with letters or servants (although as an army officer dealing with men had been a prerequisite); more likely she feared Fruity's influence with the Duke. They had shared a past long before Wallis came on the scene, they enjoyed sports in which she took little or no part – riding, skiing, golf – and a word or phrase could set them off into uncontrollable schoolboy giggles that mystified onlookers.

After an uncomfortable journey Fruity was met by an army of press photographers. At the Schloss, where he was warmly welcomed, there were only Kitty Rothschild, the Duke, Charles Lambe and Dudley Forwood, in a household run almost as if the Duke were still King. At about nine fifteen every morning Forwood would enter his bedroom, bare of personal possessions save for a number of large photographs of Wallis, to ask the Duke, then just waking up, if he had any special plans. 'Nao,' the Duke would reply in his curious half-cockney accent, 'I think we'll play a bit of golf.'

Forwood would pass this information on to the senior valet, who would set up a long table, spread with baize, on which he would place all the Duke's golf suits, each with its matching shoes, shirt and socks. From these the Duke would select his outfit, have his bath and descend in his dressing-gown to a breakfast of kippers (sent from Fortnum & Mason) and Oxford marmalade, after which he would dress. Forwood, who would have arranged a game with the golf pro, would accompany him round the course, walking the three dogs, Cora, Jaggs and Wallis's dog Slipper, all on leashes.

Back at the Schloss, the Duke would change into a suit for the light luncheon – a little cheese, some fruit – that he invariably favoured. Dinner in the evening, cooked by the French chef, was more elaborate – and meant another change of clothes. Apart from the work of the servants, whatever the Duke did required the attention of someone, at once, no matter what they happened to be doing.

'All his life he went on behaving as if he were still what he once had been,' commented Dudley Forwood. 'He could never accept that he was now, in real terms, a nobody.' In this he was aided and abetted by Mrs Simpson, who nagged him violently over the telephone about the way he was living, the people around him and her own fears and problems, all with the underlying refrain that he must stand up for his rights and extract more money from his brother.

When Fruity arrived he was delighted to find the Duke in his old friendly, affectionate, amusing form. That night, they sat up talking almost until dawn; the next morning Fruity discovered that, just as in the old days, the Duke's energy was formidable, with everything done to excess. Now that he had a skiing companion they skied until it was too dark to see, then played poker all night.

From Schloss Enzesfeld Fruity wrote Baba a series of letters that reveal an immediate and accurate grasp of the situation, from the Duke's frenetic desire to cram his days until his wedding to his utter subjugation to Wallis.

'I've never seen HRH better,' begins the first, written on 22 January 1937.

Happy, cheerful, no regrets *about anything* – he talked to W for hours after we'd finished playing poker. The conversation did *not* seem to go well. Talks of marriage early in May, no date fixed. Has NO idea of returning to England for a year or two at least. Do not think he misses England or *anything* connected with it one little bit – he seems glad to be free of it. I think Kitty has got on his nerves. She won't leave. He gets quite short with her at times. Says he wants to be with men only and doesn't want any women about. Yesterday spent the day in Vienna. Turkish bath all evening, he and I, then shopping, then big cocktail party at the Embassy. I never leave him.

Lambe left today for England but Greenacre has just arrived – he was sent out from England before they knew I was coming. I'm glad, as he does the letters etc. Tonight he was told at dinner that H.M. wanted to talk on phone to him. He said he couldn't take the call but asked for it to be put through at 10 p.m. The answer to this was that H.M. said he would talk at 6.45 tomorrow as he was too busy to talk at any other time. It was pathetic to see HRH's face. He couldn't believe it! He's been so used to having everything done as he wishes. I'm afraid he's going to have many more shocks like this.

Fruity's comment was all too true. The negotiations for a financial settlement were dragging (they were eventually resolved satisfactorily) and the Duke, who all his life had played the role of elder brother to the full, continued to telephone the new King with advice on the questions of the day which, as Walter Monckton wrote, 'often ran counter to the advice which the King was getting from his responsible Ministers in the government'. Eventually, Monckton was charged with the delicate task of visiting Schloss Enzesfeld and conveying to the Duke that these calls must cease.

The rest of Fruity's letter was equally accurate. '[H.R.H] is just living through each day until he can be with W. The 27 April is the date. He ticks off each day on a calendar beside his bed. Lots of people are marked down as never having heard from them. e.g. Hugh and Helen and Emerald he's mentioned. He tells me he didn't know till about an hour before he left England when he was going to. Goodbye dearest one, *all* my love I send you. You've been very wonderful to me and helped me so much. Without you I wouldn't be here; and this is a great success, and I am so happy I am here.'

Two days later, exhausted from day-long skiing on poor snow and talking until the small hours every night – the Duke would wander in and out of Fruity's room until 4 a.m. – he repeated that Kitty was getting on the Duke's nerves.

He is frightfully keen to have the place to himself. You know how he loves to run his own show – but the fact is she loves to be acting as hostess for him. I am very happy and HRH couldn't be a more delightful companion – he's not had one bad day since I arrived.

Of course he's on the line for hours and hours every day to Cannes. I somehow don't think these talks go well sometimes. It's only ever after one of them that he seems a bit worried and nervous. She seems to be always picking on him or complaining about something that she thinks he hasn't done and ought to do (this sounds as if I hear all the conversation – of course this isn't so but as my room is next to his and he talks terribly loudly it's awfully difficult not to hear a certain amount that he says anyway).

He is like a prisoner doing a time sentence. All he is living for is to be with her on the 27 April. As we come back every night after skiing he says 'One more day nearly over.' Never have I seen a man more madly in love. The telephone never stops and his mail is enormous, sometimes 300 letters, etc, mostly from mad people! Gosh but some of them are abusive! We never show him any of those of course. They come from all over the world. I wish you were here but there is no chance. He won't have any women at all!

The Duke's growing obsession with his financial position soon manifested itself: on 27 January Fruity's letter reported: 'HRH is frightfully close about money, he won't pay for anything. It's become a mania with him. It really is not too good. But once more let me say; HRH is a 100 per cent and the most delightful companion. If he'd remain as he is now I'd give up anything to serve him for the rest of my life. I really am devoted to him.'

Fruity felt immense pity for his friend, flagellated daily by the woman with whom he was obsessed. 'She is at him every day on the phone. He always seems to be excusing himself for something or other. I feel so sorry for him, he is never able to do what she considers the right thing. 3.00 a.m. – HRH came in and stopped till now. I will not have time to write more as we are to leave for skiing at 8.00 to do our first run.'

On 3 February Fruity wrote from the Hotel Bristol, Vienna. 'Kitty left yesterday! *Terrible* show! as HRH was late getting dressed owing to his infernal Cannes telephone call!! Missed her! *never saw her to say goodbye or thank her!* She was frightfully hurt and I don't blame her. He *is* awfully difficult at times and this is the worst thing he's done yet. I went down to the station with a letter which I got him to write to her, and that made things a *bit* better. He also never saw the servants to tip them or thank them etc, all due to more d—mn talking to Cannes. *It never stops.* Isn't it too awful? *Nothing* matters when Cannes is on the line.'

Even Fruity's sweet nature was tested. 'The evenings lately have been *dreadful*!' he wrote to Baba on 2 February 1937. 'He won't think of bed before 3.00 a.m. and now has started playing the accordion and the bagpipes. Last night there was almost a *row* on the phone. W. said she'd read he'd been having an affair with Kitty! This is d—mn funny but I can tell you it was no joke last night. He got in a *terrible* state. Their conversation lasted nearly two hours.'

A visit by the Duke's sister Princess Mary and her husband Lord Harewood made a welcome change from the exhausting routine of skiing and late nights. By early March the tensions, fatigue and stressful emotional atmosphere were beginning to tell even on Fruity, who had been there longer than anyone else in the Duke's retinue. Soon after telling Baba, 'I *love* being here with HRH but it is *very* tiring', he was writing 'I am really very unhappy at the prospect of another month at least of this life. It is a dreadful strain. I am definitely feeling it now. However he needs me and wants me so I must do it for him.'

The Duke had again refused to allow Baba to join them. Instead he wanted Fruity to accompany him to a new, more secret temporary abode – the Duke of Westminster's hunting lodge, Château de Saint-Saëns, as Fruity confided to Baba with many underlinings as to secrecy (in the event, the Duke did not go there).

Baba was in no hurry for her husband to come home; she was busy planning a motoring trip in France that would take her away shortly before his arrival. She sent him a wire suggesting he put off his return, to which Fruity replied that he had important things to discuss with her.

He explained why he did not wish to stay on longer than 24 March. 'I've carried on here and made a great success of it and HRH is very grateful to me but sweetheart I am very tired and can't stand it much longer. You have *no idea* what a strain it is. I am on duty all day and all night and no one person can stand that for long. Dickie arrived yesterday and leaves tomorrow and he will take this letter and will tell you *something* of what the life is like. Is it too much to ask you to stay in England till I get back?'

Mountbatten had been visiting his lady friend Yola Letellier in Paris and on 11 March flew on to see the Duke. The following day was devoted to discussion of the situation. What the Duke was chiefly anxious to know was when, in Mountbatten's opinion, he could return to the Fort – he still had not grasped that giving up the throne also meant giving up England.

'Talking with David and Fruity nearly all day,' runs Mountbatten's diary. 'Also wrote. Important talk with David, and possibility of return.' Next day it was: 'Breakfast at 7.15 with David. Very sad saying goodbye on both sides. Caught 9.00 plane for Prague, changed and went on via Nuremberg and Strasbourg. I was terribly sick in the storm.'

Baba refused to put off her trip despite her husband's pleas. 'I am *frightfully* sorry that I will miss you,' he wrote, 'but if *nothing* will put you off doing your trip as arranged I want you to go and really enjoy it there and have a lovely time – you deserve it after all the work you've put in at the house and as you say you're not looking well it is *essential* that you get away. It is just unlucky that I am not going to see you. I would have loved it. Is it just you and Edwina doing this trip? I'd have thought you would be very bored with her alone after a bit.'

Fruity's suspicions were correct. As well as Edwina, and Ronnie and Nancy Tree, the party included Jock Whitney.

25

'I Should Have Kissed Her but I Just Couldn't'

~

The day on which Fruity left Schloss Enzesfeld was momentous also for Irene, who took the Mosley children for the first time to her new house, 10 Cornwall Terrace, one of the Nash houses overlooking Queen Mary's Rose Garden on the south side of Regent's Park. She had left Deanery Street because the highly fashionable Dorchester Hotel, opened a few years earlier, generated so much traffic noise and its high roof took away much of the light.

Her friend Victor Cazalet was also moving. He had finally been able to buy the house he longed for, Swifts, at Cranbrook in Kent, which he planned to transform to his liking. 'Already it is utterly altered in atmosphere – orchids, central heating,' wrote another of their friends, Blanche Dugdale, who lunched there the same month in a party full of the leading politicians of the day, including Neville Chamberlain, then Chancellor of the Exchequer but known to be succeeding Baldwin as Prime Minister at the end of May 1937.

On 7 February Irene wrote Nevile Henderson a long letter of congratulations and good wishes on his appointment as Ambassador to Berlin. 'And I might have been Ambassadress there, if I had married Nevile,' her diary notes wistfully. She spent Easter with the children at Denham, giving them Easter egg hunts all over the garden. Their father did not appear. When she was preparing to leave, Nick said to her: 'I do not want you to go to London, Aunty. I want you to stay here with me.' 'I want nothing better than that to be said to me,' she wrote in her diary that night.

At the end of March she lunched with Fruity, full of news about his time at Schloss Enzesfeld. Many things had pained and annoyed the Duke, Fruity told her, such as the wholesale desertion of his servants, the abuse of Wallis Simpson by his society friends and the strictures of the Archbishop of Canterbury. 'He was determined on a royal wedding for this awful woman and Fruity says he is more punctilious than ever over HRH medals and proper procedure than ever he was as king.' Interspersed with this gossip were continual questions about Baba. 'Will she come back better pleased with me?' Fruity kept asking pathetically. 'Is she well?' Irene found reassurance difficult.

By now the Duke had left Enzesfeld to stay at the Landhaus Appesbach, a small hotel near Ischgl, in the Austrian Tyrol, where Fruity wrote to him on 27 March:

I had a dull and boring trip home with plenty of time to think over these last months, which you allowed me to spend with you. I cannot tell you how much they have meant to me, and how happy I have been. I loved every minute of my stay and never will I forget your kindness to me, Sir. I really feel awfully lonely, and miss you more than I can say, and this is true. You are a marvellous host and nothing is too much trouble for you to do for anyone you like. You have certainly proved that to me and believe me, I am awfully grateful.

Today I went to Ascot to see David [his son, almost ten] and went into The Fort on my way back. I did not see the gardener but Willis took me round. The daffodils are just coming out and the tulips are going to be very good, also the rhodos. The grass bank behind the tennis court had given way after the heavy snow but is being repaired. I went into the house but it looked so sad, all empty, that I did not stay long. I must say, every care is being taken of the place and the gardens are in perfect condition.

If there is anything at all you want done here, please make use of me. Goodbye for the present, the best of good luck and once more very many thanks for a grand time.

In mid-April Irene was asked to a large dinner party given for the Duke and Duchess of Kent. The Duke (formerly Prince George), youngest and favourite brother of the Duke of Windsor, talked to her for a long time about Fruity, the Duke of Windsor, Emerald Cunard and the rest of the circle who had formerly surrounded the ex-King. Fruity's straightforward devotion and immense loyalty to his brother were exceptional and did him immense credit, said the Duke of Kent (on whom Fruity had called several times with various messages and commissions from the Duke of Windsor).

Three days later, Tom made a surprise visit to his children at Denham. For once, sixteen-year-old Vivien was able to bask in his approval as he read her prize-winning essay on Capri and went over the exam papers in which she had done so well.

Irene was still cramming her days with activity: a speech at the annual dinner of the British Women's Symphony Orchestra at the Savoy on 20 April, a visit to the Maginot Line at Strasbourg on 22 April, where she saw the pillboxes in which humans could supposedly live for two years underground. 'There among the fresh green grass were coils and coils of murderous barbed wire, ready to unroll. Are we all insane that we go on like this?' Then it was on through the Vosges, to look at chateaux and churches, and back to Croydon airport on Wednesday evening, down to Denham on 30 April and back to London on the evening of 2 May.

She returned to pandemonium – David with a raging temperature and Fruity in a melancholic heap going off to dine alone even though Baba was back from her motoring tour. Nanny had found David motionless while Baba was on the telephone, thought he looked ill and discovered that he had a temperature of 102. 'Of course he had to be brought to me as Baba had no cook or servants there.' None of this put Baba off her evening plans and Irene had to take her sister to the theatre where Baba was meeting friends.

Irene had begun to view her sister as irremediably selfish. The moment the Coronation (on 12 May 1937) was over, Baba had whisked away Cim's tiara from her and then requested Cim's superb pearls without asking if Irene wanted either of them. This was maddening – but not nearly as ominous as a remark made by her adored nephew, Mick. Diana Guinness had visited Denham for two nights before his fifth birthday and after her departure the little boy, sitting in his bath, had asked Nanny if she was still there and then had suddenly added: 'I believe in the end Daddy will marry Mrs Guinness.'

*

In France, preparations for the wedding of the Duke of Windsor and Wallis Simpson were well under way. Wallis had moved from Cannes to the Château de Candé in Touraine, generously loaned to her (through her friend Herman Rogers) by the American multimillionaire Charles Bedaux as a place to stay until her wedding, now arranged for 3 June. It would also be a refuge from the press: at Candé, surrounded by land owned by Bedaux, it would be much easier to obtain seclusion than in the Cannes home of the Rogerses.

Although neither the Duke nor Wallis had ever met Charles Bedaux or his wife Fern, they had no hesitation in accepting the loan of his house for their wedding. The most obvious first consequence was the financial cost to the Bedaux. Fortunately Bedaux, as the originator of time-and-motion studies, had made an immense fortune by his methods of improving efficiency in industry.

From early February onwards, Herman Rogers had been writing constantly on behalf of Wallis and her requirements to the Bedaux butler, James Hale, who was handling the logistics of the visit. She wanted an important chef – the one who had been working for the American Ambassador in Paris was mooted – two nightwatchmen, one for the chateau and one for its grounds, accommodation for a man from the Sûreté and from Scotland Yard, rooms for her maid, chauffeur and Mrs Rogers's maid, a safe for her priceless jewellery, and arrangements for her truckful of luggage.

Charles and Fern Bedaux, who lived in considerable style, already had twenty-four indoor servants, grooms, gardeners, gamekeepers and a separate laundry staff. Visitors were received by a butler and two footmen but Wallis wanted more: a pastrycook, sous-chef and scullery boy, a second butler and footman, four maids and two charwomen, five laundrywomen, more gardeners, an extra chauffeur, a telephonist, a number of golf-course workers and a gatekeeper.

All this was arranged in immense secrecy. Hale (who later went to work for the Windsors) posted his letter from Amsterdam in order to avoid any connection between the Château de Candé and Wallis Simpson. On 20 February he was able to report that he had engaged the highly-qualified chef requested by Wallis for F2,000 a month. This was Alphonse Diot, chef to the Duke of Alba, who was leaving his service after fourteen years because the Duke's palace had been destroyed. Hale also assured Rogers that the rest of the extra servants requested would be arriving in two days' time.

On 3 May Wallis's decree nisi arrived at Candé. Next day the Duke arrived to join her. 'Mike [Wardell] is leaving here to fly to you tomorrow so I thought I'd send you a line,' wrote Fruity to the Duke on 8 May. 'Thank God those awful weeks of waiting are over now. It is *marvellous to see you looking* so happy *in your photos.*' Once again, telegrams, telephone calls and letters flew back and forth, in a confusion aided by Wallis's sudden and inexplicable changing of her name by deed poll from Simpson to Warfield on 12 May.

The Duke had hoped to have at least one of his brothers as supporters at his wedding although in this he was to be disappointed. The Church of England, of which the King was head, did not recognise the marriage of divorced persons and none of the Royal Family would want to be seen to flout its teachings at such a delicate time for the monarchy. Once again, the Duke turned to the old friend on whom he knew he could rely. On 17 May he sent Fruity a typewritten letter:

Dear Fruity,
First of all, Wallis and I hope that you and Baba will come here to stop for our wedding on Thursday 3 June. We suggest you arriving on Monday, 1 June, and I enclose a list of the trains from Paris in case you don't fly. The trains underlined in red are more for the information of guests who are only invited for the day.

Secondly, I want to say that I hope you will be my Best Man, so that even if Baba is unable to get away that week, you will anyway come yourself and play this important part at the ceremony.

It was nice of you to write by Mike Wardle [*sic*] and I can still hardly believe that the terrible months of separation are over. It seems too good to be true. Our plans are working themselves out gradually despite the withholding of a single helping hand from England, not that we ever expected one. But the behaviour of some people is utterly amazing.

Write and tell me soon that you will be my best man, and looking forward to seeing you on 1 June.

Yours sincerely,
Edward

A handwritten PS followed. 'We shall be wearing tailcoats at the wedding. I shall personally wear a black coat and striped trousers but a grey tailcoat suit would be all right for you if you prefer that. E'

Fruity accepted with alacrity but not everyone thought he had made the right decision. One of the Duke's oldest friends, Lord Sefton, foolishly made disparaging remarks about the Metcalfes' acceptance of the Windsor wedding invitation in front of Irene, who told him forcefully what the Duke of Kent had said about Fruity's marvellous loyalty to his brother.

The Château de Candé stood on high ground, with a view over miles of green countryside dotted with groups of tall poplars and willows. Parts of it were sixteenth century, with high towers, pointed turrets, heavily embellished Gothic doorways and huge underground vaults. The estate covered a thousand acres and included one of the best private golf courses in France; here the Duke played nearly every day of his stay and, if not, kept fit by scything the grass in the meadow.

The Bedaux had spent a fortune on refurbishing the château to the highest standards of 1930s comfort. There was American plumbing, huge refrigerators and a bar, originally the old sixteenth-century kitchen, its hooks for meat, game and hams still in place, in one of the underground vaults. In another was the dining-room, its walls covered with ancient Cordoba leather. The big drawing-room was still decorated in its Victorian red damask and the chapel in Victorian high Gothick. The Bedaux, neither of whom was Catholic, maintained this for the people on the estate but it was far too small for a wedding.

Instead, the Windsor nuptials were to take place in the pretty Music Room, used by Fern Bedaux as her sitting-room. This had Louis Seize panelling drag-painted in pale green with lavish yellow silk curtains and an Aubusson carpet patterned with circlets of flowers and cherries. For the wedding, the piano had to be lifted out of the window so that the altar could be put in its place.

As well as all the extra servants, the Duke took it for granted that his host would defray all incidental expenses. His mail was enormous and if he wanted a hundred letters put in the post, which arrived and left the château at 9 a.m., he would simply hand them over to be stamped and collected. His telephone bills continued to be colossal and if the party lunched out or visited a place of interest it was invariably Charles Bedaux who picked up the bills and tipped. The butler, Hale, had also ordered the *New York Herald*, the *Continental Daily Mail*, *Le Figaro*, the *Daily Express*, *Daily Mirror*, *Daily Sketch* and *News Chronicle*, all in the name of his employer. Perhaps because she believed Wallis was inciting the Duke to take advantage of her husband's generosity, there was little love lost between Fern Bedaux and Wallis.

In contrast with the Duke's stinginess, Wallis spent freely – on herself. In the month before her wedding, she ordered sixty-six dresses. Every weekend her favourite manicurist came from Paris, for a fee of 10s plus travelling expenses, to give her a pedicure and manicure, using only the palest of nail varnish so as not to draw attention to the large, ugly hands Wallis so disliked. For the same reason, the only gap in her otherwise magnificent collection of jewellery was rings; the exception was her platinum engagement ring with its huge rectangular emerald.

The day before the wedding, Cecil Beaton arrived at the château to take photographs, a day-long session interrupted by lunch – curried eggs, rice and kidneys – under the trees. The Duke, Beaton noticed, ate only strawberries and cream. Baba, who had arrived the night before, told Beaton at tea that she was amazed at his high spirits. Dudley Forwood knew better: he told Beaton how hurt the Duke was that so many of his friends had not come to his wedding.

From the moment of her arrival, Baba kept a diary of those historic two days.

I came here on Tuesday evening at six o'clock. I have never dreaded an arrival or visit more and would have given my fortune for the train never to stop. We were met by Ladbroke and an army of photographers. The arrival here was even more dispiriting and the castle is a rather ordinary and ugly example in quite nice grounds. Mr Bedaux met us and we were shot down a spiral staircase with one very small bedroom, entirely Empire furniture. My heart sank and I wanted to scream and break everything.

Fruity, as best man, was put next to the Duke on the ground floor, in a small suite which included a double bedroom with sitting room (occupied by the Duke) with, beyond, a shared bathroom and Fruity's room.

Wallis appeared before long [continues Baba's diary]. Not having seen her for so long I had forgotten how unattractive her voice and manner of speaking are. Her looks ensure that in any room of only moderately pretty women she would always be by far the ugliest and her figure is thin, with absolutely no line ... Wallis lost no time in explaining to me that she lived at the other end of the chateau to the Duke and he called it W1 and W2.

The rest of the party, Mrs Merriman – Aunt Bessie – harmless old girl who must have had a stroke as half of her face doesn't function and her mouth is squidgways on. Mrs Rogers – common, ordinary large-boned American. Herman, nice, quiet, efficient but unknowledgeable about what to give to the press, obviously knows nothing of England and world opinion. Mr Bedaux and Mme Bedaux are infinitely better than I expected. She is like a borzoi and is not at all common and he is brilliant and very articulate but unattractive. They are very retiring and might be guests. Wallis is paying the cheques. Dudley Forward [sic], the equerry very loyal to HRH and Wallis. We sat around and chatted in the library till HRH came in in his shirtsleeves from the office where he was competing with letters, telegrams and presents. He could not look better or be in better spirits. Outwardly he appears just the same as when I last saw him a year ago as King at the Fort.

That evening dinner (I sat between Alan the solicitor [George Allen, the Duke's solicitor] and HRH) went off very easily but one has no feeling of being at a unique occurrence or witnessing a page of history. I feel I'm passing the weekend in an ugly chateau with people (with the exception of HRH) who are unattractive and completely ignorant of what is happening and who I never want to see again. HRH is in marvellous form, obviously happy, much easier to talk to, has made not one allusion to England, family, staff or friends. Walter and he disappeared after dinner with Alan and we carried on desultory conversation till we went to bed. The telephone goes a lot and Herman makes dates to interview the press.

The list of presents is rather pathetic so far, only the Duke of Kent and one or two well-known names. He sees through Wallis's eyes, hears through her ears and speaks through her mouth. So far Kent and Gloucester are the only members of the family who have sent presents or letters.

(The Metcalfes had given the Duchess an evening bag and the Duke a St Christopher medallion from Cartier. On the wedding day itself Fruity gave him a Cartier watch.)

This morning [2 June] the parson arrived, a gallant fellow called Jardine from Darlington. He wrote and offered to come as he felt that the way the marriage was being treated by the Church, bishops etc was appalling. HRH is so pleased to be having a religious ceremony. We found a chest suitable for an altar, put a lamé and lawn tablecloth of Wallis's round it and with the aid of Mrs Spry's flowers it looked quite pretty. Cecil Beaton arrived to take photos. Herman Rogers was going to give a list of present givers to the press. Fruity got him to give up the idea. Bedaux, Aunt Bessie, Mrs Rogers, Fruity and I went to lunch at Sembeaucy, a gargantuan meal. I like the Bedaux more and more, they have done fascinating trips and are very interesting. We fetched a cross for the altar from a local church.

The Rev. Robert Anderson Jardine, vicar of the village of Darlington, near Durham, had volunteered to take the service when he saw the headline: 'No religious ceremony for the Duke of Windsor'.

At teatime Walter Monckton arrived; Baba found him charming. What her diary does not mention is that Monckton brought with him a letter from the King saying that although the Duke, notwithstanding his Act of Abdication, was entitled to the style and title of His Royal Highness, his wife was not. Monckton had argued against this but, as the King had reminded Baldwin, once a person has become a Royal Highness there is no means of removing the title – and the royal family knew little of Mrs Simpson save that this was her third marriage.

The Duke was shattered. Although the words with which he received the news were temperate ('This is a nice wedding present') it was a wound that festered for the rest of his life and, more than anything else, poisoned his relationship with his family – in part because he simply could not understand that abdication meant the complete renunciation of former powers and privileges.

Letters and telegrams pour in [continues Baba's diary]. Both Wallis and HRH appear very unrattled. She curtseys to him and calls him 'Sir' and rises slightly when he comes into a room. I gather he understood fairly well his staff, Joey etc not coming but took Perry's [Lord Brownlow, one of the Duke's oldest friends] backout the worst. Her not being made HRH was much the worst blow. At dinner last night they implied that a visit to America was in the offing and Dudley mentioned Paris in the autumn. Both would be mad.

I've never seen him happier or less nervous but try with all one's might and main when looking at her one can't register that she can be the cause of the whole unbelievable story. One almost begins to think there is nothing incredible, unique or magic about it as they are so blind to it all. Except for the press which one does not see as they are only allowed as far as the gates one might be attending the wedding of any ordinary couple.

The bitterness is there all right in both of them. He had an outburst to Fruity while dressing for dinner. The family he is through with, he will be loyal to the Crown but never to the man (the King). He blames him for weakness in everything. The friends, staff and Perry have also been awful. He intends to fight the HRH business as legally the King has no right to stop the courtesy title being assumed by his wife. Monckton and Allen agree there but let's hope he does nothing.

Wallis had lots to say about staff, Perry and HRH to me. She said it didn't matter to her, but she minds a great deal really and says Monckton has made her sign just Wallis on the documents today. She said that she realised that there was no insult that they hadn't tried to heap on her.

She thanked me effusively twice for having come, and twice said she thought it was so very sweet of me. A scene never to be forgotten, more perhaps than the ceremony: the rehearsal before dinner. A small pale green room with an alcove in one corner. The organist Dupré from Paris trying out the music in the room next door, Fruity walks in with HRH and stands on the right of the alcove, Wallis on Herman's arm comes in – under the tutelage of Jardine, large-nosed, bulging-eyed red-faced little man, they go over the service, HRH's jaw working the whole time exactly the same as I saw the King's all through the

Coronation. Walter Monckton, Allen and I watch with such a mixture of feelings. The tune played for 'O Perfect Love' is not the lovely one, so I sang it to the organist who wrote it down as easily as I am writing this. M. Bedaux keeps calling Jardine 'the Reverent'. For the guests, there were 33 chairs placed in rows, with another 15 in the library from which the chateau staff could watch. All was in place the night before.

Although the Duke had worn shorts and open-neck shirt to greet all those who arrived on 2 June, dinner that night was of the utmost formality, with the women dressed as for a ball and blazing with jewels – Wallis sported a new one, two huge quills, one set with diamonds, another with rubies.

'Dinner. Kitty and Eugene [the Baron and Baroness de Roths-child] and Randolph Churchill came to dine. I sat on H.R.H.'s right with Monckton on the other side who I could not like more. He is devoted to him. No word as yet from the King, Queen or Queen Mary and nothing is settled about the £25,000 a year.' Baba also noted that when Wallis went to bed on this last night before the wedding she shook hands with her future husband, curtsied and said 'Good night, Sir' in exactly the same way as she said goodnight to the other guests.

At seven on the morning of 3 June the police took up their places. All road traffic round the nearest village, Monts, was stopped, no parking allowed near the estate and only those with passes let in, although the villagers were permitted to line the avenue. At 8 a.m., Wallis's hairdresser arrived, carrying flowers; Wallis's hair was set, her face massaged and her nails manicured. As on the previous morning, Baba saw the Duke 'in dressing gown and tousled hair sitting on the floor going through all the mail helped by Mr Carter and his old chief clerk', sorting through some of the hundreds of letters and the 1,000-odd telegrams – including one from every member of the royal family.

At 11.47 came the brief civil ceremony, conducted by the mayor of Monts, Charles Mercier, and since it was in French with French responses, also rehearsed the night before. After this, the newly-weds withdrew briefly.

At ten past twelve, what everyone – the Duke included – regarded as the real marriage took place. With Jardine standing by the makeshift altar, which was adorned with pink and white peonies, Marcel Dupré began to play a Bach concerto, followed by a chorale.

Only seven English people were present: Monckton, Allen, Randolph Churchill (the only one in a frock-coat, a garment abolished by the Duke during his brief reign), Hugh Thomas, Lady Selby and the Metcalfes. Baba sat beside Walter Monckton, soon to become a great friend.

Baba's diary, headed 3.30, 3 June 1937, continues:

It's over and it's true. I felt all through the evening that I must be in a dream. It was hard not to cry, in fact I did. In the room itself besides the guests already mentioned there were a number of French officials and wives and five members of the press. The servants were in the adjoining room.

The civil ceremony took place first, at which Fruity and Herman R. were present. During that time we sat and waited, talking ordinarily as though nothing unusual was happening and the organ playing from the room next door. Jardine came in first, followed shortly by the Duke and Fruity, who stood two yards from my chair.

The Duke, in morning coat, dark yellow waistcoat and grey check tie, asked Fruity to hold his prayer book, given to him by Queen Mary when he was ten and inscribed: 'To David from his loving Mother'.

The diary goes on:

Wallace [sic] on Herman R's arm came in by the other door. She was in a long blue dress with short tightfitting coat, blue straw halo hat with feathers and tulle and the loveliest diamond and sapphire bracelet, which was her wedding present [her octagonal wedding ring was of Welsh gold]. Jardine read the service simply and well. 'Do you, Edward Albert George Christian Andrew Patrick David, etc, take, etc.' His responses were clear and firm and very well said. Her voice 'I Bessie Wallis' was much lower but very clear.

It could be nothing else but pitiable and tragic, to see a king of England of only six months ago, an idolised king, married under those circumstances and yet, pathetic as it was, his manner was so simple and dignified and he was so sure of himself in his happiness that it gave something to the sad little service which it is hard to describe. She could not have done it better. We shook hands with them in the salon, I realised I should have kissed her but I just couldn't. In fact, I was bad the whole of yesterday. My effort to be charming, and like her, broke down. In fact, I don't remember wishing her happiness and good luck.

If she occasionally showed a glimmer of softness, took his arm, looked as tho' she loved him, one would warm towards her. But her attitude is so correct and hard the effect is of an older woman moved by the infatuated love of a much younger man. Let's hope that she lets up in private with him, otherwise it must be grim.

After the marriage service, the Duke entered the salon with tears running down his face. The first of the 250 bottles of champagne was opened and Fruity gave the toast: 'Long life to His Royal Highness the Duke of Windsor and his bride'. The Duke laughed and said: 'I didn't know Fruity could make such a speech.' Wallis began to cut the three-tier wedding cake, plain under its carapace of icing; it took her a quarter of an hour, including all those to whom pieces had to be sent. After this, she made a good lunch, although the Duke was still so moved he could not eat.

A very nice telegram from King and Queen* and one from Queen Mary [records Baba's diary]. We all had a buffet lunch and I took a number of photos. It was easy and gay. All guests left by three and we sat around till we left for the train. She changed into a dark blue coat and skirt for travelling and they left at 6 to motor to Laroche and so to Wasserleonburg [Count Munster's chateau, where the Windsors spent most of the summer]. Lady Selby, Mr Allan, Jardine and Walter Monckton came back in the train.

When he knew Wallis was not going to be allowed to be HRH he said he wanted to give up his own title. He has written a letter to the King saying he will not *admit* the fact of Wallis not being HRH.

The hopes are that the King will give him £25,000 which with what he has already got should give him about £60,000 a year. Only an ordinary settlement has been made on her.

---

*'We are thinking of you with great affection on this your wedding day and send you every wish for your future happiness much love Elizabeth and Bertie.'

At home, on 4 June, Baba put down her last thoughts:

No one ever knew to what extent Wallis was at the bottom of every-thing. Baldwin is supposed to say that as a schemer and intriguer she is unsurpassed. My opinion is that she must have hoped to be either Queen or morganatic wife as if she had realised she would get neither she would and could have stopped him putting forward the whole idea. Although I loathe her for what she has done I'm unable to dislike her when I see her. Her hardness I find very unattractive but that is the only outstanding thing I can find to criticise, and yet there might be something more as, except for him, I would never cross the *street* to see her again.

We dined with the Kents on the night we got back at Coppins. They wished to hear every detail. I've had the impression they would have preferred to hear a bad account than a favourable one. She obviously dislikes him because of old slights and rudeness. He wrote to Queen Mary in reply to her letter to the effect that her good wishes did not ring true. Prince G said it was an awful letter.

The family loathe and abhor her so naturally are reluctant to send wishes to both. For this he won't forgive them so he replies by curt answers. The HRH question is more complicated. Terence O'Connor, Attorney General who did it all for the Government, explained it. The courtesy title of HRH was only started by Victoria and is only used by members of the royal family who are in lineal succession to the throne. Therefore when the King abdicated he was no longer in the line of succession and therefore no longer really was rightfully HRH but when he was going to make his Abdication broadcast Sir John Reith rang up and told the King he was going to introduce him as Mr Windsor. The King said no, introduce him as Prince Edward. This having been done, the step was taken and he has remained HRH although his case and the Prince Consort are the only two exceptions. Wallis's right to the HRH is therefore nil.

26

The Cliveden Set

~

By the end of 1936 the British Union was nearly bankrupt. The money from Italy had ceased, the fallout from the Cable Street affair had frightened off many supporters, and the Public Order Act, passed on 18 December 1936, forbade the wearing of uniforms and gave police the right to call off marches.

Tom's first step was to sack many of the staff; his next to mortgage his estate for £80,000 and put £100,000 into BU funds. His third, at the beginning of June, was to tell the Curzon sisters that he would be letting Savehay Farm and the children would have to spend their holidays at Wootton in future. Since no one knew of his marriage, this was the equivalent of saying that they must live with his mistress. Baba at once wrote to tell him that he had no right to put the sixteen-year-old Vivien in such a position.

On 11 June Irene was shocked to receive a telephone call from the *Daily Mail* correspondent in Berlin, Ward Price, saying that there was a report that Tom had married Diana Guinness in Berlin. She rushed round to tell Baba who sensibly told her not to burst out with this to Tom or it would make him more furious on the subject than ever. Instead, she arranged to see the Mosley family solicitor the same day, who told her that Tom had mentioned neither the question of letting Denham nor having the children at Wootton when they had met the day before.

Next morning Lady Mosley asked Irene to come round as she had a proposal from Tom to discuss with her. Before bringing it out, Lady Mosley told Irene how badly she felt about it. What Tom had suggested was that if Irene felt his children should remain in the family home, she should pay the annual running costs of

£1,500 herself and make arrangements for the children to repay her when they came of age. He justified this, said Lady Mosley, by saying that he had no more money to spend on them.

Later, at lunch, with Baba present, Tom put this to Irene himself. Irene's solicitor said it was an outrageous suggestion to which he could never agree but she asked him to reach some accommodation with Tom so that for the next few years at least the children need not be uprooted from their home.

Next day her solicitor had a lengthy meeting with Tom, who had received an offer for an eighteen-month tenancy of Denham which he wanted to accept. Her solicitor found the whole business deplorable: apart from the moral considerations Tom refused to offer any security and there was no time to make adequate alternative provisions. But Irene was adamant that the children must stay in their home so, after a long argument with Tom, she agreed to take on the costs if he would agree to a two-year tenancy.

'All hopeless and vile,' she groaned to her diary, having tried in vain to make him promise that he would not bring Diana Guinness there, 'but I took on the deal.' With additions from Baba, she compiled a letter of agreement which her solicitor refined and despatched to Tom for signature.

They were not out of the wood yet. Lady Mosley rang to report that Tom was infuriated by her letter and had called off the deal, saying that his mother and secretary could run the house instead. Once again, it was Baba who managed to make Tom see reason, eventually persuading him to put his signature to a document that covered every point raised by Irene. She may have reminded Tom that both of them depended on Irene's goodwill to look after their children during the summer holidays.

By the end of June 1937 more rumours about Tom's remarriage had filtered out but when Georgia Sitwell stayed with the Metcalfes for a weekend neither of them could confirm it. Instead, they regaled her with an account of the Duke of Windsor's wedding. 'Most interesting – pathos and bathos combined' was Georgia's response.

The summer followed the same pattern as earlier years, Irene's total commitment to the children alternating with indignation at the way both Tom and Baba seemed to take her for granted. She took the older ones to Lord's to watch the Eton and Harrow match (it was the year that Eton won by seven wickets), she went down to Hastings to see Fruity, his sister Muriel and the twins on the beach, took Nick and Mick crab-hunting on the rocks or to the big pool at St Leonards for a bathe and played spillikins with the older children after dinner. From there she went to the Isle of Wight, to spend a few days in a camp arranged for the Girls' Clubs for which she worked, returning to St Leonards in early August.

Irene's other summer travels took her to Salzburg, Greece, Crete, Delos, Myklor, by ship from Salonika along the coast, and finally back to England from Milan by train on 16 September. Next day she went to lunch with the Duke and Duchess of Kent. All of them would have been worried if they had known what their former King was planning.

While staying at the Château de Candé for his wedding, the Duke of Windsor had got on well with his host, Charles Bedaux. Unbeknownst to the Duke, Bedaux was trying to re-establish his business in Germany and was well aware of the satisfaction to the Nazi Party if the former King of England could be persuaded to tour the country – and of the benefits it could bring to himself.

Bedaux also knew that the Duke had always been interested in the working man and his conditions of labour and during their conversations the idea of an exploratory visit to Germany came up. The Duke was enthusiastic and preparations had begun soon after the wedding, with a list of conditions sent to Hitler's ADC Captain Wiedemann. On 3 September, the Duke released a statement that

he and the Duchess of Windsor would be visiting Germany and the United States in the near future for the purpose of studying housing and working conditions in these two countries.

The arrival in Berlin will be on the Nord Express on Monday morning, 11 October 1937. His Royal Highness would appreciate an attaché speaking English, this attaché to meet him in Paris by calling on Mrs Charles Bedaux at the Ritz on 30 September at 3.00 in the afternoon, and desires that his plans be kept secret until 3 October.

He and the Duchess prefer not to exceed 80 kilometres per hour in automobiles, for luncheon he eats only green salad and drinks tea –

though he would be happy to have one or two typically German luncheons in a factory cafeteria with some German workers present – he prefers receptions between 6–8 p.m. followed by a quiet dinner with a few personalities present. The party will consist of the Duke and Duchess, Dudley Forwood, the German attaché, his detective Mr Storrier, a valet and two maids.

Bedaux also corresponded on the Duke's behalf with various American private and official dignitaries. To one, he concluded: 'How right you were to suggest in April to the Duke of Windsor, who is proving himself to be as great a man as he was a King, a world leadership where what a writer has aptly termed his genius for service would be used.

'I have the personal feeling that it is going to be used and on a scale never known before. I wonder if the cruelty, the suffering, the distress are not the result of a Superior Will intent on ensuring a greater joy on earth.' The letter (dated 23 August) was, as he pointed out in the second paragraph, authorised by the Duke himself. It, too, enjoined secrecy.

Irene and Vivien left for Munich, where Viv was to be 'finished', on 25 September 1937. Viv had been worried about going to Germany – her headmistress said she thought it was because she hated fascism – but on the day itself she was perfectly calm. Irene could not help thinking of her own departure for Dresden, unaccompanied by any of her family, twenty-five years earlier, with Curzon desperately embarrassed when she burst into tears as they said farewell on the platform. On their arrival the following day she took Viv to the house where she would be staying, 16 Konradstrasse, and when she was settled in they made plans for exploring the city.

Three days later they were spectators at the arrival of Hitler and Mussolini (who was visiting Germany) at the Olympic stadium.

Goebbels in a ringing voice opened the tamasha,* followed by the Fuhrer whose voice was hard and clear [wrote Irene that evening]. He

*An Urdu word roughly translatable as jamboree.

reeled out a string of praises for Musso and his regime amid storms of applause. Musso followed and jerked his German-spoken speech out like machine gun fire. It was the better of the two – his accent was very good for an Italian.

He actually said thousands of Italians had died in Spain to save the world from Moscow. I longed to be there to see those hundreds of thousands greeting the two dictators. Throughout dinner we listened to military bands in the Stadium. I played bridge with Viv after.

When Irene left Munich on 3 October, Viv mumbled 'I am not really unhappy, Aunt,' in a way which so tore at Irene's heartstrings that immediately she got home she wrote her a long, comforting letter, with a note to the Gräfin with whom Viv was staying. 'I thank God for all the plans so far, may she be happy and safe,' wrote Irene that night. 'I think Cim would be pleased.' Back at home at the beginning of November, she found it hard to swallow both Tom's ingratitude and lack of concern over his daughter.

Tom's politics were leading him into ever deeper water. With every fresh Nazi outrage, public hostility grew towards the British Union and its continued marches and parades served as a focus for disturbance and, increasingly, violence. According to Thomas Jones, Sir Samuel Hoare (the newly appointed Minister for Home Affairs) was 'bothered by the Mosley processions but does not want to squash them in a hurry because the Civil Liberties group in the House is numerous and vocal'. At a meeting in Liverpool on 10 October, Tom was hit on the head by a brick thrown at him and was so badly injured he had to remain in hospital for a week.

While he was there, the result of a libel case brought against his newspaper, *Action*, was announced. He had lost. As Irene accurately put it, 'Tom's paper has to pay £20,000 to Lord Camrose for calling him a Jew and putting his interests before [those of] the Crown. I was amazed Tom has not got it in the neck before, his articles are such filth but Beckett has merely turned traitor to him in Court, having edited the paper at the time of the libel.'

John Beckett had not been called as a witness but had asked if he could make a statement. He said: 'When I wrote that article I believed it to be true because the information in it was given by people on whom, rightly or wrongly, I placed great reliance. To me, to tell a man that he is a Jew and that his financial interests are far greater outside the country than in it are two of the greatest insults that can possibly be offered to any man. When I discovered that so far from the information my titled friend gave me about Lord Camrose being a Jew being true, he was a Welshman – and, if I may say so, an obvious Welshman – I did not want to go into the box to justify that'.

The 'titled friend' was obviously – or so the jury thought – Tom. Lord Camrose was awarded £20,000 and costs; Beckett was unable to find the money and *Action*, owned by a company with a capital of £100, went bankrupt. To the great relief of Irene, who feared the loss of Denham, Tom could not be held liable.

On 12 October the Kents asked Irene to lunch again, at their house in Bryanston Square, this time to meet her old admirer Nevile Henderson. There were only the four of them, and Henderson held the floor about his German experiences. Almost certainly they would also have talked of the visit of the Duke of Windsor to Nazi Germany which had begun only the day before, and about which no one had known anything until the Duke's office released a statement nine days earlier.

Despite the Duke's best intentions, the visit was of course used by the Nazis as a propaganda coup. For the Windsors, it was a serious *faux pas*, as their meetings with the Goerings, Himmler, Hess and Goebbels, their gala dinner in Streicher's Nuremberg house and, finally, the meeting with Hitler at which the Duke sketched a half-hearted Nazi salute were duly chronicled – and photographed.

'There can be no doubt that his tour has strengthened the regime's hold on the working classes,' said the *New York Times*, adding that the Duke had lent himself 'perhaps unconsciously, but easily, to National Socialist propaganda'. Herbert Morrison, in the Labour magazine *Forward*, put it more strongly, saying first that the Duke had always failed to realise that in a constitutional monarchy neither the heir to the Throne nor the King can publicly express opinions on controversial matters.

'If the Duke wants to study social problems he had far better quietly read books and get advice in private. What he is going to do with his knowledge I do not know, for he cannot be permitted to re-enter public life – in this country at any rate. The choice before ex-kings is either to fade out of the public eye or to be a nuisance. It is a hard choice, perhaps, for one of his temperament, but the Duke will be wise to fade.' Unfortunately, this was not advice the Duke wished to follow.

The American tour never took place. Bedaux's drive for greater efficiency in the workplace had made him so unpopular with organised labour that an attack on him was planned, while the publicity given to the German visit had turned much of the British press and public against the Windsor visit. This time, the Duke listened to advice and on 9 November wrote to Bedaux from his temporary base, the Hôtel Meurice in Paris, regretting that he had to cancel his trip. 'If you have been embarrassed in any way I am sorry that I should have been the cause, but, as you know, I only had one aim and object from the outset, which was shared by yourself, that of learning something of the housing and industrial conditions in America today. Please let me know what expenses have been incurred that are my liability.'

But Bedaux had had enough. Terrified of the hostility, worried about his businesses, he fled to Canada and thence to Europe, never to return to America until he was flown there in 1943.*

On 24 October Irene and Baba received one of their regular invitations to Cliveden, both enjoyed and dreaded by many of those closest to their hostess. Nancy was still, as Victor Cazalet had jotted in his diary the previous year, 'a very remarkable woman. Lives on her nerves. Possesses every contrast possible. Good, bad, full of angles, incredible insights and unbelievable bad judgment. One minute offering deepest confidence, next saying most insulting thing she can think of. Very religious. Terrific energy.'

She displayed many of these qualities on this occasion. It proved to be one of the most famous of the Astor house parties, its guests

---

*Bedaux was committed for trial on a charge of treason (he had been engaged in laying a pipe across the desert to bring peanut oil to the Nazis). On the night of his indictment he committed suicide.

numbering many of those later dubbed 'the Cliveden Set'.

As well as two Astor sons, Bill and David, and relations like Nancy's niece Alice and her husband Reggie Winn, also there were the Foreign Secretary Anthony Eden and his wife Beatrice, the Speaker Captain Edward FitzRoy and his wife, the editor of *The Times*, Geoffrey Dawson, Nevile Henderson, Tom Jones (Deputy Secretary of the Cabinet until 1930, trusted counsellor to Baldwin and a great friend of the Astors), Nancy Astor's adored Lord Lothian, the Liberal peer who was appointed Ambassador to the US in 1939 and already known for his internationalist, anti-war stance, Mrs Lionel Hitchens, Philip Nichols and Sir Alexander Cadogan (Permanent Under-Secretary of the Foreign Office) and his brother Eddie (MP for Finchley until two years earlier) and Robert Bernays, now Parliamentary Secretary to the Minister for Health. Like the Curzon sisters Bernays was such an intimate of the Astor family that he spent weekends alone with them, likening himself to 'a sort of father confessor to these poor little rich boys (£25,000 a year each before they are 21)'.

With both the Foreign Secretary, the Ambassador to Berlin, senior Foreign Office men and the editor of *The Times* among the guests, the talk of course was of Germany. That night Irene wrote: 'I talked to Nevile and Bob Bernays before dinner. Sat between Nevile and Eddie Cadogan at dinner. Late in the evening, Nevile Henderson, Bill and David Astor, Philip Nichols and I, joined by Baba (after a chat with that impossible rabbit-toothed Eden) talked on Germany till 1.00 a.m. and Nevile was very interesting to the degree Baba wondered if I had been wrong in refusing him.'

After dinner Alice Winn, who shared Nancy's love of mischief, informed Irene that Nevile Henderson had proposed three times to a South American heiress. Beatrice Eden chimed in to say that he had even written to the Foreign Office from Buenos Aires to ask if he could marry an Argentine dancer.

Tom Jones wrote a description of the weekend that points up the differences between the Foreign Secretary and one of his most senior Ambassadors:

Thirty to lunch today but this includes three boys from Eton. The Edens are the highest lights and Nevile Henderson the newest. Politics all day and all night. Eden has aged since I saw him six months ago and is dog-tired at the start of the Session. I sat between him and Henderson after the ladies left last night and found they differed widely in policy. Henderson struck me as sensible and informed but without distinction. He has lived in the countries we talked about and Eden has not and this was apparent.

Eden himself thinks the Cabinet very weak and the armament programme far in arrears. On the other hand, he seems to argue that we can't do business with Germany until we are armed – say about 1940. This assumes that we can catch up with Germany – which we cannot – and that Hitler takes no dramatic step in the meantime, which is unlike Hitler. We have spurned his repeated offers. They will not be kept open indefinitely. His price will mount and he will want the naval agreement revised in his favour. It is believed that Mussolini has sold Austria to him at the recent meeting in return for what, I don't know. All this the P.M. sees and says, but I think it goes no further and that meanwhile Vansittart is trying hard to bring N.C. round to the secular F.O. view.

Grandi has been the cleverest person on the non-Intervention Committee and has put flies all over Lord Plymouth. Seems to be a duel between Grandi and Maisky [Russian Ambassador] who each try to rig the press.

Baba, who had made the most of meeting Nevile Henderson at Cliveden, was going to stay at the British Embassy in Berlin after seeing Viv in Munich. Fruity, suspicious that she would meet yet another admirer, wanted to follow her there but Irene, who knew perfectly well what Baba's reaction would be, managed to dissuade him.

When Baba returned from Germany, she was full of news. She had had a wonderful time staying with Nevile Henderson, she told her sister; also staying there was Lord Halifax, whom they had met (as Lord Irwin) briefly in India during his viceroyalty. Earlier that year he had become Lord President of the Council and would (in February 1938) become Foreign Secretary.

Halifax still believed that the Nazis were basically reasonable men with whom negotiation was possible and had persuaded the reluctant Eden to allow him to meet Hitler in Berlin under the pretext of accepting an invitation to attend a hunting exhibition and – which must have made this Master of the Middleton Hunt shudder – shoot foxes. Neither he nor Baba could have guessed how closely their lives would entwine in the future.

Less happy was Baba's disclosure a few days later that Tom did not propose to spend Christmas 1937 with his children at Denham because, wrote Irene, 'Mrs G was kicking up such a fuss. And still hangs the Sword of Damocles over our heads as to whether he is or is not married to her.' Baba, equally anxious to wrest Tom away from the Guinness influence, did her best to persuade him and soon reported success. 'T. now seems to think he might manage Denham.'

But this triumph was short-lived. A few days later, Lady Mosley told Irene that Tom had been called abroad for Christmas. 'D.G. won,' wrote Irene furiously. 'May their Xmas be black with bickerings and recriminations.'

Neither reflected that, from the unpaternal Tom's point of view, Christmas with Diana – beautiful, serene, gay, funny, adoring and gifted, with the ability to produce a near-perfect home and food – might be preferable to one spent in a household riven by quarrels, jealousy, tensions and dramas.

When fourteen-year-old Nick realised that his father was not coming he wept, Irene was told, when she arrived at Denham two days before Christmas. When the children were comforted and safely in bed, she and Nanny filled their stockings. 'I had a quiet hymn of hate at T's selfishness at going off for Xmas,' she wrote on Christmas Eve. 'But for me I was blissful.' On Christmas Day Nick performed their regular Father Christmas routine.

As the holiday wore on the simmering emotional tensions in the Metcalfe marriage resurfaced. Fruity, who had been diagnosed as suffering from a depressive illness, was planning to take a break in Switzerland but did not really want to go and talked of cancelling his hotel room; Baba wept and said nothing mattered, she would like to die if it were not for the children. Irene was relieved when they all left. That night she wrote: 'Not one word, even for New Year, from Tom. He is the utter limit.'

27

At Home with
the Duke

~

The Curzon sisters' petty squabbles were soon forgotten in the growing tension of the international situation. The Anschluss in March, when German troops invaded Austria to the cheers of the crowd that shared their language and racial background, might have had a certain logic; the threat to Czechoslovakia's Sudeten territories, with its German minority, was something far more menacing.

Over the weekend of 26 March 1938, there was another of the house parties that gave the Cliveden Set its name. Staying in the huge house were the Prime Minister and Mrs Chamberlain, Lord Lothian, the Speaker, Captain Edward FitzRoy and Mrs FitzRoy, the Conservative Whip David Margesson, Sir Alexander and Lady Cadogan, Nancy's niece Alice Winn and her husband Reggie, the actress Joyce Grenfell and her husband Reggie, Ronnie Tree, Lady Worsley, Bill Astor, Lady Wilson (the wife of Gracie's one-time lover Scatters) and the observant Tom Jones.

As soon as she arrived, Irene found herself drawn into a discussion of the international situation. As she strolled past sweeps of crocuses, the first daffodils and the magnificent Cliveden magnolia trees with her host Waldorf Astor and the American financier Sir Clarence Dillon, they spoke of nothing but Hitler; after tea, walking with Ronnie Tree, there were the same questions, the same discussions of what the Führer intended. So unnerving was the conversation that Irene slipped off to the chapel in which her sister's body had lain to pray that the sacrifices of 1914–18 had not been in vain and that the lives of the children she now regarded as her own should not be put at risk.

She felt uneasy at the composition of the party. 'I am not sure the PM should stay at the moment in a house notorious for talk with the owner of big papers and all the chat and gossip about the Cliveden group running the PM and dragooning England,' she wrote in her diary (the Cliveden Set had already been attacked by the Labour politician, Sir Stafford Cripps, and Frank Owen had written an article about it in the *Daily Express* that month).

Nor was she impressed by the Prime Minister, sitting opposite her at dinner. 'I thought the face mean, undistinguished, dead tired eyes, no vision, an ordinary cautious man whom no one could move to flights of greatness or to take any known risk for the future of the world, a very common type. Nancy lectured him through dinner as if she were running the world.' Mrs Chamberlain she found 'nice, cosy, slow, gentle but entirely devoid of the personality to make a great wife of a PM'.

After dinner, Nancy insisted upon her favourite game of musical chairs. Irene, conscious of the terrible gravity of the international situation, could not make herself join in ('What would the Nazi leaders say if they could see the PM, Nancy and others fighting and cheating for chairs? They could not believe we could ever be serious about anything'). No such scruples hindered the Prime Minister, who successfully fought David Astor for the last chair and won the game.

The indefatigable Nancy then organised another party standby, the acting out of a phrase, word or book title to be guessed by the others. Like Irene, Sir Clarence Dillon could not bear to join in at this critical moment; they watched bemused as Mrs Chamberlain crawled along the floor, to be followed by Nancy with another of her set-pieces: the clapping in of the false teeth she always kept by her in a small silver bag before launching into her two comic speeches – that of a Primrose League member and a hard-riding woman to hounds – into which she incorporated digs against the Cabinet and the Speaker.

'Are we all mad or what?' Irene asked herself miserably. She was deeply depressed at the latest round of Nazi anti-Jewish propaganda, this time aimed at the Jews of Vienna in the days following the Anschluss. 'This volatile, irresponsible, tactless crea-

42. Fruity, Georgia Sitwell, David Metcalfe, Sacheverell Sitwell and his son Reresby on a skiing holiday, winter 1938

43. Nevile Henderson, who proposed several times to Irene

44. Walter Monckton, Fruity and the Windsors on their first visit to England after the Abdication, in September 1939, when they stayed with the Metcalfes

45. The Duke and Wallis at South Hartfield House on the same visit

46. The Duke goes cycling

47.
Little Compton,
Oxfordshire

48.
Irene with Davina
and David Metcalfe
in Scotland, August
1940

49. Wartime duty: Baba in her St John's uniform

50. Lord Halifax, the Archduke
Robert of Austria and Victor
Cazalet, at Victor Cazalet's
house, Great Swifts, in 1940

51. Lord Halifax, the new British
Ambassador to Washington,
on board HMS *King George V*,
setting off for America in
January 1941

52.
Walter Monckton playing
croquet at Little
Compton, August 1941

53.
Fruity in his Royal Air
Force uniform at Little
Compton in 1941

54. The Windsors at Little Compton in 1948 (from the left: Wallis, Davina, Linda, the Duke, David and Fruity)

55. Sim Feversham

56. Irene, created Baroness
    Ravensdale of Kedleston,
    one of the first four women
    life peers, in October 1958

57. Baba with her
    CBE, in 1975

ture is the hostess for our PM in these agonising days. May God watch over it all for the best'.

Her apprehensions were realised when the party again got into the gossip columns in the *Daily Express*. Later it was discovered that the source of the leak was Lady Wilson, who had talked about it to Randolph Churchill, then working on the *Evening Standard* Londoner's Diary.

Irene's lack of faith in the Prime Minister appeared to be shared by Tom Jones. Giving Jones a lift back to London, she discussed with him Chamberlain's previous wartime role in charge of the voluntary recruitment of labour under Lloyd George and how this had only lasted seven months (Lloyd George had conceived a violent dislike for Chamberlain within days of the appointment and gave him such minimal support that he resigned). 'And this is the man we now turn to in the worst crisis since the war,' thought Irene.

She spent much of the spring of 1938 visiting Denham, on one occasion finding Tom there – 'very pleasant and friendly with the children' – before going on a motoring trip to France in April. A month later she installed Vivien in Paris with a Vicomtesse who took English girls for a final polish before their debut the following Season. Before returning to London, she and Viv met Baba at the Paris Ritz – the Metcalfes had been invited to stay with the Duke and Duchess of Windsor for the weekend at their temporary home in Versailles and Baba stayed on afterwards to take her niece clothes-shopping.

Scarcely was Irene back in England and the nursery routine re-established than another of Tom's suggestions threw the Denham household into a flutter. Lady Mosley telephoned to say that Tom wanted Irene's permission to take Micky to Wootton, 'as Mrs Guinness was not there, only her children. Nanny and I were distraught.' Irene asked for time to decide.

It was not simply that Diana Guinness and the Wootton ménage represented all she did *not* want for her sister's children; it was more that she felt it to be, as she put it to herself, the thin end of the wedge. If the principle was established of allowing Micky to spend time at Wootton whenever Diana was absent they would inevitably, sooner rather than later, overlap – and Tom would have good grounds once again to question the point of keeping Denham, their family home. Not trusting herself to speak on the telephone, Irene sent round a message saying No to Lady Mosley and went off with friends to a concert at the Queen's Hall where she was soothed by Verdi's *Te Deum* and *Requiem*.

A few days later she went to see Baba and did her best to commiserate with her over Fruity's 'nerves', for which he was going to seek treatment at the well-known spa Divonne-les-Bains on the French-Swiss border near Lake Geneva. The unhappy Fruity clung to Irene when they said goodbye. Loyal and straightforward, he found it difficult to understand why, despite the three children who should have brought them even closer together, his wife had thrust him aside in favour of a string of lovers.

Baba was extraordinarily discreet about them: her whole outward persona was one of elegance, dignity, control and fastidiousness. But moral principles stood little chance against the strength of her emotions and her libido, a conflict that manifested itself in a kind of guilty anger towards the man to whom she felt herself bound.

What unbalanced the emotional equation even further was her wealth. Years of financial dominance, of paying for their houses, lifestyle, servants, holidays, travel and the education of their children, had enhanced the strength of an already powerful personality. Fruity, who could only rely on a major's pension, had become accustomed to a wife who 'called the shots' – and found her impossible to argue with.

And now, as he left for his solitary regime, a new admirer was appearing on his wife's horizon – Michael Lubbock. Nancy had written to Baba with her usual invitation to Cliveden for Ascot but Baba had different plans. She had asked Lubbock and his wife Diana to stay with her instead. But she was careful not to offend Nancy, who was growing increasingly unpredictable and volatile in her affections, and invited the Astors and Lord Lothian to dinner soon afterwards. It was a sensible precaution. On 9 July the Astors gave their great ball of the summer, to which Irene took her niece Viv. There too was Baba who, as Irene instantly noted, 'sailed in and sailed out on a cloud of bliss with Michael L'.

That summer, the Metcalfes made their first visit to the Windsors' new house, the Villa La Cröe, near Antibes, leased for three years from Sir Pomeroy Burton. Eleven-year-old David, the Duke's godson, accompanied his parents.

La Cröe was an exotic, glamorous place, hidden away behind high stone walls and set in twelve acres of garden and woodland. A curving drive led to the large white three-storey house with green shutters. One side, with sun terrace and lawns, faced the Mediterranean and the private pool cut out of the rocks while the house itself was built round a central hall. Here the Duke's red-and-gold Garter banner from St George's Chapel, Windsor, was complemented by antique chairs with red leather seats and black-and-gold backs: on the terrace outside were black wicker loungers with crimson cushions.

The rest of the house was also full of mementoes of the life that the Duke had left behind. Much of the furniture was from Fort Belvedere. The red and white library was dominated by a large portrait of Queen Mary which hung above the marble mantelpiece, the blond oak bookshelves were filled with the Duke's presentation volumes, trophies and awards; in the library, too, was his Steinway grand piano and organ, which he would occasionally play when the Duchess was absent. From his room at the top of the house, which he called his Belvedere, he flew his personal standard. In another echo of those happier times, he would walk about the grounds in kilt and glengarry playing his bagpipes.

The drawing-room and dining-room were on the first floor and here Wallis's taste – and that of her interior decorator, Elsie Mendl – was paramount. The cornices of the high ceilings were picked out in white and gold, there were mirrors everywhere – the Duchess loved both the effect of space and looking at herself – and the Windsor monogram, WE, was on everything, from writing paper and bedlinen to the lifebuoys hanging by the pool. Entwined with the Duke's coronet, it was also on the silver buttons of the grey alpaca livery worn by the butler and footmen (in Paris they wore black suits with crimson, white and gold striped waistcoats with silver buttons, and gold-collared scarlet waistcoats for large formal dinners). Perfection reigned: the soap, towels and even the flowers in each of the six bedrooms were matched to the colour scheme.

The Metcalfes, whose fellow guests were the Colin Buists and Lord Sefton and his girlfriend Helen Fitzgerald, found life at La

Cröe both more formal and more luxurious than at the Fort. A hairdresser came daily, a manicurist twice weekly. Life ran to a daily programme, drawn up by the Duchess, just as it had when the Duke was King: '12.30 the Prince de Lucinge arrives, 12.35 we go down to bathe, a quarter to two lunch, three o'clock siesta'. Meals were elaborate: melon with tomato ice, eggs in crab sauce, chicken with avocado salad or roast beef with port wine sauce and asparagus.

All along the coast were the villas of the mega-rich: Maxine Elliott in the Château de l'Horizon outside Cannes; Somerset Maugham in the Villa Mauresque on Cap Ferrat; Daisy Fellowes, in her huge pink palace Les Zoraides in its 25 acres on Cap Martin, when not on her yacht *Sister Anne*. All of them entertained in grand style. When Somerset Maugham invited the Windsors to lunch their respective butlers negotiated over the menu and protocol for days, while at La Cröe guests were expected to curtsey to both Windsors on first seeing them in the morning and the Duke's secretary had to take dictation standing up. Part of this insistence on status was due to the Duke's desperate concern that Wallis should be treated as royal.

At the same time, the Duke's old love of informality was obvious. In contrast to the Duchess, who always wore a dress, often with one of her sumptuous jewels, or a bathing dress and matching cap, her husband would wear open-necked shirts and shorts as on the *Nahlin* cruise.

The high spirits that had disappeared during the tense months before the Abdication surfaced again in the presence of old friends, as did the Duke's love of practical jokes. One of the Windsors' wedding presents was a lavatory-paper holder that played 'God Save the King'. It delighted the Duke who, though he shared the thirties prudery over sexual jokes, loved anything lavatorial. Just before Lord Sefton arrived he said to his equerry Dudley Forwood, 'By the way, Dudley, when Hugh goes to the loo in the morning I want yer to tell me.' When Forwood tentatively asked why, he received the answer 'You wait and see'.

Next morning at nine Forwood duly went upstairs to the Duke's room and said: 'He's there, Sir.' Down came the Duke in his dressing-gown, stood silently outside the lavatory door and at the appropriate moment shouted, 'And now let me tell yeou that every proper subject stands to attention whatever he's doing!' (When Forwood once daringly asked the Duke whence came his peculiar semi-Cockney accent, he received the reply: 'I didn't want to be guttural like Mama and Papa so I went in taxicabs and learned from taxi-drivers.')

Fruity's initial hostility towards the Duchess had evaporated under her determined charm offensive, although her harsh voice still jarred on him every time she squawked, 'Die-vid!' or 'The Dook says . . .' and her ugly, gesticulating hands were an unhappy contrast to Baba's smooth white ones.

Fruity's place in the Duke's affections was as secure as ever and, despite the breaking of the Duke's promise of a job, with its unhappy financial and marital consequences, he still regarded the former King as his greatest friend. Lloyd George, staying with his wife at the Grand Hotel du Cap in Antibes to celebrate their golden wedding and entertained several times by the Windsors, commented on this friendship to Dudley Forwood, who always remembered his exact words. 'Except for the physical side,' said the former Prime Minister, 'he has a homosexual love for him. He is *passionately* fond of him.' Possibly the Duchess had sensed this element when, as Mrs Simpson, she suggested or vetoed those whom the then King should have around him in a personal capacity.

As usual, Irene spent the 1938 Season lunching and dining. In August she took a series of 'duty' holidays, one with the members of the seven social clubs for boys and girls that had started in different parts of London, a second with sixty-seven girls from the East End on the Isle of Wight, where they camped in tents pitched about a mile from the sea, a third in Switzerland with thirty-six of the older boys and girls. Tucked between the last two trips was a happy holiday at Lake Vyrnwy, in Wales, with Tom and his children.

After Tom's departure came another of the disturbing incidents that always seemed to follow in his wake. On 24 August, Mike Wardell telephoned, asking so urgently to speak to Tom that Irene gave him the Wootton number. Back at Denham two days later, she was greatly perturbed by Andrée telling her that the press had rung and rung again, asserting that Tom was, in fact, married. That weekend, staying with the recently appointed war minister Leslie Hore-Belisha at Warren Farm, she saw a story about Tom and his marriage in the Sunday newspaper *Reynolds News*. Leslie told her that it was alleged to have taken place months ago. What was the truth?

She soon forgot this latest rumour in the steadily worsening news from Europe. Tom appeared and disappeared just as suddenly, once arriving after midnight when to enter the locked house he put a ladder against the wall and climbed in through Viv's window. Next day they were joined by Baba, back from Tunis with a sheaf of photographs. Irene felt too oppressed by the international situation to stay up chatting and went to bed early, leaving Tom and Baba, as usual, alone together.

The papers were full of the crisis over Czechoslovakia, with reports of the massing of German troops on the border. 'Tom says Hitler never strikes when he makes so much song and dance about it. He does his great moves silently,' wrote Irene that night. 'I pray he is right.'

On 14 September she drove down to Denham to find Nanny in a state of alarm because Tom had asked if Irene would be 'reasonable' and allow the children to be rushed to Wootton in case of war. With reluctance, she and Lady Mosley agreed to think about it. She soothed herself by reading Mick a story, playing tennis, then bathing with the children in the river – 'dirty and beastly and the men were cutting the weed. Nanny got back at 5.30 and we had tea.' None of this calmed her fears about the war.

Then, on the news on 15 September came the momentous announcement that the Prime Minister was flying to Germany to meet the Führer. 'I wanted to cry at the splendour of the gesture,' wrote Irene that night. Sunshine next morning lifted her spirits and she went to pray in Westminster Abbey by the Unknown Warrior's tomb before waiting tensely for the six o'clock news. This included the Prime Minister's recorded remarks on his arrival back at Heston airfield. They were moving, Irene thought, 'but I still feel that Hitler has not budged'.

The sight of Fruity looking gaunt and ill as he emerged from his house did nothing to cheer her. Like all those who knew them well, Irene was in no doubt that the Metcalfe marriage was on the point of collapse – and if there was a 'crash' it would, she felt, be her sister's fault.

But the looming horror of war overrode all personal feeling. On 26 September she was writing: 'How can the Czechs accept these outrageous demands by Oct 1? It seems the two visits of the PM were of no assistance or at any rate the last one as Hitler's demands simply stiffened.' The ten-thirty news was unhelpful, saying only that President Roosevelt had sent a long telegram to Hitler and the Czech president Eduard Beneš, begging for a peaceful solution.

As one of Victor Cazalet's friends wrote to him a few days later: 'The depression was so terrible one could scarcely rise above it. We prayed and worked constantly ... The inevitableness of it all – the look on people's faces of inescapable tragedy, everywhere people standing dead still scanning the newspapers, sandbags, ARP trenches, the Green Line buses swung with stretchers evacuating the hospitals, the tenseness, the grimness, the quiet orderliness with which all the preparations were carried out. It made me so proud to be English in my heart.'

At 10 a.m. on 28 September, with Hitler's public ultimatum to Czechoslovakia due to expire at 2 p.m., the British Ambassador to Berlin, Irene's former suitor Nevile Henderson made a last-ditch telephone call to Goering (second only to Hitler in the Nazi hierarchy). At 11 a.m., Mussolini telephoned Hitler – would he prolong the ultimatum by twenty-four hours?

That afternoon Hitler's dramatic message to Chamberlain to meet him, Mussolini and Daladier in Munich at 3 p.m. the following day arrived at the House of Commons. Irene listened to the proceedings on the wireless. 'What drama in the House – men crying and cheering when the PM ended his momentous utterance, "I need not say what my answer will be".'

Robert Bernays, arriving in London from Geneva, found the capital already like a city at war. 'Laughter and even smiles have gone from it. We are like a people waiting for the Day of Judgement. Vast silent crowds are everywhere. It is horribly uncanny. Trenches are being dug in the Parks. Sandwichmen tell you where to get your gas masks. There is a dreadful notice in front of me saying: "You must not run. Turn left and follow the blue line".'

Back in his own constituency, Bernays found that children were using their new gas masks to carry home the family fish and chips.

On 29 September in a last-ditch attempt to halt the tide of war, the hastily-convened conference of the Four Powers took place in Munich at the Brown House, the Nazi Party headquarters, and after almost ten hours of talk, agreement was finally reached at 2.30 a.m. on 30 September.

Germany emerged the clear winner strategically, with the reacquisition of all her former Sudeten territories. These contained Czechoslovakia's most heavily armed frontier defences, leaving that country virtually defenceless. The Munich Agreement had bought time – but sealed Czechoslovakia's fate.

In Britain, where so many had either fought through the horrors of the 1914–18 war or had sons or daughters of an age to suffer in a new one, there was an overwhelming sense of relief at a reprieve that might – just might – prove to be permanent.

With Viv, Irene drove down to Heston on 1 October to welcome the Prime Minister on his return from Munich. Unable to get in to the aerodrome without tickets, they sat on the kerb opposite the entrance from early afternoon, buying newspaper after newspaper to shield their heads from the rain. They watched hundreds of people arrive by car – reporters, Royal Air Force officers and their wives and, a few moments before the arrival of the Prime Minister's aeroplane, the Cabinet Ministers. Lining the drive were a number of boys from Eton.

At about 6.45 p.m. the Prime Minister's plane was seen circling above. Irene and Viv were invited to listen to the radio in the car that had brought the boys from Eton. Though they did not see the Premier famously waving the piece of paper on which the Munich Agreement was written, they heard him read out this pact of non-aggression, signed by both himself and Hitler. With the boys, they rushed to the drive as he came down it in a small car accompanied by Lord Halifax (who had arrived moments before Chamberlain's aeroplane touched down).

For Irene, it was a moving experience to be surrounded by the very schoolboys who might have been sacrificed in a long war. A rainbow on the way back to London seemed a symbol of hope. At home, changing for a party at the Astors, her first euphoria gave way to disillusionment. 'I had felt all day that the Dictators had secured a triumph. That Hitler once again had fulfilled another page of Mein Kampf,' she wrote with an accuracy that escaped many.

Irene was not alone in her doubts. Duff Cooper, the First Lord of the Admiralty, resigned from the Government and Harold Nicolson made a speech bitterly condemning Britain's 'capitulation', saying that the Munich Agreement meant not peace but a respite for six months. *The Week* put it even more bluntly, saying that 'Mr Chamberlain had turned all four cheeks to Hitler'.

But life had to go on. Irene went to see a play by Bryan Guinness, former husband of the dreaded Diana ('though full of charming thoughts and poetic lines it was too static'), listened to a debate at the House of Commons, bought Elinor Glyn a sapphire paste powder box for her seventy-fourth birthday on 17 October and saw Baba, whom she thought seemed close to a nervous breakdown over her marital unhappiness. Nevertheless, Baba appeared to have had an enjoyable dinner (without Fruity) with Lord Halifax and Nevile Henderson, listening to them discuss Germany and the crisis.

At Cliveden that weekend, Irene was pleased to learn from Alec Cadogan that Nevile Henderson was considered to have done his job well – but that Chamberlain's attitude was another matter. Cadogan told her that the Prime Minister had said to him after the preliminary meeting at Godesberg that he thought Hitler was absolutely sincere, which frightened him. 'I always felt [this] would happen to the PM: that he would fall under that spell,' wrote Irene in her diary. 'It confirmed what Nevile had felt at those last two meetings [prior to Munich].'

Both the Curzon sisters made plans to travel while this was still possible. Baba was taking her daughters to Switzerland and Irene herself sailed for America on the *Normandie* on 5 November. In New York she saw friends – Condé Nast, Mrs Kahn, Neily Vanderbilt – and spent mornings at Saks buying Christmas presents. On 27 November, after being royally entertained, she left for Washington, to be greeted by the news that she and Baba had dreaded for so long.

In the last days of the month the news broke that not only was Tom married to Diana Guinness but that they had had a son (on 28 November). While the papers were full of allegations and denials, Irene waited apprehensively. Then, when she came home after dancing at the Waldorf with Douglas Fairbanks, she found a cable from Baba. 'What we heard is true, will be published Thursday: birth of son Saturday. Children's position won't change.' She felt rather sick.

Back in London on 22 December she hurried at once to lunch with Lady Mosley, as appalled as Irene was by Tom's secrecy and his method of breaking the news of his marriage. Both his older children had learned it from the press, as had Baba, still at that time his mistress, and all three were devastated by the deception.

'Sweet Nick had noticed Mrs Guinness's huge size at Wootton in August,' wrote Irene, 'and gallantly had never breathed to a soul though agonised at the situation. Oh! why did Tom not tell us all at Lake Vyrnwy. And poor Ma with the child born on a Saturday – Tom only came in to see her on the Monday when the Press started suggestions! She looks a liar to all the BUF who will never believe she did not know. She said Baba had been like a raving lunatic.'

Baba, who had read the news in the train on a brief visit to Paris, was so shattered that she fled the country and took refuge in Gstaad. A sense of being thoroughly and humiliatingly duped must have been intolerable to someone as conscious of her own dignity as Baba. Her mortification was such that she even omitted the conventional courtesies – she did not write a formal note of congratulation on Tom's marriage or on the birth of his baby.

Irene, by contrast, and for the sake of his children, made the best of this fait accompli. She felt a little happier when Zita James, one of Cim's great friends, called on her. 'Of all amazing things she [Zita] feels this marriage of Tom's and the child may relegate Cim's children more and more to me. Pray God it is so.'

28

Fruity Speaks His Mind

~

The shock suffered by Mosley's children on learning that their father had secretly married the woman so disliked by their aunts brought out the best in Irene. There was no criticism, no repining. She encouraged Vivien's natural loyalty to her father, listening to the girl she thought of as a daughter explain, in words she must have heard from her father, how inevitable the marriage was. Diana had given up so much for Tom, said Vivien, and her services were so necessary to him – 'besides, she adores him'. Viv was showing great sensitivity and unselfishness, thought Irene. It must have been worse for Nick, surrounded by everyone at school. When Tom arrived at Denham, dinner passed smoothly as Irene chatted about her recent US trip; afterwards, she took advantage of the moment to discuss Vivien's debut – Vivien wanted to 'do' the Season thoroughly, from presentation at Court to coming-out ball.

After the Mosley children had gone to bed, it was impossible to avoid the subject of Tom's marriage to Diana any longer. Irene told Tom that all she wished to say was that the loyalty of his children after the cruel shock they had received was amazing and he must never betray it. Tom took this well-deserved reproof calmly and went on to talk about Denham. He had never wanted Diana to 'butt in' there, he said; he simply wanted everything to go on as before. 'I think he feels ashamed how it all came out and took place,' she wrote that night. 'I definitely know God kept me in the USA away from Baba so I could come back calmly and talk it all out with Tom and get matters settled whilst she is out of the country.'

Tom was grateful for Irene's rational approach, as his mother told Irene when she arrived at Denham on Christmas Eve. Tom himself only arrived after lunch, in time to do his Father Christmas act and join in the Christmas tea and carol-singing.

Against all the odds, she felt that their Christmas had been a happy one – she had never known Tom so amenable, or sweet to the children, or so sensible in planning for the future. He even agreed to relinquish Cim's bedroom to Viv, who longed to have it as her own.

When the meeting with Diana took place, on 27 December 1938, Irene was psychologically prepared to meet her brother-in-law's new family. Her first impressions were not of Diana's beauty but of the affectedness of her voice: the Mitford drawl, with its up-and-down inflections, prolonged vowels ('orfficer' and 'lorst') and idiosyncratic 'exclamations' was at its most pronounced when Diana was nervous. She was surprised that Diana called Tom 'Kit' (Diana had done this almost from the start, because her brother was called Tom) and how bad the tea was ('just bits of bread and butter and a tiny Xmas cake') for what was after all an important meeting. But they chatted easily about Wootton, Diana's new chef, shooting and, of course, the baby.

As always, Irene's heart was softened by the sight of a child. Alexander, she thought, looked big and strong for his age, more like a baby of nine weeks than one just over a month old. When Diana's mother, Lady Redesdale, joined them later the surreal aspect of the encounter struck her forcibly. 'How that battered washed-out woman could have produced those six hooligan girls I do not know,' wrote Irene. 'What a curious picture of Tom – wife, baby, mother-in-law and monthly nurse, very domestic but somehow not fitting.'

Irene and Nick both thought the meeting had gone well; buoyed up, Irene wrote to Baba in Gstaad, exhorting her to put her own feelings behind her and accept the situation. She read the letter to Lady Mosley and, at midnight, had a long and satisfactory talk with Nanny, who told her how Micky, now almost seven, had reacted. When he read the announcement in the evening paper he said, 'This must be some rot or else Daddy would have told US.' When Nanny explained that it was in fact true he said philosophically: 'Well, I am no longer his youngest son.'

A moment later he asked what he should call his father's new wife. If he addressed her as Lady Mosley, they would think it was Granny, if Diana, it would be too like friends of his own age, and she couldn't be Mummy because she was not his mother. Nanny also told Irene of a revealing incident. Micky, already in bed when Tom called at Denham for dinner on his way to Wootton one evening, was told by Nanny Hyslop to call out a greeting to his father but refused, saying it would be an embarrassment as he had only seen him about four times in his life.

Having discussed with her solicitors Tom's proposal to ask the Court for £1,500 a year more and to request a further sum to pay for Viv's coming-out expenses, Irene returned to America early in 1939, accompanied by the future Czech Foreign Minister Jan Masaryk who was an old friend. Both were desperately worried at the threat to Poland's three million Jews and were to discuss the question of emigration. Before leaving she put a notice in the papers to say that she would be bringing out her niece, Miss Vivien Mosley, from 10 Cornwall Terrace, Regent's Park.

With family plans settled, Irene seized the opportunity to enjoy what she felt might be a last season's hunting. It was brought to an abrupt end when her horse came down with her on slippery mud after jumping a post and rolled on her, breaking her collar-bone and four ribs. When found by one of the field she was hanging head down and unconscious from the saddle – fortunately her horse was standing still or she would have been badly dragged and possibly killed. By 14 January she was back in Cornwall Terrace, bruised all over and suffering pain from her broken ribs, but delighted to be home.

In Switzerland the unhappy atmosphere between the Metcalfes was more noticeable than ever. 'Fruity with us grumbling endlessly about his life and Baba's unkindness to him,' wrote Georgia Sitwell early in January. 'Tea with Metcalfes in their villa, which is absurdly small – poor Fruity'. 'Sach, Reresby and I drove in sleigh to see ski jumping. Very exciting. Talked about Metcalfes, of course.' And again on 10 January: 'Fruity came down and talked sadly for ages.'

Baba's return in mid-January brought the inevitable family dis-ruptions as she now immersed herself in the business of Vivien's coming out, disputing everything from the financial aspects to

Viv's clothes which, she said, were not 'right' – a judgement that caused the eighteen-year-old Vivien much anxiety. Even Georgia Sitwell, fond though she was of Baba, commented, 'She is spoilt, irritatingly self-assured and bossy,' though she added, 'but not intentionally'. The fact that Irene was conscious that Baba's taste was far superior to hers did not help matters. However, she was soon in command of the field again as Baba went off on a trip to Tunisia with the Sitwells ('I resent being treated as Baba's lady-in-waiting', wrote Georgia crossly, though when Baba actually arrived, on 15 February, all was forgiven).

The 'small' dance for 150 which Irene gave for her niece on 10 February (there would be a big ball in the Season proper) passed off well. Viv looked superb in a dress of oyster-grey satin, its short jacket embroidered with red; Gracie Curzon wore black velvet and Irene, supervising from a bathchair, was resplendent in rubies. The first-floor ballroom at Cornwall Terrace was decorated with white tulips and white irises; there was supper in the Chinese room on the ground floor and a bridge room for the chaperones at the top of the house. The party ended at 2.30 a.m., with a wild race by the young men and girls from room to room, leaping over sofas and chairs. Two days later, the effort caught up with Irene: her right lung collapsed and two pints of fluid had to be drained from it.

It was back to bed, nurses and doctors again. Tom visited her, spending an hour discussing the international situation. 'He said the Italians were very inflammable and might ask for a lot but that Musso could not stand a war and it depended if Hitler could control him,' wrote Irene. Tom also told her that he found Hess the supreme party technician, that Diana was greatly impressed by Himmler but that they all hated Streicher – and that what Hitler enjoyed about Goebbels was his wit. Since Diana had been visiting Germany regularly, and had numerous tête-à-têtes with the German leader, this obviously came straight from the Führer himself.

A few days later Irene was visited by Nevile Henderson, re-covered from an operation for cancer of the tongue and preparing to return to Berlin. The reason Chamberlain was so insistent that Britain would always come to the aid of France, he thought, was partly to frighten Mussolini, whose alignment with the Nazi regime was becoming ever clearer. Grandi was summoned to Rome for a few days at the end of March to be told he had lost touch with Italy and fascism, and reproved for not wearing the new fascist uniform designed by Il Duce himself.

Irene's injuries took a long time to heal. She was too ill to go to Melton to present the bouquets to the principals in *The Student Prince* (she was still president of the Melton Operatic Society) and by the end of February she knew she should give up any thought of hunting that year – and possibly for ever.

Another visit from Nevile Henderson, soon after the invasion of Czechoslovakia on 16 March 1939, seemed to confirm these fears. 'He was sad, disillusioned and could see no daylight. He definitely felt the out-and-out lefters, Goebbels, Streicher and Himmler, had rushed Hitler into this,' wrote Irene that night. 'Though he realises all about honour, obligation, etc, he is very chary of having several million Englishmen killed for Rumanians, Slavs etc, to resist wars of different nations who could be run over by Hitler in a few hours – long before we could gather strength.'

The visit of the French President in March duly emphasised Franco-British solidarity. Robert Bernays, attending the gala performance of the opera in cocked hat and ministerial uniform in the place of Walter Elliot, wrote of one of the last diplomatic flourishes of peacetime: 'It was like pre-War Vienna. The incomparable Opera House was blazing with uniforms and tiaras. There were rows of scarlet-breeched footmen on the grand staircase and the loveliest women in England.'

The bickering over who would 'run' Viv's season continued. Baba was determined to have the final word, saying that she knew best – an unkind dig – through having children of her own. Irene comforted herself, and gathered her strength for the forthcoming Season, with her usual remedy: a cruise, visiting Greece, Istanbul and Italy.

Shortly after her return at the end of April she went down to Denham, to find a dozen fascist drummers, young women who traipsed up and down in the pelting rain, rehearsing for forthcoming marches, while their clothes got soaked and their high heels sank in the mud. The drums were a mild irritation compared with what came next: a request from Tom that Diana and their new baby should spend the month of July at Denham. Irene took advice from Andrée and Nanny before finally deciding that Cim would have probably wished this, if only to ensure Tom's continuing good relations with his two elder children.

With the start of the Season and her niece's debut Irene's life was packed, her days full of dressmaker fittings and luncheons as well as a succession of committee meetings and concerts. In the evenings were the parties: Queen Charlotte's Ball on 17 May, where each girl was presented with a red satin heart on a ribbon and a bottle of scent, Sibyl Colefax's party for the American novelist Thornton Wilder, her own supper party, with the band of the Four Hundred, attended by many of her old beaux like Bobby Digby and Miles Graham.

On 8 June came the event for which Irene had been planning for months: Vivien's ball. At ten thirty the guests began to swarm into the flower-bedecked rooms. Baba arrived on her own as Fruity was having a hernia operation. The Duke of Kent arrived at twelve fifteen and after one dance with his hostess settled down to discuss with her first Baba and Fruity, then Tom and Diana, and finally the King's speech versus that of the Duke of Windsor. The ball ended at 4 a.m. 'Baba, Viv and I came home in her car, jubilant and happy at the glorious success of the party.'

The social events seemed more numerous than ever as the last Season of peace unrolled. Irene took her niece to Paris for another round of parties: racing with Sir Charles Mendl at Longchamps and a huge ball given by the immensely rich Daisy Fellowes. There the Duke of Windsor came to talk to her. 'He chatted a lot about Fruity and said he would never get a job because he would not be serious and concentrate on anything,' wrote Irene, apparently oblivious of the fact that exactly the same charges could be levelled at the Duke.

Back in London, the Season wound to its frenetic climax. There was a dance at Londonderry House, its Rembrandts, Raeburns and Gainsboroughs looking serenely on as the debutantes shook their hips to the latest craze, the Big Apple; a ball at Sutton Place, floodlit for the occasion; a weekend at Walmer Castle in Kent; the Henley Regatta; Mrs Clifton Brown's ball in Eaton Square; the Cubitt ball at Holland House, where the pile-up of guests' cars in Kensington High Street was such that Irene and Viv walked the final mile through drizzle, clutching their trains and tiaras.

The ball at Blenheim a few days later was so wonderful that Irene was thankful Viv had come out that year – perhaps the last time that anyone would see such a spectacle. Guests danced in the huge library, with its organ at one end; the floodlighting, which could be seen for miles, turned the façade of the palace a glowing amber, illumined the cedars, the stone water garden with its two Cleopatra's Needles, the borders of rambling roses and the lake faintly gleaming through a pearly mist. Small supper tables were set on the flagged terrace, where chefs grilled food to order and any chill was dispersed by two large braziers; inside, there were powdered footmen in red velvet, the beautiful Duchess of Kent surrounded by a mass of young men, and supper in the Painted Room.

Four days later Viv was presented. As only married women (who had themselves been presented) could in turn present a debutante, this had to be done by Baba, to Irene's frustration. The pair set off at 7 p.m., equipped with sandwiches, brandy and smelling salts and, for Baba, elegant as ever in grey organza and aquamarines, her Red Cross examination books, so that Vivien could question her during the long wait in the Mall. With the threat of war increasing daily Baba with her usual thoroughness and efficiency was training to be a nurse.

Reality intruded with a jolt when the faithful Nevile Henderson next called on Irene.

He is bitterly out of sympathy with the Government's policy with Poland, Rumania and Russia. He thinks Hitler knows well enough we would fight over Danzig and will behave unless he gets convinced that we want to fight him anyhow and that then he might steal a march while he was still ahead in armaments. It pains me how Nevile dares say the occupation of Czechoslovakia was right and that the Czechs are rapidly turning pro-German. He thinks Danzig should go back too. He agrees with me that Winston Churchill in the Govt would convince Hitler we were going to fight against him and he implored the P.M. not to put him in. He does not see the Germans' faults enough. His spectacles are too rosy and it pains me.

On 16 July 1939, Tom held his last and greatest meeting in London. He had managed to hire the enormous new auditorium at Earl's Court and filled it with an audience of more than 20,000. Irene attended with Viv, Nick and Lady Mosley, Baba with Mike Wardell. There was the usual panoply of banners and standards of the various fascist 'districts', stewards, rousing pipe and drum bands and Tom's solo march down the centre aisle in the beam of spotlights to mount the high rostrum. Speaking, as usual, without notes, against the background of an enormous Union Jack, he talked of how the whole of Britain's international trading system, foreign policy and even Britain's various conflicting political parties were 'maintained for one reason; and for one reason alone – that the money power of the world may rule the British people and through them may rule mankind'. His audience were in no doubt that it was 'international Jewry' to which he was referring.

Even more contentiously, he went on seemingly to defend Hitler:

I am told that Hitler wants the whole world. In other words, I am told that Hitler is mad. What evidence have they got so far that this man, who has taken his country from the dust to the height in some 20 years of struggle – what evidence have they got to show that he has suddenly gone mad? Any man who wants to run the whole of the modern world with all its polyglot population and divers people and interests – such a man is undoubtedly mad and I challenge my opponents to produce one shred of such evidence about that singularly shrewd and lucid intellect whom they venture so glibly to criticise.

Somewhere about this point in the two-hour oration Winston Churchill's son Randolph, sitting with the dancer Tilly Losch directly in front of the Denham party, got up and walked out. For those who stayed, there was a spectacular peroration extolling the splendour and virtues of Britain and its historic past and saying that no true Britons would die 'like rats in Polish holes'. It was an extraordinary and hypnotic speech that brought the crowd roaring to its feet – and it said in the clearest possible terms that Britain should not go to the aid of Poland.

Afterwards, the family went back to Lady Mosley's flat for supper, where Baba joined them. While they were eating, to their surprise Diana's brother Tom Mitford arrived without warning. At 11.45 Tom Mosley appeared. Then, at 12.15, there was a mass irruption of Mitfords: Diana, who had been giving interviews to

German reporters, her mother, her youngest sister Debo and a couple of friends. Baba, unable to face her successful rival, left at once.

The hypnotic spell woven by Tom's oratory quickly wore off and Irene seized the chance of what she was increasingly coming to think might be a last foray abroad: a quick trip through the Low Countries and Scandinavia. On her return she heard that Dino Grandi had been recalled to Rome.

This was because, on 22 May, the 'Pact of Steel' – the military alliance between Hitler and Mussolini – had been signed. The last thing the popular Grandi wanted to see was war between his country and England; when ordered by Mussolini to make a speech publicly and uncompromisingly justifying the Duce's policy, the Ambassador at first refused. Then, under threat of being outlawed by his own country, he delivered the words he had been sent. Though only the staffs of the Italian and German embassies were present, Mussolini's son-in-law and Italy's Foreign Minister Count Ciano had already released the text to the Rome newspapers, whence it was picked up by the naturally hostile British press.

Next day Grandi called on Halifax, now foreign secretary, who (according to the count's memoirs) said: 'Dear Grandi, don't take it to heart. Everyone understands. All that matters is that you should stay to work with us for peace.' But Halifax's good wishes were of no avail and Grandi received a cable ordering him to leave for Rome forthwith. From Rome the count wrote a 'touching' letter to Irene dated 9 August; to his adored Baba he wrote elegiacally: 'There are moments which mean a whole life. An afternoon at Kew Gardens in early spring. Two children playing at life, hand in hand. Blossoming trees, a golden rain of blossoms everywhere. Your dress, I remember, was designed with blossoms too. Both happy like birds. Was it a mistake not to end our day like birds do? It was.

'And you again, smiling, forgiving, heavenly, lovely and beautiful, on the dark platform of a station, going away for ever...'

That last summer of peace, the Metcalfes had again been asked to stay with the Windsors at La Cröe so that Fruity could recuperate from his hernia operation. He was well aware that the gilded life, with its make-believe royal court, continued as if in a sealed capsule, with dinner parties in the white-and-gold dining room, neighbours like Maxine Elliott curtseying to the Duchess, the Duke scrutinising every bill for possible economies while showering the Duchess with jewels and furs, and therefore wrote to warn his friend that he would be a bit of a 'washout' as a guest. 'I am still walking with the aid of a stick ... then I have to go to bed every night at 10.30. I would have to bring my servant and I would have to ask you and Wallis if you would permit me to wear a soft silk shirt and short coat [dinner jacket] as I just couldn't face dressing up with a stiff collar or shirt etc. In other words your old friend Fruity would be an infernal nuisance and not worth the trouble and would only occupy one of your much-sought-after rooms and give little in return!'

The Windsors were undeterred by Fruity's caveats and the three Metcalfes duly arrived at La Cröe. After Baba and David left at the end of July, Fruity stayed on, fulfilling, as he had done so many years earlier, the duties of a temporary ADC.

On 1 August he described in a letter to Baba

terrible wailings coming from the woods and first of all thought that one of the little dogs had got a slight go of rabies but after listening intently I heard the bagpipes. At 6 p.m. some very strange people arrived, evidently some 'old time' friends of Wallis's, and the Rogers family. Then H.R.H. appeared, escorting Wallis (I having acted up to this as ADC in waiting, introducing etc). His appearance was magnificent if a little strange considering the tropical heat. He was completely turned out as the Scotch laird about to go stalking – beautiful kilt, swords and all the aids. It staggered *me* a bit and I'm getting used to blows and surprises. Then from the woods rushed what might have been the whole Campbell family, complete with pipes and haggis etc. I was told they were Folk Lore dancers, here to promote better international feeling. Personally, I think that if they got into Germany I wouldn't blame Hitler attacking anyone ...

Over the next three weeks, the Riviera emptied. On 19 August, Hore-Belisha, who had been over for cocktails a day or two earlier, flew back to London. Walter Monckton had to cancel the visit to La Cröe that he had planned for the end of August; in London he sought to make arrangements to bring the Windsors home in the event of war. Irene, staying with friends in York, learned that Lord Halifax had gone south from his estate of Garrowby 'in acute worry over Danzig'. The arrival of Vivien from Wootton just before dinner struck a further note of gloom: she told her aunt that her father was very worried as Diana, having recently seen much of Hitler, said he was determined to seize Danzig. Irene was further depressed by the description of the telephone system at Garrowby. 'It seems inconceivably incompetent for a Foreign Secretary. A private phone rings in the Tower, which is seldom heard, or Halifax is too bored to go up to it. I gather Chamberlain has no phone at all.'

The crisis escalated at terrifying speed. On 21 August came the news that destroyed the last faint hope of peace: Hitler had concluded a non-aggression pact with the Soviets. All hope of an alliance between Britain, France, and Russia vanished and, with his eastern front secured, so did the sole remaining obstacle to Hitler's plans. From now on, war was a matter of days away – although there were still those who refused to believe it. The King had no illusions, leaving Balmoral for London on 23 August for a Privy Council and visits from his Prime Minister and Foreign Secretary. Halifax gave a talk on the radio that evening which Irene found trite and uninspiring.

The countdown began. On 25 August all British nationals still in Berlin and all Germans in England were asked to leave. Passages to America and Canada were fully booked and the Admiralty closed the Mediterranean to British shipping. The roads out of London were congested: many were getting away while they could before the evacuation of one and a half million people commenced in a few days' time. The telephone system ground almost to a standstill with the number of calls, which took up to six hours to be put through by the overworked operators. The Emergency Defence Act was rushed through, giving the Government the authority it needed to put the country on a war footing and the acting Socialist leader [Arthur Greenwood] gave Labour's assurance that the House would stand united against aggression. 'The peril of war is imminent,' the Prime Minister told the House, 'but I still go on hoping.'

Irene drove to Denham on 26 August, to find Nick and Diana

there with Tom, who asked her to take his mother, Viv and Nick up to Wootton the following day – he expected air raids to start the moment war broke out. Back in London she packed up her pictures and collection of crosses and sent them down to Denham. Next day her chauffeur drove them all to Wootton, which she thought Diana had furnished very badly ('only one small window in each bay opens so one suffocates'), perhaps because she so resented the sight of Hitler's photograph by Diana's bed. She removed the photographs of Goering and his baby from the sitting-room mantelpiece.

By 29 August the tension was palpable. German troops were massed on the Polish border and the midnight news reported that Nevile Henderson flew back to Berlin after the Cabinet meeting and was still with Hitler and Ribbentrop at 11.30 p.m.

On 1 September Hitler struck, his troops invading Poland at dawn. Britain and France instructed their ambassadors to inform the German government that unless Germany withdrew, their respective countries would be forced to fulfil their obligations to Poland. In Britain the Navy, Army and Air Force were mobilised, blackout orders were given and the evacuation of mothers and children from large cities began. Irene learned that a group of six would arrive at nearby Uttoxeter from Birmingham the following day and somehow managed to find and hastily furnish a suitable cottage for them.

On her return to London she learned that James the footman had been called up; after saying goodbye to him, she and the cook covered the hall light and all the passage lights with blue paper to dim them, took out every plug in the drawing-room and morning-room and decided to live in the dining-room with its thick curtains. 'I feel that dear Viv is suffering very deeply underneath,' she wrote that night. 'It is so cruel that she is facing what I did in 1914 – all my world in ashes round me. How can such horror triumph? An unbounded conviction like Hitler's moves mountains. I loathe his photograph by Diana's bed and long to smash it to atoms. I wonder what Tom and Diana are thinking of their hero?'

At La Cröe there was nothing to indicate that either Windsor realised the true gravity of the situation. True, the Duke had sent a personal telegram to Hitler, followed by one (on 29 August) to the King of Italy, asking him to intervene for the preservation of peace. Even when he was told on 1 September that the Germans had invaded Poland, he still refused to believe that Europe was teetering on the edge of war. 'Oh, just another sensational report,' he said impatiently. When, that evening, the Duke received a message from the King of Italy telling him that Italy intended to remain neutral, he was jubilant. The Duchess was so convinced that the crisis would blow over that she was making arrangements to have the new butler's wife brought out from England.

Fruity was under no illusions. That afternoon, he drove first to Cannes to see the British Consul and then to Nice, to visit the travel agent Thomas Cook where, through charm, persuasiveness and the Duke's name, he managed to reserve a compartment on the 7.30 a.m. train to Paris the following morning for seven of the Duke's servants, his own valet and a secretary. Apart from the Windsors, only Fruity, the Duchess's Swiss lady's maid and a few French servants were left at La Cröe.

On Sunday 3 September the Duke, about to have a swim, was told that the British Ambassador was on the telephone from Paris. Ten minutes later he came back. 'Great Britain has just declared war on Germany,' he said – and dived into the pool.

The Duke's solipsistic approach to a war that might see the end of his country, let alone of millions of lives, finally proved too much even for the loyal Fruity. As he wrote to Baba that momentous Sunday: 'Certain people here are quite extraordinary. No one could understand how their minds work. On Friday it had all been settled for a plane to come out early Saturday morning to bring us home etc. At about 1 a.m. or 2 a.m. Walter [Monckton] spoke again. The conversation had to be in French which didn't help any as Walter is about as bad as the Master here! It went on in the library. I went on reading my book in the drawing room as I did not think that anything could go wrong.'

Walter Monckton was telling the Duke that he would arrive the following morning at ten in a plane to escort them home. The Duke asked him petulantly why he, Walter, was coming since (as Monckton's notes record) 'he would take up space that could be occupied by the Duchess's luggage'. When the Duke was told that he would be staying with the Metcalfes he said he would only come if his brother and his wife were prepared to have them at one of their houses; informed that this was impossible, he refused to leave. Fruity's letter describes what happened next:

... Well anyhow they came in to me after about half an hour and said 'We are *not* going – the plane is coming for you and Miss Arnold [secretary] tomorrow.' I looked at them as if they really *were* mad – then they started off – 'I refuse to go unless we are invited to stay at Windsor Castle and the invitation etc and plane, are sent personally by my brother etc'. I just sat still, held my head and listened for about 20 minutes and then I started. I said: 'First of all, I'll say that whatever I say is said speaking as your best friend. I speak *only* for your good and Wallis's – *understand that*. After what I've said you can ask me to leave if you like but you're going to listen now.

'You have just behaved like two spoilt children. You *only* think of yourselves. You don't realise that there is at this moment a war going on, that women and children are being bombed and killed while *you* talk of your PRIDE. God, it makes me sick. You forget everything in only thinking of yourselves, your property, your money and your stupid pride. What you've now said to Walter has just bitched up everything. You talk of one of H.M. Government's planes being sent out for Miss Arnold and for me!! You are just 'nuts'! Do you really think for one instant they would send a plane over for me and Miss Arnold? It's too absurd even to discuss.'

I said a lot more in the same strain. They never uttered. After this I said: 'Now if this plane *is* sent out to fetch you, which I doubt very much, then get into it and be b——y grateful.' I went to bed then, it was 3.15 a.m. Well at 7.15 I was wakened by *her* maid telling me to get up! To arrange for a car to go to the flying field etc. Then at 8.00 'he' came into my room fully dressed and said: 'We've decided to go on the plane'. I said: 'Okay – *if* it comes – and now I'll have a bath!' Of course there never was any plane as I knew they'd never send it – of course Walter would have repeated all the rot talked on the phone to the Head Boss in England.*

The Lady (?) here is in a panic, the worst fear I've ever seen or heard

---

*Immediately after his conversation with the Duke, Monckton told Sir Alexander Hardinge, now the King's Private Secretary, of his former master's decision; Hardinge's response was: 'The King's plane can't be sent unless they are coming themselves.'

of, all on account of the aeroplane journey. Talks of jumping out etc. Every half hour it's 'I won't go by plane! We will motor to Paris! Or Boulogne etc' I point out the impossibility of doing this – roads blocked with troops, no hotels, etc. Today there is talk of a destroyer being sent out. Oh God, it's such a madhouse. Now Winston is head of the Admiralty he will I think send a destroyer if the little man asks for it. It seems *she* would rather go by boat. We've got no servants here except Marcel and Robert and a pantry boy and two French maids. You should see 'him' packing – it really is funny.

I am to go with the boss here, *wherever* he will go in this war, so *please do this for me*. Get in touch with Scotland Yard and let Major Whittle or Whattle (the awful thing is his correct name has gone clean out of my head) know that I am going to do this for the war and therefore *cannot* do Special Constable. I hope he will understand – speak to him yourself.

Fruity had made his choice. Fortuitously he had cut the cords that knotted him and Baba in such an unhappy tangle of emotions. By casting in his lot with the person who was, in one sense, his first love, he had released the two of them from the miseries and jealousies of their life together. Above all, while remaining married to the woman he adored, without either scandal or humiliation he had made it possible for each to lead their own life.

29

Britain at War

~

Britain's war began with the dropping of three million leaflets over the Ruhr, Germany's with the sinking of the passenger liner *Athenia* by a U-boat, in direct contravention of the rules of submarine warfare. If nothing else, it showed the direction the war would take.

At Wootton, Irene had listened with horror to Chamberlain's broadcast announcement of war. That night she sang 'Onward Christian Soldiers' with Micky when she put him to bed. After the ten-thirty news she and Nick walked in the moonlight that streaked the long avenue and lay in a broad band across the lawn. She dreaded the idea of Diana's arrival, with her devotion to fascism and Hitler.

Irene spent the first few days of the war searching out blackout material for Wootton's huge windows. She eventually managed to find 56 yards of black cloth at 1s 6d a yard, which she took back to Wootton in triumph. Then, helped by Nanny and Grimwood, the Wootton chef, she began the laborious process of taking down all the curtains, stitching the black material in as a lining and rehanging them, often wobbling perilously at the top of a shaky ladder as she fixed pelmets near the high ceilings. When the material ran out she used black paint to cover the windows. She had the bumpers and running boards of her car painted white and its headlights filtered to give only a dim glow. She wrote to Campbell Steward, Chairman of the Bureau of Information, and Harold Holt, organiser of concerts all over England, to ask if they might have a job for her. In London she offered a room in her house as a rest room for VADs and reduced her own living space to a dining-sitting-room to save light, fuel and work.

On 11 September Diana sent a wire – to Vivien, not Irene – to say she was arriving that evening with her two boys, Desmond and Jonathan. After dinner they all listened to the news. 'I felt Diana hated it and it made me uneasy,' Irene wrote that night. 'So I listened to the Lord Mayor's appeal for the Red Cross nervously, much more so Anthony Eden's 20-minute address on the enormities of Hitler and his regime, which drew a protest from Diana. She talks blandly of Tom carrying on the Movement during the war. I felt very strongly I could not be with her for long because of that attitude.' Irene left the following day.

After the Duke of Windsor had refused the offer of a royal aircraft Walter Monckton had flown to Antibes in a dilapidated Leopard Moth on 7 September, partly to persuade the Windsors to leave France and partly to discuss what the Duke was going to do during the war. Monckton had spent much time in England lobbying on behalf of a suitable and fitting job for him.

The King had first thought of a civilian post under the Regional Commissioner for Wales, then of an attachment to the British Military Mission which was shortly to leave for Paris. The King's advisers did not want to give the Duke too central a role: Queen Elizabeth feared lest her brother-in-law, with his well-known charm and glamour, would overshadow her husband at this most difficult time. Everyone felt that if the Windsors returned to the Fort they would be a good deal too close for comfort and possibly the focus of a rival court.

It did not take the Duke long to decide that he would prefer the Military Mission, although it meant – temporarily at any rate – giving up his rank of Field Marshal. He now asked for a destroyer to transport them instead of a plane and the long-suffering Monckton flew back to arrange this. A message was sent to the British Embassy in Paris informing them: 'The Duke of Windsor should be ready to embark at 1700 at Cherbourg on Tuesday 11 September'. When Baba had heard from Fruity that no accommodation had been offered the Windsors by anyone, anywhere – least of all by the royal family – she invited them to the Metcalfe house in Ashdown Forest. As all the arrangements had to be made from

Downing Street and as Monckton could not speak French, she was called on constantly to help.

The Windsor party left Antibes in three cars, spending two nights en route. One temporary chauffeur drove the Windsors and Fruity, with the dogs, in the Duke's car, another drove the Duchess's car, with the lady's maid and another servant, a third drove a Ford station wagon piled with luggage. In Paris, the Duchess's invaluable secretary, Mrs Bedford, had bought extra suitcases, packed the clothes they wanted to take, despatched what she could through the British Embassy and even managed to get the Duchess's precious furs out of store. Then they sent off for Cherbourg, where they were met by Randolph Churchill, in the uniform of the 4th Hussars, representing his father, and the Duke's cousin and old friend Lord Louis Mountbatten, commanding the newly-built destroyer HMS *Kelly*. First the luggage and the Duke's car were loaded on board, and finally the party, the Duke carrying one dog, the Duchess another, and the lady's maid the third, walked up the gang-plank.

On 12 September Baba drove Walter Monckton down to Portsmouth in her Buick, followed by her chauffeur with a van (no car, either, had been made available to the Windsors). They arrived about half past six in the evening and went to the Queen's Hotel where they booked for the whole party – it would be a dreadful first night back in England, thought Baba. Fortunately, Admiral James, C-in-C Portsmouth, had offered to put the Windsors up.

At eight thirty a message came to say the *Kelly* would arrive in about an hour. The party went down to the dock, in inky darkness except for a faint blue light, and stood on the same jetty from which the Duke had so hurriedly and secretly left England almost three years earlier. With relief they saw that one gesture at least had been made to his former status: a red carpet flanked by a guard of honour of a hundred men with tin hats and gas masks – a tribute from Churchill to his friend and former monarch.

At last, out of the velvety blackness ahead appeared a tiny yellow-and-green light. It slowly approached until the *Kelly* slid into view alongside the dock. Baba and Walter Monckton were first up the gangway, followed by the Admiral. They were greeted by Mountbatten, who took them down to his cabin for a glass of champagne with the Windsors.

Once ashore and after the reviewing of the guard, the Windsors were taken to Admiralty House in Portsmouth while Fruity and Randolph Churchill accompanied Baba and Monckton to the Queen's Hotel. Next morning they collected the Windsors and, with Baba driving them in her Buick – the chauffeur had gone to fetch the Duke's car – and Fruity driving the luggage van, they set off at a steady 50 m.p.h. behind a police car.

They arrived at South Hartfield House, Forest Row, at 1.30, to find the press already at the gates. There was a brief photocall in front of the Metcalfes' house and after a short statement from the Windsors the reporters and photographers left.

'The Duke never *once* gave the impression of feeling and sensing the sadness of his return with the dramaticness of departure,' records Baba's diary. 'Like with everything in his life, the blind has been drawn down and the past has been forgotten with its many memories. The visit has gone easily and well on the whole. There have been moments when the ice has seemed dangerously thin and ominous cracks have been heard but the night has brought a thickening up and we have skated on the next day okay.'

The Windsors went to London most days, using the Metcalfes' town house, 16 Wilton Place, which had been closed for the war and its furniture dust-sheeted. The Duke worked in a small sitting-room, his papers on a single table, the Duchess had her hair done in Baba's empty bedroom with its shrouded furniture. 'Clerks, secretaries, War Office officials, bootmakers, tailors and hair-dressers stream in and out,' Baba's diary continues. 'We have sandwiches and tea from a Thermos.'

It was from Wilton Place, on 14 September, that the Duke went to see his brother the King at Buckingham Palace – the first time the two men had met since the Abdication. The King reported to their younger brother, the Duke of Kent, that 'the meeting went off all right but it was very unbrotherly.' However they did discuss the Duke's future employment, with agreement that the Duke would join the Military Mission in Paris.

He saw the King, a stag party, and nothing personal crossed the lips of either [Baba's diary recalls]. P.M., Winston, Belisha and Edward [Halifax] have all been visited with uneventful success. His job has materialised and Fruity is on his personal staff. This was done as usual not with tremendous grace. Fruity flew over to France to make adequate arrangements. The first few days 200–300 letters arrived a day and there were only six bad ones. Fruity and I got only a few bad ones and many charming ones. One IRA saying they would blow up the house and another incredible one to me from a sex maniac. Walter has had to be with his son so we have had everything à quatre. It's been difficult on more than one occasion not to shout 'Stop! Stop! Stop! You've got everything all wrong'. But considering all, they have been very grateful and sweet and completely simple. If the Duke goes to say goodbye to his mother, it will be at my door for good or bad the plan can be laid, as during one of our lengthy talks I put it over strong to Wallis.

I do think the family might have done something. He might not even exist but for the one short visit to the King. Wallis said they realised there was no place ever for him in this country, and she saw no reason for him ever to return. I didn't deny it or do any pressing.

They are incapable of truly trusting anybody, therefore one feels one's loyalty is misplaced. One has no real affection for either of them, as his selfishness and self-concentration is terrifying. I don't know why one goes on 'playing'. It must be for what he was, as what he is today, as a personality and friend, is not worth the candle. What I am finding difficult to put into words is the reason for his only having us as real friends instead of legions. He is so dreadfully disappointing.

From the Windsors' point of view, the visit had been a success. The Duchess wrote Baba a charming letter of thanks ('This is a small effort from the Duke, three dogs and myself to try and thank you for all your hospitality to us and being able to remain calm in the face of such an avalanche of guests') with an amusing description of their arrival back on French soil after a horrible crossing.

'The Channel turned itself inside out for us and the Express lay flat on it first on one side and then on the other. We arrived looking green and drawn to be met by quite an ovation from the British troops on the quay. I wanted to cry and be sick at the same time and regretted my sallow appearance, realising that several hundred men and a goodly smattering of nurses were wondering "How could he have done it?"'

In London Irene, worried that she had left Viv in what she saw as a hotbed of Nazism, was greatly relieved to hear from her niece that she wanted to go and work in Norfolk. She gained the agreement of Tom, who wanted her to contribute £1,000 p.a. to the upkeep of Wootton – 'according to him, the two children want Wootton to be kept going more than Denham' – but the rest of his conversation left her even more deeply alarmed.

> He predicted the likelihood of Germany and Russia winning; it was by no means so sure we would. Hence his mission to get a peace while the Empire was still intact ... I asked him his views on Hitler etc and he said he was only out for Britain and a safe peace for her, but I think he sees in himself a potential smasher-up of all our capitalist systems when the disruption of communism creeps over Europe and towards us, and with anti-Semitism as his pillar of hate he will arise from the ashes of conservatism and profitmaking. We talked earnestly on the curious thing that great fanatical faith has to have hate to work on.

Next day, during lunch with his mother and Irene, Tom expressed his views more strongly. 'They were venomous and alarming and vitriolic,' wrote Irene. 'He cursed this Government for the betrayal of our nation and said he would work on the people to get them out.

> If Tom had his way and he was in power he would at once make peace with Hitler, letting him have his huge bloc to the Mediterranean if Hitler leaves us and our empire alone, but if he touches it we fight. Ma said in vain: 'But do you want to see such a regime all over Europe and all-powerful?' but I fear he does not mind the Poles, Rumanians, etc being sacrificed. He argues he could make England so strong Hitler would never dare touch her, how could he when she holds a colossal part of the globe and so forth.
>
> He raged on about the audacity of Chamberlain saying Hitlerism must be wiped out – cannot 80 million Germans choose their Government and would we stomach Hitler butting in here and condemning our Government and telling them he would fight to exterminate them?

Irene found listening to this tirade so horrendous that she was even thankful when Diana arrived with her eldest son, Jonathan. She also decided that she would prefer to do her duty vis-à-vis the children by looking after Denham rather than Wootton – she did not see why Diana should gain financially at her expense – and wrote to Tom to tell him so – 'tho' I fear he will not like this'.

She was right. When he received her letter there was another of the furious rows, that everyone round him dreaded. Of lunch the next day with Tom and his mother she wrote:

> It was one of those awful interviews with Tom when he was so wild with rage he tore up and down the room in a filthy blasphemous state, with dear Ma trying to calm him. I gave out some pretty stiff heated rejoinders and that simpering ass Diana never uttered. The situation was so bad when D. rang for lunch I begged to leave but Ma winked that I should stay and we both wasted a lunch we could not swallow.

Throughout lunch Tom threatened that owing to Irene's intransigence the children would have to live like workmen, Wootton would have to go, Nicky leave Eton and Micky be put in the care of Baba and then in the spring to school. Irene repeated her offer to pay for Denham; Tom would have none of it.

Irene was under no illusions. With a father who had misappropriated her own income she was quick to recognise the same motive in another. Tom, she knew perfectly well, wanted her to subsidise his children so that even at this desperate time he could continue to pour funds into fascism, and was using her love for them and fear that they would be taken away from her as emotional blackmail. She had a miserable, sleepless night but her view was confirmed next morning by both Lady Mosley and Baba.

A couple of days later, Tom capitulated. Realising that he would get nothing more out of Irene and that if he were intransigent would lose Denham into the bargain, he called on her solicitor to say that he was happy to continue with the Denham arrangement as before.

'It is as I predicted,' wrote Irene triumphantly. 'He would come crawling back when he saw his interests being damaged.' She added a note of thankfulness that her sister Cim was no longer alive to see Tom behaving like this; and, when she saw Nick at Eton, briefly outlined the dispute and his father's propositions for Denham so that seventeen-year-old Nick, as eldest son, could make up his own mind on the future of their home.

On 28 September – the day before the Duke of Windsor left for

Paris and his new job – Irene gave a luncheon party for him to meet Nevile Henderson: tea and apples for the Windsors (the Duke seldom ate more than an apple for lunch and the figure-conscious Duchess often followed suit) and sandwiches and drinks for herself and Nevile. The conversation was disjointed, ending with abuse of the Ministry of Information by the Duke. The Duchess said little. 'I came to the conclusion what a common little man he really is,' wrote Irene. 'Nevile stuck to the point he thought this [the Nazi] regime would hold the floor unless the Reichstag rebelled, and cracked.'

Fruity returned to France with the Duke on 29 September. After leaving the Duchess at the Windsors' house in Versailles they went straight to the Military Mission at Vincennes, commanded by Major-General Sir Richard Howard-Vyse. 'Arrival very full of good cheer,' wrote Fruity to Baba on the 30th. 'All the boys in red from the highest quarters down to welcome us. I knew one or two of 'em from the last war. We got off at 9.30 today and got to Suchet at 1.30 – they go by themselves to Versailles till Monday. I'm *so* glad. It's a great relief for me. I'm delighted to get a day or so *without* the Windsors. Mrs Corrigan claimed me almost as a prisoner of war on my arrival here. I shall escape believe me.'

Once in Paris, the Duchess re-engaged Gertrude Bedford, her efficient secretary (who lived there), began to work for the French Red Cross, and concentrated on decorating the Windsors' new house at 24 Boulevard Suchet. Almost at once the alert Fruity spotted a source of potential trouble.

At present and probably for a little time it is quite all right for Nibs to stay at Suchet with Mrs Nibs [he wrote to Baba on 3 October 1939]. I say at present because he *is* seeing and talking to important civil and political people. BUT it must not last for too long otherwise he is finished. The French press are very quick to spot things and it will have a very harmful effect if Nibs is known to sleep with Mrs Nibs etc while the boys are going through it. One other reason: he must get off on his own away from that influence, away from household worries. Now I want this 'offensive' to start in a matter of a week. I suggest Walter starts the game. You could do a little to Mrs N but be very careful – use all your famous tact.

Fruity's comment about 'household worries' – an unlikely phrase to use about a couple as well serviced as the Windsors – was justified. Anything pertaining to the Duchess, however trivial, immediately received the Duke's absolute, undivided attention, no matter what more pressing concerns were in the offing. As Fruity wrote exasperatedly: 'His Nibs is utterly impossible to deal with. If one has something really important to tell him and he is at Suchet, we'll say, he will suddenly get up to notice a door has jammed and does not properly open or shut, or that the water does not run hot, or that Mrs Bedford has to pay a bill for $7\frac{1}{2}$ yards of linoleum for the back stairs etc.'

It was quite different, save in one particular, when they visited a section of the French front, where the Duke inspected fortifications and anti-tank defences and met the generals of various divisions, with whom he was greatly impressed. 'Everyone was delighted to see HRH and the visit could not have gone off better,' wrote Fruity. 'This was very important to His Nibs as you can well imagine. Then we proceeded to another French section and saw their front etc. Again we were impressed. HRH was all through absolutely delightful company. No one could have been a more interesting or amusing companion – how we laughed at many incidents. All through he was in splendid form.

'The only few minutes I hated and when he was "all wrong" was when I had to get the hotel bills and get them paid, and then he was *frightful*.'

The Duke's preoccupation with money had increased to an extent that embarrassed all those around him: in contrast with the lavish lifestyle and the Duchess's extravagance, every account was minutely scrutinised and, if possible, chiselled down, and friends were expected to pick up the bill for any entertainment.

I found W. looking like an old apple, a very old wizened one and a terribly sour one. I said Good Morning Wallis, had a look at her and went out [he wrote to Baba on 9 October]. 'You ask in your letter is my position secure or "groggy" – when I see W. I wouldn't know anything! She is like a kaleidoscope – different every time you look. All I know is, I feel sure I am doing him absolutely the best and that no one could do him better, or nearly as well.

I know *nothing* of Gray Phillips coming out to join HRH's staff. It is complete news to me. He has not said a word about it and of course neither has she. I've hardly seen them since we arrived in Paris because they went off at once to stay in the hotel at Versailles. I *believe* they are coming up tomorrow to Suchet for good. They have got Marcel and Robert and are now arranging to get the Chef sent to them. The Chef had been mobilised and sent to some unit in the S. of France but they've been upsetting the whole ruddy army to get him and today when I saw HRH he looked a bit sour and said there had been some stupid misunderstanding with the French about the Chef and that he must go out to the Mission to put it straight. He said it was not a Major General's job but if people under that rank couldn't do certain things *he*, as a Major General, would have to personally deal with it!! They say that the Germans are bombing the Maginot Line and that the French are replying and losses are taking place on both sides but the battle of HRH's chef is making more noise than all the shelling.

The fact is that when he is off without 'Mrs' he is excellent. With her or near her he's not worth 2½d and then you can't trust him a yard.

As a letter from the War Office made clear, Fruity could not look to the Government for remuneration for his work for the Duke of Windsor. 'I am directed to inform you', it ran, 'that your appointment as ADC carries no emoluments from public funds.'

The next blow was to learn that Gray Phillips would be joining the Duke's ménage.

HRH tells me (now!) that he will be in uniform. I wonder what uniform and what rank? He is to live at Suchet. I gather he is to act more or less as Comptroller etc and at times HRH will take him on tour. I suggest he brings a few suits of *civilian* clothes. HRH wishes me to get out some. I wouldn't mind my new grey striped flannel suit or my new blue flannel, a few decent shirts to go with them, collars attached and long sleeves, also one or two ties, my Regimental one and two or three new ones that I recently bought, also some medium weight grey or blue socks. I have the necessary shoes. My new little soft grey hat might also be necessary. These damn civilian clothes – I personally would never bother about this but he has several times mentioned it.

I shall remain at Ritz when in Paris. The Mission is utterly impossible, it is 45 minutes from Paris and Suchet. I must be near HRH as long as he insists on living in Paris. Be very careful when you or Walter write or speak to either of them at Suchet re HRH staying there. If he thinks there is any pressure or advice being given *nothing* will move him. Re Wallis: of course I don't let her see what I feel. I am exactly the same as always.

Irene and Baba had immersed themselves in war work. Baba was now fully qualified and nursing, mostly the old, at the Princess Beatrice Hospital in Earl's Court where, at first, her unmistakably upper-class voice and elegantly-fitting uniform caused the 'career' Sisters to suspect her of dilettantism. But her hard work and uncomplaining stance soon won them round.

Irene spent much of her time at the Kennington Day Nursery and concerning herself with the future of children generally. When she first saw the evacuees sent to Wootton she was horrified by their stunted growth, general ill-health and dirty, ragged clothes. 'What is really shameful is that our system has allowed such creatures to grow up,' she wrote to *The Times*. 'There is a serious deficiency somewhere in training and outlook. Our educational methods seem to have failed miserably, and such children, through evacuation, have been brought mercifully to the light of day.' She went on to beg for legislation to stop the parents taking them back to the damp, verminous and despairing conditions from which they came, feeling that life in the freedom and tranquillity of the country would give them a far better chance.

An imaginative gesture was to offer sanctuary to the ten men of a Regent's Park barrage balloon unit. She had seen them out of her bedroom window in Cornwall Terrace and wondered where they went when off duty. On hearing that no one else invited them in at night, she put her former music room at their disposal, with its circle of easy chairs, tables, radiogram and well-dimmed lights, telling them to ask their wives and girlfriends along if they wished. She also gave them the use of a bathroom so that they could have a hot bath after work. Around half a dozen turned up most nights between 6 and 10 p.m. Typically, Irene was not satisfied with this single act of kindness but urged her friends to do the same for their local defence units.

In those first months of the war the hectic social pace of the upper classes scarcely faltered. Many still had servants, though half the number they had had earlier in the year as the young and fit were called up or left to do more fitting war work. London restaurants like Quaglino's and Claridge's were packed every evening as those home on leave or with new jobs in the Admiralty or War Office or who were staying in town overnight – trains were packed with troops moving about the country – went out to dinner as usual. Irene, working at the day nursery, going to concerts when she could, would give lunch to her friends the Eshers or the Masseys at Claridge's, go to Sibyl Colefax's parties, or be entertained by Miles Graham or Nevile Henderson.

Miles Graham, now a general, drove her down to one of the Cliveden weekends that still continued and at the end of November she took Vivien to Eton in driving rain to watch the famous Wall Game in a sea of mud. 'It really is miraculous that in War this fantastic drollery goes on,' she wrote. 'Elliot [the headmaster] and all the masters out in top hats and tailcoats and rolled umbrellas, including the Provost. Photographers nipping about everywhere and waterlogged boys struggling in the mire.'

She was temporarily on excellent terms with Baba. They discussed another of Irene's admirers, Leslie Hore-Belisha ('Baba told me that he asked someone lately whether if he married a baroness he would become a baron!'). When Belisha told Irene about an evening spent with the King and Queen and that he had suggested Fruity as ADC to the Duke of Windsor she wondered if he was telling the truth or was simply trying to please her.

That autumn Baba bought Little Compton, in Oxfordshire, an exquisite Tudor manor house on the eastern flank of the Cotswolds which had once belonged to Archbishop Juxon, the cleric who had accompanied Charles I to the scaffold to pray with him in his final moments. She furnished its panelled ground-floor rooms with the rosewood-and-gilt side cabinets and walnut wing-chair that had come from Kedleston, oak tables, piles of books, pretty table lamps and rugs over the polished wood floor. Upstairs, in her white-painted bedroom with its high, barrel-vaulted ceiling, was the painted and lacquered furniture which later became the hallmark of her taste.

Soon after Baba moved in she received a letter from Wallis, its tone of mild complaint ranging over everything from the uniform she had to wear for her work with the Red Cross to her servants.

You are lucky to have your friends around you and be in your own country. I have a great longing for America – war makes one like a homesick child perhaps. I have signed up with the Section Secretaire Automobile of the French Red Cross and been given an ambulance. I tried in every way to do things for the English but I was far from welcome. The uniform is like all feminine ones – hideous but pratique. The Duke is well but as disheartened and discouraged about everything as I am.

I hope the house is getting on – I can imagine the endless difficulties. I am still struggling with the butler question – we have an ape at present. Fruity will be home for Christmas. We haven't decided what we will do as I don't know if the Duke will get enough leave to make opening La Croe worth while. Why not come over some time – it would be fun to see you once again.

In Paris, Fruity was finding life with the Windsors more and more difficult. He no longer felt that, as formerly, the Duke's affection for him was rock-like. This, he could not help thinking, was due to the Duchess's influence. When he and the Duke set off for a tour of Strasbourg and then the Front he told Baba that the atmosphere at first was chilly.

'But by slow degrees as we progress further and further from Paris and the environs of Suchet we begin to thaw, gradually, slowly, as another mile is put between us and Suchet!! HRH is extraordinary. By the afternoon we became NORMAL and again he became a really delightful companion, one with whom one would go away anywhere (*slight* lapses when a bill has to be paid!).'

They inspected gun batteries, saw a battalion of tanks that had seen action in September, lunched with the general in command and then reached Strasbourg. 'We entered a City of the Dead,' wrote Fruity on 30 October 1939. 'Picture it in your mind, a wonderful city of over 200,000 inhabitants now completely empty, with at most 1,500 people in it. It was weird. One felt one was entering a city that had been struck by plague. One found shops with all their stock in the windows ready for sale, hotels with the lounges all prepared. One expected to see rats running from the houses across the street. Grass is sprouting between the tramlines, the roads are uncleaned, stray dogs run about. Given another couple of months Strasbourg will be but a name. All the inhabitants left in 36 hours.'

They motored on to the Rhine, then into the Vosges Mountains, where snow prevented a view of the Siegfried Line, and then to one of the largest fortresses of the Maginot Line. 'A veritable underground city, it is terrible, something uncanny – H. G. Wells,' wrote Fruity to Baba. 'Think of 1,500 men locked in an iron box under the earth.' Before he signed off, he told her once again that HRH had been *wonderful* all these days – missing nothing and seeing everything'.

Once back in Boulevard Suchet the easy, affectionate camaraderie that had inspired such deep devotion in Fruity disappeared and the frosty chill reappeared. '*It always will be the same* I believe as long as she is alive, and *she* makes him the same way,' wrote Fruity to Baba on 30 October. In the same letter he told her that the Duchess's war work had been shelved: 'The hospital business is off as there is no need for hospitals at present (the other reason is she doesn't really want to do it – it *would cost money*!)'

There were further reasons for discontent. As someone whose only income was his major's pension, pay was a matter of importance to Fruity, and so far he had received none. To expedite matters, he wrote privately to Hore-Belisha, whom he had met and dined with several times in Cannes. He also felt that having dropped everything immediately to accompany the Duke when needed, on the understanding that he was acting as equerry, and having worked hard and to the best of his ability, he was gradually being pushed to one side.

His disenchantment with his employer increased when, dining alone with the Duke one evening, he showed him a letter he had received from the Military Mission saying that the War Office had no authority to pay him at all. 'I showed HRH the letter and he said – nothing. He then looked at me and said: "Didn't they tell you at the W.O. you wouldn't get any pay?" I said: "Good God, no." He looked just fishy. Christ, I am fed up. What beats me is that HRH is quite prepared to do nothing for me at all. He is the frozen limit. I really think I can't stay on with him without any *authority* or *pay*. In lots of ways I won't be sorry.'

Fruity had one more underlying worry. Ever since Baba's blatant infidelity with her brother-in-law that had caused him such misery, he had focused on Tom Mosley as the cause of their growing estrangement. While her subsequent affairs were conducted with reasonable discretion, Tom Mosley flaunted his conquests, Baba included. In France, away from her, knowing that she was out most evenings, the idea of this tortured him.

'I've wanted to say something *VERY* important to you,' he wrote on 3 November. 'I do not want to have a row on paper, and any unpleasantness, but I will just say that I sincerely hope and trust that you are not seeing *anything* [underlined eight times] of Tom Mosley, and that you will not do so.'

30

'My Idea of a Perfect
Evening'

~

Baba was becoming close to a man as different from Tom Mosley as
it would be possible to imagine. Edward Wood, Viscount Halifax,
former Viceroy of India and now Foreign Secretary, was a politician out of a sense of duty rather than the burning ambition and
lust for personal power that inspired Mosley. His twin passions
were High Anglicanism and foxhunting. Immensely tall and distinguished-looking, he had been born without a left hand; instead,
he had a false fist with a thumb over which he wore a leather glove
in black or brown (according to whether he was in London or
the country). It was impossible to imagine him doing anything
dishonourable; he was so admired by the King that His Majesty
had given him the unique privilege of walking through the gardens
of Buckingham Palace to the Foreign Office.

Baba had kept in touch with Halifax ever since she had first met
him with Nevile Henderson in Berlin. She had entertained the
Halifaxes in London and been to stay with them at Garrowby,
their estate in Yorkshire, and all three had soon become close
friends. But although Baba was extremely fond of Dorothy Halifax
her real closeness was with Dorothy's husband. As the Foreign
Secretary was known for his austere reserve such an intimacy was
all the more surprising – and noticeable to observers. It was a
friendship that developed while she was still conducting her affair
with Dino Grandi: to be the favourite female companion of both
the British Foreign Secretary and the representative of Mussolini's
fascist regime was an irony unremarked on at the time.

Apart from an occasional lunch the first significant milestone in the friendship between the Foreign Secretary and the young woman who was to mean so much to him occurred on 4 October 1939, when Halifax wrote Baba a short note: 'I was on the point of writing to you to say that Dorothy had had to go up to Yorkshire till Saturday and to beg you to come and cheer my solitude when your telegram came. So I jumped at Friday evening, which I hope may be all right for you, if you don't mind plain fare and if you really don't mind being tête-à-tête! It will be very good to see you. Will 6.30 do? And I will try not to have too much work to do after dinner!' It was of that evening that Baba wrote in her diary: 'Dined with Edward tête-à-tête – my idea of a perfect evening'.

As Foreign Secretary Halifax spent much, if not most, of his time in London, while Dorothy was often at Garrowby. He and Baba would dine together, or go for walks in the Park. With her interest in politics, her flattering attention and her lucid comments, she was a stimulating as well as attractive companion; for her part, mixed with her liking and admiration for his nobility of character was the enjoyment of feeling herself at the very centre of things.

As they became more intimate, she poured out all her misery over her marriage and her worries about Fruity and the future. For Halifax, the presence of this beautiful, unhappily married young woman who obviously adored him was irresistible. It was not long before London society, buzzing with wartime scandal, wondered if she was sleeping with him. If it had been any other man, the answer would have been yes, but the exact nature of the relationship was a mystery even to those closest to both of them, from Irene on the one side to Halifax's close friend Victor Cazalet and Private Secretary Charles Peake on the other.

Yet although Halifax was undoubtedly romantically obsessed with Baba, a physical liaison is unlikely. He was deeply devoted to his wife, he was a man of honour and his religious principles were such that if he had contravened them in this way he would have been tortured by guilt and remorse – and there is no trace of either in the many letters he wrote her. Holding hands during one of their interminable walks through the woods at Garrowby or Little Compton would not have troubled even the Foreign Secretary's rigorous conscience.

Halifax's feelings for Baba can perhaps best be compared with those of Asquith for Venetia Stanley: the adoration, the age gap, the flood of letters that poured out political secrets and gossip with complete trust in the discretion of their recipient. Dorothy, wise and understanding, ensured that the marriage could accommodate this other love – in one of Halifax's letters to Baba there is a reference to a long discussion which he had had with Dorothy about his relationship with Baba – 'disinfecting' it by maintaining her own close friendship with the younger woman.

From Baba's point of view Halifax represented stability, an older man on whom she could rely utterly; his approach to life provided a compass that helped to guide her through the moral maze in which she so often found herself; his faith helped and underwrote her own – they would pray together – and he exuded that heady, intoxicating scent of power and inside knowledge which she found so deeply satisfying.

At the same time, she was seeing both Michael Lubbock, her affair of the previous year, and Sir Walter Monckton. Monckton was well known to have a weakness for women; he was also an extremely clever and attractive man. Baba had liked him from the moment she met him at the time of the Windsors' wedding and their joint involvement in the couple's affairs had frequently brought them together. As most of those close to Baba knew that she and Fruity now led virtually separate lives, she was usually asked out on her own. With a string of admirers, she was seldom at a loose end.

Irene was as busy as ever. Her health, never very good, was not improved by her drinking bouts, characterised as 'neurasthenia', 'cramps in my tummy' or even 'lumbago', which became more frequent when she was worried. But they never stopped her seeing friends, conducting committee meetings – or worrying about Denham. Like a running sore, the question of its future continued to dominate her: Nick, who had won an examination prize at Eton for the fourth time running, told her that he had never been told he was going up to Wootton after Christmas; Nanny refused to discuss the future, and Baba smiled pleasantly and told her not to worry. Irene resorted to bed and a course of colonic irrigation.

Nevertheless, the first Christmas of the war began well. Irene, always generous, had given a champagne party and a Christmas dinner, cooked in her kitchen, to the barrage balloon unit and their wives and girlfriends; her staff and the nurses got turkeys and a bottle of whatever drink they liked, the VADs received 10s apiece so that they could take their boyfriends to the theatre. At Denham, she did her best to keep up the spirit of past Christmases with a tree, presents and the tradition of Father Christmas down the chimney performed by Nick. On Boxing Day evening they listened to Lord Haw Haw attacking the British Government from Germany. Irene told the Mosley children, accurately if tactlessly, that this was William Joyce, who until recently had been one of their father's chief fascist executives – a piece of news to which they reacted defensively.

Fruity, in Paris, told Baba on 30 January 1940 that the Duke was going to GHQ for a few days and was very pleased about the proposed trip, which he described to Fruity as 'the thin end of the wedge'. 'I am glad for him,' wrote Fruity. 'I too think something better will come up fairly soon for HRH and then, I guess, I disappear.'

In the meantime, it was Fruity's turn to accompany his employer. 'I'm off on a very interesting and exciting tour of a section of the French line,' he wrote in a letter of 19 February. 'I'm *very* pleased at being taken. They are in wonderful form. I am getting to really like her. I find I can do a great deal with her, much more than with him, and so I get things done.' Confidently he added: 'She likes me now'.

Baba was not so sure. Fruity was hoping for some home leave and she wrote an alarmed postcard to Walter Monckton. 'I have a sinking feeling it may forbode [*sic*] bad news as something tells me that our dear friends may be planning the dirtiest ever!' Monckton replied reassuringly, though wrongly: 'I do not think you will find the news from the Suchet front as bad as you expect'.

At Denham, the alterations to 'halve' the house and thus cut down on the rates were in full swing. Nanny and Micky, there on their own apart from a daily governess, found themselves without heat or hot water during one of the coldest months of the year while boiler and pipes were removed, shut down or replaced. For Nanny, the discomfort was aggravated by uncertainty about the future. She had given her life first to the Curzon daughters, then to Cim's children; in Irene's absence, she was wholly responsible for Micky. Yet she only discovered matters that affected her deeply at second-hand. With the arrival of Diana's nanny and two-year-old son Alexander and, soon, Diana's second child (Max, born in April) she foresaw herself being pushed into a subordinate position. She felt that Tom was too cowardly actually to sack her but hoped that constant pressure, overwork and humiliation would eventually force her to leave. All this she poured out to Irene in a painful interview at the end of February.

Putting these worries to one side, Irene went to stay with her sister, seeing Little Compton for the first time and finding it spectacularly beautiful. 'Baba seems to get a very satisfying life,' she wrote in her diary on 24 February. 'I wonder where I make the error – perhaps through too much work and thought, giving no time to men and social leisure. She has her regular dinners every week with her two beaux, Sir Walter Monckton and Lord Halifax. I have nothing of that and oh! If I had the ear of Lord H on church questions. She is interested in none of these things.'

Fruity, just returned from his French tour, had received the Duke's permission to go on leave, 'H.R.H. was *absolutely wonderful* all through,' he told Baba. 'I think he was better this tour than ever before. He was remarkable. He *never* gets tired and he was never in a bad temper or a bad humour and interested in *everything*. There is no question, at jobs like this he is unbeatable.' Soon, these views would alter drastically.

Relations between Wallis and Baba, who kept up a sporadic correspondence, were cordial. On 8 April Wallis wrote from La Cröe, suggesting that Baba came out later in the year. 'We have had a *lovely* second honeymoon. We are delighted to hear that Fruity feels so much better and has gone to England – the Duke wired him to stay as long as he could because it must be a most dreary life at the Ritz marking time for the war to begin. We always want him for dinner at Suchet but that is not very gay – but nothing really is now with this lowering over us always. When will it stop and what then?'

It was a question that was about to receive a terrible answer. All over Europe there was chaos. Britain watched in horrified disbelief as the Nazis invaded first Norway and Denmark (on 9 April) and surged towards the Low Countries. Rumour and counter-rumour were rife; as the Nazi forces drew nearer the coastlines of the North Sea and Channel the wildest stories abounded – German paratroopers floating down dressed as nuns, a 'fifth column' of spies and traitors who secretly informed Hitler of British plans – and those with any kind of official position were eagerly sought for what they could tell.

Fruity, close to the French GHQ through the Duke of Windsor, was one of these, and making the most of it. When Georgia Sitwell met him on 14 April she found herself writing: 'Fruity is now so much "in the know" no one else can speak – what the generals think etc.' Baba, too, relished her inside knowledge. When Georgia visited her at Compton she noted that Baba was able to state firmly that although the Prime Minister had said, 'Hitler has missed the bus', and a number of enemy warships had been sunk, the withdrawal from Norway was inevitable. 'She had seen Halifax and Walter Monckton and they both said it was no good going on; the Norwegians offered no co-operation and did not want to fight.'

On 10 May, German forces invaded Holland, Luxembourg and Belgium. Neville Chamberlain resigned and Winston Churchill became Prime Minister in his stead, leading a coalition wartime government. The Home Guard was formed, as Britain's last line of defence against invaders. Five days later, the Duchess of Windsor left Paris for Biarritz. The Duke accompanied her and then returned to the Military Mission.

As the Dutch surrendered and the French defences were pierced (near Sedan) the threat of invasion was in everyone's minds. Posters went up warning that 'Careless Talk Costs Lives', the Home Guard drilled with what weapons they could muster, and contingency plans were laid to prevent the Royal Family and senior politicians falling into the hands of the enemy.

Tom Mosley, as Britain's fascist leader and a man who passionately believed that the war was a mistake, appeared to many an obvious Quisling figure. Even Baba, still in his thrall, had recorded of her first wartime political conversation with him (three months earlier): 'I find his attitude quite dreadful; you can't make him admit Germany is to blame.' On 16 May, Irene visited Sir John Anderson, the Home Secretary, at his request. Anderson asked her if she had any evidence that Tom would betray his country at this moment of its greatest peril, through the 'fifth column' or otherwise. Irene replied that, although she had none, 'if Tom thought such a thing was good for England in conjunction with Hitler's regime then he might do anything if he got angry and thought we were mucking the whole thing.

'I gave him bits of conversation from Tom and Diana and I said I had been useless as we had not met for weeks. He said I had given him all he wanted.'

Public opinion had swung violently against Tom. When he spoke on behalf of a British Union candidate at a Lancashire by-election on 19 May he was booed and the BU man polled a mere 418 votes to the Conservative 32,063.

It was clear that France would soon fall – the Germans were turning from the coast to Paris – but the Duke, accompanied by Fruity, continued to visit various sectors of the Front. By 19 May German troops were approaching Paris; by the 21st they had captured Amiens and Arras. 'It really is a case of all to stand or die,' wrote Irene that day. 'If the Channel ports go, England is bombed and invaded at once.'

On 22 May the Government rushed through an Emergency Powers Act that gave them almost unlimited authority over the lives and property of all British citizens. One of its regulations, stemming from an earlier Emergency Powers Act, was that labelled 18B: this empowered the Home Secretary to detain anyone 'whom he had reason to believe' was of 'hostile origins or associations' or thought to have been involved with anything 'prejudicial to public safety or the defence of the realm'. This regulation was now strengthened to include powers of detention over any members of an organisation that in the Home Secretary's view was 'subject to foreign influence or control' or whose leaders 'have or have had associations with persons concerned in the government of, or sympathetic with the government of, any power with which His Majesty is at war'.

The fascist newspaper *Action* the following day brought matters to a head. 'The question has been put to me why I do not cease all political activity in an hour of danger to our country,' Mosley wrote. 'The answer is that I intend to do my best to provide the people with an alternative to the present government if, and when, they desire to make peace with the British Empire intact and our people safe.'

Poised to act, the authorities now swooped. That afternoon the

BU offices were raided and over forty people detained. Tom was not among them. An evening newspaper headline announced that the Conservative MP Captain Maule Ramsay had been arrested that afternoon.

When Irene arrived home the telephone was ringing as she walked through her front door. It was Viv – to say that her father had been arrested at Dolphin Square in Pimlico and taken to Brixton Prison. Irene begged her niece to come and stay but she said she would rather remain at Denham and that she would tell Nicky.

Irene passed the news on to Baba and Lady Mosley, then went to the dinner party to which she had been invited. 'I felt that if I chucked they would think I was in sympathy so with black grief in my heart I went out. On my way back I saw a light in Donald Somerville's room and I rang to ask him his thoughts of Tom. He told me to impress on Viv and Nick it was not a disgrace but a precaution. I could only see one thing clearly: Thank God Cim was dead.'

Tom's detention in prison raised several questions. Who would decide things for the children? Would Diana become their guardian as well as their stepmother? This thought prompted Irene to ask the Canadian High Commissioner Vincent Massey, with whom she was dining, if he did not think Diana was as dangerous as Tom. Should she write to Sir John Anderson to that effect? Massey agreed. Feeling in any case was running high: the Mosley Day Nursery in Kennington was vandalised, its glass sheds and sun parlour smashed.

Baba, still in a state of nerves over her children, was doing what she often did when strung up: flailing out at those nearest to her. The first to fall victim to her black mood were Irene, who had argued strongly against sending the children to America, and Fruity, who was castigated for not writing. His reply, on 24 May, contained an unusual touch of sarcasm.

Well, I really should have thought that knowing you are always so well informed with the news, you would have understood why you had not received any letters. Perhaps the short line I did send you, at the first opportunity, explains this, if you have not been getting much war news.

These last few weeks have been a great strain. Today the situation is much the same, if anything it is worse. I am very busy, going anywhere at a moment's notice, day or night. Each night (and day) we have been expecting the German bombers and tanks to arrive. We have two or three alerts each day.

You ask me if I will still remain in Paris! Good God, I don't know if there will be a Paris in 24 hours. What or where I will go to God again knows. You speak of an interesting time. Yes, it is all that and more. A lot more. Re your remark about the German tanks having wings or part of the French Army having them, well the latter is very true, unluckily.

As you now know, the 9th Army could not 'take it'. The General and all his staff are now either shot or prisoners of war. It has been a terrible shock and surprise. I fear there are bigger shocks to come. HRH came back two days ago. I am uneasy about him. He might do *anything*. Anything *except* the right thing. I live from hour to hour, fearing to hear the worst. He talks of having done enough. Of course do not repeat any of this. Gray P is no use in an emergency. None at all. Anything he says is the worst advice possible, or else he sits mute, which is even worse and more dangerous. I do not know what will happen. W. is like a magnet. It is terrible. I have seen a great deal and hear everything. I can't yet work out what Thomas and I will do, or where even to try to make for, if the situation changes much worse (I refer to one's life and also should HRH make his fatal decision). I'll write when I can.

By 25 May the British Army was separated from the French and Boulogne was in German hands. As the Channel ports fell one by one, Britain waited in suspense. Everyone believed that invasion was now days rather than weeks away. In Paris, Fruity followed the routine set up by the Duke. Sometimes the arrangements for the following day were already known or could be made the evening before; when this was not so, Fruity would telephone the following morning for orders.

One evening towards the end of May Fruity said his usual 'Goodnight, Sir. See you tomorrow.' When he made his customary telephone call the following morning at eight thirty and asked to be put through to the Duke he was answered by a servant who said: 'His Royal Highness left for Biarritz at six thirty this morning.'

Fruity, who had worked for months without pay, doing everything he could to support the Duke and make the lives of the Windsors easier, found himself abandoned without a word by the man he considered his best friend, to find his own way home as best he could.

He wrote to Baba at once, a letter that was a paean of rage, misery and disillusionment. After advising her to take the children for safety at once to Cornwall or Devon where, with luck, there would be sun, bathing and tranquillity, he went on to say that his own situation could not be much worse.

Re my Master, he has run like 2 rabbits. He never made one single mention of what was to happen to me, or his paid Comptroller Phillips. He has taken all cars etc and left not even a bicycle!! He intended to go at 6.30 a.m. the morning *before* he did go *without even telling me he was going* but was held up for petrol or something. He has denuded the Suchet house of all articles of value and all his clothes etc. After 20 years I am through – *utterly* [several underlinings] – I despise him – I've fought and backed him up (knowing what a swine he was for 20 years), but now it is finished.

Live at Suchet, you suggest. No thank you – I've been busy doing anyone's job, taking papers etc, but only used when there was *no one else*. Everything is packed up at the Mission. I cannot yet figure out where I go or what I do – but I will do something, believe me. I have ideas, as I always have, I guess they will not come off but it will not be for want of trying! Our rifles are at Purdeys – get them. I am like a sheep without any fold – Mission No 1 is not on the map for me. Now no more. Fondest love to you and the children.

PS Re Walter M I cannot of course advise him to any kind of action. But, I say this, if Walter works once again or does anything for HRH then I say he is demented. The man is not worth doing anything for. He deserted his job in 1936. Well, he's deserted his Country now, at a time when every office boy and cripple is trying to do what he can. It is the end. He said to Gray something about coming back later on!!! Yes, he'd come back and her when things are OK. F

To the Duke he wrote briefly from the Travellers Club in the Champs-Elysées on 3 June:

I am leaving for England this evening. I hope there to work in some way more actively than I have been able to do for the past few weeks. I do not mind *what* I get to do but I will then feel that I am helping my country more than I have been doing lately.

My position here since you left has been impossible and one I cannot stand. I have had not one word from you, Sir, and so can only surmise that you intend to stay where you are now.

I am sorry, Sir, to leave your service, but I feel sure that it is the *only* thing to do. I thank you, Sir, for all your past kindnesses to me, also for helping me to come out to France with you in September.

I will say Goodbye, Sir, and wish you and Wallis the very best of good luck. Please remember me to Wallis.

He ended the letter 'Yours ever'.

Baba never forgave the Duke for abandoning Fruity in Paris. She felt he had behaved appallingly and it increased her protectiveness towards her husband – although it did not alter her behaviour one whit.

As for Fruity, he struggled back to England, arriving on 5 June. The effect on him of this total and unexpected betrayal by the man he had loved, trusted and faithfully served was disastrous. At a stroke, he had lost not only one of the two main pillars of his life but a job that had given him back much of his self-respect after years spent helplessly watching his wife's affairs with other men.

Irene's days passed in committee meetings, war work, good causes and speeches – to the Federal Union Club, the Sisterhood in Lees Hall, the Canning Town Settlement, where she spoke as the sponsor of a movement called Responsibility, which aimed to inculcate in everyone a sense of personal responsibility. 'I am convinced that we must put our own house in order, during this tragic conflict, before we try to tidy up Europe after the war,' she said, using as example the poor housing, nourishment and education brought to light by the mass evacuation of under-privileged city children. She spoke well and fluently, with all the force and passion of someone who believes deeply in what she is saying.

With Tom in prison, the question of the guardianship of his children came up. On 10 June – the same day that Italy declared

war on France and the Windsors, now in La Cröe, were entertaining Maurice Chevalier – Tom's lawyer, who had seen him in
Brixton Prison, told Irene that Tom had said he would have nothing
more to do with his children if their guardianship was taken from
him – and Denham would be barred to them. Next day Irene's
lawyer met Tom's, who took a more sober line than his client
by suggesting joint guardianship between Tom and Irene. Irene's
response was that she thought the difficulties of the situation and
their divergent views would make this unworkable, an opinion
strongly endorsed by her solicitor. The matter, he said, would be
settled in court.

Less than a week later the first German troops entered Paris,
making the collapse of France a virtual certainty and Britain's peril
even greater. All that Tom Mosley stood for was more than ever
abhorred and, as stories of the infamous behaviour of the Nazis
in occupied countries began to trickle back to England, those
in authority who knew of Diana's close friendship with Hitler
scrutinised her more closely than ever.

When Irene saw her close friend (and former father-in-law to
Diana) Lord Moyne he told her that he felt Diana was more
dangerous than Tom but that she was to be allowed to continue
her life at Wootton 'in case she was useful to the Home Office'.

On 25 June Irene's solicitor passed on the guardianship verdict.
Although the judge was willing to waive all question of guardianship and co-operate with Tom on important issues, Tom had
flatly refused this. 'He wanted entire and complete control of the
boys – he was not interested in the girl!' reported the solicitor.
As Tom had said that he wanted sole guardianship – obviously
impossible from prison – or nothing, after much deliberation the
judge had no other course but to request guardianship from
outside. Irene's name was put forward and accepted. Tom's reaction was to send Irene a message that he would never again have
anything to do not only with the guardianship but with the care
of his children.

That night, Irene wrote in her diary: 'God in his inimitable way
has handed me Cim's children. May they see the possibilities and
not blame me and may Cim from afar be assured I will do my
duty.' What effect this total rejection from their surviving parent
might have on the children she did not speculate.

That evening, 30 June, Diana was arrested at Denham and taken to Holloway Prison, leaving behind her Alexander and her second son, eleven-week-old Max, whom she had been breast-feeding. No one knew how long she would be detained but it looked as if the problem of Denham would soon be resolved: the War Office had sent someone down to inspect Savehay Farm with a view to renting it. Agreement came through in a few days and, stifling her revulsion, Irene kept all Diana's jewellery, brought up by Andrée, in her own house for safety.

In July 1940, after the Windsors' flight to the South of France had taken them through Spain, Portugal and a series of indiscretions, the Duke was reluctantly offered, and as reluctantly accepted, the governorship of the Bahamas. The Duke, ran one of the protocol instructions that preceded him, was to be accorded a half-curtsey, the Duchess was to be called simply 'Your Grace'.

As her husband's late employer sailed with his duchess for Bermuda, Baba took her family to Scotland. Here Lord Halifax wrote to her, gossipy letters full of inside knowledge. 'Hitler hasn't invaded us yet. The latest date to be tipped is [July] the 11th when I hope to be at Garrowby. Full moon 15 or 17 and the waning moon doesn't suit. So I am counting the days off till 17th!'

For Irene, a bank holiday visit to Cliveden and to a nearby military hospital churned up some painful memories of that earlier war in which she had lost so many friends and potential suitors. 'I could not face the ward, the medics, the nurses, the blue uniforms of the wounded, the sickening smell of ether again – the whole of me revolted in anguish.' After this wretchedly evocative experience, she too set off for Scotland; here, much of the time was passed in inconclusive but increasingly angry rows about the various possible permutations of Micky's schooling, punctuated by outbursts from the unhappy Fruity – 'a most ugly diatribe on Baba's selfishness in not wanting to come north and when he was ill spending all her time with Lord Halifax'.

Fruity's complaint that Baba deserted him to spend time with Halifax was well founded. She left him in Scotland to return to London on 21 August, to dine with the Foreign Secretary ('His sweetness and love for me is touching,' she wrote in her diary.

'Thank God for it as otherwise I would feel very lonely at present'). The tête-à-tête dinners continued, followed by a visit by both Dorothy and Edward to Little Compton in early September. 'My dearest Baba,' wrote Halifax after it. 'The weekend was delicious ... that perfect walk. It was wonderful being with you and I loved every moment.'

Baba was determined to do what she could to secure Tom Mosley's release from prison. One obvious route was Halifax, who saw the Prime Minister and Herbert Morrison, the Home Secretary, at every Cabinet meeting. 'I saw Herbert this morning and he was quite friendly. He said he hadn't heard about the phlebitis [a recurrent problem for Tom Mosley]. So perhaps something may happen; but I think it is wiser to appear fair so did not press him unduly. He seemed still to be a good deal impressed by the political difficulties of release. More on this when we meet and meanwhile you had better say nothing to anybody.'

Halifax's caveat about the political difficulties of releasing Mosley was an understatement. Not only would the whole of the Left have risen against it (as they were to do three years later); moderate opinion too would have been outraged at a time when Britain was fighting for her life. All through that long hot summer, the Battle of Britain raged overhead. The only barrier between the might of the Luftwaffe and probable subsequent invasion were Britain's pathetically few pilots (on 21 August, Fighter Command had a total of just 1,377 pilots at its disposal and on a bad day anything up to twenty were killed).

Irene arrived back in London on 6 September after a nightmare journey from Scotland, to witness the beginning of the Blitz – 7 September saw the first large-scale night air attack on London. During the following twenty-two days and nights nearly 7,000 tons of bombs were dropped on the capital and the Docks blazed almost every night. Within days, she and Baba were part of a loose coterie of friends whose focal point was the London hotel known to them as 'the Dorch'.

31

The Dorch

~

The Dorchester was believed to be the safest hotel in London. Opened in April 1931, it had been built of reinforced concrete from the basement to the top of its eight floors. These were soundproofed with blankets of seaweed (as used by the BBC to deaden sound in their studios) and the walls with cork so that the three hundred bedrooms were exceptionally quiet and although the building shook slightly when a bomb dropped nearby the explosion was muffled. When war was declared, the hotel's entrance was hidden by a high screen of sandbags, its curtains lined with heavy black cloth, and the roof covered with a layer of shingle. For those who sheltered in the Turkish baths below the main building, there were thus twelve feet of concrete between them and any bombs that might fall.

As the air raids began, some of the hotel's regulars evolved into a 'sleeping colony'. Irene's friend Victor Cazalet was a director of the company that owned the Dorchester and he sometimes invited a few friends down to the ladies' Turkish baths – the Halifaxes, who stayed there when in London, usually in a suite on the sixth floor, the Duff Coopers, Sir George Clerk, Oliver Lyttelton, Lord Portal (Chief of the Air Staff), Oliver Stanley, Walter Monckton, Irene and Baba. Robert Boothby would often join the party when the raids were bad, more for company than anything else. On any one night there might be as few as three of this shifting population or every corner might be crowded. Beds were behind screens and everyone ignored each other's snores – though some were more difficult to ignore than others. 'Victor and Duff snored like bulls,' wrote Baba in her diary. 'They went through the whole scale of snores, bass, falsetto, bubbles like a boiling kettle and the swallowing kind. I thought I would go mad but had to stick it out.

'Edward [Halifax] only takes three minutes before he is asleep but manages to yawn loudly and incessantly as a prelude to dropping off into this bottomless, childlike slumber, out of which nothing wakes him.' Woken by the cleaners at 7 a.m., everyone would put on dressing-gowns, pick up their washing things and move upstairs – Cecil Beaton talked fastidiously of the hotel's 'expensive squalor'.

Some of the regulars treated the Dorchester as an extension of their own home or estate. The immensely rich Edwardian hostess Maggie Greville gave dinners here from her wheelchair, supplementing the Dorchester kitchens with eggs and cream from her home farm (she died in the hotel in 1942) and Sibyl Colefax continued to entertain freely. Emerald Cunard, who had gone to America at the beginning of the war, returned to live on the seventh floor when her house at 7 Grosvenor Square was bombed. Her suite had a large sitting-room, bedroom, bathroom and maid's room and was crammed with as much of her own furniture as possible, from Buhl cabinets, Louis Quinze chairs and sphinxes to eighteenth-century bookcases, crystal bibelots and console tables resting on gilt eagles. When bombs fell she retreated under the table with a volume of Proust.

Wartime controls allowed restaurants to charge a maximum of 5s per meal, which could be of no more than three courses; luxury establishments like the Dorchester could add an extra 'cover' charge to cover the cost of linen, butter, rolls and so forth and a further 2s 6d if there was music and dancing. At first, Dorchester menus still included oysters, cold lobster, smoked salmon and roast grouse and even as late as 1942 there were delicacies like gulls' eggs, salmon trout, quails, asparagus, ices, savouries and fruit. By 1944, the sandwiches contained tasteless soya paste.

In September 1940, on the fourth night of the Blitz, the two Curzon sisters slept in the Turkish baths for the first time, sharing a cubicle. Both had lunched with Edward and Dorothy Halifax in their suite, with the Russian Ambassador and his wife, M. and Mme Maisky, Sir Horace Seymour and the Ambassador to Denmark, Mr Malet. At five o'clock Victor Cazalet rang to ask Irene and Baba to dinner, where the other guests were the Halifaxes and Archduke Otto of Austria; and at midnight, with bombs falling, Victor had suggested sleeping in the basement. Down everyone went, carrying water, glasses, candles and pillows.

As the Blitz continued, both sisters did what they could to help. Baba worked in her St John's uniform hard and long at London Bridge tube station, where about eight thousand people congregated every night; Irene took victims of the Blitz to Baba's house or her own, bringing them mattresses, candles and food. Afterwards she frequently dined at the Dorchester, where long evening dresses were still worn ('Diana Cooper very unsuitably dressed in black lace with roses in her hair') and spent the night in the Turkish baths where the drone of German planes, bomb explosions and deafening barrage from the anti-aircraft guns in Hyde Park, could scarcely be heard.

The night of 13–14 September was particularly dreadful. Irene spent it fully dressed in a dugout near her house, with the men's lavatories too close for comfort and the thud and crash of exploding bombs until first light. At 5 a.m. she got up and helped make tea and sandwiches for those in the air-raid shelter and the ARP wardens – exhausted and dirty-faced beneath their tin helmets yet unfailingly cheerful. At 5.45 she went out and saw what had so shaken and deafened them the night before: the hospital opposite was badly hit on two floors, an office building damaged and nearby Radcliffe Street a shambles – 'One woman was dragging out stuff from her shattered kitchen and yelling with rage at the Germans'. A few days later, walking to Selfridges to buy a siren suit, she noted that all the windows of Londonderry House had been blown out and Mrs Leo Rothschild's house and garden, 5 Hamilton Place, had had a bomb in the garden.

Baba still managed to get down to Little Compton most weekends, where Fruity was living while waiting for a job he had been promised with the RAF, his former sweet nature soured by recent events. When Georgia Sitwell went to stay for the weekend of 25 September, finding not only Baba but Fruity, David and his tutor there, she noted: 'Fruity more absurd and less agreeable than usual.'

Irene was not the only person intrigued by Baba's relationship with Lord Halifax. 'Discussed with Victor Cazalet Baba's extraordinary power over Lord H and that she rang him at any moment over minor things and that he always responded and that it was always Baba first and then his family,' recorded Irene. Victor responded crisply that it was Dorothy Halifax who was the saint, not her husband.

Halifax was doing what he could to help Baba in her pursuit of freedom for Tom Mosley.

My dearest Baba [he wrote on 16 September]. I saw Herbert M this evening at the Cabinet and told him that the 'indefatigable young lady' had shown me the latest report on O.M. which looked as if he might well die if not let out, and that I could not suppose that he wanted that and that if it happened it would be a scandal. He began by saying that their prison doctors had not always formed the same judgment as the outside consultant and I said that of course he could check up in any way he liked but that having myself seen the report of the consultant, who was presumably a responsible man, I could not myself doubt what was the right course. You have certainly done all *you* can. I loved our evening together.

Much as Irene longed to see Micky, she wrote to Nanny at Wootton to tell her not to return to Denham yet – Andrée reported that there were German bombers overhead every night. Micky, setting off for school, was told simply to say 'yes' and nothing more if asked whether he was Oswald Mosley's son.

The busy social life at the Dorchester continued non-stop – bridge parties with Duff Cooper, Loelia Duchess of Westminster, Bob Boothby and Lady Beatty, chats with Jean Norton and Hutch [Leslie Hutchinson, the glamorous coloured piano player who had been a lover of Edwina Mountbatten], Lady Maureen Stanley's cocktail party where the hostess was tipsy. Whenever Irene ran into Lord Halifax, as at lunch at the Chinese Embassy, where he was guest of honour, she noticed that he brought the conversation round to her sister.

Not everyone found Baba so intoxicating. When she went to stay with Georgia, taking David but not Fruity, her hostess found her irritatingly determined to visit her lover, Michael Lubbock; when he put her off she decided to stay on with the Sitwells instead. 'Baba is so charming and I am very fond of her,' wrote Georgia.

'but oh! she is so catty, so smug, so condescending about so many things.'

Baba had some reason for complacency. In the midst of his busy ministerial life Halifax was writing to her constantly, affectionate little notes that made it clear how much he relied on her company. 'I am hoping to do pictures and cinema with you on Saturday. I have alas! been summoned to Chequers on Saturday evening to talk U.S. with Winston and Philip L[othian]. But I needn't start down till four or five if you are free to play about till then.' He confided to her his war aims: 'I wished to fight long enough to induce such a state of mind in Germany that they'd say they'd had enough of Hitler! The real point is, I'm afraid, that I trust *no* settlement unless H is discredited.'

'Edward never tires of asking me why I like him,' records Baba's diary of those months. 'I answered: "because you make me feel sunny all through". When I asked him what he liked about me he said: "I can't put it in any crisp phrase like that but I love you very much." '

Their affection was so apparent that Walter Monckton, another of her admirers, referred to Halifax as 'my hated rival'. Fruity, now in the RAF and stationed near Reading, was nowhere in the equation: although he appeared at the Ritz from time to time, his life and Baba's had become essentially separate.

When Baba's busy social life, with its amorous overtones, threatened to overflow into Irene's 'territory', it aggravated Irene's jealousy of her sister. Not yet the constant, corrosive emotion it was to become, it nevertheless began to colour her attitude. Irene had always thought of Victor Cazalet as *her* friend; now that he had become so close to the Foreign Secretary that he accompanied him every Wednesday morning on his daily walk to the Foreign Office to feed him gossip, Cazalet included Baba in his parties more often than Irene.

Because of her friendship with Lord Halifax, Baba met Foreign Office mandarins and visiting dignitaries – exactly the sort of people who fascinated Irene. One of these was Gaston Palewski, Chef de Cabinet to the young General de Gaulle who was rallying the French Resistance movement from London under the banner of France Libre. (De Gaulle's first, historic broadcast to the French people had been made on the evening of 18 June, concluding with an inspiring call to arms: 'Whatever happens, the flame of French Resistance must not and shall not go out'.) Palewski, who later had a love affair with Diana's eldest sister, the novelist Nancy Mitford, was clever, entertaining and an inveterate womaniser: that autumn, staying at Little Compton, he attempted to seduce Baba but was rebuffed.

Irene's feelings were exacerbated by the way Baba casually made use of her, as she had done so often in the past. She treated Irene's room at the Dorchester as her own, frequently hogging the hot water and the telephone. 'Very dirty and quite exhausted I came in from the East End to find all Baba's things strewn there. I could have wept – no place of my own.' 'Her consternation and acidity on my simple dirty East End toilette passed description. Tried to answer some letters while Baba phoned and phoned.' 'Victor was pretty indignant at Baba always taking Sir George Clerk's vacant bed in the baths.' 'Traces of Baba were in my room in orchids and silver foxes left behind.'

At the end of November Irene paid a visit to her stepmother, Gracie, living at Blanche Farm near South Mimms, Hertfordshire, in much reduced circumstances. Gracie was commendably frank about her own responsibility for her misfortunes. Against a background of guns and the distant crump of bombs both women talked more freely than ever before. 'She made a full and frank confession of her follies with Scatters, her financial difficulties and his ruining of her,' wrote Irene. 'How Edwin Montagu and Rupert Becket had each loaned her £500 to tide her over her difficulties, that Scatters lost her £20,000 in the City, and yet though people told her again and again of his betrayal of her, even King George, she deliberately carried on, till finally some squalid behaviour broke her spirit.'

Cliveden was a sharp contrast to the cottage at South Mimms. With twenty guests, jewels, pearls, blazing fires, soft beds, servants, delicious food, the usual earnest talk and belief that most problems could be solved by discussion among the influential *bien-pensants* who gathered there so frequently, it was difficult to believe there was a war on. When Tom Jones gathered everyone in the library before dinner on 30 November 1940 so that people could air their views on the war, the consensus of opinion was that the Government had no clear war aims and Britain was bound for defeat. After breakfast next day the same group assembled for the same discussion, with an article by the military historian Basil Liddell Hart, which completely dismissed any hope of a British victory, lending weight to the argument. When Nancy brought out her false teeth and did her imitations after dinner the usual Cliveden atmosphere was complete.

Back at the Dorch, Irene found that gossip was rife about her sister and Lord Halifax. Her friend Alice Massey warned her that it looked bad when Baba rang him in the middle of dinner with other people present who might talk. The very next night, the Prime Minister, who always kept late hours, wished to get hold of Lord Halifax at 12.45 but could get no reply: Halifax was so sound a sleeper and the door of his cubicle was locked. Without hesitation, the Dorchester telephone operators rang the person they believed had the greatest access to him – Baba, who was sleeping next to Irene.

Baba acted with commendable briskness. Pulling on a dressing-gown, she found Halifax's detective and sent him in search of a key. Eventually a night porter was found – Irene meanwhile holding the receiver to keep the connection with the Prime Minister's office open – and Baba slipped in to wake the snoring Foreign Secretary. Finding Halifax (who was suffering from an infection) drenched in perspiration, she gave him aspirin, changed his sheets and made him change his pyjamas, finally emerging from his bunker half an hour later. 'What must the detective and porter have thought?' wondered Irene.

It appeared to her such a compromising situation that next morning when Baba was dressing to go to early church with Lord Halifax she expostulated. When Baba flared up, saying that he had restored her religious faith and that their relationship was on the highest moral plane, Irene pointed out that she had only meant that their emerging together so early in the day was not fair on Halifax: people in the hotel could so easily put the wrong construction on it. Baba went to church alone.

Halifax was sublimely unaware of these nuances. On 10 December he was writing to Baba from the Foreign Office: 'I think I shall have to stay up here on Friday night so come up and do your Christmas shopping and bring your knitting for after dinner in case I have a lot of work. There will be a fire in my room after tea on Friday so let me find you there on my return from the office. Would you like to suggest that we give Leo [d'Erlanger, whom Baba had asked to stay as 'chaperon' at Little Compton that weekend] a lift down in the car or can we manage to keep it to ourselves? I look forward to the weekend very much. Perhaps we could have a walk on Saturday?' Afterwards he told her that it had been 'a very perfect two days'.

On 12 December came news of the death of Lord Lothian, British Ambassador to Washington. Like his beloved Nancy Astor, he was a Christian Scientist and, when he developed uremic poisoning, refused the orthodox medical treatment that would have cured him. Speculation as to who would succeed him was feverish. 'Nancy says one me, two Waldorf,' Halifax told Baba. It was Halifax.

When the appointment was confirmed he told Baba at once, writing to her sadly on 21 December: 'How hateful this last 24 hours has been, with all that it means, redeemed only by being able to share the first feelings of it all with you, and by the knowledge that we should not be as far away from each other as outward things would appear.'

Baba was shattered by the news. Irene's journal for the following day records: 'In my post a heartbroken letter from Baba saying she had had two days of agony in London and that she did not know what it would do to her with him gone to Washington.' Irene went straight to the Dorch to see Halifax, who told her that he thought his appointment a mistake but that Dorothy had failed to convince Churchill of this. Irene concluded by telling him how sad she was for Baba, adding, in a parallel that may have startled Halifax, 'I only hope she will look upon it as Nancy looked upon Philip Lothian going there – as God's will.' Lothian had been the man closest to Nancy Astor for many years.

32

An Unexpected Proposal

~

For Baba, the New Year of 1941 was overshadowed by the departure of the Halifaxes for America. 'I dread their going,' she wrote
in her diary. 'It seems like the bottom falling out of my present
world . . . no letters, no dinners, no heavenly cosy evenings, besides
the interest of knowing a bit what goes on in the world. I'm sure
his success is certain and he may well be the key to getting America
in finally, but it is a hard price to pay.' She was with them constantly
in London before they left, only taking time off to drive herself,
Irene, Nick and Vivien to Brixton Prison on 13 January so that
the children could see their father for the first time since his arrest
and detention eight months earlier. But their visit was fruitless.
'Did everything possible to see him but without success,' records
her diary.

That evening Victor Cazalet, together with the builder of the
hotel, Sir Malcolm MacAlpine, gave a huge farewell party for
Edward and Dorothy at the Dorchester. He sent the Curzon sisters
corsages of orchids with which they bedecked themselves but it
did not make the entertainment any more appropriate, in Irene's
opinion: '47 people they would never want to see on their last day
in England.'

The Halifaxes left on the morning of 14 January. Baba went to
church early; on her return, there were constant telephone calls
as the final packing was completed and last-minute government
messages came through. All the while Baba went backwards and
forwards between Irene's room and the Halifaxes, getting whiter
and tenser by the minute. Finally, they had to part. 'We were all
three crying so much it was impossible to speak,' wrote Baba later.

'The sweetness of Dorothy has been unbelievable. She might well have been bored by my friendship with Edward; instead, the things she said about what it had meant to him, and them both, made me want to cry.'

Baba came back from seeing them off just after eleven, fell into Irene's chair and wept so copiously that Irene shed tears in sympathy. Sensitively, she left her sister alone for a while, going off to pay her bill and talk to people in the hall. At 11.45 Walter Monckton called in for ten minutes to report that the Halifaxes had sent a final farewell to Baba as they were being seen off at the station by the assembled Cabinet.

Both of them wrote to Baba that day, Dorothy to say how she treasured Baba's friendship and Edward Halifax a more intimate note from the train.

> I have just opened your note, Baba darling. It has made it seem a little less beastly in one way wishing you goodbye this morning and in another infinitely worse. You need not be afraid that I will forget you or stop loving you, for I don't think that would be possible, and the memory of you, and knowing you are remembering me in your thoughts and prayers, will be of quite untold help.
>
> You were *so* good and brave this morning, with that horrible Miss Bennett and everyone else buzzing round. But we both knew what we both were thinking and, hard as that made it, it yet helped, for we were so very close together.

The Halifaxes crossed on the new British battleship, the *King George V*, to Chesapeake Bay. A letter from Charles Peake, the witty diplomat who was Halifax's Private Secretary, suggested that all those close to Halifax were aware of how much Baba meant to him. 'Edward sent you a letter in a cigarette tin which was soldered up, tied to a buoy and a flare, thrown overboard and subsequently picked up by a destroyer.* Most romantic I call it. I wish for many reasons you were here and think you will have to end by coming if the mission is to be a real success and he is to be happy.'

Peake's letter was followed closely by one from Halifax himself,

---

*This was the method used to send royal letters home from mid-Atlantic when the King and Queen had visited the US the previous year.

written on 2 February. 'You can guess how I am longing for a first letter from you. I tell myself that one *might* come any day now if they had sent a bag by air mail. It seems perfectly ages and ages since we said goodbye to each other in the Dorch. Anyway it is three weeks nearer the time when we shall see each other again.'

Baba was well aware that Halifax showed her letters to Dorothy. Certainly the letter which she wrote to both Halifaxes from Cliveden on 24 January was noticeably different in tone from Halifax's, expressing simple friendship only, without the endearments and longing that thread his. 'Here it is relatively peaceful and Nancy in a sweet mood. She thinks that it was a pity Waldorf and she were not sent to Washington as they could have carried on with Philip's work as every connection he made and everything he knew of the U.S.A. was what she had taught him!

'Apparently the Pooh [their nickname for Winston Churchill] asked the hectic Corgi [Lloyd George] to join the band wagon but he refused except on his own terms which were a cabinet of five and an early meeting every morning with ministers fresh from their slumbers.' From Ditchley [the home of the Trees] two days later she wrote: 'Everything heard at Cliveden proved to be wrong! The Corgi will never be a member of the Government as there will not be a war cabinet and anyway he hates the war.'

Halifax tried to counter their separation by maintaining a regular flow of letters, all numbered so that they would not be taken out of order, sometimes accompanied by extracts from his diary, sometimes giving her news from the US ('I am sending you cuttings from the papers this morning on Wally's operation for face lifting! To judge by the photographs she would have been better to leave it alone, I think! I am hearing mutterings about the Governor of the Bahamas wanting to come up here. With the face-lifted one? I suppose so.')

All the letters breathe love and longing. 'Jan 14 seems a terribly long time ago,' he wrote on 10 February, 'and all I have had of you since then is your photograph which looks at me as I write, and your last note, that I keep locked up but look at from time to time.' The epistolary log jam was soon broken. By mid-February he had received several letters from Baba.

He advised her on her marital difficulties.

I have thought a lot about your problem, darling, about how much you should say to F when he is doing something that is likely to put him wrong with other people. I would have thought you certainly should say what you thought, and why, very nicely. After all it takes two doesn't it (or perhaps it doesn't) to make a row and I would think that you could say your say in unprovocative form and when you saw a row likely to begin, step off and refuse to be drawn, saying that you had only thought it right to tell him how it might strike other people etc. Anyway I loved your asking my advice about it.

He added a cryptic sentence implying that some of their correspondence was shielded from Dorothy's eyes: 'Your little note where you abandoned the high tone of respectability pleased me much as you can guess. When you do abandon respectability, put it on a separate sheet from your regular letter (although your letters come to me unopened all right) ... You are seldom out of my thoughts, my dearest, and I pray for you every day. May God continue to let us bring happiness to each other.'

The cold and her hard work took their toll of Irene's health but she continued to go to her committee meetings and to visit canteens. In mid-March, she paid a visit of a different kind, driving Nick over from Eton to Denham. Here they were met by the charming Colonel O'Shea, in charge of the intelligence work taking place in the house, so sensitive that they were not even allowed to walk through the gardens. The house was in excellent condition, the barn had been rebuilt and one of the cottages had even been fitted up with electric light and telephone.

As one of the Dorch inner circle, Irene naturally saw a great deal of Victor Cazalet, so she was not surprised to receive a confidence from him. He was, he told her, going to America in three days' time with General Sikorski* for a short visit. Her first thought was that it would make Baba green with envy. She was, however, greatly taken aback by the next development. She had imagined that Victor would be going by the usual route, by clipper from Lisbon [the commercial air service to the US], so was sur-

*Victor Cazalet was British Liaison Officer to the Polish Government-in-exile.

prised to receive a letter from him in Scotland. She was even more surprised by its contents: a proposal of marriage.

It took her several days to come to a decision. She was very fond of Victor. Almost a year younger than herself – she was just forty-five – he was good-looking, intelligent, cheerful, rich, gregarious and, as Conservative MP for Chippenham, the friend of many ministers. They had much in common: Irene was passionate about music, Victor was a talented pianist; she greatly enjoyed tennis at which he was a near-professional; even more importantly, his faith was as deep as her own. She had many Jewish friends and intensely disliked any form of anti-Semitism; he was a keen Zionist and friend of Chaim Weizmann, Israel's future President. Victor's sister Thelma was perhaps Irene's greatest woman friend.

Baba begged Irene to consider Victor's offer but she finally decided against it, even though she was fundamentally lonely despite her life of ceaseless activity. One reason was probably her suspicion that Victor was not really 'the marrying kind'. So, on 27 March, she wrote her refusal, sealed it up, and gave it to Baba to enclose in her letter to Halifax (which went by the diplomatic bag) as the quickest and surest way to reach him.

Devoted though she was to Halifax, Baba did not let his absence inhibit her lively social life. In fact her sister had so many admirers, who rang at all hours, that Irene found sharing her Dorchester room with her difficult. The three chief beaux, who seemed to be constantly on the telephone, were the American diplomat Averell Harriman, Walter Monckton and Leo d'Erlanger. Sometimes she would ask one or more of them down to Little Compton in a house party for the weekend; often they would take her to whatever gathering they had been invited to – generally something important or glamorous, as when she arrived back very late one night having dined in a large party with Walter Monckton, Lord Beaverbrook, Brendan Bracken, Averell Harriman and others. 'She certainly gets "in" on much more than me and gets all those people to do her bidding,' Irene noted enviously. 'I had a bad morning of loneliness, fears and hopelessness,' she wrote on 29 March, two days after turning Victor down.

To the outside world she appeared frantically busy. She worked daily in the East End, running a busy food centre serving meals to the bombed-out. She also visited nurseries, where the warmth she always felt for children could be given free rein. 'The children much enjoyed your visit,' wrote Father Edwyn Young after she had visited a children's home in Wapping. 'And this is not because you are who you are, but because they love your natural and friendly approach, and because they'll always look on you as a friend, and a friend in the best sense – i.e., one who came to see and cheer them up when they most needed a little cheerfulness.'

But in her bouts of depression Irene wondered why she did not manage other more public achievements, such as speaking on the BBC like Violet Bonham-Carter, or why she did not have such devoted friends as Baba. 'She can order them to do anything she wants. What is wrong with me that I fail on these lines? But I suppose if the poor and lonely love one as their friend it was like Christ and I am grateful.' For Irene, though, it was not enough, and gradually she began to turn to her old comforter, the bottle.

At the British Embassy in Washington, the possibility of a visit by the Windsors had been mooted, a prospect viewed by Halifax with barely concealed repugnance. 'You will be amused to hear about the Windsors,' he wrote at once to Baba. 'He telegraphed home to say he thought of coming here and I was asked my opinion. I said that I deprecated it but if it had to be we had all better pretend to like it and do him well.'

Fortunately for the Halifaxes, the Duke had just given an extraordinarily indiscreet interview to the American magazine *Liberty*. Sitting amid the white satins and chintzes of his drawing room in the Bahamas, dominated by a portrait of his wife over the mantelpiece, he had lamented the fact that he had never met Mussolini. Although he acknowledged that Churchill and Roosevelt were greater than either Hitler or Mussolini, he went on to say, 'There will be a new order in Europe whether it is imposed by Germany or Great Britain'. The Duke even advocated that the United States should keep out of the war as it was 'too late' to make any difference, adding that he himself could later act as mediator between the two sides. Churchill reacted immediately with a stinging telegram of rebuke. 'The appended passage from the article in *Liberty* which has not been repudiated by Your Royal Highness gives the impression and can only bear the meaning of contemplating a negotiated peace with Hitler. That is not the policy of HMG nor is it that of the Government and the vast majority of people in the U.S.' Churchill requested the Duke not to go to Washington; the Duchess's spending habits on visits to Miami were already incurring criticism.

The Windsor visit averted, Halifax turned to other matters in his letters home. All refer to his hoped-for visit from Baba, made more likely because his enquiries had led to someone who could fix her a return passage either by clipper or in a bomber. He was, he assured her, constant in his affections. He updated her on the war front.

Roosevelt is declaring the Red Sea open which means American ships can start carrying stuff to Suez. He is also I fancy considering direct convoying but I doubt whether he will get there just yet. And I guess he will start showing the fleet up a bit more in the Atlantic, with the object of knowing where raiders are not, which will help our hunting groups. They are also going to get hold of the foreign ships tied up here and this will influence South American states. So there is a good deal to put against the sinkings, and they are of course building as hard as they can.

I don't like this Balkan scene a bit, though Egypt looks a bit better. As regards the Balkans, even if we get kicked out altogether I expect it will be less bad than if we hadn't *tried* to help the Greeks. Morale is what is going to count in the long run, and the moralities. And this country I would guess will be moved by our desperate efforts to save Europe and the world. I fancy they are more and more feeling a bit self-reproachful while we are suffering, to be only making money ... the real reason I should like to come [home in August] – apart from private reasons! – is to get in touch with what Pooh [Churchill] and Co are thinking, so that one can be intelligent here.

Baba in her turn regaled him with gossip, telling him of Victor's proposal to Irene even before Victor knew he had been turned down. 'First and foremost Victor!!!' wrote Halifax on 17 April. 'Dorothy and I have done nothing but smile whenever we have thought of it. Somehow it never would have occurred to me. I did not know he might be thinking on those lines. I would give a great deal to hear your nocturnal discussions on this with Irene. I see she has written to him and I have duly forwarded it. Do tell me if you can when you write as to the decision. I should hate to think of his poor little feelings being hurt. But it certainly is an odd idea.'

In early spring the Luftwaffe stepped up its night raids on London and the South-east while Germany's success in other theatres of war kept the thought of invasion alive. Raids or not, Londoners did their best to lead normal lives and Baba's admirers were no exception. Walter Monckton, with whom she had been on terms of friendship since first they met, seems now to have become a would-be lover. After they had both dined with the Willingdons in Lygon Place, Walter Monckton came back with Irene to the Dorchester to see Baba, and as Irene recorded: 'After talking in my room they went into her bolthole and lay on the bed and chattered till all hours!!!' A letter from him in April certainly hints at a sexual relationship.

'Darling Baba, *Not* "hurtingly faithless!". How can *you* say that when you keep me tantalisingly suspended between frying pan and fire. The fire just doesn't begin to burn. The frying pan fries only too efficiently. But I agree toto corde with Edward. It is your bounden duty as a friend to extricate me from these perils. But it is *you* who are faithless. You extricate the Averells and the Bills but you allow this poor old man to sizzle – with cool detachment.'

After nine months, came the last and greatest raid on London. On 10 May 1941, in the bright moonlight that became known as 'bombers' moon', 550 German bombers dropped hundreds of high-explosive bombs and over 100,000 incendiaries. Fourteen hundred died that night – the most for any single raid – every railway station was hit and the Chamber of the House of Commons reduced to rubble. It provoked from Fruity, who had come to accept their separateness, a passionate plea to Baba, begging her in the name of sense and judgement not to come to London. He wrote to her from White's Club because his room at the Ritz, where he had spent the night, was unusable.

It was terrifying – a foot of ceiling and windows all over my room, rug, chest etc crashing into the passage buried in a heap of rubbish. No lights, no phone, no *anything*. One bomb dropped when I was in bed in the garden outside my window. The streets today are a foot deep in glass.

It is not fair on your three children if you do come up. *Please* believe me and act accordingly. Death is round *every* corner here in a night like last. It is *even money* if you escape, with at least your eyesight gone through broken glass. I implore you *not* to make the excuse of 'dining with Walter', 'hearing Walter speak' or dining with Cazalet or people like the Halifaxes. These people have *got* to be here, doing their work. If you had work to do then I'd say do it and stay but having absolutely none it is very wrong for you to come near London.

That is all I can say. Your life is your own and you can throw it away if you so wish – it is your choice. But remember you are the mother of three children.

A few days later, the windows of Irene's house were blown out again.

As the raids tailed off, work in the shelters diminished and Irene, with her experience of public speaking, began giving talks. She spoke on Abyssinia at various army camps and depots, lectured on East End shelters and Christianity at Malvern College, and addressed the joint annual meeting of the Lincoln branch of the National Council for Women and the Central Girls' Club on the need for a religious faith as powerful as the German people's belief in Hitler. She always tried to look smart and when, on 1 June, clothes rationing was announced in the Sunday papers, she could not help regretting the number of clothes she had given to the maids at the Dorchester.

Gossip about Halifax in Washington filtered back through their friends. While Dorothy, warm, charming, tactful and hard-working, had become a favourite, Halifax's reserved, patrician manner gave the appearance that he was standoffish and uninterested. As he was known as a foxhunting man, he had been invited to have a day with a pack in Pennsylvania about which he had written enthusiastically to Baba ('a very nice-looking pack, huntsman an Englishman who used to be with the Warwickshire, whipper-ins American, all very well turned out, a great many people in red coats'). No doubt this enthusiasm had made a sharp contrast with his usual rather aloof persona, for the press had lambasted him for indulging in such a luxury pursuit in wartime.

Victor Cazalet unhappily confirmed this. 'He will never slip into the easy ways of P. Lothian, who was beloved by everybody,' he wrote in his private diary; and he urged Halifax one evening to ring up Roosevelt 'just for a chat. Americans love this.'

Whether or not the Ambassador did attempt such an out-of-character move is not known, but his long letters to Baba continued, filled with news and comment as well as plans to see her again. When Hitler invaded Russia he wrote, 'I hope that as in the past, Russia may prove an unprofitable investment for invaders.' In another letter he noted presciently: 'The U.S. Navy is all ready, as they think, for a scrap and most of them are just longing for some incident that will settle it. I shall be surprised if they don't get it.'

At home, Irene had driven down to Eton on 28 June and, after watching cricket, had taken Nick to Denham, where Colonel O'Shea walked them round the house and garden. Everything was in apple-pie order: O'Shea's men were making a trout farm in the gravel pit, the lawns were mown, and where two bombs falling nearby had hurled debris all round Cim's sarcophagus the holes had been filled in and everything smoothed away.

A few days later she went to a dinner at the Dorch given by Mrs Ronnie Greville. They were joined by Victor Cazalet, who had arrived back a week earlier from the US after a ten-hour flight from Gander, Newfoundland, in a converted Liberator bomber. After dinner he took Irene back to his room, where they discussed his proposal of marriage. For the romantic Irene, who longed for love if not passion, what Victor offered seemed an unhappy substitute: it appeared that he was yet another of the men who saw her as a powerful aid to his career rather than as the love of his life.

'He said such bald cold things: that he knew he would get a governorship if he had a wife. But he was scrupulously fair about his side of the bargain – one's freedom, etc. I asked God to give me ten days over it.'

Less than a week later, after she had presented the prizes and certificates at Parson's Mead School, given them a talk and retired to bed weary, her mind was made up. Victor appeared in her room at 11 p.m. in his dressing-gown; when he attempted the mildest physical contact she felt repelled. 'Sickness when he wanted to shake my hand and offer me some small kiss of affection. It is no good. It cannot be done. I was frozen stiff. I could scarcely touch him.' Next day she wrote a final letter of refusal to Victor, then went out to Harvey Nichols and bought two hats.

With the Blitz over, London was much safer. Baba reappeared, having rung Irene to ask her to fix a dinner party for her, and then went to visit Tom at Brixton. As often after she had seen him, she returned uncommunicative. Her emotions on seeing this ex-lover who had so grossly deceived her must have been a jumble of remorse, longing and guilt; and when he told her he hoped to go to France with Diana after the war 'to achieve some measure of happiness' it must have struck deep.

Yet she continued to do her best to achieve his release, or at least secure better conditions for him in prison, attempting through Halifax to reach the Prime Minister and Herbert Morrison. Though Halifax had been thoroughly in favour of Tom's deten-tion – 'I am glad to say we succeeded in getting a good deal done about fascists, aliens and other doubtfuls, Tom Mosley being among those picked up,' he had written in his diary in May 1940 – his devotion to Baba meant that he commiserated with her over not being able to get Tom's situation improved.

Irene found staying at Little Compton difficult. Baba's authori-tarian approach jarred on her, especially when it came to dealing with Nanny – a friend and virtual member of the Curzon family for over forty years. Baba wanted Nanny to stay at Little Compton and look after the Metcalfe children as well as Micky, and Andrée to get a job for the duration of the war; Irene felt Nanny should do as she wished. Neither wanted to stay at Little Compton, though they agreed to do so for the moment, and Irene's maid Ida also gave notice, saying 'she did not like the Compton atmos-phere' – Irene felt it was because too much work had been piled on her.

She also found it difficult to still the undercurrent of envious resentment when Baba read extracts from the letters sent by Halifax and Dorothy. 'Why does she get all this priceless and exquisite adoration, in its richness and splendour, but it does not come my way? I must be at fault somewhere. She gets the best of both worlds, even though her life with Fruity is misery.'

There was no doubt about the adoration. Halifax was – for him – in a fever of anticipation at the thought of seeing Baba again. 'I just can't imagine what it will be like when I first see you again in the old Dorch,' he wrote from Washington on 27 July 1941. 'Do pray very hard that nothing may interfere.' A week later he was telling her: 'I shall aim at getting off with a Friday night at Chequers and spending Sunday with you. Unless I arrive Saturday or Sunday I shall go straight to London and hope to find you in the Dorch!'

Baba's relationships were a dominant theme in the lives of those who knew her well. Like the rest of the world, Irene and Nanny were mystified as to the exact nature of her friendship with Halifax. 'We could not fathom the Halifax–Baba thing. Baba was in a secret glow of delight as the Foreign Office phoned her Lord Halifax was coming in a bomber and would arrive today and stay in London [Halifax's return was in fact delayed for several days]'. When Irene dined with Leo d'Erlanger, a Little Compton habitué, they spent hours talking about her sister – d'Erlanger said that Baba 'should have grabbed Jock Whitney and got a good settlement for Fruity'. And when Irene drove the brilliant lawyer William Jowett to London after a weekend at Little Compton Baba's situation came up again. Jowett's advice was that if Baba really wanted a legal parting of the ways she should offer her husband a two-years separation and, if he refused to co-operate, cut off his money.

Baba, meanwhile, was seeing as much of the Halifaxes as she could and, Irene felt, keeping them unnecessarily to herself. Once again, she felt hurt, this time when Baba refused to allow her to accompany their party to see the air-raid shelters at Bermondsey – Irene's stamping ground – saying it would make too many. Even Victor Cazalet recognised Baba's proprietorial attitude to the Halifaxes and when he asked them to dine invariably asked her too – often without Irene. Despite their failed romance she was seeing as much of Victor as ever. In August she stayed with him at Great Swifts, his country house at Cranbrook in Kent, and in early September dined with him to meet the Chaim Weizmanns as well as often seeing Victor informally.

The Dorchester was still central to all their lives, more so now that Sibyl Colefax, for whom entertaining was as much a part of life as breathing, had hit upon the simple but effective idea that became known as 'Sibyl's Ordinaries' – dinners, generally on a Thursday, after which guests would receive a discreet bill the following morning. As the war drew on, the cost of the Ordinaries rose from 10s 6d to 15s, the wine served was Algerian and, eventually, sherry ceased to be offered before dinner.

The first of these paid dinners was on 18 September. Round the table at the Dorchester was Lady Colefax's usual eclectic mix of politicians, writers and personalities. Irene, Adrienne Whitney, Juliet Duff, Gladwyn Jebb, Thornton Wilder, Mrs Gilbert Russell, Sir Roderick and Lady Jones (the writer Enid Bagnold), Roger Senhouse and Robert Montgomery. Harold Macmillan failed to turn up and Baba, also invited, turned her down in favour of an evening with Victor Cazalet and the Halifaxes – soon to return to America.

At the end of the month, largely to further Baba's efforts on behalf of Tom Mosley, the Halifaxes gave a small dinner party consisting of the Prime Minister and Mrs Churchill, the Chief Whip David Margesson and Baba. 'Winston started by coming and plumping himself down on the sofa at once and speaking of Tom,' runs Baba's account of it. 'I had asked Edward to talk to him about the prison and efforts to get them moved to the country. This had been done and Winston was charming, most ready to listen and saw no disadvantages in putting the couples together but Herbert Morrison [the Home Secretary] will be the stumbling block. He is hard, narrow-minded and far from human in a matter like this, and in any case he has a special dislike of Tom.

'One rather telling remark I thought was when I said it was awful to see someone like T in prison and Winston said: "Yes, and it may be for years and years." '

The Halifaxes returned to Washington on 20 September 1941, flying first to Lisbon, where Halifax wrote to Baba, 'I so long to hear your news, and your voice on the telephone at Bristol seems a terribly long time ago. But I build my castles for February [when they hoped to return to England].'

Back in Washington, the long, numbered letters resumed, with their adoring messages. 'I long to get your first letter and I am marking off the days again until the time comes for my next trip over. I am keeping your last note for a little longer until I know it all by heart. Then it shall be destroyed!'

With the Halifaxes gone, Victor Cazalet had more time for his other friends. On 10 October Irene again went to stay with him at Great Swifts where they were joined by her other admirer, Leslie Hore-Belisha. After lunch Hore-Belisha and Irene had a long walk, discussing Victor. 'I sniggered inside to think of two beaux in one weekend whom I might have "taken unto myself" but I am sure God guided me not to. Victor says Leslie is only absorbed with himself but I am not sure that criticism could be applied also to the person who made it.'

Victor, unaware that Hore-Belisha was a rival, summed him up more prosaically. 'Leslie can be very agreeable but he is getting far too fat,' he wrote in his diary. 'I was rather doubtful if I had enough of the right food for him. However for one dinner he had soup, two goes of chicken, two helpings of pie and all the butter and biscuits he could collect.'

After dinner all of them were depressed by listening to Lord Haw Haw telling them how the German army was advancing, it seemed inexorably, on Moscow. Gloomily, Hore-Belisha predicted a great victory for the Germans in the Middle East, after which, he said, 'They will then switch to us'.

Irene was still doing all she could for the Mosley children: discussing his future with eighteen-year-old Nick and entertaining for Vivien, now twenty. That October she took a party of Vivien and her friends to the Lansdowne to dine and dance, followed by a nightclub. She felt that she should visit Tom in Brixton Prison but when she suggested it, both Nick and Baba failed to respond – though they took her car to visit him the following day.

Balked of a visit, on 26 October Irene sent Tom a long letter full of the news she had meant to tell him in person of Nick's future plans and about Micky who had started at St Ronan's that term. Four days later, she received a brutally brief reply. It was a single line, written by Tom's solicitor Oswald Hickson, saying only that a year at Oxford was better than a half [a term] at Eton.

Irene was disgusted both at Tom's rudeness and his lack of interest in his children. 'I shall take no more trouble with him,' she wrote in her diary, underlining the words heavily.

33

The Halifax Letters

~

The threatened Windsor visit to the US took place in October 1941. The Duke and Duchess were accompanied by the Duke's valet, two lady's maids, a chauffeur and secretary, their Comptroller Gray Phillips, their three cairns, now so bellicose that the Halifaxes' dog, Franklin, had to be shut away to avoid attack, and seventy-three pieces of luggage, too much even for their sumptuous suite at the Waldorf Towers, New York, so that the passage outside was lined with half-unpacked trunks. Their visit to the Washington Embassy was marked by a similar lavishness. 'They were both most amiable and – except for their ridiculous amount of luggage, of which the papers were so critical – behaved most decently and ordinarily,' wrote Dorothy Halifax, adding: 'I was a little outraged by being presented with a bill for £7.10 for hire of a lorry to take their luggage to and from station – it did seem a little unnecessary for a 24-hour visit.'

Lady Halifax was too charitable to mention that a luncheon for twenty-two had to be cancelled at the last minute, the Duchess preferring to send out for food and the Duke to drink tea and eat fruit in his bedroom. But a dinner party went well and their general comportment was praised. Both, it was thought, behaved impeccably, with particular kudos going to the Duchess at one gathering where she refused the offer of tea or cocktails and drank a glass of water instead – 'tea would have been too English and cocktails too fast!' noted Halifax approvingly of this subtlety.

Halifax sent Baba a full description of a tête-à-tête with the Duke, who had asked himself to luncheon and stayed until five thirty. They talked generalities for some time, and then the Duke launched into a discussion of his own position.

355

Whatever people thought of the Abdication, that was bygones, and if it had not been for the attitude of his own family – whom he never wanted to see again – things might have worked quite smoothly [wrote Halifax]. The Bahamas was exile, etc etc. He would stick to them for the war but then? He had thought he could have lived in England but he was not going to expose himself or the Duchess to insults and humiliations from the family. And so on. You know it all by heart.

I said that I well knew all the difficulties and tried to be as sympathetic as I could – but I thought he ought not to mistake the friendly welcome that he received from people here. Different feelings were still smouldering and excessive prominence before the public would quickly bring them out. People had thought, rightly or wrongly, that he had 'quitted' on his job, and quite apart from that were very critical of her. In what way? he asked. Because of their feelings about divorce, said I, and so we talked for two hours.

He made it pretty plain that he does not look any more, unless his family have a change of heart, to settling down in England. He thinks France will be pretty difficult after the war but likes the New World if it wasn't so expensive! He said that he was, as he looked, extremely happy and 'had a wonderful wife'.

I must say I was very sorry for him and thought he was a very pathetic figure. Not that I change my general feeling either about his coming back to England or her being HRH.

As to the Duchess, reported Halifax, she was very agreeable and very anxious to justify their abandonment of Fruity in Paris. He conceded her chic, but thought her hands, 'always a most revealing test of quality, dreadfully common, stumpy and coarse. No, I wouldn't have given up my Empire for her!'

The Halifaxes had been worried in case the Duke talked indiscreetly to the wrong people, especially about his future prospects. 'We were all on tenterhooks,' Dorothy wrote to Baba. Halifax, who had always believed the visit would be a mistake, had his opinion confirmed by the unfortunate publicity which the couple generated. 'The general press roundup on the Windsor visit has come out pretty badly and I think the visit certainly did harm. Extravagance [the Duchess had fallen on the shops]; pleasure; England being bombed; where did they get the dollars from? Lease

Lend money? I hope it may not become a biennial affair, sorry as I am for them in their St Helena.'*

In November Fruity was posted to Cairo. Irene gave him a farewell lunch in the Savoy Grill where Fruity, fifty-four, out of the second job he had really loved and surrounded by younger men sporting decorations, wings, crowns or red tabs, admitted that he felt 'a bit down' at still being only a flight lieutenant, overtaken by younger men who seemed to become squadron leaders with ease. Irene's sympathetic heart was touched and she sent round a collection of the best new books to Claridge's Hotel where he was staying. He left the following day, after saying a brief goodbye to Baba and fourteen-year-old David who had come up from Eton.

When Baba dined with Irene that evening, the old irritation surfaced. Irene was by now a considerable personality on the wartime 'talk' circuit, lecturing, doing some broadcasting and speaking to schools on subjects like 'Youth in Wartime', so her younger sister's automatic dismissal of her views did not go down well. 'I am maddened by the cocksure way Baba downs anything one ever says about Charles Peake, the P.M. or anyone as if one's own views were puerile and not worthy to be pronounced.'

Baba's assumption of superior knowledge was, as ever, founded on the confidences of her devoted admirer in Washington. Halifax wrote to her almost within minutes of the bombing of Pearl Harbor on 7 December 1941:

Ten minutes before [I was] going out for a ride, the President rang me up from the White House to say that the Japanese were bombing Hawaii and asked me to pass it on to London as quickly as I could. So that's that. If war was to come with Japan I can't imagine any way in which they could have acted more completely to rally, unite and infuriate American public opinion. The report is of pretty severe damage to ships and aeroplanes but most of the fleet was at sea already and none of their newer ships in harbour.† I have no doubt we shall

*When the US Ambassador to France had asked the Duchess when they were leaving for the Bahamas, she had replied: 'We sail for our St Helena tomorrow.'
†Five battleships and fourteen smaller ships were sunk or seriously damaged as well as two hundred aircraft, and over 2,400 people killed.

all have some ugly surprises but I also have no doubt that the Japs will learn that they have made the biggest mistake in their history. It will be interesting to see whether Germany follows suit in declaring war on the US.

Four days later, Hitler did exactly that.

In the same letter, Halifax showed how aware he was of Baba's own concerns, putting aside his personal feelings about Tom Mosley to advise her to tackle the Prime Minister direct. Then, at Christmas, he was able to give her some welcome news: at last, something was being done about Tom. 'On December 23 Winston led us apart in the White House in the evening to say that he had settled up Tom Mosley's business, he had had to have a special meeting of the War Cabinet and read the riot act to H. M[orrison] and that he (Winston) had had to assume his most "puppy dog" attitude. He said he had not written to you but wished me to tell you! I hope it really is an improvement. It was not very clear from what he said exactly what had been done.'

What had happened was not the release Baba had hoped for – but Tom's reunion with the woman she still continued to detest.

Churchill, for whom imprisonment without trial or charge was, as he later put it, 'in the highest degree odious', had written a strong note to Morrison stating that 'internment rather than imprisonment is what was contemplated' when Defence Regulation 18B was put into effect. The result of this was that those internees who were married were, at last, allowed to be together. For most of them this meant the Isle of Man (where many of the wives were already). For Tom Mosley this was not an option: it was felt that to place the Leader among his devoted flock would only lead to trouble – but it was clearly unfair to keep the Mosleys apart when other couples were allowed to be together. Accordingly, on Sunday 21 December Tom was taken from Brixton to Holloway Prison, where he and Diana, and another couple, were accommodated in a small separate block. It was, wrote Diana later, 'one of the happiest days of my life'.

At Little Compton, New Year's Eve was celebrated in the traditional way. Friends came to dinner and afterwards everyone happily played 'the Game'.* 'Baba doing the Immaculate Conception was a scream and Viv Great Expectations with a cushion up her tummy was wonderful,' wrote Irene. 'The suddenly [Colonel] Ted Lyon got up and did Every Dog has his Day by crawling round the room and lifting his leg on us and the furniture. Just before midnight we went outside and saw the New Year in with Auld Lang Syne. So ended a dreadful year of stress and strife.'

As 1942 opened, the hail of letters from Lord Halifax continued. 'An interesting visit this morning from Steinhardt, the late US Ambassador to Moscow,' he wrote on 1 January. 'He said that the Russian cold didn't really begin before January and expressed his opinion that unless the Germans could get out fairly quickly, they were in for what he called as ghastly a disaster as history had ever seen. It sounds a dreadful thing to say, but I devoutly hope he is right.'

His next letter described how he had cheered himself up when he had flu – a remarkably aggressive fantasy for a man of such devoutly Christian principles. 'If and when we are winning I am bound, I think, to realise my great ambition of seeing Hitler shoot himself or be shot! For flight is impossible, apart from the fact that it is discreditable for a Dictator. Where can he fly to? Do let us pray we live to see him having to make his horrible choice of method of suicide.'

On 2 December 1941 Ernest Bevin, the Minister for Labour, announced a massive mobilisation of womanpower (something which Nazi Germany, extraordinarily, never contemplated even when calling up boys and old men): all single women between twenty and thirty were to be conscripted for some form of war work. Vivien wanted to work in a factory and left Little Compton to live in a comfortable hostel with two girlfriends doing similar work, taking with her Andrée, who would look after them all. Baba too was leaving: as the Blitz had virtually stopped, she had decided to return to London to nurse in Bermondsey. Before she left, she received an unexpected letter – an olive branch from the Duchess of Windsor, who wrote on 31 January 1942:

*A version of charades.

Dear Baba,

I have been sorry not to have had a word from you all these months. Even if the Duke and Fruity have agreed to disagree I hoped *we* haven't. I am afraid British Mission No. 1 was never Fruity's affair – from the moment he looked it over and returned to Harefield House with the reports of the personalities there, and I am happy he has been fortunate in finding a suitable and interesting job.

The Duke has not been as fortunate – *this* gift from the 'gods' was anything but welcomed and was in fact most heartbreaking for both of us. The story of Lisbon is too bad, but I am afraid our book will be filled with chapters like that as long as we have anything to do with officialdom and naturally the war has placed us in that position. However we have accepted the exile and have tried to do the small and trying, due to its very provincialness, job as well as possible with the motto 'Do thy part – therein all honour lies'.

It was divine to get away from here but the trip to the U.S. was spoiled by crowds everywhere – though they were *most agreeable* we longed for a private life. And then the press, always so really terrific and following one everywhere and whether one is kind or rude to them, they invent more lies and silly notions – however that is the great U.S.A. and one must learn to take it.

I am afraid Ld Halifax has had quite a beating from them, also the Embassy from the Washington press where he is certainly far more popular than the members of his staff. He was magnificent with the eggs and tomato throwing in Detroit and only the throwers were ridiculous. Now that the U.S. is at war however all these things will cease as we are now *really* allies ...

Baba replied immediately, in terms that made it clear she had neither forgotten nor forgiven the Duke's appalling behaviour to Fruity.

Dear Wallis,

I know nothing about the Duke and Fruity agreeing to disagree and I'm sure this explanation would come as a complete surprise to Fruity. Anyway, between friends of 20 years that friendship is not broken because they 'disagree', especially when on one side so much devotion and loyalty has been given. True friendship is very rare and I feel it calls for better treatment than this. Although it does not directly affect me I can't help feeling sad and shocked that the Duke should have felt it unnecessary to communicate with Fruity in any way since the day he motored out of Paris in June 1940. He did not even warn him he was going the night before.

Perhaps my views of the obligations of friendship and what it involves are too high. I am surprised you should not understand my feelings and where my loyalties are bound to lie as I thought we rather agreed on these matters.

Baba

The war news was appalling. Germany was pushing back the 8th Army in the Western Desert, the Allies were unable to halt the advance of the Japanese through Malaya, and on 15 February 1942, the 'impregnable' fortress and great naval base of Singapore surrendered to the Japanese. Irene, dining with Victor Cazalet, heard of his visit to Malta, which had suffered over 2,000 raids by Nazi bombers and where Valletta harbour was full of wrecks.

At the same time, there was a glimmer of hope: the first American soldiers had arrived (in Northern Ireland), Britain had signed a treaty of alliance with Russia and, in the air, was at last able to go on the offensive with a devastating raid on the shipbuilding Baltic port of Lübeck.

The country was tightening its belt. Losses from convoys across the Atlantic to Hitler's wolf-pack of U-boats were huge and people were doing what they could to alleviate food and clothing shortages. On the government-issue Utility clothing, skirts rose and turnups on trousers disappeared, while women were using beetroot juice as lipstick and gravy browning to tint their legs to save on stockings, the seams drawn in with eyebrow pencil (Halifax thoughtfully sent Baba some American nylons).

Nor was Buckingham Palace immune; here a five-inch 'hot-water line' had been painted round baths and, as Halifax informed Baba: 'I got a letter from the King last week, who ended with a P.S. to the effect that they were getting rather short of a certain class of paper; generally sold in packets of 500 and beginning with B.* Signed G.R. I think that would make an interesting footnote for future historians!'

*A well-known make of lavatory paper called Bronco.

'Carrying on' had become the great British virtue, covering everything from growing vegetables and keeping livestock, making wedding dresses from parachute silk and painting cardboard wedding 'cakes' to attempting to stick as closely as possible to known patterns of life – for Irene, this meant taking her niece Vivien to the annual Queen Charlotte's Ball, still featuring the pulling of a giant 'cake' and a procession of debutantes and giving a Dorchester luncheon for the Grand Duchess of Luxembourg.

Once again, Irene's drinking had become a problem. She was reasonably good at handling it, usually withdrawing to her room at the Dorchester when she realised she had had more than was good for her. But several times recently she had been so drunk in public that Vivien was seriously worried. Not only did she often take Viv and her friends to parties or restaurants where there was dancing; she was shortly giving a twenty-first birthday party for her – and Vivien was terrified that her aunt might become embarrassingly tipsy.

Not daring to tackle Irene about it herself, Vivien told Baba, who had no such reservations and was in any case extremely scornful of her sister's weakness. 'I simply can't understand why Irene just can't stop,' she would say. Now she wrote Irene a severe letter about her 'failure'. Chastened, Irene replied that she was giving up alcohol for Lent. A week later she was able to write with satisfaction that 'my dinner for Vivien's 21st went off beautifully. Baba had decorated the cake with sugar roses, candles and a silver key. Viv cut it half way through the evening. When they had all gone Baba and I had a most helpful and non-critical chat about my failings and sadnesses and she was really quite human'.

Irene's summer began with a visit to Victor Cazalet at Great Swifts. It was looking marvellous, its walls clad with wisteria above beds of wallflowers and forget-me-nots and rhododendrons in full bloom. Except for the damage to the park by tanks, and the troops under canvas in the woods, it would have been easy to forget the war, but as Victor pointed out, it was better than having the Germans there.

Halifax's letters now contained the constant theme of his return. 'It was nice to hear you speaking of the end of June, which is only a short way off,' he wrote at the end of May. 'Do you remember our dripping walk together, back from Harold Nicolson's odd tea party?' And on 4 June, 'We have just been having a large Fourth of June dinner here and I have slipped away from it on plea of work to write to you. One didn't feel very much like a riotous 4 June dinner as you may guess with this Libyan fighting in full swing.*

The Windsors have descended on us – really on Dorothy – for a night on Monday. They are very silly I think to keep on showing up here. Much wiser for them to give everybody ample time to forget. Goodnight my dearest Baba, I can't tell you how I look forward to seeing you.

Irene spent much of June travelling round Wales, Plymouth and Swansea, talking at meetings on behalf of the Anglican Church, speaking at a Youth Rally at the Congregational Church in Pontypridd, and even giving sermons. She returned to London on 13 June, saw Micky ('my loved one came up from St Ronan's with Nanny and had tea with me in Victor Cazalet's sitting room he kindly lent us') and went with Victor to an Allies Club reception. At Sibyl Colefax's dinner the next day she met the usual literary and political figures – the novelist L. P. Hartley, the Gladwyn Jebbs, Roger Makins – and 'a badly burned pilot, Hillary, who has written a much talked of book.'†

One June evening came an unsettling hint of more family trouble. Walter Monckton, who knew everything, ran into Irene in the hall of the Dorchester as she returned from an outing. He told her that he had had bad news of Fruity in Cairo – the actual words he used were 'he's up to no good'. For the moment, Irene kept this item of news to herself – in any event, all Baba's attention was focused on the imminent arrival of the Halifaxes. They arrived by air on 5 July 1942, to be met by Baba, who spent the evening with them in their suite at the Dorchester, which only occasional other visitors were allowed to use.

Irene found it hard to stifle her envy of a sister who effortlessly

---

*Rommel had just launched a devastating offensive; less than three weeks later Tobruk fell, with 25,000 Allied troops taken prisoner.
†The fighter pilot Richard Hillary had just written *The Last Enemy*. Later, after insisting on flying again, he was again shot down and this time killed.

had central place in the affections of one of the most distinguished and influential men of the age. So when, ten days later, Victor Cazalet gave a big dinner for the Halifaxes, she was delighted to be seated in the place of honour between Halifax and Ed Morrow ('a position I fear coveted by Baba'). But when Baba began to talk of the coming weekend, which she was to spend with Victor Cazalet and Halifax, Irene was disturbed: as well as more unworthy feelings, she was genuinely worried about her sister's reputation. 'This going round with Edward H. I don't like it.'

For the moment, the worry of Fruity put it out of her mind. In Cairo, it appeared that he was drinking too much; Halifax had heard that he often had to be carried home. Baba, who could not bear the thought of scandal, was anguished. With Irene, she discussed three possibilities: that he should be encouraged to return to some kind of life in London or nearby, or warned in solemn terms by letter of the consequences of his excessive drinking – or left to suffer the consequences.

Never one to be borne along passively by the current of events, Baba acted decisively. She first sought the helpful advice of Fruity's sister Muriel, after which she wrote a long letter of warning to Fruity. Then, feeling slightly sick at the speed of events, she took the plunge of sending the twins to boarding school before going to stay with the Halifaxes at Garrowby. Here she spent much of the time walking and going for long rides with Edward. 'I feel more than ever dependent on him and he seems even fonder of me and is touching in his wish and longing to help,' records her diary on 3 August. 'But what can help: *nothing*! Irene rang up in the evening and broke my only thread of hope.'

Irene had telephoned because Louis Greig had told her that Fruity was being sent home to receive his dismissal from Sir Archibald Sinclair, the Air Minister. Baba left Garrowby at once. Back in London, she wrote to Sir Archibald, whom she knew, and as she informed Irene a few days later, 'had a most odious conversation about Fruity with Louis G at Air Ministry'. Louis had been inadequate and offhand on the telephone: he had said, she reported, that from the first Fruity's Commanding Officer had found him hopeless. Baba's reaction was instantly to leap to the defence of her husband against what she described to Irene as 'unjust attacks'.

Greig, aware that Baba had rejected everything he had said outright, came to see Irene at the Dorchester on 11 August. To her he explained that Fruity had only been taken on in the Cairo job because of his, Louis's, influence and that he could not help him any more. Nor could Archie Sinclair, at the Air Ministry, interfere.

But for Baba all was not doom and gloom. One of her admirers, the American General Cliff H. Lee, in charge of all service supplies for the American Army, told her that he could put in for Little Compton as a leave and rest centre for American officers if it helped her. Baba agreed gratefully: this constant, well-paid supply of up to half a dozen presentable young officers at a time requiring accommodation meant that she could keep on not only her butler, cook and lady's maid but also employ a parlourmaid and house-maids – a staff almost unheard of in wartime.

A few days later came another boost to Baba's morale. Jock Whitney, the rich and glamorous American she had contemplated marrying, arrived in England as Intelligence Officer to the Eagle Squadron.* Jock had recently remarried but his wife, the former Betsey Roosevelt, was in America so it was not long before Jock, too, was one of the men circling her.

Halifax, now back in Washington, gave Baba what comfort he could, as well as his usual avowal of undying affection. 'It is not at all nice having to begin this writing business again,' he wrote on 26 August. 'It is a poor substitute for the other. And I long hungrily for the first of yours. One other thing, I want you to send a telegram when anything definite occurs about Fruity's return or dates. I would like to be with you in thought at the time.'

At the beginning of September the Duke of Kent, who had been another ardent admirer of Baba's – so much so that marriage had been in the air – was killed in a plane crash in Scotland. 'Your account of Marina is very shattering,' wrote Halifax. 'The bed business sounds like Queen Victoria and Albert. Poor woman. Is it really the fact that his head was cut off? Who told you that? And how do they know about the plane hitting, bouncing, etc? Has the solitary survivor been able to tell them much? They will never know I suppose why they were there at all.'

---

*The famous air squadron of Americans who had joined Britain in her fight before their own country had declared war.

Fruity arrived home at the end of September and Baba's first action was to wire this news to the Halifaxes. Edward responded immediately, writing on 10 October, 1942:

I can't tell you, darling one, how great a relief your letter was saying the first 48 hours had at least gone off smoothly. The important thing you have got to do if things get difficult is to harden yourself against minding what is said from the other side, discounting it in advance, so that when and if it comes its hitting power is diminished.

And secondly, keep your own temper under very firm control. No one can work up a successful quarrel if the other party won't play! You know, I think, my dearest, how much love surrounds you as a kind of moral armour plate protection and there is much more to be called into service as you need...

34

Sisterly Jealousy

~

That autumn, the Halifaxes needed all their strength to survive two devastating blows. The first was the news that their second son, Peter Wood, had been killed on 1 November 1942 in the Battle of El Alamein. Halifax wrote to Baba on the day this news was received. 'I can't write you a proper letter because I'm so snowed under with letters from kind people about Peter.'

El Alamein had seen the defeat of Rommel and the tide of war turning – up to 40 per cent of the Axis shipping between Italy and North Africa was being sunk (leaving Rommel's Afrika Korps desperately short of supplies), Tobruk had been recaptured, and the Soviets had begun their counterblow at Stalingrad. But for the Halifaxes there was another tragedy.

On 30 December 1942 their youngest son, Richard, who had only just joined his regiment in the Middle East, lost both his legs in an attack by a Stuka dive-bomber.

At first, Fruity's arrival at Little Compton went well. But coming back to England must have been a desperate disappointment to him – as Cairo itself had been, despite his high hopes. No turn of events could have underlined more forcefully just how completely his life had been derailed.

Wartime Cairo was a fashionable place to be. In neutral Egypt, it suffered few if any of the privations endured by countries actively waging the war. It was a focal point for young officers on leave as well as for the women who wanted to follow their men as close to the theatre of battle as possible. In the bars and nightclubs a spirit of frenetic gaiety prevailed among those who would, perhaps next morning, return to the dangerous and dirty business of war. Everyone who had business in the Near East passed through the city, spies as well as soldiers, and it was the headquarters of command operations in the vicinity.

The most famous hostess in wartime Cairo when Fruity had arrived there in November 1941 was Maud ('Momo') Marriott, the rich, elegant American wife of Brigadier Sir John Marriott. She entertained constantly, presiding over a wartime salon that drew everyone of interest. As she was a great friend of Baba's, Fruity naturally expected at least to be invited there on a fairly regular basis, if not to become one of the habitués of the house. But Momo made it clear that he was not important enough. He was a humble flight lieutenant whereas every other man of his age wore crowns, pips or wings; and he was being cold-shouldered by the very people from whom he could have expected friendship.

Fruity must often have reflected on the decline from the bright fulfilment of his younger days, from being the beloved husband of a well-known society beauty to deceived spouse, from chosen companion and devoted servant of a prince to this position on the sidelines, from a promising career in the Indian Army to a junior rank in a Service he had come to hate.

It was hardly surprising, in a man formerly so convivial, that the drink to which he turned for solace now tightened its grip; and that, by now set in his ways, he made few concessions to changed wartime circumstances. When he arrived back at Little Compton the servants to whom he had been accustomed all his adult life, first in India and then during his marriage to Baba, were still there; his wardrobe was still intact; and rationing had made little impact on him. With nothing to do, almost a visitor in a house in every respect run by his wife, there was no real pattern to his life. General Lee, as good as his word, produced an unending supply of American officers so that the Little Compton household ran on oiled wheels, much as it had done before the war, except for the new emphasis on vegetables and livestock. The ducks survived but Baba soon gave up her attempts at rabbit breeding.

By the end of January 1943 Fruity had found a job, working for Filipo del Guidice, owner and founder of Two Cities Films, in the Public Relations Department, living at the Grosvenor House

Hotel during the week and coming down to Little Compton at weekends.

The Halifaxes were looking forward to a visit from Victor Cazalet; more importantly, their son Richard was reported to be steadily improving. 'We had a long letter from him last week – very cheerful – coming here perhaps to get fitted up and then all home together,' wrote Halifax on 25 January. For the next two months, his letters consisted largely of news on Richard's progress.

Irene, in her mid-forties aware, that her 'chances' were slipping away and that the children she had looked after for so long would soon be leading independent lives, had a fit of misery and regret when Victor took her down to spend the weekend at Great Swifts. Looking out of her window at the dazzling display of yellow crocuses on his lawn she tortured herself for her haste in turning down Victor's offer of marriage – 'and yet I cannot!' She cheered up later when two other guests arrived, Victor produced champagne, sloe gin and brandy and they had some good bridge after dinner.

At Little Compton – now the only real centre of Curzon family life – she listened while Baba read out to her and Charles Peake and his wife two letters that were so intimate that they showed perhaps more than anything else how strongly Halifax felt about her. One was from Peter, the son who had been killed, and the other from Richard, describing how his legs had been amputated in a small tent in the middle of the desert. Irene could not restrain her tears. 'The heroism and cheerfulness of it was fantastic,' she wrote that night. 'As if he had had a small scratch – full of jokes. Oh! the gallantry of these young men. Then I was shown Peter Wood's letter to his parents in case he was killed (which he always felt he would be.)'

Despite his bereavement, Halifax's flow of letters to Baba continued unabated. Many featured the sort of intimate political gossip she loved, such as Anthony Eden's suggestion that he, Halifax, should go to India as Viceroy after the war – presumably to preside over partition. 'Whatever else might be said, I'm sure I would be in an impossible position with Winston as P.M., whatever assurances he might feel like giving.' He was also anxious that she keep some part of their correspondence secret: 'Let Victor see my diaries but not any PSs.'

In April Irene listened avidly while Nick, on leave from France, where he was an officer in the Rifle Brigade, told her about his regiment, his men, his reactions to fighting and his talks with his father, whom he now visited in prison as regularly as he could. She was glad when Nick told her that he found Tom's company encouraging and inspiring and delighted that although his men knew he was Oswald Mosley's son, no one attempted to take it out on him in any way.

Back at the Dorch, Victor reappeared. Yet again, he proposed to Irene. 'But if I could not stand him round me when I am ill,' she wrote reasonably, 'it is certain he would still get on my nerves as a husband and permanency.'

On 11 May 1943 Churchill arrived in Washington for talks with Roosevelt. Winston's visit, Halifax told Baba, was exhausting but very worthwhile because he was getting to know the President well. 'Your account of Tom Mosley is grim,' he added. 'I wonder whether he will ever find his movement reviving after the war.'

He went on to revert to the question of absorbing interest to them both. As the daughter of the man who had been arguably India's greatest Viceroy, and as a former holder of the same great office, Baba and Halifax enjoyed speculating as to who would become India's first post-war Viceroy, with all that the position entailed in terms of the delicate political negotiation required in the run-up to Independence, straightforward organisation and 'image'.

India is causing Winston a lot of worry [Halifax wrote on 27 May]. And I gather he has been and is quite seriously considering Anthony for it and that A is quite seriously considering it for himself. Not necessarily to be a peer and therefore ineligible for future leadership. But it would leave the Pooh still less controlled than at present. For Heaven's sake keep all this to yourself. With all his faults of egocentricity, total lack of the right sort of humility and utter inconsiderateness for anybody but himself I do take off my hat to the sheer confidence, vitality and vigour of the man. There is nothing artificial about it and the stream seems quite inexhaustible. It's that that impresses people here.

One morning at the beginning of June Lady Mosley telephoned Irene to tell her that Tom was so ill his doctors said he would die if he was forced to remain in Holloway. In Baba's absence, Irene left a message with the Little Compton butler and dashed off to the House of Commons, largely to hear the Prime Minister report on his American visit but also to lobby whatever influential friend she saw there about Tom's desperate situation.

Baba was insistent that only the Prime Minister could order Tom's release and that it would carry more weight if Irene appealed to him rather than her, as everyone knew how much Irene disliked Tom. She added that Tom had said he was not interested in Micky and that Irene could keep him. Far from feeling relieved that her loved one would not be taken from her, Irene was again deeply shocked by Tom's parental indifference.

A few days later the Mosley family doctor, Dr Kirkwood, telephoned to say that Lady Mosley had got everything out of proportion: he had never said that Tom's life was in danger – although he would certainly be better out of Holloway.

The question of the new Viceroy continued to exercise both Baba and Halifax.

> I think you can allay your anxieties about India [he wrote to her on 6 June], but Dickie Mountbatten is certainly a new idea. Pooh I guess is thinking rather more about some super-Minister of State to heat up the war effort there, and recognise Burma, than about trying to govern India and find a way out of the log-jam.
>
> If this is his idea I think he is wrong, for the Viceroy is going to have to make an awful lot of difference to the war against Japan, whereas he ought to be able to do quite a lot for better or worse on the political side. If I were dictator I might try somebody like Peter Fleming – though Freya Stark would be good!

Ten days later Halifax, though delighted at the prospect of a visit from his former Private Secretary Charles Peake, was writing sadly: 'A telegram came last night telling me of Wavell as Viceroy. How your father would have spat. And I cannot help thinking, though perhaps for different reasons, that he'd have been right. I think between ourselves W is a bad choice, tantamount to saying: "We don't care a d—n about the political side." Still, I'm glad it isn't John Anderson, or Anthony or Duff Cooper – and still more that it isn't me.'

When Irene ran into Chaim Weizmann in the lobby of the Dorchester on 4 July, he gave some news that desolated her. Both Victor Cazalet and General Sikorski had been killed in a plane crash on leaving Gibraltar.* Irene was so stunned she scarcely knew what to do. In a daze she allowed the friends who were taking her to lunch at the Bagatelle to carry her off, thinking that perhaps the best thing was to control herself and carry on.

After lunch she rushed back to her hotel room to telephone Baba with the news, then thoughtfully rang Victor's household at Great Swifts, thinking that the shock would be terrible for them if they first heard it on the evening news bulletins. Later on she went to a cocktail party but could not face the chattering crowds so walked back with someone who understood how she felt – the banker Henry Tiarks who had just lost his baby son.

Upstairs in her room, she finally broke down and wept bitterly, her sobbing intensified by the sympathetic friends who telephoned her to express their sorrow. She found it difficult to come to terms with this sudden, arbitrary tragedy. 'Dear Victor only did good in this sad world even though I failed him in not being able to marry him and it was the last thing he said to me – he would hope again when he returned.'

She felt battered and alone. Louis Greig told her the details of the accident: the big Liberator had only just taken off when all four engines apparently failed and it crashed 300 yards out from the Rock, with everyone still waving farewell. Of the 17 passengers and crew the only survivor was the Czech pilot.

'Victor's loss comes very close to us all, doesn't it?' wrote Halifax on 8 July. 'We laughed a lot [at him] – but there was solid virtue behind what we laughed at. And he was such a good friend, loyal, devoted, unselfish, humorous.'

As July wore on, Halifax's thoughts were turning increasingly towards home. From Portland, Oregon, he wrote to Baba on 19 July with another reference to the mysterious 'PSs' – 'I loved your PS and only distance and the uncertainty of how long this letter

---

*The General, as Commander-in-Chief of the Polish Army as well as Polish Prime Minister in London, was flying to the Middle East to inspect Polish forces there.

will take to get to you prevents me answering like with like!' –
before discussing holiday plans, the prospect of a night or two in
London, and how he could time his stay in Garrowby for a date
when Baba would be free to come up there. 'If you don't meet us
(as I dream constantly with prayers that you will), leave full
instructions at the Dorch for us to make contact at the earliest
possible. I think of little else.'

At Little Compton, Irene's underlying resentment of Baba had
resurfaced as a result of her sister's attitude to her struggle against
alcohol. Victor's loss, with all that it implied, had no doubt hit her
harder than she realised as her drinking had since become more
persistent. Although Irene despised her own weakness, even more
did she loathe Baba's strictures. When she received a long letter of
reproof she replied that Baba's constant surveillance had a worse
effect on her than anything; what she, Irene, needed, was cheerful
co-operation in her attempt to break her habit.

Fruity's presence, however, altered the balance of the sisters'
emotional equation, providing a focus for their joint annoyance,
with his silences, his view that rationing was for others and, almost
the worst crime in those days of desperate fuel shortage, his
hogging of the hot water. Although Baba had forbidden them all
to have baths because of the water shortage Simpson (the butler,
who also acted as Fruity's valet) would run deep baths for Fruity.
Furiously Irene tackled him about this, to which Simpson replied
that if he had demurred Fruity would have paid no attention and
done it himself. 'How I got through dinner I do not know.'

Micky, infected by the general malaise, chose this moment to be
unexpectedly rude to Irene, the episode not made easier by the
twins remarking that if it had been them, Baba would have sent
them upstairs for the rest of the day. Then, after an afternoon's
croquet, all the children had to be sent out into the hall as Fruity
would not stand for noise in the drawing-room and Irene had to
listen while one of the Americans spent twenty minutes on the
telephone to his girlfriend.

The Halifaxes returned in mid-August. Shortly afterwards, they
asked both Curzon sisters to a luncheon party at the Dorchester –
the other guests were the Halifaxes' son Richard, their daughter

Anne (married to Lord Feversham) and Charles Peake. Neither Baba nor Irene could have foreseen that this innocent invitation would trigger a quarrel so bitter that it is doubtful if their relationship ever recovered.

As the luncheon was held in Victor Cazalet's former sitting room, it put Irene into an unhappy mood from the start, no doubt exacerbating the loneliness of which she constantly complained in her diary. 'I felt embarrassed from beginning to end as the whole thing was so intimate with Baba's asides to Edward that I felt like an outcast. I wonder what Anne and Dorothy really feel about her?'

Nick's departure after embarkation leave did not make Irene any happier. She was also worried about her health; her doctor, who thought she might have a small internal polyp or cyst, had sent her to a nursing home to await an X-ray. Lying in bed there she had been delighted and touched to receive a basket of tomatoes, eggs and fruit from Baba. Few presents could have been more welcome; fresh eggs were a real luxury. It was the last surge of pure, uncomplicated sisterly affection.

Back at the Dorch, Irene's pleasure at Baba's recent thoughtfulness disappeared when she found Baba using her room to make a stream of telephone calls. She told her sister that as there was no space for her in her own room, she would go to Viv. Her remark was a flashpoint. Baba flared up and told Irene not to be a martyr. Irene responded that Baba was too fond of her own comfort and extremely selfish – and then came out with the accusation that set the tinder alight: 'I said if it had not been for one or two loyal friends to protect her, her name was mud over Edward Halifax.'

Then, in Irene's words: 'Baba hit me savagely in the face and I told her to get out.'

It was the biggest breach the sisters had ever had. In the immediate aftermath, Irene rushed down to her friends the Masseys and on emerging ran into Charles Peake, on his way to see Baba, who advised Irene to be patient 'and things would sort themselves out'.

Irene, made frantic by what had happened, took her telephone off the hook, as she could not face the thought of a broadside from Baba before a broadcast she was due to do on 3 October. Balked of the telephone, Baba wrote a furious letter to her sister. Irene managed the broadcast successfully but was so nervous of Baba that she returned to the shelter of the nursing home.

On 7 October, when she was back at the Dorchester, Viv came to see her. The message she bore was that Irene had allowed the wonderful platonic friendship Baba enjoyed with Edward Halifax to become smutty, like the minds of those around her.

The estrangement continued. At the Requiem Mass of Gracie's son Captain Hubert Duggan MP at Farm Street Catholic church in early November, the sisters sat together but did not speak.

Rumours of Tom Mosley's imminent release were spreading. When this was confirmed, Halifax wrote tenderly to Baba: 'I see by the papers that Tom is being let out. From your letter, I fear you will feel it is too late. But with all my heart, I pray it may not be so and that better and changed conditions may work favourably. Do let me know how things go with him and how you feel about it.'

The news that Tom would be released was the signal for country-wide protests. Trade-union workers marched on Downing Street and the Home Office. Factory workers downed tools and questions were asked in Parliament. So great was the uproar that when the Mosleys were finally released, at 7 a.m. on 20 November 1943, it was through the unobtrusive side entrance of Holloway Prison, known as Murderers' Gate, to a car with its engine already running, with an unmarked police car ahead and behind. A thick fog aided the small convoy's unnoticed departure.

Irene was bombarded by the press, who did not know where the Mosleys had gone. At any other time this would have driven her to distraction but the breach with Baba overshadowed everything else. She barely noticed when Fruity telephoned, furious at the idea of Tom's release and no doubt worried in case Baba's affair with him would be resumed.

There were constant consultations with the Masseys over sending a letter to Baba. Then a ready-made reason for writing presented itself: concern over Vivien. Would the machine shop in which she worked use her presence as a pretext for another of the strikes which Tom's release was currently causing? Back came another screed from Baba, so angry and astringent that Irene posted it straight on to the Masseys.

As the papers filled with the row over Tom, Halifax wrote to Baba on 25 November: 'I fear [this] may be worrying you a bit. What asses people are, and to what an extent emotion governs human thought. No wonder Herbert Morrison was a bit nervous, if he foresaw this storm. I long to hear from you what happened to him and what you judge of the "hullabaloo".'

The controversy over Tom's release raged so furiously that a debate on it was scheduled in Parliament. Churchill, writing to Halifax from Cairo on 26 November, said he was 'burning to take part in the debate on 18B and if I were at home now I would blow the whole blasted thing out of existence. So long as Morrison presents the case as exceptional treatment for Mosley naturally he is on difficult ground and people can cry "Favour"! He really would lose very little to sweep the whole thing away, which he could do by the overwhelming arguments I have mentioned to him in the various telegrams which you will have seen by now.'

(The most telling one enshrined the principle close to Churchill's heart: the importance of the Habeas Corpus Act. Urging the abolition of Defence Regulation 18B, he wrote: 'The national emergency no longer justifies abrogation of individual rights of Habeas Corpus and trial by jury on definite charges.')

Much of the country thought otherwise. On 28 November a huge crowd marched to Trafalgar Square carrying placards demanding Mosley's return to prison. Many of the trade unions were up in arms and the TUC, representing six million workers, deplored the Home Secretary's failure to take public opinion into account – Mass Observation polls showed 77 per cent against the Mosleys' release. MPs all over the country received deputations from their constituents urging continued detention.

The Parliamentary debate, on 1 December 1943, was an extraordinarily heated affair. Irene went to listen and was sickened by the venom of many Members. So many Labour MPs revolted against Morrison's ruling that at one point it seemed as if they might force him to leave the Government. What distressed Irene most was thinking that Viv and Micky would read these speeches about their father.

'The Tom M row must surely be dying down,' wrote Halifax to Baba on 9 December. 'Charles [Peake] told me he thought Herbert M made a very good case but the trouble is that nobody – or very few people – are judging these things rationally. I shall be much interested if and when you see Tom to hear how he feels towards society in general as the result of his treatment of the last few years. I suppose he must be very bitter – at least, I guess I should be. But perhaps he just feels flat, and glad to be out of prison.'

The rift between Baba and Irene was not really papered over until Vivien lunched with her aunt on 11 December. However tactless and over-emotional Viv thought Irene had been, her loyalties lay with the woman who had been a devoted mother figure for most of her life. Irene, in her turn, realised that behind the messages Viv transmitted from Baba lay the girl's genuine, desperate appeal for Irene to be with them as a family in the Christmas holidays. She wrote a letter that she hoped was sufficiently humble to satisfy Baba, posted it and slept until the afternoon of the following day – when the second post brought a stiff response from her sister, almost, though not quite, refusing her olive branches and demanding further apologies. The Masseys advised swallowing her pride and giving Baba what she wanted, if only for the children's sake, and a second, grovelling letter went off. Christmas was saved.

On Boxing Day Viv and Mick went over to see their father for the first time since his release. He was living at the Shaven Crown, a semi-derelict inn near Moreton-in-Marsh in Gloucestershire which he and Diana had rented. With them were not only their two small sons, five-year-old Alexander and three-year-old Max, but also Diana's sons by her first marriage, Jonathan and Desmond Guinness.

Diana and Tom – who had spent much of his time lying in bed – looked thin, tired and ill and the four boys were incubating whooping cough. It was scarcely surprising that Viv appeared extremely depressed when she and Mick returned at eight o'clock.

It was a highly social holiday, with a constant flow of visitors for lunch, tea, drinks and dinner as well as General Lee and the American officers. Even so, Irene did not enjoy it: in addition to her other sufferings, she had become plagued with breathlessness, perhaps resulting from the strain of the past months.

Worse still was the loneliness that seemed to have taken root at the core of her being – even in this crowded house she felt isolated and apart. 'I am so breathless I cannot get a word out; no one is good and warm to me. I might be a bit of driftwood. It simply breaks my heart and I prayed and prayed over that note to Baba [on arrival she had left a note on Baba's bed].'

Her letter did little good. When Fruity and David left the house early on the morning of 28 December to spend the day with champion jockey Steve Donoghue at Didcot Baba rounded on her sister, demanding yet more explanations and apologies, insisting that Irene took back things that Irene equally adamantly denied having said.

Irene wept bitterly; Baba told her furiously that her tears were nothing but cheap drama. Speechless with sobbing, Irene left the room. At dinner she managed to chat and laugh with Fruity over reminiscences of their days at Melton and, later, had a helpful talk with Viv before bedtime. 'But I fear somehow Baba is still very frigid.'

The diary ends sadly on 31 December: 'I think for a while I must keep away from Baba and Fruity.'

35

Peace but not Accord

~

Irene's public persona was still impressive. Handsome and upright, her somewhat shapeless figure shown to best advantage by the skills of Nancy Astor's corsetière, Illa Knina of 30 Bruton Street, her sonorous voice at its best in the public speaking at which she was remarkably effective, it was not easy to forget that she was the daughter of one of the century's towering figures. The subjects of her numerous talks and lectures – to Women's Guilds, Mother's Unions, Boys' and Girls' Clubs or rallies – invariably had a strong moral theme which added to this impression: 'What is Club Service', 'How to become a Club Leader', 'The Adventure of Youth', 'Faith is No Longer an Adventure', 'God is an Adventure', 'What the East has taught me in Club Life', 'Service is the only true Dignity', and so on.

In private it was a different matter. Warm-hearted, generous, emotional, she had done her best to be a mother to her dead sister's children and, though she knew they responded to her love, two of them were now leading independent lives and she had been accused of surrounding the third, thirteen-year-old Micky, with too much petticoat influence. She worked extraordinarily hard, largely at activities to benefit others, she tried hard to be good and do the right thing, yet she felt unrewarded and unfulfilled. Whenever she looked at her younger sister, married, with children, glamorous, alluring, magnetic to men, confident and sure of the path she wished to pursue, she was reminded of what she longed for.

Baba, in her turn, was too proud to present anything but an immaculate image to the world. On the rare occasions that this gleaming surface cracked, both felt the old closeness. But in general, to Baba Irene, or Ne-ne (pronounced knee-knee), as she always called her sister, was faintly ridiculous so that her attitude seemed offensively patronising to the sensitive Irene. 'There was much talk at Denham betwixt Viv, Baba and me in the afternoon,' she wrote on 24 February 1944. 'I felt considerably crushed and trampled over by the indifference shown by Baba to anything I had to say on the matter, considering I paid several thousands to keep it going for the children when Tom was nasty from 1937–9.'

For Irene, jealousy of her younger sister had become a constant underlying emotion. In particular, she envied Baba her close relationship with Lord Halifax. Since the bitter breach with her father all those years ago, there had been no semi-paternal figure to take his place. Halifax would have filled this role to perfection – older, as distinguished morally as he was politically, a man whose faith she knew would have inspired her and, perhaps of more significance than she realised, a former holder of the same great office as her father.

As the last, weary years of war rolled on, each month brought a victory or gain. In January 1944 the Allies landed at Anzio and the biggest-ever bombing raid on Berlin took place. In March hundreds of Allied troops landed in Burma and within twelve hours had made an airstrip in the jungle for fighters.

On 25 May Halifax wrote excitedly to Baba from the Waldorf Astoria:

> Here is a bit of personal news I would like you to have but which you must keep strictly to yourself. I was astonished two days ago to get a telegram from Winston expressing a desire to submit my name to the King for an Earldom!! Don't laugh too much. Confidence, good work, gesture to Americans etc. My first reaction was definitely adverse. Incongruous in wartime and likely to be equally incongruous when we are all living in a bankrupt new world afterwards. And moreover one felt that one was contributing comparatively little in effort and sacrifice by the side of thousands of others. So it seemed to me slightly discordant and ridiculous.
>
> Dorothy however took the view that, while one was still doing the job, it was rather a compliment to me and the U.S., which it would

not have been if it had been offered when one was pushed out or retired, and that the world at large would take it as a recognition of the importance of the job, etc.

So after much debate, and not without some doubt, I have telegraphed to W assenting. I shall be anxious to know whether you will think I have been a fool or not, when you have finished smiling! I'm sorry to let go Viscount, which I think is a nicer title, and which my father and grandfather had made respectable, but I think the main point is that the name itself remains.

On 4 June Rome was liberated by the Allies and on 6 June the invasion of Europe began with D-Day. A week later the Germans hit back with the first of a new type of weapon, the V1 flying bomb. It was jet-propelled, pilotless, flew at low altitudes and, when it ran out of fuel, exploded. Nevertheless, on 22 June Halifax was able to write: 'Malcolm Macdonald tells me that many of the intelligent, in the know people in London are confident that Germany must crack before October'.

His return to London in July meant another ecstatic reunion. 'I hated going away this morning,' he wrote to Baba (on 22 July), a telling sentence since he wrote from his beloved Garrowby. 'It is perfect being with someone like you who shares everything and with whom one has no reserves or lack of understanding. A very perfect companion, you are. So good altogether that it is spoiling and life seems to lack much of its spice and savour when you aren't there.'

On 25 August Allied troops, led by the French, marched into Paris. By now the Germans were calling up old men and children; boys of fifteen were captured in the front line. The British Government had begun to plan for post-war education and a free medical service for everyone. 'Oh! How I rejoice at seeing the Germans getting their own stuff back,' wrote Halifax as the Allied advances continued. 'As the NY Times says: "One has the sensation of seeing a motion picture in reverse".'

Once again the Germans retaliated with a more deadly version of the V1: a long-range, powerful rocket that travelled faster than the speed of sound and exploded on impact. In September the first of these V2s landed on London (most of the smaller, earlier V1s had fallen on south-east England). But nothing could halt the inexorable Allied advance.

With the end of the war now seemingly only months away – something made even more likely when the first German city – Aachen – fell to the Allies on 20 October 1944 – the Halifaxes' plan for a holiday in England was postponed: it would not do for the Ambassador to be away from his post when victory was declared.

Instead, Halifax began to urge Baba to visit Washington, perhaps for Christmas or certainly soon afterwards. 'I don't think I shall come home – unless sacked – before May,' he explained, adding in the same letter: 'Have you been reading about the mass massacres in concentration camps at Lublin?* Have you ever read anything more utterly bestial in your life?

'More and more I find myself wishing that lots of Germans may be killed before this job is over, from top to bottom, for I believe justice would best be served by their feeling something of what either directly or by acquiescence they have done to other people.'

On 21 September, Mussolini was lynched in Rome. Baba's old friend and former lover Count Dino Grandi had played a large part in Il Duce's overthrow the previous year, framing the resolution that divested him of much of his power in the Grand Council in July 1943. The next day Mussolini was arrested and imprisoned and a Prime Minister installed, though it was not until he tried to escape to the German lines after the liberation of Rome that he was caught and killed.

By the beginning of 1945 Irene's health was poorer than ever. The diary is full of complaints about her 'nerves', poor sleeping and breathlessness and the writing, always difficult to read, is much wilder. Her feeling of psychological distress must also have been exacerbated by the tensions between Baba and Fruity. Even thirteen-year-old Micky was unhappily aware of these. 'He told me Fruity and Baba went at each other day and night.'

Whereas, previously, Irene had usually managed to cover up her

*The first death camps had been found in Poland on 27 July, a discovery soon followed by others equally hideous.

drinking and she had never been seen the worse for wear on any of her public engagements, now it was impossible to ignore. Her story that she had been hit on the head and fallen into a basement area was disbelieved by most of her family. 'She simply got drunk and fell over,' said Fruity when he heard it.

As always, she was penitent, remorseful, ashamed and biddable, agreeing to go into a nursing home for another cure during the month of January 1945. She hated every minute of it – the lack of privacy, the constant presence of watchful nurses, the whole paraphernalia of pills and injections designed to ease the process of withdrawal. 'It made me desperate like a caged lion and I only wanted to escape and do bad things,' she wrote in her diary. She went home, tried a different treatment and then, as a last resort, went down to Little Compton, where Baba was briskly kind and understanding.

In the outside world, the war in Europe was moving into its final phase. On 14 February Dresden was reduced to a smoking ruin and victory after victory brought the Allies nearer to Berlin. In the Bahamas, the Windsors were looking forward to the end of their 'exile'. The Duke had announced his resignation from the post of Governor from April 1945, a few weeks before the end of the traditional five-year term. Their thoughts naturally turned to France, their only real home since their marriage.

When Baba heard that they were leaving the Bahamas she wrote at once to the Duchess – the first time since her previous acrimonious letter – a stiff little note asking about some pottery she had bought just before the war. Wallis's reply showed that she was anxious to get on terms again.

Dear Baba, [she wrote on 25 February 1945]
Gray has told me about your Juan-les-Pins pottery. Here is the situation. La Cröe has been occupied by the Italians and the Germans, has been shelled from the sea by us and last but not least ruined by the Germans. The Americans are now dealing with the latter and we ought to be able to have our representatives inside of the gate shortly. I hope your things are not among the missing. We have lost quite a bit of our possessions. I do not think the pottery ever got to the Paris house somehow but must admit to being a bit vague on this score. Gray is writing to our old and frozen butler at Suchet to enquire and

look among the mess there. If it is in Paris it is safe – but La Cröe I can't say.

I was sorry not to hear from you after my last letter and hope there was nothing in it that could have caused a misunderstanding. If so it was certainly unintentional on my part – as I have always appreciated and valued our friendship.

Yours ever,
Wallis

At the end of April Hitler committed suicide in his underground bunker and at 2.41 a.m. on 7 May the Germans signed the instrument of unconditional surrender. Finally, after more than five long years, the war in Europe was over.

Like everyone else, the Curzon sisters celebrated. Baba collected a group of friends outside White's Club and with thousands of others they walked the streets escorted by Fruity – now a special constable – who found his progress impeded by constant questions from passers-by about bus and Tube routes. The late evening found them, exhausted, sitting on the traffic island opposite the Ritz, shoes kicked off to ease their aching feet, watching the jubilant play of the searchlights after listening to the King's broadcast at 9 p.m. from loudspeakers at the front of Buckingham Palace.

Halifax's feeling that the Duke of Windsor was after his job was justified. The Duke was anxious to arrange his post-war future, which stretched blankly before him and, if he could not have his first choice, the Embassy in Washington, hankered after a position as Ambassador-at-large. Meanwhile, to fill the immediate aftermath of their departure from the Bahamas the Windsors decided to take a holiday in the US. They left for Miami on 3 May 1945, letting it be known that they would then return to France.

The problem was that a man who had renounced the Throne could not very well represent the reigning monarch, while the return of the Windsors to England raised the spectre of a second 'court'. When the new Labour Government was elected on 26 July 1945 it, too, agreed that a roving Ambassadorship would lead to inevitable trouble. As Halifax wrote: 'It would almost certainly cause embarrassment to the Ambassador and the Consul, each of whom would be likely in different degrees to find it difficult to keep the Duke on the approved line or correct him if he got off it.'

The chief difficulty was that both Windsors were massively mistrusted. Halifax was worried that official telegrams would not remain secret. 'I should myself feel little confidence in his discretion in this field,' he minuted. He also felt that their constant party-going would soon count heavily against what popularity they enjoyed in America. Once again, it was left to the King to tell his brother that a US-based job would not be possible.

Even the Windsors' return to France caused apprehension. 'I confess I regard without enthusiasm his intention of returning to Paris,' wrote the new Foreign Secretary Ernest Bevin. 'His friends there turned out to be for the most part collaborators and he will expect to live there in luxury amidst great poverty.' When the Duke visited Lloyds Bank in St James's Street at the beginning of October and asked for an overdraft of £5,000 to be transferred to Lloyds in Paris so that the Duchess could draw from it whenever she wanted, alarm bells rang in both the Treasury and the Bank of England, powerless to stop the transaction. 'They naturally feel hesitation about large sums of money being made available to the Duke in France when ordinary British subjects there are severely restricted,' wrote a senior Foreign Office official.

Money, jobs and readjusting to a life of peace were also the prime considerations of millions of the Duke's former citizens. Irene began work for charities that sprang up in the first months of peace, like Aid to Greece, got her pearls out of the bank ('after all these War years!'), gave luncheons for Danny Kaye – unfortunately he preferred Baba's company – bewailed the fact that Virginia cigarettes seemed unobtainable and visited her stepmother Gracie who was now living with, and caring for, her son Alfred Duggan, the future novelist and biographer. Irene still found it difficult to adjust to the idea of the Marchioness of Curzon, noted for the grandeur of her lifestyle even in an era of extravagance, doing the dirty laundry. But she was immensely impressed by the skill with which Gracie had made her small house in South Mimms, Hertfordshire, so pretty.

That August Irene saw Diana again for the first time since she had been to admire her new baby in 1940. The Mosleys, then living temporarily at Crux Easton, near Newbury in Berkshire, had bought Crowood House, near Hungerford, its farmland and piggery worked by some of Tom's ex-fascists. Tom not only believed firmly in the importance of growing one's own food but also that it was the best way to build up his and Diana's health after the privations of prison.

Baba, at Little Compton, was planning a trip to America, her clothes packed and ready in Irene's house, when the sisters became victims of a cunning robbery. At the beginning of September Annie, Irene's maid, was rung up with the news that her mistress had had an accident and lost her key and would Annie leave hers by the dustbin in the basement area. The caller went on to tell Annie that if she would collect Irene's luggage from the Dorchester (still treated by Irene like a club), he would bring Irene up to see her doctor. When Annie returned from the Dorchester she found Irene's room in complete disorder and much missing. With any new garment only obtainable through the few clothes coupons allowed annually, the loss of even one's oldest clothes was a serious matter.

Baba's terror that her furs, left in Irene's room packed and ready for America in a cardboard box, had also been taken affected Irene so deeply that it almost made her disregard the disappearance of her own silver fox fur, camiknickers, stockings, coats, hats, dresses and silk underwear, dressing-case and wireless. Yet her very real concern did nothing to prevent the jealousy that was now endemic. 'Dear God! I was envious of her as a VIP going to Washington. Fruity was not complimentary of her privilege in getting out there through Halifax when tragic cases cannot get back.'

Irene filled her life even more frantically with people and good works. She turned in desperation to the music that was so much a part of her life, going alone to the Albert Hall to hear Yehudi Menuhin, but the aching inner void remained and she stifled tears most days. She sat on endless committees, dealt with great tranches of Club business, attended the World Congress of Faiths and the War Workers' Committee meetings and opened a bazaar for the Salvation Army in Shepherd's Bush. She took Micky and the twins shopping in Bond Street, followed by tea and a theatre for which Fruity joined them, gave constant lunches to her friends at the Dorchester or Quaglino's and suppers at the Savoy. It was a life that many would have found fulfilling. But in Irene's eyes, everyone else was better off – especially Baba.

Baba returned on 6 December 1945, to be met at Waterloo by

Fruity with a large van borrowed from the Dorchester for the sixteen cases stuffed with American booty. For once, the sisters had a cosy evening alone together, talking of Irene's many friends in America and those Baba had met. Both were distressed when Tom Mosley held a fascist reunion party in Russell Square, followed by a dance for a thousand supporters. 'Why cannot the man keep quiet?' wrote Irene crossly.

Christmas, predictably, was a matter for despair to Irene, especially when the contents of Baba's sixteen cases were revealed. 'Baba brought back trunks of clothes, hats, shoes and stockings for the twins. The children got furs, boots, wristwatches from Lady Halifax, pretty presents. I came up after breakfast and cried my heart out, I desperately am in need of all these things and have not got one. A green summer dress length from Baba, a pair of black gloves, pink sequin bedroom slippers and oh! the dress I bought with my own money was nowhere near what I wanted. I cannot see why I am so desperately unlucky in gifts. Baba had exactly what I wanted.'

Two days after Christmas Fruity and David left Little Compton. Though regarding her brother-in-law as an irritation factor was now almost axiomatic for Irene, she noticed at once that with Fruity's departure all gaiety had gone from the house. 'There is a barrier invisible all the time to naturalness and a stifled atmosphere pervades the place,' she wrote. Another rare evening of warmth with her sister, when the barriers of restraint were lowered and the old intimacy returned merely pointed up the normal sad difference. 'Fruity lays down the law on plans, Baba gets argumentative on anything he says, the twins do not utter, David half reads a book and I am apprehensive from beginning to end,' she wrote. The beloved little sister of those early years at Hackwood seemed to have vanished as if she had never been.

36

Envoi

~

After the war, the sisters' lives diverged. Irene's never regained the vivid momentum, the sensation of being close to great events or involved in deep emotions, of earlier days. Seeing less of Baba also meant that the discrepancy between their lives was less of a cause for unhappy comparisons.

The war and Tom's imprisonment had put an end to the Mosley family home, Savehay Farm at Denham, which was sold by Tom on 1 January 1946. Irene mourned its loss as a place to which the grown-up Mosley children would return like homing pigeons. Her own large, rather gloomy house at 9 The Vale, in Chelsea, with none of Denham's childhood associations, did not exert the same appeal. It was, though, a good base for all her committee and Club work, and for the numerous speeches she was still asked to make. 'I could not be my father's daughter and not inherit a small part of his great power of public speaking,' she wrote of this part of her life.

She missed Denham for another reason. At Denham, she was at the heart of the household. It might not have been her house, but it was largely her money that had maintained it, and when there was any decision that had to be taken she was the one consulted by Nanny or Andrée; more importantly, her presence there was pivotal to the children. At Little Compton, which had replaced Denham as the family centre, she felt marginalised.

Her jealousy of Baba, which to a large extent ruined the latter part of her life, continued virtually until her death. She felt that her sister both dominated – 'Baba bosses everything' – and ignored her, making it less and less possible for her to keep on an even emotional keel. She sought psychiatric help, usually returning after such consultations to the womb of the Dorchester rather than to her own house. One psychiatrist told her that she was running away from herself, another diagnosed her sister as the trouble ('He thought I had become completely defeatist largely because of Baba and that I must not leave this question but face it squarely').

It was a verdict that troubled her so much that she began to be physically ill. Sensibly, she came to the conclusion that 'these delvings into the past do no good'. Irene herself put her troubles down to the difficulties of her relationship with Baba, years of overwork and her 'ageing years' (the menopause had affected her badly). 'All have taken their toll and temporarily I have cracked and am bankrupt of health and belief. It mortifies me beyond belief.'

The relationship with Micky, the son she always wished she had had, was no longer straightforward as it had been when he was the lovable cuddly baby or uncomplicated small child who had ruled over her heart since she first took responsibility for him; he was now a boy entering adolescence, with an adolescent's need for privacy. As the 1950s passed, she felt lonelier than ever: she was well into her fifties, her sexual life was over and the admirers had dropped away, she was childless and the family she had made her own – though their love for her was as strong as ever – had grown up and were leading their own lives, while Baba had begun increasingly to regard her as a tiresome irrelevance.

The tippling in which Irene had always indulged increased again – this time she turned to sherry – but again, it did not stop her constantly seeing friends, travelling or pursuing a successful public career. She worked busily for her Clubs, she went to conferences all over the country and she was in great demand as a church speaker – she was an excellent orator on a simple, revivalist level. Once, her nephew Nick was travelling down Piccadilly on the top deck of a bus when he heard her sonorous voice booming out over a loudspeaker. Looking down, he saw her preaching outside St James's Piccadilly, with a large lunch-hour crowd gathered round her.

'She inherited something of her father's oratorical powers,' said *The Times* in its obituary, 'and what she lacked was balanced by her manifest intensity of feeling and conviction.'

She went on travelling, often with Micky. They would set off for Africa, South America or Indonesia, spending anything up to three months on such a trip. She also wrote her first and only book, *In Many Rhythms*. The publisher George (now Lord) Weidenfeld, whose habit it was to suggest to any attractive or important woman who sat next to him at dinner that she should 'do a book' for him, absentmindedly issued this invitation to his old friend Irene. It struck an immediate chord. Next morning she was on the telephone to his office and a book was duly published by Weidenfeld and Nicolson in 1953. Although it sank instantly without trace, Irene was delighted with it.

She was now chairman of the Franckenstein Memorial Musical Scholarship, run by the National School of Opera, for an advanced singing student or professional singer of either sex, with a knowledge of German and a reason for desiring a period of study in Austria. Irene took immense trouble in finding teachers in Vienna for the winner, Miss Joan Edwards, and gave a farewell party for her.

The Life Peerages Act in 1958 marked a dramatic change in Irene's status as a result of the work she had carried out virtually all her life – as chairman of the Highway Clubs, vice-president of Girls' Clubs and Mixed Clubs, treasurer of the Musicians' Benevolent Fund and joint president of the London Union of Youth Clubs. As well as creating the first life peers, the Act (which received Royal Assent on 30 April) was also the first recognition of a woman's right to sit and vote as a peer, something for which Irene had always campaigned. She became one of the first four life baronesses in the country – the others were Stella, Marchioness of Reading (widow of the first marquess), Katharine Elliot (widow of Walter Elliot, Minister of Agriculture in the pre-war National Government) and Barbara Wootton (Mrs Wright), a former Professor of Social Studies at London University and a well-known broadcaster. 'We must be cautious and wise because we have taken twenty-five years to get in,' said Irene in answer to congratulations. 'We must have caution and dignity and only speak on those things we know about. I might not speak in the House for months, unless it has anything to do with a subject I know a lot about, like schools or the Wolfenden Report. If the grammar school question comes up, for example, I might bound up and make my maiden speech right away. Or I might not say a word for five months or so.'

Two years later, in a debate on the Street Offences Act, she made a speech that generated more publicity than anything she had hitherto done. Speaking of the prostitutes who frequented the disreputable clubs and cafés in the East End she knew so well, she told her fellow peers authoritatively: 'These girls charge a fiver for a long spell and £1 for a quick bash.' Her elegant appearance, said one newspaper, 'was a strange contrast to the deliberately strong language with which she jolted the men Peers into attention'.

Irene's later life brought her much more happiness and fulfilment, but sadly her health had begun to decline. On 9 February 1966, at the age of only 70, she died, her deep religious faith sustaining her to the end. 'No one could have been a more inspiring and active president [of the World Congress of Faiths],' said *The Times* in its obituary. 'She was a tower of strength ... her warmth and understanding of the religions and philosophies of the east were invaluable.' And, in a sentence that summed up her whole life, it remarked: 'In everything she did she was passionately involved.'

Baba's life after the war continued to be as social as ever. There was a rapprochement – less than willing on Baba's side – with the Windsors. The Duke and Duchess had returned to Paris in September 1945, to find that the freehold of their house in the Boulevard Suchet had been sold and that they had to vacate it by the end of April 1946. They then moved south to the Villa La Cröe, which had survived the war remarkably unscathed, although the windows had been blown in by shellfire, the sea front mined and the sheltering trees cut down to provide a clear field of view.

The Duke at least was pleased to be back there: to him it was more of a home than anywhere he had lived since Fort Belvedere. It was more relaxed, the entertaining there was less formal than the grand Parisian luncheons and dinners given by the Duchess, he could wear his kilt, practise his bagpipes and wander freely around the grounds. Within a few weeks they were back to almost pre-war levels of comfort – almost anything was available for those who could pay for it. The Duke was also able to slip across to England unobtrusively to visit his family, in particular his mother.

It was on the first of these trips, in the autumn of 1946, that Walter Monckton approached Fruity one day in White's Club with the words: 'The Little Man would like to see you.' The indirect approach through Walter was, perhaps, to save the Duke's face in case of rebuff – it was the first contact since the brutal abandonment in Paris six years earlier – or possibly because he feared that a telephone call might find the implacable Baba at the other end of the line.

Fruity agreed at once. He took with him his son David, the Duke's godson, arranging for David to wait in a side room at Marlborough House, where the Duke was staying, so that the two former friends could meet alone. When father and son returned to Wilton Place, Baba was waiting in the drawing-room.

'*Well?*' she demanded, putting all the intensity of her question into the single word. 'How was it? Did he apologise?'

Fruity, his son remembers, looked embarrassed and said: 'Well, he just held out his arms wide and said' – here Fruity imitated the Duke's tone of deep emotion – 'Oh, *Fruity!*'

'Is that *all* he said?' asked Baba.

'Yes, Babs, that was all he said,' replied Fruity.

Baba gave a furious snort of disgust and turned away. But the ice was broken. As far as Fruity was concerned, all was forgiven and forgotten and the old affection restored.

Baba could not hold out on her own, especially when the Duchess wrote from La Cröe in May 1948: 'Dear Baba, Being here once again has brought back so many pre-War memories that the Duke and myself wondered if you and Fruity could come out to stop with us for a bit. We shall only be here until August 15 as we are giving up La Cröe.'

The relationship continued cordial and in April 1949 the Duke was writing to Baba warmly.

Dear Baba,

Thank you a million times for our lovely visit with you and Fruity. We could not have enjoyed being with you all again more and seeing your enchanting house and all those gems of Cotswold villages and gardens.

It was all a great treat. The comfort was of a high order and the fare delicious in spite of your predictions. I do hope you won't have to part with Little Compton; that would be a great shame and maybe you will be able to resolve the financial and domestic difficulties.

But I must confess I was a little shocked over the state of Fruity's wardrobe. Not that I find his morale low or in need of building up; but after all it is 'debutante year' [the Metcalfes' twin daughters came out in 1949] and I believe I have been able to work something out to help him!

We do hope we will all meet this summer and please tell us your plans as soon as you have made them. Thanking you again and with our love to you all.

There was also an affectionate letter from the Duchess. After saying 'how delightful it was to be with you both and to have the pleasure of knowing your "grown up" family', she urged Baba to retain Little Compton. That summer Baba, who oversaw every detail of her daughters' debut, had decreed that there was not enough room for the entire family at Wilton Place, despite its six bedrooms and three bathrooms. She installed Fruity and David, who had just come out of the Army, together with a butler, in a house in nearby Motcomb Street, buying its lease for £3,000, although their life was still based around Wilton Place, where they dined most evenings. Nancy Astor offered her house in Hill Street for the twins' debutante ball.

Baba sold Little Compton in December 1949 for £30,000. When asked the reason for the sale by the *Evening Standard* she replied: 'The usual one in these days – high taxation.' She had also begun to travel widely. Her first visit was to Rome where her friend Frank Giles, there with his wife Lady Kitty, was correspondent for *The Times*. But before this, there was a meeting with a former love.

'Left London on February 28, 1951,' runs her diary. 'Grandi met me at Gare du Nord (endless conversations and wires had been coming). His looks are incredibly changed, no beard and face over life size, otherwise the same. I rather dreaded the meeting as so much has happened and I wasn't sure how he would be. The worry was wasted. No one could have been more charming and there never can be a more delicious companion, talker and laugher so the journey was perfect.'

For Grandi it was something more. As his son confirmed, he remained in love with Baba all his life. 'Meeting you at le Gare du Nord and being together in Rome has been simply wonderful,' he wrote to her afterwards. 'I see you there in the high carriage in the winter dim light, greeting me, recognising me: "Hello, Ge".

'Yes it would have been paradise to go to Sicily together. But we must be grateful to Providence for having given us a Roman week, a "bit" of us together every day of a whole week. Do you not think so?'

A week was all Grandi could spend with Baba: his home was now in Brazil. He had played a large part in the downfall of Mussolini in 1943 and had escaped any consequences by settling in Lisbon until the end of the war, when he moved to Brazil and re-established himself in business.

As Baba's diary records: 'G leaves for Brazil tomorrow – such fun renewing our friendship – a rather terrifying thing to do but this week has proved everything I have thought in the past more than correct and I admire and am terribly fond of him.'

For Grandi it was more. He wrote to her from Rio, to assure her of his devotion. 'No darling, I am not a "monster of faithlessness" as you say in your last short note. You are always in my thoughts and in my heart. You always have been, believe it or not. Always. From long ago, from a sunny day in Kew Gardens a million years ago. Age, tragedies, have meant nothing.'

Grandi was not the only man in Baba's life. Some time at the end of the 1940s she embarked on the last serious love affair of her life.

It was a choice that seemed extraordinary to virtually everyone who knew her: Viscount Feversham, the son-in-law of her devoted admirer – and in the eyes of many, probably lover – Lord Halifax, a man so deeply moral that he would not have a divorced person to stay at Garrowby (unless he happened to be a Master of Foxhounds). 'How does Baba think she can get away with it?' was the general reaction. One theory mooted was that Halifax was the man Baba had most loved in her life but because he was essentially 'out of bounds', as well as a semi-father figure, she turned instead to the engaging Sim Feversham. In any case, Halifax's romantic passion for her had waned and the old closeness had vanished, even though they remained friends.

Baba and Sim Feversham had first met in the late twenties. He was two years younger than her, a good-looking man with the gift of making everyone he talked to feel that they were the only person in the world he longed to see. He had been brought up by a mother who had had numerous lovers and had trained as a probation officer; and both aspects were reflected in his attitude to life. He spoke in the House of Lords, he was President of the Probation Officers' Association and Chairman of the Mental Health Association; and he believed in enjoying oneself.

They made no secret of their relationship. They went on antiques-buying trips together, Baba helped to organise his daughter Clarissa's large coming-out dance at Syon House – even choosing her dress for her – and she spent as much time with Sim as she could. They travelled frequently together. In Palermo in 1951, in the diary packed with the spelling mistakes about which Halifax had taken her to task in their wartime letters, Baba wrote, 'Sim is the most perfect travelling companion and sightseer, we think and laugh alike and therefore adore every minute of each day.' After that month-long trip she set off home 'with every mile anxiety growing. One couldn't expect such a blissful month without having to pay for it.' Later that year, they visited France and Venice together.

He shared with Baba her feeling for perfectionism: it was Sim who did up the house; Sim – rather than his wife Anne, the Halifaxes' daughter – who ordered the food when smart guests like the Duke and Duchess of Kent came to stay; Sim who had a passion for gardening. He was fun, amusing, imaginative and possessed of overwhelming charm.

By this time, Baba's life with Fruity had degenerated beyond repair. It was time for a discreet parting. Advised by her lawyer, Baba went abroad for a full fiscal year so that she could save enough money in income tax (the top rate was then punitive) to set Fruity up in a flat on his own in St James's Court, an apartment block just off Piccadilly, from which he could easily walk to White's. She left in January 1952 and did not return until April 1953. While she was away, Fruity was temporarily installed in Bepton, four miles outside Cowdray, in Sussex. He found it very lonely and David would drive down in the family Humber at weekends.

Baba's year abroad took her first to New York and then to South America and the Caribbean, where she was joined in March by Sim. By June she was in Paris, en route for Athens, where her old friend Charles (now Sir Charles) Peake was Ambassador. She took Freya Stark's house in Greece for August and September. Sim was her first visitor, for a long weekend; soon afterwards, she saw Grandi again. 'Since Roma last year Grandi Ge has had a bad year,' she wrote in her diary. 'Brazil is killing him. He speculated and lost most of the money he had made; his health went to pieces, so he was harassed and depressed. Ge was only here a few days, dashing to Milan and Rome before flying to Brazil.' October to February 1953 was spent with her daughter Linda in Rome and at the end of February she moved on to Tripoli (where Sim came out on the 28th).

Her travels did not end after her return. Her next visit was to the Peakes. It led to what would become the most important work of her life. While she was there, in August 1953, the Ionian earthquake struck. The plight of the survivors – 1,000 had been killed, 4,000 injured and 10,000 made homeless – especially the thousands of children wandering lost and crying, struck her so forcibly that she joined the Earthquake Committee. It brought her in touch with another earlier admirer. 'I will work with Michael Lubbock when I return,' notes her diary. 'How strange that our paths should cross again like this.' More importantly, it was to lead to what absorbed her for the rest of her life: her work with the Save the Children Fund.

In 1954 she went back to the Caribbean, and in the summer to Italy, Greece, Elba and Corfu. The following year she finally decided to divorce Fruity. For many years they had led separate lives but divorce was a radical step and, apart from running counter to the advice given her by her beloved Edward Halifax, was a public admission that she had failed in one vital aspect of her life. It was done as quietly and unobtrusively as possible – and, once again, Providence was kind. Baba's uncontested divorce from her husband of thirty years took place during the three-month newspaper strike in 1955 (25 March–20 June) and so went virtually unreported.

Her family believed that her divorce was in order to leave herself free for remarriage with Sim Feversham but that he, happy with their present arrangement and with no desire to divorce his wife, took fright and left her.

It was not quite as simple as that. The trouble was that, for all his charm, Sim was an inveterate gambler. Although he did not gamble on the Stock Exchange he did on just about anything else. He backed horses at impossible odds, played roulette at the Clermont Club, for which he would travel to London several times a week, and played games of chance through the night for high stakes in private houses. Several times on family holidays he found himself unable to pay household bills because he had gambled everything away at a casino the previous night; once he asked a friend to buy him half-size cocktail glasses 'as I can't afford to pay for the Martinis'. As women of all ages found him irresistible he was invariably forgiven but his habit meant that any serious lady friend had to be able and willing to foot all the bills.

Baba had been prepared to do up his cottage, Pennyholme, on the Yorkshire moors, either buying or lending him what it needed, as it was their joint love nest. Though she and Sim went on seeing each other after her divorce and he accompanied her for part of the time in 1955 on her travels to Greece and the Middle East, the end of the affair was in sight. One day, he pushed his luck too far. 'Money's your God,' said a disillusioned Baba, who was by nature somewhat tightfisted. It was the end.

For Baba this was a shattering blow. She thought she had found love again; instead, a deep humiliation was added to the guilt she felt at having divorced Fruity. When, only two years later, he was diagnosed with lung cancer, she returned at once to his side to nurse him. She was unstinting in her care: years later, she told her niece Vivien that the early years of her marriage were the best of her life, so good that even after the difficulties that came later 'I would do it all over again tomorrow'.

When Fruity died on 19 November 1957, one of the first calls was from Sim Feversham. 'It's Sim – do you want to speak to him?' Baba was asked. 'No. No,' she said, covering her face instinctively with her hands. 'He's absolutely the last person I want to talk to.'

Fruity's death was mourned by many. When the news of his illness had leaked out, his figure was immediately included in a conversation piece being painted by Simon Elwes of the Coffee

Room at White's Club (on the commission of Lord Camrose). Only twenty-four hours before he died he had spoken to the Duke of Windsor, who had been telephoning regularly for news and indeed had come over to see him on 9 November (when Harold Nicolson met him dining with Baba). He returned for Fruity's funeral and from the Windsors' house in the Bois de Boulogne came a letter from the Duchess.

'Dearest Baba, we are sad about darling Fruity. We never had a better friend and the Duke really loved him as you well know ... Thinking of you so much these days and talking over old times and laughs with Fruity – I send you my love and understanding and let me know if I can do anything for you. With my deep affection.'

The year after Fruity's death, Baba moved from the Wilton Place house into an elegant flat in 65 Eaton Square (the house used for the television series *Upstairs Downstairs*). Apart from family and friends, the main thrust of her life was her work for the Save the Children Fund, a commitment that lasted for more than forty years.

Into it she poured time, energy and much of her own money. When the Dalai Lama left Tibet with 80,000 followers in late 1960 and the Indian Government asked the Fund for help with the children who accompanied them, it was Baba who went to Simla in early 1961 at her own expense (as she did on all her travels for the Fund) to discuss with the Dalai Lama what could be done for them. A school, he thought – and she began to look for premises.

By an extraordinary coincidence, the first house offered was the one that her father had used at weekends more than half a century earlier. It was not entirely suitable and eventually the Fund bought Stirling Castle, where Baba had lived during her early married life in India, which could house five hundred children. From Lord Sieff (owner of Marks & Spencer) she begged five hundred suits of clothes and five hundred pairs of new shoes for the children, which he generously gave. As head of the Fund's Overseas Department she travelled all over the world, often at extremely short notice, to scenes of earthquake, flood and typhoon. She went to South Korea in the 1960s, and regularly to Saigon and Da Nang during the Vietnam War.

In 1968 she became vice-chairman of the Save the Children

Fund. Two years later, she flew out to India again, and spent seven days travelling by helicopter round the relief centres of a disaster area where a cyclone had struck.

In 1979, the year after her vice-chairmanship ended, she travelled to America with Nigel Nicolson, who was going on a lecture tour. She was still every inch her father's daughter, both in her readiness to accept unexpected discomfort – as Curzon had in his travels in the Pamir mountains – despite her love of creature comforts (she travelled when possible with her own silk sheets) and in her expectation that officialdom was at her beck and call. Baba, noted Nicolson, always had the grand manner. 'Her Save the Children official comes to arrange our onward trip and helps with motels and air tickets. Baba treats him like a servant.' In 1975 she was awarded a well-deserved CBE.

Baba had an enormous number of friends, attracted by her vitality, her interest in other people, her elegance and gift for entertaining, because she liked to laugh and rarely complained – and because of her immense loyalty to friends. Yet even those who loved her most were aware of the obverse of this: an unforgivingness that neither the passage of time nor altered circumstances could change.

Its chief manifestation was in her hatred of the Mosleys, who had settled in France in 1951. Of Diana, the woman whom she believed had taken her sister's husband away from her, she refused ever to speak. For Tom it was a hatred of the 'Hell has no fury, like a woman scorned' variety: despite all her efforts at helping him during the war he did not, as she had hoped, return to her afterwards. Instead, prison had brought him and Diana still closer. Tom, who would have liked to have seen Baba again, finally persuaded her to lunch with him and Diana in 1956. The meeting was a complete disaster.

Baba died on 7 August 1995, aged 91. At her memorial service (on 12 October 1995) Lord Carrington said: 'Baba Metcalfe was a supreme example of someone who, right up until her death, interested herself in everything that was happening around her; in public affairs and personalities, and of course particularly in the future of children all over the world ... she had, even in old age, great beauty, a commanding presence, composure and serenity; she had wit, and humour, and a very well-developed sense of the ridiculous which belied her somewhat imperious manner. She had style and taste, a keen mind and intellectual vigour right until the end ... she was a grande dame in the best and proper sense.'

Like her two sisters, she had for years given time, energy and unstinting effort for the public good. After the tumult of their early years, this was the true heritage of their father.

Note on Sources

Most of the material on which this book is based is taken from the diaries and private letters of the Curzon sisters and interviews with those who knew them. Irene Ravensdale not only kept a Hunting Journal but a comprehensive daily diary, vividly describing her feelings and emotions and the behaviour of those nearest to her, written up every night however late the hour. Baba's diary, written sporadically, recorded important or interesting moments in her life. Fruity Metcalfe wrote comprehensively to his wife when he was away from her; also in the Metcalfe archive are a large collection of letters from Lord Halifax, some from Count Grandi (others were supplied by the archives of the Italian Foreign Office), and letters from the Duke and Duchess of Windsor. The diaries of Georgia Sitwell, Victor Cazalet and Robert Bernays supplied other valuable contemporary documentation.

Material on Curzon's life is readily available from the numerous biographies about him, especially the magisterial life by David Gilmour and the excellent earlier work by Kenneth Rose. His papers, from the private letters to the last detail of his household accounts, are in the Oriental department of the British Library. The Souls are described by Violet Bonham Carter in *The Listener* of 30 October 1947, by Anita Leslie and in Ann Fleming's letters. Wilfrid Scawen Blunt describes the Crabbet Club in *My Diaries*. Mary Leiter's early life is admirably detailed in Nigel Nicolson's *Mary Curzon*. The details of Mary Leiter's marriage settlement are in file F112/67 of the Curzon papers. There is a description of the engaged couple in the *St James's Gazette* of 5 April 1895.

Mary Curzon's will can be found in the Principal Registry, First

Avenue House. Her letters and Curzon's to her tell much of her story. The story of the dog at the Durbar is in Wilfrid Scawen Blunt's diaries. Curzon's early letters to the children are in the British Library and others are in the possession of Lord Ravensdale.

The story of the 'I see ...' game was described to me by Baba's daughter Linda Mortimer (Baba had also done the same thing with her own children). There is a full description of Hackwood in file F112/715 in the British Library. Cimmie's school is described in Janet Morgan's *Edwina Mountbatten: A Life of Her Own*. There is an essay on her childhood by Irene Ravensdale in *Little Innocents*, edited by Alun Pryce-Jones.

Elinor Glyn wrote copiously of her feelings for Curzon, both in her diary, and in writings about him, detailing the ups and downs of their relationship. Much of Curzon's relationship with Nancy Astor is revealed in their correspondence; Nancy Astor's papers are held at the University of Reading.

Linda Mortimer described the selection of Baba's dog, a story she had often heard from her mother. Grace Curzon's letters to Curzon are all in the British Library, as is the correspondence over Cimmie's back problem (file F112/685). Curzon's views on 'woman suffrage' (apart from those printed in the newspapers of the day) can be found in file F112/39. Full details of Irene's coming-out ball are in file F112/687. Comte Willy de Grune, in attendance on the Belgian royal family at Hackwood during the 1914–18 war, reminisced of them and of his love for Irene and how well she danced to Baba's daughter Davina Eastwood, when she and her sister visited them in Belgium. Artur Rubinstein describes his weekend at Hackwood in his autobiography. Cynthia Asquith's description of Curzon is illuminating, as is his own brief self-description (in file F112/531).

Grace Curzon's autobiography describes much of her early life with Curzon and his letters recount the long battle to achieve an heir. Details of the balls given by Curzon for his daughters can be found in the British Library, with further descriptions in *The Lady* and other society magazines. The account of Curzon's proposal that Oliver Lyttelton should marry one of his daughters is in the memoirs of Lyttelton (later Lord Chandos).

Contemporary descriptions of balls and parties can be found in publications like *The World*, *The Lady* and society papers like *The Tatler* and *The Bystander*. Baba's coming-out ball is described in *The Times* and in *The Lady* as well as in the Curzon papers; and she frequently appears, with Grace Curzon, in society magazines. Her presentation at Court is described in *The Lady* of 15 June 1922.

Post-war society life is admirably described in Loelia Duchess of Westminster's *Grace and Favour* and in Cynthia Asquith's *Remember and Be Glad*. Grace Curzon describes fully the life at Carlton House Terrace in her memoirs. Scatters Wilson's military career is listed in contemporary *Who's Whos*.

Fruity Metcalfe's military career is documented in the Public Record Office and there are further details in the Imperial War Museum and there is also material in the autobiography of his niece, the broadcaster Audrey Russell. Lord Mountbatten's diary gives a very full description of the Prince of Wales's Indian tour. Nancy Astor's tactless remark to Grace Curzon is described by Frances Stevenson in her diary, held in the House of Lords Library. The episode when Prince Henry cracked Curzon's dining-room table is described by Baba in an unscreened Channel 4 interview.

Lord Ravensdale described the initial meeting between his mother Cimmie and Tom Mosley. Elizabeth Winn explained that her aunt Phyllis Brand had found Mosley so attractive that she persuaded him to come and canvass for Nancy Astor in Plymouth – where he remet Cimmie. Tom Mosley's military career is listed comprehensively in the Public Record Office. The letters between Curzon and his wife give a full account of their movements and feelings, and of Baba's movements. Grace's appearance at St Moritz in January 1923 is described in several contemporary newspapers.

The important balls, the Buckingham Palace Garden Party and the Prince of Wales's incognito trip to Le Touquet are all described in various issues of *The Lady* magazine. The Prince's letters to Fruity Metcalfe are in the possession of his son David Metcalfe, who also holds the compact, written on paper headed Sea Meads, Sandwich Bay, Kent, to cut down on smoking by the Prince of Wales, Prince George and Fruity. Baba wrote 'I never got the £100 as they kept the pledge,' on the envelope in which it is kept.

The Story of Melton Mowbray by Philip Hunt and *Melton Mowbray in Old Photographs* by Trevor Hickman provide a comprehensive picture of this little hunting town in the twenties. Irene's Hunting Journal is full of the incidents and accidents in the major hunts, many of which are also mentioned in the *Leicester Mercury* and in Michael Clayton's *Foxhunting in Paradise*. There is much about Craven Lodge in *Melton Mowbray, Queen of the Shires* by Jack Brownlow. The Local History Archive of the Melton public library also has much of interest about Craven Lodge, the town, and the Prince of Wales. The late Miss Monica Sheriffe added personal reminiscences of that time.

Lady Glyn (born Susan Rhys Williams, the daughter of Elinor's youngest daughter Juliet) recorded that after Elinor died, Cimmie told her mother Juliet that Curzon had asked to see Elinor Glyn when he was dying but that no message had been received. 'I asked my mother why the message was never given to Elinor,' wrote Lady Glyn to the author. 'She said: "Cimmie thought it was his wife who prevented it. She was jealous".' Curzon's wills and codicils are, of course, freely available.

The description of Cimmie 'in costly furs' is by a German newspaperman, Egon Wertheimer, who attended a meeting of the Labour Party in the Empire Hall in south-east London. Irene describes her love affair with Gordon Leith in her diaries; interviews with Lord Ravensdale fleshed it out further. Lord Holderness described the affection his father, Lord Halifax, had for the encampment of Naldera, near Simla; the Metcalfes' lunch with the Halifaxes is recorded in Lady Halifax's diary. Savehay Farm is described in a private publication by its present owner, Mr Frank Cakebread, and there are other descriptions in the biography of John Strachey by Hugh Thomas.

Grace Curzon's attempt to prevent her daughter Marcella marrying Edward Rice was recounted to me by Marcella's daughter Lady Plymouth. Tom Mosley's many infidelities were confirmed by his son and biographer Lord Ravensdale.

The *Leicester Mercury* describes the Melton Ball of January 1929. Thelma Furness recounts her love affair with the Prince of Wales in her autobiography. There are descriptions of Fort Belvedere in both the Duke and Duchess of Windsor's memoirs. The Hon. David Astor talked to me about his mother and Cliveden and there is much family material in James Fox's *The Langhorne Sisters*. Cimmie's election campaigning is recorded in Irene's diary and the local Stoke newspapers. Her parliamentary speeches are in *Hansard*.

The biography of Oswald Mosley by Robert Skidelsky covers the Mosley Memorandum in full. The diaries of Beatrice Webb and Robert Bernays describe the atmosphere of that time. Irene Ravensdale's diary as ever provides a full account of the life of the three sisters.

There is a full account of the New Party in *John Strachey*, Nicholas Mosley's biography of his father, Robert Skidelsky's Mosley biography and several others. The *Birmingham Town Crier* and the *Manchester Guardian* describe Cimmie's resignation from the Labour Party. Mosley's sending of emissaries to Germany is reported in the *Daily Herald*. Statistics of the Nazi Party vote are in the October 1998 issue of *History Today* ('Who Voted for the Nazis?' by Dick Geary).

Diana Mosley writes about her relationship with Tom Mosley in Venice and after in her autobiography *A Life of Contrasts* and has also described it to the author in interviews. Much information about Artur Rubinstein was supplied by Lady Weidenfeld, who knew him for many years. The story about Tom Mosley recounting to Robert Boothby his confession to Cimmie of his mistresses is in Nicholas Mosley's biography of his father and was confirmed to me by Lady Boothby. Vivien Forbes-Adam and Nicholas Mosley confirm that the 'sister' referred to was their aunt Irene and not, as most people supposed, Baba.

Miles Graham's letters, the diary of his mother Lady Askwith and Irene Ravensdale's diary give a full picture of their engagement and of Cimmie Mosley's death. Tom Mosley's love affair with Baba Metcalfe was confirmed to the author by her close family, who were able to throw much light on her feelings about it. Baba Metcalfe confirmed to the author her continuing hatred of Diana Mosley and her belief, shared by those around her, that from the start Diana had been determined to wrest Tom Mosley away from her sister; Diana Mosley in several interviews confirmed that this had never been her intention and that Mosley had told her he would never leave his wife.

There is a great deal of information about Jock Whitney in press articles such as the *Saturday Evening Post* (1 June 1957) and *Vogue* (1 February 1965).

The best descriptions of the events leading up to the Abdication are in Philip Ziegler's official biography of Edward VIII and Lady Donaldson's *Edward VIII: The Road to Abdication*. The recent release of some of the Monckton papers has added further detail. Alfred Shaughnessy recounted to me the stories he had heard from his stepfather Captain the Hon. Piers ('Joey') Legh, equerry to the Prince of Wales, who sailed with him when as Duke of Windsor he went into exile, and I am obliged to the Royal Archives for passing on to me copies of several of Fruity Metcalfe's letters.

Walter Monckton's papers are in Balliol College Library. Betty Hanley furnished me with a full description of the Château de Candé in the time of her aunt, Fern Bedaux, together with papers and letters (many from the Bedaux butler, Hale) describing the household the Duchess wanted and the cost to M. Bedeaux of much of the Duke's behaviour, together with letters concerning the visit to Germany. Baba Metcalfe's diary gives the fullest, most immediate eye-witness account of the Windsor's wedding.

Descriptions of life at La Cröe can be found in several books, notably Dina Wells Hood's account of her life with the Windsors and Harold Nicolson's diary. Much other information was given to me by both David Metcalfe and Sir Dudley Forwood; there are also additional details in Lady Loughborough's unpublished memoir. There were many pictures and descriptions of Little Compton and its furniture in a Sotheby's catalogue of September 1999. Accounts of the fuss the Windsors made about leaving Antibes in 1940 are in the Monckton papers and Fruity Metcalfe's letters.

Details of the construction of the Dorchester, its early years, guests and menus are contained in the hotel's own files. The Public Record Office holds details of correspondence leading up to the Mosleys' imprisonment, internment and eventual release, as well as letters and papers relating to the Windsors' return to France after the war.

Bibliography

Amory, Mark (ed.), *The Letters of Ann Fleming* (Collins, 1985)

Asquith, Cynthia, *Diaries 1915–1918* (Hutchinson, 1968)

Asquith, Cynthia, *Remember and Be Glad* (James Barrie, 1952)

Asquith, H. H., *Letters to Venetia Stanley*, edited by Michael and Eleanor Brock (OUP, 1982)

Birkenhead, Lord, *Contemporary Personalities* (Cassell, 1924)

Bloch, Michael (ed.), *The Wallis and Edward Letters 1931–1937: The Intimate Correspondence of the Duke and Duchess of Windsor* (Weidenfeld and Nicolson, 1986)

Blunt, Wilfred Scawen, *My Diaries* (Secker, 1932)

Blow, Simon, *Fields Elysian* (J. M. Dent, 1983)

Bradford, Sarah, *Sacheverell Sitwell* (Sinclair-Stevenson, 1993)

Brett, Maurice (ed.), *Journals and Letters of Reginald, Viscount Esher 1903–1910* (Ivor Nicholson and Watson, 1934 and 1938)

Brownlow, Jack, *Melton Mowbray, Queen of the Shires* (Sycamore, 1980)

Campbell, Nina, and Caroline Seebohm, *Elsie de Wolfe: A Decorative Life* (Panache Press, 1992)

Chandos, Lord, *Memoirs* (Bodley Head, 1962)

Churchill, Randolph, *Lord Derby* (Heinemann, 1959)

Clayton, Michael, *Foxhunting in Paradise* (John Murray, 1993)

Collis, Maurice, *Nancy Astor* (Faber, 1960)

Cooper, Artemis, *Cairo in the War* (Hamish Hamilton, 1989)

Corbitt, F. J., *Fit for a King* (Odhams Press, 1956)

Crathorne, James, *Cliveden: The Place and the People* (Collins and Brown, 1995)

Curzon, Grace Elvina, *Reminiscences* (Hutchinson, 1955)

D'Abernon, Viscount, *An Ambassador of Peace: Pages from the Diary of Viscount d'Abernon* (Hodder and Stoughton, 1929)

D'Abernon, Viscount, *Portraits and Appreciations* (Hodder and Stoughton, 1931)

Dennis, Geoffrey, *Coronation Commentary* (Dodd, Mead, 1937)

Donaldson, Frances, *Edward VIII: The Road to Abdication* (Weidenfeld and Nicolson, 1974)

Egremont, Max, *Balfour: A Life of Arthur James Balfour* (Collins, 1980)

Fox, James, *The Langhorne Sisters* (Granta Books, 1998)

Furness, Thelma and Vanderbilt, Gloria, *Double Exposure* (Muller, 1959)

Gilmour, David, *Curzon* (John Murray, 1994)

Glyn, Sir Anthony, *Elinor Glyn* (Hutchinson, 1955)

Goldsmith, Barbara, *Little Gloria, Happy at Last* (Macmillan, 1980)

Hardinge, Helen, *Loyal to Three Kings* (Kimber, 1967)

Hardwick, Joan, *Addicted to Romance: The Life and Adventures of Elinor Glyn* (André Deutsch, 1994)

Hart Davis, Duff (ed.), *Letters and Journals of Sir Alan Lascelles: End of an Era, 1887–1920* (Hamish Hamilton, 1986)

Hart Davis, Duff (ed.), *Letters and Journals of Sir Alan Lascelles: In Royal Service, 1920–1936* (Hamish Hamilton, 1989)

Hickman, Trevor, *Melton Mowbray in Old Photographs* (Alan Sutton, 1993)

Jebb, Miles (ed.), *The Diaries of Cynthia Gladwyn* (Constable, 1995)

Jones, Jack, *Unfinished Journey* (Hamish Hamilton, 1957)

Jones, Thomas, *A Diary with Letters* (OUP, 1954)

Langhorne, Elizabeth, *Nancy Astor and her Friends* (Arthur Baker, 1974)

Lees-Milne, James, *Harold Nicolson* (Chatto and Windus, 1981)

Lees-Milne, James, *Prophesying Peace* (Chatto and Windus, 1997)

Leslie, Anita, *Edwardians in Love* (Hutchinson, 1951)

Lowndes, Susan (ed.), *Dairies and Letters 1911–1947: Marie Belloc Lowndes* (Chatto and Windus, 1971)

MacKenzie, Norman and Jeanne (eds), *The Diary of Beatrice Webb*, Vol 4: *1923–1943* (Virago, 1985)

Maxwell, Elsa, *Celebrity Circus* (Appleton, 1963)

Morgan, Janet, *Edwina Mountbatten: A Life of her Own* (HarperCollins, 1981)

Mosley, Diana, *A Life of Contrasts* (Hamish Hamilton, 1977)

Mosley, Leonard, *Curzon: The End of an Epoch* (Longman, 1960)

Mosley, Nicholas, *Beyond the Pale: Memoirs of Sir Oswald Mosley and Family* (Secker and Warburg, 1993)

Mosley, Nicholas, *Rules of the Game: Memoirs of Sir Oswald Mosley and Family* (Secker and Warburg, 1992)

Nicolson, Harold, *Curzon: The Last Phase* (Constable, 1934)

Nicolson, Nigel, *Mary Curzon* (Weidenfeld and Nicolson, 1977)

Olson, Stanley (ed.), *Harold Nicolson Diaries, 1930–1964* (Collins, 1980)

Philpott, H. R. S., *The Rt Hon. J. H. Thomas* (Sampson Low, 1932)

Pryce-Jones, Alan (ed.), *Little Innocents: Childhood Reminiscences* (Cobden-Sanderson, 1932)

Ravensdale, Irene, *In Many Rhythms* (Weidenfeld and Nicolson, 1953)

Reed, Douglas, *Insanity Fair* (Cape, 1938)

Rhodes James, Robert, *Bob Boothy: A Portrait* (Hodder and Stoughton, 1991)

Rhodes James, Robert, *Victor Cazalet: A Portrait* (Hamish Hamilton, 1976)

Roberts, Andrew, *The Holy Fox: The Life of Lord Halifax* (Weidenfeld and Nicolson, 1991)

Rose, Kenneth, *Superior Person: A Portrait of Curzon and his Circle in Late Victorian England* (Weidenfeld and Nicolson, 1969)

Rose, N. A. (ed.), *Buffy: The Diaries of Blanche Dugdale, 1936–1947* (Valentine Mitchell, 1973)

Rubinstein, Arthur, *My Young Years* (Cape, 1973)

Russell, Audrey, *A Certain Voice* (Ross Anderson, 1984)

Sachs, Harvey, *Arthur Rubinstein* (Weidenfeld and Nicolson, 1995)

Shaughnessy, Alfred, *Both Ends of the Candle* (Peter Owen, 1978)

Shaughnessy, Alfred, *Sarah: The Letters and Diaries of a Courtier's Wife 1906–1936* (Peter Owen, 1989)

Sheean, Vincent, *Between the Thunder and the Storm* (Macmillan, 1944)

Skidelsky, Robert, *Oswald Mosley* (Macmillan, 1975)

Smart, Nick (ed.), *The Diaries and Letters of Robert Bernays, 1932–1939* (The Edwin Mellen Press, 1998)

Soames, Mary (ed.), *Speaking for Themselves: The Personal Letters of Winston and Clementine Churchill* (Doubleday, 1998)

Sykes, Christopher, *Nancy: The Life of Lady Astor* (Collins, 1972)

Thomas, Hugh, *John Strachey* (Eyre Methuen, 1973)

Wells Hood, Dina, *Working for the Windsors* (Wingate, 1957)

Westminster, Loelia, *Grace and Favour* (Weidenfeld and Nicolson, 1961)

Windsor, Duchess of, *The Heart Has its Reasons* (Michael Joseph, 1956)

Windsor, Duke of, *A King's Story* (Cassell, 1951)

Ziegler, Philip, *Edward VIII: The Official Biography* (Collins, 1990)

Ziegler, Philip, *Mountbatten* (Collins, 1985)

Index